THOMAS HARDY'S NOVEL UNIVERSE

For Victor, Will, Christian, and Olivia: for love, joy, and light.

For my parents and grandparents: for life, faith, and courage.

Thomas Hardy's Novel Universe

Astronomy, Cosmology, and Gender
in the Post-Darwinian World

PAMELA GOSSIN
The University of Texas-Dallas, USA

ASHGATE

Published by
Ashgate Publishing Limited
Gower House
Croft Road
Aldershot
Hants GU11 3HR
England

Ashgate Publishing Company
Suite 420
101 Cherry Street
Burlington, VT 05401-4405
USA

Ashgate website: http://www.ashgate.com

British Library Cataloguing in Publication Data
Gossin, Pamela
Thomas Hardy's novel universe : astronomy, cosmology and gender in the post-Darwinian world. – (The nineteenth century series)
    1. Hardy, Thomas, 1840-1928 – Criticism and interpretation 2. Hardy, Thomas, 1840-1928 – Philosophy 3. Hardy, Thomas, 1840-1928 – Knowledge – Cosmology 4. Hardy, Thomas, 1840-1928 – Knowledge – Astronomy 5. Cosmology in literature 6. Astronomy in literature
    I.Title
    823.8

Library of Congress Cataloging-in-Publication Data
Gossin, Pamela.
Thomas Hardy's novel universe : astronomy, cosmology, and gender in the post- Darwinian world / by Pamela Gossin.
    p. cm. — (The nineteenth century series)
    Includes bibliographical references and index.
    1. Hardy, Thomas, 1840-1928—Knowledge—Astronomy. 2. Hardy, Thomas, 1840 1928 Knowledge—Cosmology. 3. Hardy, Thomas, 1840-1928—Criticism and interpretation. 4. Astronomy in literature. 5. Cosmology in literature. 6. Literature and science—History. I. Title.

PR4757.A79G67 2007
823'.8—dc22

2006018480

ISBN: 978-0-7546-0336-8

Printed and bound in Great Britain by MPG Books Ltd, Bodmin, Cornwall.

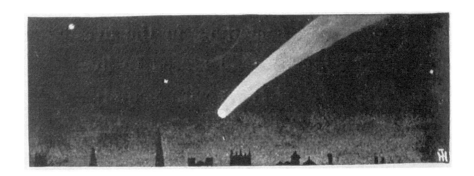

I learn to prophesy the hid eclipse,
The coming of eccentric orbs;
To mete the dust the sky absorbs,
To weigh the sun, and fix the hour each planet dips.

I witness fellow earth-men surge and strive;
Assemblies meet, and throb, and part;
Death's soothing finger, sorrow's smart;
– All the vast various moils that mean a world alive.

— Hardy's "A Sign-Seeker," stanzas 4 and 5

Contents

The Nineteenth Century Series
General Editors' Preface

The aim of the series is to reflect, develop and extend the great burgeoning of interest in the nineteenth century that has been an inevitable feature of recent years, as that former epoch has come more sharply into focus as a locus for our understanding not only of the past but of the contours of our modernity. It centers primarily upon major authors and subjects within Romantic and Victorian literature. It also includes studies of other British writers and issues, where these are matters of current debate: for example, biography and autobiography, journalism, periodical literature, travel writing, book production, gender, noncanonical writing. We are dedicated principally to publishing original monographs and symposia; our policy is to embrace a broad scope in chronology, approach and range of concern, and both to recognize and cut innovatively across such parameters as those suggested by the designations 'Romantic' and 'Victorian.' We welcome new ideas and theories, while valuing traditional scholarship. It is hoped that the world which predates yet so forcibly predicts and engages our own will emerge in parts, in the wider sweep, and in the lively streams of disputation and change that are so manifest an aspect of its intellectual, artistic and social landscape.

Vincent Newey
Joanne Shattock
University of Leicester

List of Illustrations

Acknowledgments

My work in literature and the history of astronomy and much of the research for this book has been supported by grants and fellowships from both the humanities and the sciences. I am especially grateful to Professor Ralph Alpher and the Dudley Observatory, Schenectady, New York, for timely support received in the form of two grants (1993, 1995) which allowed me to develop fully a research program initiated during a Rockefeller Fellowship in Interdisciplinary Humanities in the History of Science Department at the University of Oklahoma (1990–91). I also received direct support for this project from the National Endowment for the Humanities (summer stipend, 1997), a Howard Foundation Fellowship in the History of Science (Brown University, 1997–98) and a Special Faculty Development Assignment from the School of Arts and Humanities, University of Texas-Dallas (2003–2004).

I have been the fortunate recipient of encouragement from true scholars and even truer teachers in a number of disciplines who made this experiment possible as well as pleasurable. First and foremost, I must thank the members of my doctoral committee at the University of Wisconsin-Madison: David C. Lindberg, Michael Shank and Robert Siegfried in the History of Science; and Phillip Harth, Leah Marcus, and James Nelson (a student of Marjorie Nicolson's), in English. At the University of Texas-Dallas, I have had many fun and enlightening exchanges with Marc Hairston of the Hanson Center for Space Sciences, as well as Patricia Howell Michaelson, Michael Wilson, Gerald Soliday, Theresa Towner, and Dean Dennis Kratz, all of the School of Arts and Humanities.

I have been heartened across the miles (and across the years) by the inspiration and insights of Mary Jo Nye, Robert Nye, Howard Weinbrot, James J. Bono, Edrie Sobstyl, Jim Lattis, Robert Brain and Catherine Peterson. Heartfelt thanks are due also to all of my beloved students, graduate and undergraduate, across the disciplines in Literary Studies, Historical Studies, Aesthetic Studies, the History of Ideas, Medical and Scientific Humanities (MaSH), neuroscience, molecular biology, physics, and computer science, who have all come to share my belief in the power of "Brave Combos" (and nuclear polka), especially Tim Haynes, M. Wayne Cooper, M.D., Michele Marshall, Tonja Wissinger, Patricia Chogugudza, Jamie Wheeler, Christopher Speck, Patrick Dennis, Deborah Scally, Nicholas Boeving, Darby Grande, Shari Childers, Jaime Jordan, Suzanne Gabriel, Adrian Cook, Kaj Lubag, Evelyn Montgomery, Matthew Braddock, Dietrich Volkland, Mark Dixon, Yongzhao Deng, Jonathan Wade, Kristi Wesloh, Sharon Duncan, Karen Bartlett, Natalie Delker, Akiko Inoue, Royce Davidson, and the incomparably energetic Mona Sadeghpour and Amelia Potasznik.

I am grateful to have had the use of the general collections and the special History of Science Collections at the University of Oklahoma's Bizzell Memorial Library. The OU circulation librarians bent the rules of physics for me to extend time and space for my use of their books and journals over several years – thank you for understanding. I deeply appreciate, also, the generous assistance and invaluable advice of Professors Marilyn Ogilvie and Kerry Magruder in the History of Science Collections, especially for Kerry's help in selecting and preparing digital images for use in this volume. For their keen advice and kindness, I owe thanks to editors Ann Donahue, Erika Gaffney and Meredith Coeyman at Ashgate Publishing. I will always be mindful, too, of the useful comments and suggestions offered by Ashgate's anonymous readers.

In addition to my husband, children, parents and grandparents to whom I have dedicated this project, I am increasingly aware of how much my thoughts, feelings, values and world view have been shaped and enriched by my siblings, Patricia Gossin Crisler and Jill Gossin Jensen, Jeff and Paul. Finally, I thank psychologists, Dr. Richard Moreno and Angela Anthony, whose good counsel gave me new perspectives on the power of human perception and personal narrative at a crucial point in this project.

I gratefully acknowledge Indiana University Press for granting permission to reproduce material from my article, "'All Danae to the Stars': Nineteenth-Century Representations of Women in the Cosmos," pages 65–96 of *Victorian Studies* 40.1 (Autumn 1996). Routledge/Taylor and Francis Group granted permission to reprint materials from chapters that first appeared in volumes produced by Garland Publishing: copyright © 1996 from *History of Astronomy: An Encyclopedia*, John Lankford, editor, pages 307–14 and copyright © 2000 from *Encyclopedia of the Scientific Revolution: From Copernicus to Newton*, Wilbur Applebaum, editor, pages 367–71. The cover art for this volume, William Dyce's "Pegwell Bay, Kent: A Recollection of October 5th, 1858," is reproduced by permission of the Tate Gallery, London. The frontispiece illustration and all other illustrations are reproduced with permission, copyright the University of Oklahoma Libraries and the History of Science Collections, University of Oklahoma Libraries, respectively.

Notes on Texts and Style

With the general readers' convenience in mind, I have elected to cite editions of Hardy's primary works that have been readily available in the past and are likely to remain so in the future. In the case of *Two on a Tower*, one of the novels that stays in print only irregularly, I have, for the purposes of textual stability (if not accessibility), cited the 1895 edition.

Only those markings that have direct significance for the meaning of the passage cited have been reproduced from Björk's edition of Hardy's *Literary Notebooks*.

Author's Preface

Nay, from the highest point of view, to precisely describe a human being, the focus of a universe, how impossible!

– The Woodlanders

When Ernest Brennecke published his book, *Thomas Hardy's Universe* (1924), he hardly intended the title to be taken literally. Indeed, Brennecke's conception of Hardy's "universe" required no understanding of nineteenth-century astronomy, cosmology or astrophysics, nor any appreciation for what Hardy may have thought about them. Instead, Brennecke's volume proffered, as the subtitle clarified, "A Study of a Poet's *Mind*," in which he aimed to examine "the closest intellectual affinity" between the *world views* of Hardy and Schopenhauer.[1] Attending to verbal, topical, and thematic echoes in the texts of the two men, Brennecke made as strong a case as he could for the "influence" of Schopenhauer's philosophy upon the metaphysics of Hardy's poetry and novels. While Hardy knew better than to depreciate the sincere efforts of such a serious reader, he immediately recognized the failings of such an approach and expressed his concerns in a letter to Brennecke, written June 21, 1924. Deflecting his most pointed criticism of Brennecke's study by citing an unnamed third-party reviewer who remarked that "it was a little too much like a treatise on Schopenhauer with notes on Hardy," Hardy continued, with pained politeness:

> and though that was a humorous exaggeration, what the critic meant, I suppose, was that Schopenhauer['s] was too largely dwelt upon to the exclusion of other philosophies apparent in my writings to represent me truly - that, as my pages show harmony of view with Darwin, Huxley, Spencer, Comte, Hume, Mill, and others (all of whom, as a matter of fact, I used to read more than Sch. [sic]) my kinship with them should have been mentioned as well as with him. Personally I have nothing to say on this point, though I share their opinion to some extent.
>
> (Hardy to Brennecke, as in Brennecke, frontispiece)

After praising Brennecke for his astute observation regarding the absence of Bergson's thought in his work, Hardy corrects several other matters of fact and complains (while maintaining that he is not) about the author's "attempt to trace imitation . . . in a purely

---

[1] Ernest Brennecke, Jr., *Thomas Hardy's Universe: A Study of a Poet's Mind* (1924; New York: Russell and Russell, 1966) 14, emphasis added. Hereafter: Brennecke.

accidental resemblance" and frequent "tendency to find influence in chance likenesses."

That any case study of the influence of a single figure upon Hardy – whether philosophical, literary, historical, scientific, or otherwise – would meet with similar criticism goes without saying. No monolithic approach could "represent . . . truly" the full range of "influences" upon Hardy's life and thought; nor, really, should Hardy have hoped for one to. Having been subjected to more than his fair share of misrepresentation and misunderstanding over the course of his career, he no doubt developed an unusually strong sense of what their opposites might feel like, were he ever to experience them.[2] The overall tone of Hardy's letter to Brennecke seems to hold in uneasy tension a grateful solicitousness for all that his study intends and a disappointed resignation over its all-too-inevitable falling short.

Although Brennecke's attempt to chart *Thomas Hardy's Universe* is only rarely cited in current critical discussions, even eighty years later his project can still usefully remind us of the extent to which crises of influence and representation continue to vex Hardy scholars today. No matter how meticulously textual or conscientiously contextual, no matter how widely or deeply biographical, philosophical, social, political, Marxist, feminist or masculinist, new critical, new historical, new new historical or postmodern, no matter how faithfully committed to consideration of form and function, poetics, plot and character, narrative and narrator, no one of us has fulfilled Hardy's heart's desire to have his life, work and thought represented "truly." Of course there is, perhaps, no one who could better empathize with the ineluctable futility of our efforts than Hardy himself, whose every work was a failed experiment in representing "truly" life and the universe within him and around him.

Additionally, Brennecke's conflation of Hardy's inner and outer "universes" highlights another set of concerns of continuing importance to readers of Hardy: the fundamental and unresolvable philosophical problems inherent in describing the relationship of perception to reality, subject to object, individual self to the social realm and the physical world beyond. To whatever extent we might ultimately agree with Hardy's assessment of its overall success and relevance, Brennecke's study directly engaged (and, inadvertently expressed) questions still at the center of all interpretative work: how to relate the meaning(s) to be found upon (or made from) an author's pages to the understanding he or she formulated in his or her mind and, how the reader's "universe" relates to them both. Like Brennecke, who brought his personal reading of Schopenhauer to his reading of Hardy, all of Hardy's readers necessarily make ontological cuts in his already ontologically unique universe and bring eclectically cut universes of their own to the task.

In *Thomas Hardy's Novel Universe*, I mean to take the "universe" literally and personally – in reference both to his understanding of past and contemporary

---

[2]   For one scholar's view of the critical reception of Hardy's works, see: Edward Neill, *Trial by Ordeal: Thomas Hardy and the Critics* (Columbia, SC: Camden House, 1999).

astronomy and cosmology and in relation to the internal spaces of Hardy's mind and my own. Drawing upon my own eclectic background and training in the history of science, and the history of popular astronomy and cosmology, in particular, I hope to bring a unique contextualization to my reading of Hardy's novels. Interpreting his major and minor fiction against the background of how Hardy and his contemporaries may have conceived of the mid- to late-Victorian cosmos, I hope to convey some sense of how and why Hardy's apprehension of humanity's place in time and space was "novel" in its originality and power as well as uniquely encapsulated in the form and setting of his novels *per se*.

In the three chapters that constitute Part I, I describe the critical, literary and historical frameworks that form and inform my interpretative approach to Hardy's life, mind and work. In the Introduction, Chapter 1, I discuss the historically uneasy scholarly relationship between literary history and criticism and the history of science and explain why I have chosen to mediate between their professional, philosophical, and disciplinary differences by focusing on their shared term, "history," rather than turning toward discourse theory or cultural studies, among other possibilities. Through what I am pragmatically calling a "literary history of science," I attempt to combine elements of both disciplinary outlooks and interpretative methodologies. Bringing methods of analysis and values of historical inquiry from the history of science to literature seems an apt choice for close reading of primary texts which themselves display – as Hardy's texts do – the deep integration of historical, scientific, and literary materials and concerns. A renewed faith in the power of the word to embrace and express our literary, historical, and scientific understanding can offer literary scholars and historians of science alike a sanctuary from cross-disciplinary conflict and contention. In such an open literary and historical interpretative space, we can freely offer our best approximations of Hardy's understanding of cosmology in the configurations that seem to have held the most immediate personal and cultural meanings for him.

In Chapter 2, I survey the history of astronomy's engagement with literature and literary history's engagement with astronomy and cosmology from the ancient world through the Victorian era, situating Hardy's personal synthesis of astronomy and cosmology within both traditions. The vast range and seeming ubiquitousness of literary uses of astronomical phenomena never fails to surprise most readers, once they are made aware of them. Even those whose study of individual works has otherwise been exhaustive are often astounded to discover to what extent they have taken for granted the astronomical imagery and allusions in their favorite poems and novels. Many of these texts, of course, are well-established as strong literary models for Hardy's poetry and fiction. Safely distanced in time from the later (and still on-going) wrangling of interdisciplinary critics and historians over such materials, I suggest that Hardy drew on his inheritance of primary "astronomical literature" for his own purposes, in his own eclectic way, fashioning a uniquely personal philosophy of life that considers the "facts" of the universe boldly, offering significant biological and cosmic implications for his readers as individuals and for their shared surrounding culture.

In the third chapter, I provide a brief history of astronomy and cosmology from their ancient Greek origins through their manifestations within Victorian observational and theoretical astronomy, cosmology and early astrophysics, in preparation for Part II's discussion of how and what Hardy knew of these developments and discoveries and how he applied that knowledge within his own cosmological narratives. Significantly, the most sophisticated astronomical observations and theories produced by a particular culture have not always been in lockstep with that same society's most prevalent world view or most influential cosmological myths and stories. Hardy's broad-ranging familiarity with natural philosophy, drama and literature – classical to contemporary – prepared his mind to detect substantial resonances between ancient Greek world views and the cosmological – philosophical, social and political – significance of the astronomy and astrophysics (as well as geology and natural history) of his own space and time.

In Victorian culture, popular astronomy and cosmology took many forms, including popular illustrated texts for gentlemen, ladies and children; periodical and newspaper coverage of astronomical discoveries and theories; cartoons, poetry and novels; public observatories and international expeditions. None of these forms, however, rivaled in imaginative impact the "real-life" stories and tangible discoveries of astronomical heroes and heroines like William, John, and Caroline Herschel. Current ignorance of the pertinent history of nineteenth-century astronomy may largely be to blame for the lack of scholarly recognition of, and critical appreciation for, the extensive presence of astronomical concepts, allusions, symbolic associations and deep cosmic metaphors in Hardy's literature. Without a basic knowledge of the most important astronomical phenomena of the period, Hardy's modern readers have been hampered in their ability to identify and interpret astronomically influenced plot devices and tropes. As a result, the literary and philosophical significance of these elements has, for the most part, remained unexplored and seriously underestimated.

In the first chapter of Part II, Chapter 4, "Reading Hardy's Novel Universe," I survey some of the extant evidence that suggests how Hardy accessed contemporary popular astronomy and cosmology for himself and how he integrated that knowledge and information into his personal world view and aesthetic framework. In the next three chapters (5, 6 and 7), I give new close readings of both major and minor novels against the background of Hardy's knowledge and use of popular contemporary astronomy and astrophysics. My analysis treats seven works: *A Pair of Blue Eyes*, *Far From the Madding Crowd*, *The Return of the Native*, *Two on a Tower*, *The Woodlanders*, *Tess of the D'Urbervilles*, and *Jude the Obscure*. Paying special attention to narrative structure, scene setting, plot devices, characterization and issues of gender, I analyze the multiple levels of astronomical allusions and tropes that Hardy incorporates into each text. In unexpected and sophisticated ways, reading Hardy's astronomy enriches Darwinian and feminist perspectives, extends formalist evaluations of Hardy's writerly achievement, and provides fresh or alternative interpretations of enigmatic passages and scenes.

Like many of his literary contemporaries with interests in natural history and astronomy (Tennyson, for one), Hardy considered biological (organic) evolution over geological time as a continuation of the inorganic evolution of stellar and galactic objects described by the nebular hypothesis. In the novels I examine, Hardy explores the possibilities and limits of human existence within the terrestrial *and* celestial spheres, countering the worst potential consequences of social Darwinism with an alternative "moral astrophysics." The primary bearers of the astronomical and cosmological message of Hardy's fiction are the female characters through whose narrative lives he appears to express a striking and intense appreciation for morality and sympathy in the godless universe, rather than the heartless scientific pessimism so often attributed to him.

In the Conclusion, Chapter 8, I suggest broader social and cultural contexts for how literary tradition and the history of astronomy converge in Hardy's "personal construct cosmology" through which he offers new myths for the lives of Victorian men and women. By juxtaposing astronomical narratives of failed potential with visions of new possibilities, he creates "novel" universes in which the fates of his female characters are directly linked to their knowledge and skills in observational astronomy. Indeed, the fates of his fictional women, in particular, are often directly connected to their knowledge of the astronomical "truths" of the universe, including awareness that divine presence may be hostile, indifferent, or nonexistent. Playing out their lives within these literary thought-experiments, Hardy's cosmic heroines fail personally and socially to resolve the "big questions" of the modern cosmos: how to reconcile instinct with intellect, empathy with technology, creativity with entropy. Yet despite their losing encounters with the ignorance, prejudice, and injustice of human individuals and society, Hardy significantly depicts his primary female characters as active agents within their earthly environments, not passive victims beneath the stars. Offering a critique of contemporary concepts of human progress available in then-current evolutionary theory and anthropology and suggesting imaginative recombinations of the feminine and masculine, Hardy's cosmological narratives effectively model ways in which readers (male and female) may actively participate in the shaping of their own life stories as well as the cultural evolution of their species.

"I treated Art as the supreme reality, and life as a mere mode of fiction."

Oscar Wilde, *De Profundis*

PART I
CRITICAL METHODOLOGY, LITERARY AND HISTORICAL BACKGROUND

Chapter 1: Introduction

"Convergence of the Twain"
A Personal Perspective on the Interdisciplinary Study of Literature and Science

When two scholarly endeavors are drawn together from different directions into a single interdisciplinary study, the enterprise need not shipwreck. Although Hardy commemorated the sinking of the Titanic by conceiving of "convergence" as the coincidental collision of opposing forces – Nature/Culture, Fire/Ice, Male/Female, Human Vainglory/Immanent Will – there are other thematic associations available for other incidents of convergence. Although by no means a typical path into Hardy scholarship – and plenty accidental in many respects – my experience with the interrelations of literature and the history of science has enabled me to appreciate, and in some ways even to reenact, aspects of Hardy's quest to understand the natural world and human life within it.

While Hardy is as interdisciplinary a writer as one could ever hope to meet, and that fact alone may adequately justify taking an interdisciplinary critical approach to his work for some readers, such a choice remains problematic for others. Somehow the linkage of "Hardy and philosophy," "Hardy and psychology," and "Hardy and Darwinism" all seem more natural than the unlikely pairing of "Hardy and the history of astronomy and cosmology." For one, that last combination implies a cooperation between literary studies and the history of science (especially the history of the *physical* sciences) that few practitioners in either domain have encouraged over the years. Indeed, for much of their separate histories, the professional distance between the two disciplines has actively worked against joint interpretative ventures.

Disciplinary History: Literary Studies and History of Science

As professional academic disciplines, literary criticism and History of Science emerged along lines different enough. The two fields developed, by and large, as segregated scholarly communities, with students striking out for careers in one, very early abandoning all hope (or at least, focused interest) in the other. During the first half of the twentieth century, historians of science generally received their initial training as research scientists and grew into their profession in other buildings, on the opposite side of the campus from classically trained and liberally educated literary scholars. Working from within their science specialties out, the first few generations of historians of science were more often self-taught in history than trained, modeling their research concerns, interpretative approaches and techniques, as well as their writing styles, on the finished products of the previous century's "Great Men of Science" hagiographies and "History of the Empire" tradition rather than shaping them to critical methods, historiographical concerns, and philosophical frameworks offered by theorists. Conversely, during roughly the same time period, literary criticism had already evolved into just that. Biographies of canonical writers and histories of literary forms and techniques were necessarily foundational to a literary critic's work, but such projects did not provide his/her primary driving force, let alone final purpose. Increasingly, literary exegesis and analysis produced case studies of primary texts the central goal of which was to test and demonstrate the strengths and potentials of various literary theories. By the time they entered the working world of academe, newly minted early-twentieth-century literary critics and historians of science were firmly set on divergent tracks of education, professionalization, and socialization. Whether in university classrooms, offices, archives, at conferences, on academic governance committees or editorial boards, they rarely encountered evidence of each other's existence, either in print or in person.

During the 1930s to 1960s, the two endeavors made intermittent contact through the methods and concerns of intellectual history, as evidenced in studies by such scholars as Arthur O. Lovejoy, C. S. Lewis, Francis R. Johnson, and Marjorie Hope Nicolson. Nicolson's "science in literature" studies, in particular, inspired an imitative explosion among literary scholars seeking the alchemical, astronomical, botanical, zoological and/or medico-historical "keys" to "the" interpretation of works of literature with strong scientific content. The exchange of ideas and information from history of science to literary studies via the channel of intellectual history was generally positive, with historians of science expressing polite surprise and some bemusement that their archival studies of primary works of science should be of use to literary critics; although that revelation did not inspire any obvious push to discover to what extent the reverse might also be the case. Once the first rhetorical bombs of the Two Cultures debate fell, however, further chances to negotiate that channel without suspicion of professional or disciplinary disloyalty were temporarily lost.

But not forgotten. Within the past two decades or so, literary studies and the history of science have met up again as a small but potent part of a larger interdisciplinary academic enterprise, Literature and Science Studies. Both Nicolson's "science in literature" and the Two Cultures' "Science vs. Humanities" perspectives influenced the founding in the early 1980s of SLS: the Society for Literature and Science (recently renamed, SLSA: the Society for Literature, Science and the Arts). During its inaugural meeting, the society's officers duly and repeatedly honored Nicolson's contribution to interdisciplinary "literature and science studies" although they simultaneously distanced themselves from her – to their minds – unsophisticated atheoretical approach to the analysis of primary materials, both literary and scientific. As a professional interdisciplinary organization, SLS made it a central purpose to bridge the "two cultures gap" by inviting research and teaching scientists, physicians, computer scientists, and engineers to participate in its conferences and join its membership. Now, however, after twenty years of professional existence, the society still bears clear marks of the aftermath of the two cultures debacle, with a strong majority of its members working within the arts and humanities, from literary or various cultural studies perspectives. The two cultures dichotomy is present also in the annual conference program, as many plenary speakers and session and panel presenters continue the attempt to define what the "and" in "Literature and Science Studies" can and should mean; whether "a" theory of "Literature and Science" is possible (or desirable); and, if not, what kinds of partial and provisional theories might be most promising and useful.

Yet, as the founding of SLS/SLSA both indicates and encourages, more literary scholars than ever before are aware of and are working with the primary materials once considered the purview of historians of science. Most currently import those materials under the aegis of interdisciplinary Science Studies or Cultural Studies and eschew the more conservative purposes and internalist/externalist confines of the discipline of the History of Science, as traditionally defined. Similarly (and in an appropriately Kuhnian way), while a fair number of younger historians of science use contemporary literary critical theories of discourse, linguistics, and rhetoric as part of their normal research programs, older scholars harbor distrust of such approaches, fearing that they may be but fleeting fads driven by academic politics rather than firm foundations for reliable new paradigms of analysis. Ironically, then, while awareness and exchange of each other's materials and methods seems to be at an all-time high at both individual and institutional levels, the two approaches to understanding human creative activity seem more at odds than ever, with literary studies and the history of science embracing different epistemologies, differing notions about the nature of evidence, the relevance of influence, issues of authority, the stability of language, the limits and potential of representation, and other theoretical and practical crises of scholarship.

Very recently, scholars from both fields exhibited their disciplinary differences in very public displays of academic swagger, theoretical drawing-of-lines-in-the-sand, rhetorical jabs, flaming email posts and ripostes during the various skirmishes of the so-called Science/Culture Wars.[1] Fought with pens, PCs, and parody, the conflict

---

[1]   Alan Sokal, "Transgressing the Boundaries: Towards a Transformative Hermeneutics of Quantum Gravity" in *Social Text* 46/47 (Spring/Summer, 1996) 217–52 and "A Physicist Experiments with Cultural Studies" in *Lingua Franca* (May/June, 1996) 62–4. See the first response of Andrew Ross and Bruce Robbins in the following issue, *Lingua Franca* (July/August 1996). For a blow by blow recounting, see: *The Sokal Hoax: The Sham that Shook the Academy*, edited by The Editors of *Lingua Franca* (Lincoln: University of Nebraska Press, 2000). For subsequent discussion, see: Andrew Ross, *Science Wars* (Raleigh-Durham: Duke

wounded and weakened combatants on both sides, giving and taking offense, leaving both positions more disfigured than represented, more defensive than defended. As matters stand, the model of war itself may have done more conscriptive harm than descriptive good. Historically, of course, the binary system of adversarial pros and cons has been inherent throughout the rhetorical tradition, and by incorporation, in academe itself. Now, however, more is at stake than taking honors in debate. In many ivory-towered environments, inter- and cross-disciplinary surface tensions and territorial disputes are directly linked to departmental and programmatic funding levels as well as rates of survival during tenure and promotion reviews. The academic marketplace has become an embattled state, where potential hires are evaluated less on their creativity and fresh perspectives than on their ability to make immediate contributions to the political fire-power of senior faculty needing new defenses for long-held positions. Life-and-death competition between academics has become so commonplace that it seems virtually inevitable, almost natural.

Yet should our territorial imperatives, economic sanctions, political maneuvering, and selfish genes will out? Two wildly divergent branches may spring from the same stem and be nurtured by the same roots, grounded in the same soil. Might the current emphasis on how far apart literature and science studies have grown be obscuring clear sight of underlying shared realities and values? At the center of this stormy culture clash may there not be a place where unity may emerge amidst diversity and multiplex influences flow toward confluence?

A Personal History of Literary Studies and History of Science

I might well have remained among those academics eternally skeptical about the possible existence of a shared interpretative space between literary studies and the History of Science had I not been fortunate enough to experience it personally. In completing the course work for a double Ph.D. in the History of Science and English at the University of Wisconsin-Madison, I had myriad opportunities to observe the values and mores of students and professors of those two endeavors in action and in close juxtaposition. Through that joint educational process and experience, I found consilience between literature and science (to borrow E. O. Wilson's coinage) at the same place that, I believe, Hardy found it – at the level of primary expression of lived history and thought.

Every weekday for more than five years, I carried the lectures, reading, professorial quips, and off-hand remarks of my fellow graduate students from one

---

University Press, 1996); Paul R. Gross and Norman Levitt, *Higher Superstition: The Academic Left and its Quarrels with Science* (Baltimore: Johns Hopkins University Press, 1997); Alan Sokal and Jean Bricmont, *Fashionable Nonsense: Postmodern Intellectuals' Abuse of Science* (New York: Picador, 1999); and Noretta Koertge, ed., *A House Built on Sand: Exposing Postmodern Myths about Science* (Oxford: Oxford University Press, 2000).

discipline into the next, testing the beliefs and biases of one set of mentors and friends against the real-life evidence found in the texts, classrooms, offices, hearts and minds, of the other. At the time of my graduate studies, the faculty in the two departments were split by a central disagreement concerning the extent to which scholars ought to dedicate their studies to the analysis of texts and discourse (assuming the concomitant "death of the author") or ground their work on some greater faith in the recoverability and "reality" of the past. As I was soon to learn as I read more deeply into the scholarly literature in both areas and began attending and presenting papers at national and international conferences in both fields, this was far from a local dispute. Pressured by sensible arguments from peers and professors in each discipline to reject the "nonsense" of the other, the problem felt overwhelmingly insoluble, one only amenable to choosing-up sides, not synthesis.

The more I interacted personally on a day-to-day basis with literature professors and historians of science, all of whom I liked and respected as people and as scholars, the more the only reasonable choice seemed to be to postpone choosing as long as possible. In the time that indecision bought me, I observed that although both *groups* seemed committed to maintaining a professional, disciplinary posture of mutual exclusion and disregard (if not, occasionally, outright disdain and contempt) *individuals* regularly expressed cross-disciplinary interest and cautious curiosity, frequently stopping me in the hall to clarify points of information for them or to ask me to "translate" something they had read from literary into historiographical jargon, or vice versa. Being caught in the middle of the two disciplines gave me a unique opportunity to develop bilingual communication skills. Although acquiring passing fluency in both at once seemed more than twice as difficult as learning them sequentially, the double immersion experience proved invaluable. For a good long while, it was just plain confusing to hear the concerns and claims of one discipline simultaneously filtered through those of the other; but gradually, what had sounded cacophonous, clarified to counterpoint.

The more I observed practitioners in both fields' work and heard them talk about what they did and why, the more I began to sense that literary studies and history of science were two scholarly communities divided by a common language as much as they were by their philosophical, social and political differences. The commonalities seemed especially apparent at their level of personal engagement and professional praxis with primary materials, whether literary or scientific. There, I heard scholars in both fields speak with equal passion about the past and describe themselves as employing many of the same interpretative processes in their work with authors/scientists and texts, although they did so with heavily different accents, speech patterns, and diction. What I came to understand was, that whatever intricate, internecine interdisciplinary debates over issues and approaches to texts and contexts raged within and between literature and science studies at the metalevel, at the more local, aboriginal level, two subsets of those larger enterprises – Literary History and History of Science – still preserved a fundamental interest in, and respect for, the shared term at which they intersect, namely: history. Listening to how both sides approached history from different directions, I accumulated a sense of the shape and substance of the two endeavors and began to see that some of the uncertain narrative lines in one could be reinforced by the clearer lines of the other and, together, the interpretation of the past they might collectively produce could prove richer than those they could fashion alone.

At base, both literary history and history of science have as their primary purpose the goal of describing and explaining Δ / t (change over time). On the surface, the content and materials of the two fields may seem as incommensurate as the personalities and training of the professionals who engage in their study, but the primary lines of inquiry they are inspired by are identical: Who did and/or knew what when? How? Why? What did it matter to them? How may it matter to us? Literary history and the history of science share essential values that begin with scholars' deep and abiding interest in and compassion for the individual human life of the past. By association, scholars extend that interest and respect to their subject's quest for knowledge and his/her expression of the process and results of that quest. Literary historians and historians of science alike inquire about the resources and challenges their subjects faced, which inquiry necessarily leads them to wonder about the peoples, places, and events of the past that comprise the historical, social, political and intellectual contexts in which their subjects lived, worked and thought. Although their responses to epistemological dilemmas do widely vary, scholars in both disciplines exhibit an equally serious engagement in discerning the limits and potentials of human knowledge, both in our own minds and times, and in those of the people of the past. Both groups employ similar working models of knowing – a continuum from the unknowable/uncertain/impossible through increasing probabilities to certainty – but each discipline emphasizes the importance of different points along that continuum. In general, literary scholars mind the gaps between the unknowable, possible, probable, and certain; while historians of science commit to closing them by employing a provisional, instrumentalist fine-tuning of the probabilities with ever-firmer appearing data. Though one set of scholars seems to focus on how much *may* be knowable and the other, how much may stay *un*knowable, both groups are aware that their projects approach the knowability of any past or present actor/agent, idea or event only *as a limit* (in the mathematical sense). The resultant core humility informs both.

Whether in literary history or the history of science, we may not know the thoughts, actions, and milieu of another human, living or dead, any more surely than we may know the mind of God. However, in both, we do have (to paraphrase Galileo's argument to the Vatican in defense of natural knowledge as ancillary to revelation) the "book of human nature" to guide us – and we can come to "know" that book both as readers of it, and as contributing authors to it. It is precisely at just this point – where the grateful living meet the remains of past works and days – that I have come to believe that a convergent "literary history of science" may help us bear witness.

A Personal Essay Toward a "Literary History of Science": Primary Texts as Methodological Models

Like many readers brought up within the western intellectual tradition, I first encountered the primary texts of what I call "literary history of science" through Judeo-Christian religious accounts and Greek and Roman classics, especially the Old Testament story of creation and the cosmological myths and early natural history of Hesiod, Homer, Aratus, Lucretius, Ovid et al. As my reading extended through a broad range of medieval to early modern works, and beyond, I met many more writers who crafted texts that combined the natural knowledge of their day with poetic, aesthetic, dramatic, and fictional forms and elements. Dante, Copernicus, Donne, Kepler, Margaret Cavendish, Milton, Aphra Behn, Darwin, the Herschels and Hardy himself (to name a mere few) all offered poetic cosmologies and natural histories or cosmological and natural historical poetry, plays and dramatic fictions that seemed to me to operate continuously, and contiguously, within the same literary genre. Although both literary history and the history of science have long claimed separate disciplinary ownership of these primary materials, to me it just made immediate sense to recognize the existence of "literary history of science" as a natural hybrid in both form and content from the earliest beginnings of written artifacts. By extension, it also seemed pragmatically apt (not to say polite and considerate) for us – as literary scholars and historians – to approach equally literary and scientific artifacts in ways that draw upon the best of their authors' dual worlds, matching our critical and interpretative methods and apparatus to our subjects' multi-disciplinary madness.

For the texts that held the most immediate attraction for me – the literary history of astronomy and cosmology – the one interdisciplinary scholar who had attempted a comprehensive analysis of their literary and scientific form, content and contexts in relation to each other, was Marjorie Nicolson. Yet, even as a young scholar, I recognized that her project to navigate the history of science *in* literature, left the reverse current open to exploration. So in my early work, I attempted to extend and retool her approach by bringing literary materials into the historiography of science.[2] The importation was not too taxing, as within both disciplines many of the same critical methods and techniques had equal currency: close exegesis of primary texts; attention to the language usage of individuals and communities; recognition of past transmission and influence; tracing of scales of context, from the life and mind of the writer or scientist, to those of his/her coterie or circle, professional community, public audience, and his/her social and political milieux. Since the history of science already encompassed studies of popularization, transmission, translation and scientific biography – all of which could fairly be dubbed "literary" history of science, it was not too much more of a stretch to argue that more overtly literary forms – such as poetry and fiction – might serve as raw materials as well. My initial essay into crafting

---

[2]   Pamela Gossin, *Poetic Resolutions of Scientific Revolutions: Astronomy and the Literary Imaginations of Donne, Swift and Hardy*, diss., University of Wisconsin, 1989.

literary history of science as a critical methodology, then, was essentially an extension of the history of science's traditional project to study popularization and the history of popular science, especially astronomy and cosmology, from the Copernican and Newtonian through Astrophysical Revolutions.

Yet my interdisciplinary interpretative and analytical approach did not really develop as a mere variation on Nicolson's literary scheme. My deepest interest in and curiosity about the interrelations of literature and the history of science arose independently of my education and training in either discipline, emerging more fundamentally from the confluence of my personal experiences, perceptions and observations of how language, history and nature seem to operate and make meaning in my own life and from a direct engagement in the vicarious experiences offered by other authors' primary texts in which they expressed their personal experiences, perceptions and observations of language, life-in-time and life-in-nature. Although vital to my understanding of and participation in professional, disciplinary discourse, my awareness of the analyses and theories of Nicolson and numerous other interdisciplinary critics, historians and philosophers were superadded, and quite of secondary significance, in my efforts to craft my own philosophy of life, literature and history of science.

It is impossible to recapitulate this process as I lived it (as, of course, it is impossible to do so for another, like Hardy); but I believe that whatever limited understanding of the interrelations of the phenomena of literature, history and science that I have been able to form, it was primarily forged by reading and re-reading words like these:

> Hers is the head upon which all "the ends of the world are come," and the eyelids are a little weary. It is a beauty wrought out from within upon the flesh, the deposit, little cell by cell, of strange thoughts and fantastic reveries and exquisite passions. . . . All the thoughts and experience of the world have etched and moulded there . . . / She is older than the rocks among which she sits; like the vampire, she has been dead many times, and learned the secrets of the grave; and has been a diver in deep seas, and keeps their fallen day about her; and trafficked for strange webs with Eastern merchants: and, as Leda, was the mother of Helen of Troy, and, as Saint Anne, the mother of Mary; and all this has been to her but as the sound of lyres and flutes . . . The fancy of a perpetual life, sweeping together ten thousand experiences, is an old one; and modern philosophy has conceived the idea of humanity as wrought upon by, and summing up in itself, all modes of thought and life.[3]

Melding form and content, Pater's words attempt to express the interrelations he perceives between art and reality, the individual and the universal, the present and the past. His interpretation of this single aesthetic artifact is simultaneously (and necessarily, for him) historical and philosophical. His poetical prose, in turn,

---

[3]   Walter Pater, "Leonardo Da Vinci," *The Renaissance: Studies in Art and Poetry*, 1893 text, ed. Donald L. Hill (Berkeley: University of California Press, 1980) 98–9.

aestheticizes his view of history and philosophy. The cognitive craftsmanship necessary to such syntheses of form and content intrigues me as a reader and inspires me as a writer. The sort of sensory and syncretic way with words that Pater achieved was a long time in the making, and was, perhaps, incipiently present within the earliest origins of human communication.

Human language may well have developed as a technology of survival. Among its many uses and purposes, language retains a primal connection with the preservation of life. Awe-struck or stricken with the sense of our own mortality, we record that we exist in the handprint of a petroglyph, autobiographies, diaries, and letters. Beyond our "Kilroy was here" statements, we use language in myriad social, economic, and political applications, in a motley array of workaday pleasure and practicality. We also, all of us, encounter life experiences that we recognize as requiring – that seem to call out for – extraordinary speech. Here in Oklahoma, in the aftermath of the Murrah Federal building bombing, we were overwhelmed with poetry. Thousands of poems in every conceivable form, from senders of every description from all over the world, poured into the state. Crises of sympathy demand the muse. In birthing rooms, in the company of a dying friend, in righteous anger or mercy, we feel an urgent impulse to speak or write words, to express thought and feeling in such a way that their meaning impresses itself upon the soul of the listener or reader like the scent of rose petals crushed into the palm of a lover's hand. Poetic forms of language are necessary. We may speak and write to live.

Less immediately intelligible are reasons why the living read the words of the dead. Historically, our motivations have been many: the search for *prisca sapientia*; the need for practical guidance in the structure and administration of social and political systems; curiosity about the experience and activity of human cultures and individuals; need for inspiration and hope, or admonishment and warning; the private desire for explanations of sorrows our parents did not share with us. For me, opening a book written so long ago that the author cannot still be alive, weighing its words, sends a tremble up my forearm, in acknowledgment: he lived, he died; I live, I will die. But (with my apologies to James G. Frazer), it is not the fear of death, nor the fear of the dead, that starts the tremble. No guilty morbidity keeps the book open. The affinity begins with the awe of vitality. I hold an artifact of a life in my hands.

Reading is potent communion; a mutually willed violation, an offering and a taking. Opening a book, there is a tacit recognition that the writer's words – willed into existence and an order – are being reconstrued into my own understanding. Tracing out lines of another's thought and experience, I wonder at the immediate sense the words make for me and the simultaneous estrangement I feel from the meaning they made for their maker. I felt the same way when I stepped into my grandmother's farmhouse for the first time after her death. Joining the distressed busy-ness of the other grieving women in the kitchen, I picked up an old wooden spoon. I was startled by its perfect fit, my fingers and palm matched the subtle woman-made curves of its handle: she was here. Stirring in haste? With what joy? Despite what heartache? *Lacrimae rerum*. I had to set it down. It felt right in my hand, but I had no right. Her tool, her life; not mine.

Many of the people I love have been dead hundreds of years. Sensing an author's life within a text, I know that I could not look into his or her eyes without weeping. She had immortal longings in her. These are the pearls that were his eyes. Such lives are as real and tangibly tender as they are remote and forever vanished. How do we ever presume to enter the existence of another? How can we bear to blunder into understanding of another? To have another blunder in toward us? What else is there to do? We work, make love, make life, live to tell about it, hope someone else will care. Writing and reading are both acts of empathy.

Reader and writer are bound by the mutual need for companionship across time. Situated as we are within this cosmos, our physics and physiology constrain our experience of each other. Time separates with a tantalizing pang. Transfixed in a transient present, you and I slide frictionless between the vanishing points of the past and future. Looking through the one-way mirror of a text, we can faintly see the author looking upon the surface in which she sees her own image reflected in infinite regression toward invisible readers whom she could not predict and cannot prevent. Her predicament evokes pity and terror.

In the desperate straits of time, so much to think and feel, writing and reading are urgent matters. Some writers staked their lives on the durability of their verbal artifacts – letters in a bottle tossed upon the sea. Yet one's quest for immortality is contradicted by another's concession of futility: Shakespeare's poetic monuments are eroded by Catullus's breath upon the wind. When they do endure, and for as long as they survive, verbal artifacts preserve life. Every reading revives the writer's creation of the text. Through readers, writers have their lives incorporated and multiplied; through writers, readers experience manifold lives. Like Pater's *La Gioconda* (the *Mona Lisa*), our lives perpetuate, and are perpetuated by, all we read and write. We sweep together ten thousand experiences and live and die many times.

~

My personal conception of the potential of a literary history of science, then, has been directly shaped by a sense of the power of words to preserve and convey human thought, emotion and experience across the vagaries of space, time and chance. From a personal desire to know, from a personal need to feel less alone, I developed a personal faith in literature, history and science: as academic disciplines and professional fields, to be sure; but more so as ways of knowing and as modes of expression – three particular and versatile means of representing knowledge about life, the universe, and everything. I truly believe that in every human communication, the most casual verbal exchange, the very next text I read, I will receive some insight into the meaning of life. I continue to hope that by reading primary texts in literature, history and science, I might compile a hitchhiker's guide to the "big questions" of the universe: What is out there? What is in here (my heart and mind)? And, who, by the way, are you? What can we mean to each other? Is there really no exit? Literature, history, and science present themselves to me as different manifestations of common human quests, three cognate languages in which the purposes and results of those quests are communicated and expressed.

Recalling the various influences of texts of the past, I hear a fugue of different voices that sounds something like this:

"History never repeats itself. Historians repeat each other."

*

"I must create my own system, or be enslaved by another man's."

*

"The history of every country begins in the heart of a man or a woman."

*

"Her full nature . . . spent itself in channels which had no great name on the earth. But the effect of her being on those around her was incalculably diffusive: for the growing good of the world is partly dependent on unhistoric acts; and that things are not so ill with you and me as they might have been, is half owing to the number who lived faithfully a hidden life, and rest in unvisited tombs."

*

"The nominal subject [of this book] is North American cotton tenantry as examined in the daily living of three representative white tenant families.

Actually, the effort is to recognize the stature of a portion of unimagined existence, and to contrive techniques proper to its recording, communication, analysis, and defense. More essentially, this is an independent inquiry into certain normal predicaments of human divinity."

*

"The world is made, it is powered by science, and for any man to abdicate an interest in science is to walk with open eyes into slavery."

*

"I am become death."

*

". . . Thus the interest of their sidereal observation led them on, till the knowledge that scarce any other human vision was traveling within a hundred million miles of their own gave them such a sense of the isolation of that faculty as almost to be a sense of isolation in respect of their whole personality, causing a shudder at its absoluteness . . . . Having got closer to immensity than their fellow-creatures, they saw at once its beauty and its frightfulness. They more and more felt the contrast between their own tiny magnitudes and those among which they had recklessly plunged, till they were oppressed with the presence of a vastness they could not cope with even as an idea, and which hung about them like a nightmare."

Exactly. How to cope with the nightmare, and the ideas? What to do with all the voices in my head that keep me up half the night? Beauty. Truth. History. Mortality. Oh, my. These literary, historical and scientific voices all seem to me to make sense, seem to me to be telling the truth, some of the truth, some truths, about life, the universe, and everything. For all I know, literature, history, and science may well be the most effective means by which human cultures have made sense and continue to make sense of existence and the world. Yet, for all of their effect on and within culture, for all of their strengths as social, intellectual and professional forces, my private engagement with literature, history and science resides primarily (or to be more accurate, primally) at the level of my own personality, psychology and neurobiology. Most likely, I think in the particular way I do about the convergence of literature, history and science for reasons I have only limited awareness of, if, indeed, any at all.

I am aware that I have strong cognitive preferences for mathematical and aesthetic pattern-seeking and analogy. I know that I am attracted to primary materials rich in such patterns (of course, I do not *think* I am just imposing them), but I do know that I infuse them into my own interpretative writing and analyses. When I ask myself: What function of x (literature) will tell me something about history of science? What function of y (history of science) will tell me something about literature? I just *like* the fact that those insoluble problems have complex feedback loops and each set of values feeds into the other, the shape of things coming into increasing focus with every term plotted. If pressed, I would venture to say that those types of problems seem "more real" to me than other kinds of problems; that is, they seem symbolically in accord with what I think the state of human knowledge in the universe is. Working with apparently simple problems that infinitely and elegantly replicate themselves from a micro to macro level also satisfies some inner aesthetic intellectual craving I have that I cannot satisfactorily explain. I do know that my attention is drawn in and held by complex multilayered structure, relations of form and content, the accrual of provisional, partial, insights. In my thinking and writing, I employ metaphors of harmony and correspondence within professional modes of cooperation and communication, especially translation and popularization. It has not escaped my attention that all these preferences display, lead to, or imply various kinds of fusion of literature, history, and science.

Although I recognize that this is not a particularly typical or even sensible way for me to express my interest in literature and science, any number of neuroscientists, neuropsychologists, neurophilosophers (Roger Penrose, Gerald Edelman, Patricia Churchland, for example) would see such a description as no revelation to them. Current work in neuroscience suggests that human beings are ready-wired to perceive similarities across a wide range of phenomena, to conceive of the universe in terms of mathematical relations.[4] So, I imagine, that at some point in my cognitive

---

[4]   See, for example: Roger Penrose, *The Emperor's New Mind: Concerning Computers, Minds, and the Laws of Physics* (New York: Penguin Books, 1991) and *Shadows of the Mind: A Search for the Missing Science of Consciousness* (Oxford: Oxford University Press, 1994); Gerald Edelman, *Neural Darwinism: The Theory of Neuronal Group Selection* (New York: Basic Books, 1987) and *Bright Air, Brilliant Fire: On the Matter of the Mind* (New York: Basic Books, 1992); Patricia Smith Churchland, *Neurophilosophy: Toward a Unified Science of the Mind–Brain* (Cambridge, MA: MIT Press, 1986) and *Brain-wise: Studies in Neurophilosophy*

development, I identified commonalities in literature, history, and science, accumulated complex educational experiences, was exposed to environmental stimuli that eventually led me to seek consensus in contention, friendship in competition, and whatever else it is Darwin would predict relatively defenseless academic tree shrews do to survive and with any luck, get their books done and get tenure.

I know that it will always remain impossible for me to identify with absolute certainty the causal factors of nature–nurture, cognition or psychology, mathematics or aesthetics that may have shaped my choice to combine literature, history, and science in my life and work. While I know that I took classes in calculus, the historical novel, art history, the writing of poetry, and descriptive astronomy in fairly close succession, that is as close to a probable sequence of cause–effect events as I can reconstruct. Given my family's origins on the farmlands of central Nebraska, it should not be overly surprising that I trust the insights of the Great Plains psychologist, George Kelly, who described human beings as born-scientists, meaning-making animals, interacting with their post-Turnerian frontiers, observing phenomena, formulating predictions, testing; creating their own personal constructs of the world, all the better to live in the world.[5] My own personal constructs, then, may account for why Kelly's description of born-scientists instantly appeals to me as a nice definition of born-poets, born-novelists, and born-historians, too.

Given that our self-knowledge and our chances of reconstructing our own personal histories and personal constructs are so inherently limited, and given the ultimately personal and ultimately unknowable aspects of all our attempts to understand ourselves and the world through literature, history, science, or by any other means, it seems to me that we could dissipate much disciplinary discord by accepting the fact that we all share in those limitations and gracefully grant that the most we should humanly ask of each other (as critics, scholars, historians, friends) is that we speak and write as truly as possible about what we care about, and how and why we care about it. If we let the personal and aesthetic authenticity of our words reflect those of the primary texts we love, much conflict and contention could be set aside and what we hold most dearly in common about the human experience and human expression might come into clearer focus. Decommissioning our militaristic metaphors, we might consider more organic alternatives. Like Darwin's famous tree of life, among the many branches of literary, historical, cultural, and science studies, some flourish, some have weakened, others have died; those remaining have grown far apart, but that distance makes room for diversity, complexity, symmetries, balance, and has a beauty all its own. I know that I did not come to the study of literature and the history of

---

(Cambridge, MA: MIT Press, 2002); Francis Crick, *The Astonishing Hypothesis: The Scientific Search for the Soul* (New York: Scribner/Maxwell Macmillan International, 1994) and Christof Koch, *The Quest for Consciousness: A Neurobiological Approach* (Englewood, CO: Roberts, 2004).

[5] George Alexander Kelly, *The Psychology of Personal Constructs*, 2 vols. (New York: Norton, 1955).

science because of any winning claims of one competing critical approach over another, any particularly compelling new methods of analysis, philosophical systems, or historical program(me)s, and no one Scottish or French, or any postmodern anywhere shares the credit or blame. The extent and the results of my trafficking with the words of postmortals, however, is another story:

Perhaps the most authentic statement I can make is that when I read words written by people long since dead, like those I quoted above, I see embedded in their words truths about history, poetry, cosmology, science, and astronomy that I take to heart in my own life and try to apply to my work professionally. For Oscar Wilde, part of the beauty of history is its originality, while the downfall of historiography is the lack of it. William Blake senses the dangers of system-building in philosophy and cosmology and hopes to effect his escape through visionary poetry. Willa Cather and George Eliot create autobiographical and regional narratives to convey their sense of the historical significance of women in relation to the natural environment. Jacob Bronowski's and J. Robert Oppenheimer's urgent testimonies of the presence of science in the world flash in bold relief against James Agee's equally urgent desire to fuse authentic, self-conscious artistic representation to the actual. All have shaped how I feel about life and interdisciplinary studies. All have bearing on my reading of the final passage quoted above in which Hardy depicts two lovers apprehending the beauty and terror of their place in the universe.

So, to the extent possible, and in so far as it is within my power, I would like to avoid knowingly falsifying my own history. However theoretical signposts may have reassured or turned me away from certain methodological pathways, none was prior to the fundamental personal values I developed from reading primary materials in literature, history and science. I learned from Blake before Kuhn; Wilde before Latour; Cather before Haraway.[6] Many of my friends and colleagues in both disciplines have directed their research and thinking by applying the various theories and methodologies of literary critics, linguists, philosophers of history and science, and sociologists of science, often with an intelligence and diligence I greatly admire. I have followed with keen interest their work in new literary history, formalist criticism,

---

[6]   Although subsequent engagement with their works has also proven invaluable, see: Thomas S. Kuhn, *The Copernican Revolution: Planetary Astronomy in the Development of Western Thought* (Cambridge, MA: Harvard University Press, 1957), *The Structure of Scientific Revolutions*, 2nd ed., enlarged (Chicago: University of Chicago Press, 1970), and *The Essential Tension: Selected Studies in Scientific Tradition and Change* (Chicago: University of Chicago Press, 1977); Bruno Latour and Steve Woolgar, *Laboratory Life: The Construction of Scientific Facts* (Princeton: Princeton University Press, 1986), Bruno Latour, *Science in Action: How to Follow Scientists and Engineers through Society* (Cambridge, MA: Harvard University Press, 1987) and *We Have Never Been Modern* [*Nous n'avons jamais été modernes*], trans. Catherine Porter (Cambridge, MA: Harvard University Press, 1993); Donna Jeanne Haraway, *Primate Visions: Gender, Race, and Nature in the World of Modern Science* (New York: Routledge, 1989) and *Simians, Cyborgs, and Women: The Reinvention of Nature* (New York: Routledge, 1991).

representational theory and art history, anthropology, cultural studies, and gender and science. Rather than attuning myself to their methodologies, however, or somehow adapting their critical apparatus to my projects, I have tried to develop my own style of analysis by modeling *primary* texts – working to craft my own empathetic mode of historiography and literary interpretation.

To literary scholars, the methods of my literary history of science may most resemble those of close reading, reader-response criticism, intertextuality, or psychological and biographical criticism. Historians of science may note similarities with the history of ideas, theories of narrative history or Gerald Holton's concept of *themata.*[7] To some extent, my methodological preferences may be attributable to unconscious modeling of the critical approaches of other scholars. In making conscious critical choices, though, I have extrapolated from my personal experience of reading and writing to the professional tasks of literary exegesis and historiography. Observing my own use of narrative, metaphor, and analogy, I assume that if I have developed identifiable patterns of interpretation and expression, my subjects, like Hardy, probably have as well. At base, I try to let each author teach me about his or her texts. I try to attend to the visible evidence they have left of their thought, beliefs and feelings in their imagery, metaphors and analogies, the relation of form and content in their narratives, their symbolic repertoires and recurrent thematic motifs.

Literary theorists have long examined the processes and products of creative writing in light of theories of archetypes, theories of mind, the psychological insights of Descartes, Freud, Jung, James, Lacan. Some historians of science have ventured psychological readings of their subjects' work as well. Similarly, elements of personal construct psychology and neuronal group selection inform and support my approach. According to proponents of neural Darwinism, as synaptic networks develop and are reinforced by the stimuli of a human being's experiences, they emerge in consciousness as metaphoric and narrative patterns that order, store, retrieve and assign meaning to the chaotic phenomena of life. In therapeutic practice, the narrative therapist's role is to learn from the client's telling and retelling of stories and compose a profile of his/her personal set of meaningful associations (in contrast to interpreting them according to preestablished Freudian or Jungian sets of symbols). The neurophysiological origins of metaphor and narrative and the psychology of personal constructs may lend intelligibility to the attempt to account for how and why individuals' personal narrative constructions of natural knowledge (especially in cosmology, religion, gender) correlate or conflict with the social constructions around them.[8] When something seems to be "in the air" or in shared discourse, it may also be transmitting itself in the ether between our ears.

---

[7]   Gerald James Holton, *Thematic Origins of Scientific Thought: Kepler to Einstein*, rev. ed. (1973; Cambridge, MA: Harvard University Press, 1988) and *The Scientific Imagination: Case Studies* (Cambridge: Cambridge University Press, 1978).

[8]   For a wide variety of instructive descriptions of possible applications of such methods of analysis, see: Robert A. Neimeyer and Jonathan D. Raskin, eds., *Constructions of Disorder:*

If history results from the butterfly effect of human agency, it makes sense to prefer a correspondingly corpuscular model of historiography, tracing the visible evidence of contact, however minute, between human actors, the exchange of books and meetings of minds. While the "truth" may be "out there," consensus about the nature of reality – past, present, or future – will almost certainly remain out of reach by any means human beings may develop to apprehend it, literary, historical, scientific, or otherwise. I do not believe that the impossibility of *fully* knowing relieves us from the desire or need to know, nor should it discourage us from trying. As far as I can tell, the thoughts and feelings, the actualities, of the formerly living are only in the slightest degree more occult than those of the living breathing husband and children I have dinner with every night. I have about the same tools at my disposal for learning about both: words, and the shared experience of human existence. What I learn about my grandmother's life in the letters, poems, and stories she left tied in tidy bundles is different from what I learned from the stories she told me across her kitchen table or the songs she sang as she worked. I am grateful for both. I feel the same gratitude for the written artifacts of Donne, Kepler, Behn, Hardy et al., and hope to extend to them the same familial respect and courtesies. That my grandmother has been gone over ten years, and they have been gone three or four hundred, makes no essential difference to the kind of curiosity I have about their lives, the empathy I feel for them, or the ways I can discern and imagine their existence.

Another crucial aspect of my notion of a literary history of science – the personal relation of researcher to historical subject – has been substantially shaped by the empathetic mode of narrative voice employed by certain historical novelists and particular authors of nature writing and experimental documentary fiction. Writers from my native state, Willa Cather and Wright Morris, simultaneously evoke a sense of place, historicity, and self-consciousness in their writing – a poetics of history.[9] Perhaps the simple power of the Nebraska landscape, the tangible sensation of being the lone verticality upon an endless plain/plane, lost in so much space, always

---

Meaning-making Frameworks for Psychotherapy (Washington, DC: American Psychological Association, 2000); Michael F. Hoyt, ed., *The Handbook of Constructive Therapies: Innovative Approaches from Leading Practitioners* (San Francisco: Jossey-Bass, 1998) and Glenn Roberts and Jeremy Holmes, eds., *Healing Stories: Narrative in Psychiatry and Psychotherapy* (Oxford: Oxford University Press, 1999).

[9]   Willa Cather, *O Pioneers!* (1913. Boston: Houghton Mifflin, 1941), *The Song of the Lark* (Boston: Houghton Mifflin, 1915), *My Antonia* (New York: Houghton Mifflin, 1918), *One of Ours* (New York: A. A. Knopf, 1922), *A Lost Lady* (New York: A. A. Knopf, 1923), and *Death Comes for the Archbishop* (New York: A.A. Knopf, 1927); Wright Morris, *The Home Place* (1948. Lincoln: University of Nebraska Press, 1999), *The Field of Vision* (New York: Harcourt, Brace, 1956), *Ceremony in Lone Tree* (New York: Atheneum, 1960), *God's Country and My People*, (New York: Harper and Row, 1968), *Plains Song, for Female Voices* (New York: Harper and Row, 1980), *Will's Boy: A Memoir* (New York: Harper and Row, 1981), and *Photographs & Words / Wright Morris*, ed. James Alinder (Carmel, CA: Friends of Photography, 1982).

unavoidably facing the verge of the horizon, endows Great Plains writers with a special appreciation for the universal dilemma of life on this pale blue dot and whatever spirit or art its inhabitants are able to raise within, against, and upon it. Similarly, I see a poetics of science in the work of Barry Lopez, John Janovy, and Loren Eiseley (the latter two also from Nebraska), all of whom perceive and experience nature while self-consciously interpreting and expressing what they see.[10] The personal and subjective representation of Cather's and Morris's "literary" history and the poetic science of Lopez, Janovy and Eiseley, suggest alternative, or additional desirable facets often absent from an impersonal "objective" historiography. Some of the legitimate work of historiography is the search for the means of representing the past with aesthetic and personal authenticity. I have found the most inspiring exploration of the relation of the subjective/aesthetic to the actual/historical in James Agee's and Walker Evan's *Let Us Now Praise Famous Men* (1941).

For Agee, perceiving the human dilemma and writing about it were extensions of the same problem. In writing documentary fiction (as all history is to various degrees), Agee sought a way to use words to communicate "the cruel radiance of what is."[11] He found the whole process of representing life through words "curious, obscene, terrifying and unfathomably mysterious" and recognized that none of us are capable of achieving it, or fully appreciating the efforts of others who try. For me, Agee's fusion of poetry, history, and actuality, provides an apt model for literary history of science. His deep and empathetic apprehension of life, I try to grant to the formerly living. I appreciate his commitment and struggle to use words in a poetically precise mode of representation. I share his recognition of the inescapable inadequacy of words, the ultimate futility of such a struggle; but I also share his belief in the essential meaning and value of the effort; despite all the restraints and limits and virtually guaranteed failures, the attempt itself partakes of, and contributes to, the beauty of history.

*   *   *

It is in the shared spirit of such efforts – far from the collision course of cross-disciplinary conflict – that I offer this attempt to observe and describe Thomas

---

[10] Barry Holstun Lopez, *Of Wolves and Men* (New York: Scribner, 1978), *Winter Count* (New York: Scribner, 1981), *Arctic Dreams: Imagination and Desire in a Northern Landscape* (New York: Scribner, 1986), and *About this Life: Journeys on the Threshold of Memory* (New York: Knopf/Random House, 1998); John Janovy, Jr., *Keith County Journal* (New York: St. Martin's Press, 1978) and *Yellowlegs: A Migration of the Mind* (Boston: Houghton Mifflin, 1980); Loren C. Eiseley, *The Immense Journey* (New York, Random House, 1957), *The Invisible Pyramid* (New York, Scribner, 1970), *The Unexpected Universe* (London: Victor Gollancz, 1970), *The Night Country* (New York: Scribner, 1971), *The Innocent Assassins* (New York: Scribner, 1973), *All the Strange Hours: The Excavation of a Life* (New York: Scribner, 1975), and *The Star Thrower* (New York: Times Books, 1978).

[11] James Agee and Walker Evans, *Let Us Now Praise Famous Men* (1939, 1940, 1941; New York: Ballantine, 1976) 11.

Hardy's novel universe. In creative, cultural and philosophical continuity with past mythopoetic and natural historical narratives, astronomical and cosmological accounts, I believe that Hardy's unique mind and personality worked together to fashion a set of new myths encapsulating his view of humanity's place in the universe. One can only hope to respond in kind to the literary history of science that Hardy himself creates in his novels – a realistic assessment and compassionate understanding of the multifarious ways that cosmic forces converge, for good or ill, in our common human story.

Chapter 2

Literary History of Astronomy and the Origins of Hardy's Literary Cosmology

The primary subject matter of this chapter can be approached in at least two ways depending on how one chooses to combine and stress the first three principal terms of the title: a literary *history of astronomy* or, a *literary history* of astronomy. The former has generally been considered the purview of historians of science specializing in the "exact sciences" of mathematics, astronomy and physics, with personal interest in the humanistic contexts of their subjects' work; whereas the latter has primarily been undertaken by literary scholars and critics with amateur interest in popular astronomy and cosmology. Although the two groups often treat the same primary materials, they rarely emphasize the same scholarly questions or arrive at similar conclusions about their significance. On his own Hardy studied the literary history of astronomy and cosmology from *both* perspectives, creating a unique understanding of their interplay in human history and consciousness that is evident in the settings and emplotment of his novels.

Literary *History of Astronomy*: Actual and Potential

Traditionally trained historians of astronomy and physics have earned their reputations as the most conservative practitioners of history of science. Focusing their studies almost exclusively on the technical aspects of observational–experimental and theoretical astronomy and astrophysics, they scan and scrutinize observational data in tablets and tables, retrace sight lines and calculations, test instruments and their measurements, and confirm astronomical laws and theories. Attempting to see through their subjects' eyes with as close to the same optics as possible, such scholars often conduct their research, and frequently write about it, in the language of mathematics – geometry and calculus. Their efforts yield exquisite understanding of the descriptive, explanatory and predictive power of astronomy as it has developed over time. Given the high level of commitment to an internalist approach within the field, it is hard to imagine a less literary subdiscipline within the history of science. Many historians of astronomy themselves accept this characterization, although part of their own disciplinary history belies it.

Literary *history of astronomy* is not a part of mainstream history of science, but it has taken many forms over the past one hundred years, from trivial homage to serious engagement. Historians of technical astronomy generally travel the whole length of their careers without noticing the creative literature they pass by, although occasionally a strict internalist may footnote a useful "transdisciplinary" study or set the tone and central theme for a journal article or book chapter with a quotation from a poet, dramatist, or novelist. While most syllabi for graduate and undergraduate history of astronomy courses tend to have conservative reading lists, some include satires, poems, novels or plays with astronomical subject matter to supplement (and offer diversion from) other required readings. Historians of popular astronomy, by contrast, have found literary works essential, mining them for direct and indirect evidence of the dissemination of astronomical concepts and discoveries across wide audiences. Often they choose literary or artistic examples to illustrate the social context of, or individuals' response to, particular scientific ideas or events.[1] The histories of archaeoastronomy and ancient and medieval astronomy and cosmology, likewise, would scarcely exist as fields if their practitioners had not acknowledged the importance of – and widely used – literary source materials. Indeed, for those time periods, and across many cultures, literature and astronomy share much of the same history within many of the same artifacts and texts (as we will see in the next section below).

Among historians of astronomy who study the early modern period to the present, it is somewhat rarer to encounter deep engagement with primary literary resources. As the forces of the Renaissance and Scientific Revolution progressed across several centuries, the seven Liberal Arts were gradually redefined as the "Arts and Sciences" and a similar split is reflected within the ranks of the scholars who now study them. The intense interdisciplinary training undertaken by historians of astronomy in mathematics, astronomy, physics, foreign languages, and historiography typically affords them little opportunity to acquire additional corollary expertise in literary and rhetorical studies. Where critical analyses of literary materials have been relevant and enriching to their projects, historians of early modern and modern astronomy usually do not venture their own interpretations of the primary literary texts, but cite, instead, the analyses of scholars specializing in literature and language studies. In such cases, historians of astronomy seek out "literature and science" books and articles, literary critical biographies, or interpretative studies of individual literary writers who achieved a high degree of scientific literacy and employed sophisticated scientific images and themes in their work. For example, they may refer to the works of C. S.

---

[1] To note just a few such relevant studies: Michael J. Crowe, *The Extraterrestrial Life Debate 1750–1900: The Idea of a Plurality of Worlds From Kant to Lowell* (Cambridge: Cambridge University Press, 1986); Sara Schechner Genuth, *Comets, Popular Culture, and the Birth of Modern Cosmology* (Princeton: Princeton University Press, 1997); and Stephen C. McCluskey, *Astronomies and Cultures in Early Medieval Europe* (Cambridge: Cambridge University Press, 1998).

Lewis or A. O. Lovejoy or consult collaborative literature and science surveys (such as Alan J. Friedman's and Carol C. Donley's joint study of the "myth" of Einstein) to get a sense of "what was in the air" in a particular culture during a time period they study. They may quote specialists such as Stephen Fallon or Harinder Marjara to indicate what the current "lit. crit." take is on Milton's references to Galileo in *Paradise Lost.*

The downside of this dependence upon secondary literary scholarship is that historians may inadvertently recycle literary critiques that are misinformed, outdated, and themselves dependent on recycled and outdated histories of science. Thomas Kuhn, himself, offers one of the most influentially notorious examples. While Nicolson's *Science and Imagination, Breaking of the Circle* and *Newton Demands the Muse* (among others) provide valuable interpretations of early modern literature read against the background of contemporary science, they are best read, too, against the literary and historical contexts in which she wrote them. Drawing upon Nicolson's studies (and inadequately mindful of other intellectual and religious influences she describes), historians of science like Kuhn (and others) have supported the argument that Copernican astronomy engendered a revolutionary "crisis" in the surrounding culture. Literary scholars joined in determining the degree and kind of scientific crisis detectable in astronomical literature; not asking *whether* (as Donne put it) "new philosophy calls all in doubt" – but *how*. To some extent taken in by the "two" world systems propaganda of Milton and Galileo, scholars in both fields have over-simplified the cosmological choices culturally available to literary writers (Ptolemy *versus* Copernicus). Thus, much astronomy in literary works has been misidentified, scientific perspectives skewed, and interpretations of literary responses to astronomical developments obscured. The "doubt" of Donne, for example, has been read as ambivalence over, or hesitancy to choose between, geo- and heliocentric models; when, quite probably, he had moved beyond such debates to embrace a sophisticated Keplerian cosmos.[2]

To avoid losing themselves in such interpretative mazes, perhaps, book-length studies of the interrelations of literature and astronomy by historians of astronomy have been few and far between. For such reasons, J. D. North's monograph, *Chaucer's Universe* (1988), may remain unique (in more ways than one) among the scholarly products of historians of astronomy. There can be little doubt that Geoffrey Chaucer's eminent place in the astrological–meteorological poetic tradition has been in no small part established by North's expert analysis of the poet's command of technical astronomy and astrology. While few historians of science have matched the depth and scale of North's project, they have produced many journal articles and book chapters that utilize literary resource materials and concerns. Among such projects are

---

[2] See: Gossin, "Introduction," "Astronomical Allusion and Analogies in Donne's *Ignatius His Conclave* and Selected Poetry" and "Donne's Poetic Adaptation of Complex Astronomy in 'Good Friday 1613. Riding Westward,' 'The First Anniversary' and others," in *Poetic Resolutions of Scientific Revolutions* 20–8, 81–144, 145–204.

rhetorical studies of the prefaces of primary astronomical or cosmological texts, investigations of the translation and transmission of primary works through various language groups and cultures, analyses of matters of audience and influence in the popularization of astronomy and physics, examinations of the hermeneutics of scientific metaphors and language, and discourse studies of primary astronomical texts.[3]

Although historians of astronomy have long been aware that historically and scientifically germane content is embedded in poetic, dramatic, and fictional literary forms and subject matter, as of yet, interpretative and historiographical engagement of literary materials within the discipline is still more potential than actual. The reluctance of historians of astronomy to utilize literary sources more fully may be owing both to the perception that literary materials require specialized literary forms of analysis and a concomitant distrust of those forms, especially new historicism, reader-response criticism, deconstruction, semiotics, and post-structuralism. Nonetheless, some historians of science are discovering that the interpretative latitude afforded literary works need not be appreciably wider (or fuzzier) than that granted other types of historical documents or scientific texts. Literary and historical exegetes often assign meaning by working within virtually identical sets of hermeneutic parameters, exploring issues of authorship and audience, biographical detail, professional and personal aims, cultural and technical contexts, and rhetorical and stylistic traditions. Indeed, historians of science bring unique backgrounds and skills as proficient readers to the interpretation of primary works of creative literature. By doing so, we perform an invaluable exegetical service: roughly recapitulating contemporary audiences' experience of literary and scientific writing.

Historians of science, in general, and historians of astronomy, in particular, have much to gain both personally and professionally by employing a fuller, and more explicit, consideration of literary sources, concerns, and methods in our research and writing. Literary texts provide insights into the achievements, goals and interpersonal relationships of scientific actors as individual thinkers and as members of culturally distinct groups. Literary works record, illuminate and inform the social and political contexts, institutional settings and popular perceptions of scientific activities. Poets, dramatists and storytellers express the interests and concerns of the culture at large and their subjects often directly involve discoveries and developments in astronomy and

---

[3]   See, for example, the general argument and especially the final chapter in James R. Voelkel, *The Composition of Kepler's Astronomia Nova* (Princeton: Princeton University Press, 2001); Robert S. Westman, "Proof, Poetics, and Patronage: Copernicus's Preface to *De Revolutionibus*" in *Reappraisals of the Scientific Revolution*, eds. David C. Lindberg and Robert S. Westman (Cambridge: Cambridge University Press, 1990) 167–205; various essays in *Astrology, Science and Society: Historical Essays*, eds. Patrick Curry (Woodbridge, Suffolk, Eng.: The Boydell Press, 1987); and James J. Bono, *The Word of God and the Languages of Man: Interpreting Nature in Early Modern Science and Medicine, vol. 1: Ficino to Descartes* (Madison: University of Wisconsin Press, 1995).

natural philosophy. These texts record their authors' awareness of and responses to astronomy in general as well as to particular developments. Since many of the key players in the history of astronomy belonged to intellectual societies with wide interests and broadly literary and philosophical social circles, it seems appropriate for historians of astronomy to study their subjects' discursive universe in a form as close to the inherently interdisciplinary original as possible.

A ready familiarity with the literary history of astronomy enables robust interpretations of contemporary discourse employed by astronomers and their peers. Formal conventions, motifs, wordplay, and figures of speech encountered in astronomical texts and other historical documents often have established patterns of meaning within *literary* tradition. Awareness of the existence of literary conventions in astronomical imagery can add sophistication and caution to historical conclusions about how particular astronomical concepts may have been transmitted and popularized. Is a natural philosopher comparing a human heart to the sun because he is a knowledgeable heliocentrist (probably knew Thomas Digges or William Harvey) or had he participated in the coterie circulation of metaphysical poems that played off of that trope and one or more of those *poets* knew, or knew of, Digges or Harvey?

Literary *history of astronomy* can help map a range of culturally available meanings for diverse forms, styles, themes and ideas as they are encountered in various kinds of texts. Such contexts can help distinguish when an astronomer is employing an original or derivative concept, establishing an important variation-on-a-theme or idly repeating a commonplace. A heated online discussion by the members of the History of Astronomy listserv (hastro-l) a few years ago illustrates this point as a number of members worked their way to the conclusion that Isaac Newton's famous "standing on the shoulders of giants" remark accumulates significance both from its allusion to past usages of the image by other writers and by its adaptation of prevailing literary techniques of *ad hominem* satiric attack.[4]

The literature of astronomy can provide a complex knowledge base for interpreting the nature and purposes of literary production within emergent scientific and literary communities. In many forms of literature, fundamental nomenclature and the popular meanings of astronomical terms and concepts shift as they enter and travel through different intellectual populations and social classes. The degree of literacy and learning possessed by authors and their audiences greatly influences the sophistication of literary references to scientific developments. For example, popular almanac writers' discussions of Aristotelian–Ptolemaic and Copernican astronomy do not generally emphasize that these systems are rough equivalents as symbols of the *limitations* (as opposed to the glorious achievements) of human reason, but that *is* Milton's perspective.

When we read the literature of astronomy in explicitly literary ways, we can supplement our awareness, as historians of astronomy, of formal style, rhetorical

---

[4] For the archives of the History of Astronomy Discussion Group see: <http://listserv.wvu.edu/archives/hastro-l.html>

principles, and their applications. Not all uses of rhetoric go by the book, Aristotelian or otherwise. Then, as now, grammar, rhetorical style and literary technique were primarily learned through usage rather than university instruction. Through careful attention to the structure of primary texts, and much practice, readers develop an "ear" for style, and learn to recognize personal trademarks of diction and the jargon of intellectual peers. We can discern when nuances of tone indicate genuine emotional response or a quick bow to literary convention – personal regard versus courtly compliment, honest reluctance to publish versus stylish authorial false modesty. Such distinctions can directly shape our interpretations of texts because persuasive strategies, argumentative styles and fashionable forms of irony all exhibit faddish change within intellectual coteries.

In their writing, astronomers appropriate and modify language and concepts from literature and other types of writing in the surrounding culture. Our understanding of Kepler's and Newton's cosmologies can be supplemented, for example, by examining how their writing draws upon disparate aspects of theological poetics. Astronomers also draw upon literary models outside their own subject matter to engage in debate with their contemporaries and historical predecessors. These dialogues often betray themselves in the subtext, that is, at the level of tonal echoes, parodic allusion and imitative formal structures. Applying literary reading skills to historical and scientific texts, historians of scientific controversies and priority disputes (often central to the history of astronomy) can gain insight beyond texts' superficial content that can prove invaluable for understanding the form and function of the verbal assaults natural philosophers launched upon each other. Jonathan Swift and Alexander Pope offer brilliant case studies of how men of letters used writing to negotiate complex public and private quarrels, campaigns for and against competing professional styles and disputes concerning political, social and moral values. Read in light of these literary pyrotechnics, the dark shadows of priority disputes and bitter correspondence between Newton and Hooke, Newton and Flamsteed, Newton and you-name-him take on new significance. The enlistment by prominent *scientific* actors of networks of correspondents and discursive champions who pledged their pens to defend their cause is likewise usefully highlighted by the important strategic advantages commanded by *literary* figures with strong coffeehouse followings and large popular readerships.

The literature of astronomy creates explicit and structural astronomical analogies that describe human emotion, political intrigue, philosophical dilemmas and religious faith; it memorializes the heroes of the history of astronomy and mocks them. Literary treatments of cosmology and the space sciences create complex social, political and religious allegories and explore still unresolved tensions in humanity's powers of imagination and reason. By including creative writing among the resources of the history of science, we extend the range of the discipline's research as well as enrich its repertoire of reading skills. The predictable cadences of descriptive prose, the unexpected presence of a narrator's voice, the exotic melodies of poetic prosody – rarely encountered in most texts and documents used in the history of science – offer a refreshing break to scholarly reading habits. The versatility and subtle precision with which creative writers employ literary devices remind historians of science of the importance of actively selecting and creatively shaping the meanings of the literary forms and tropes we employ. As writers, historians of science have constructed an array of narratives and devised various metaphors to describe and explain the development of astrology, astronomy and astrophysics. Examining how literary form and style operate in primary literary texts of the time periods we study can raise professional self-consciousness about how and why to deploy literary devices and strategies in our own historiography. Have we constructed one of our own narratives as a contest, murder mystery or coming-of-age story with conscious purpose or by subconscious default? Is a certain governing metaphor historically apt or anachronistic? Has the momentum of plot development compelled the characterization of a set of scientific actors as heroes or victims? Why? Periodically as historians of science, we reappraise the meaning of our own working metaphors ("revolution") and consider whether developmental models themselves need reconfiguration or replacement in our narratives. Attending to how narrative structure, characterization, tone, analogy and metaphor operate in primary literary texts can help us think in literary ways about the words we use to write history – which, in turn, can help us, literally, think about history. Just as importantly, such approaches may enhance our ability to communicate and promote our epistemological and philosophical values to our students and the general reading public as well as to others working within the growing and increasingly diverse interdisciplinary academic community. The wealth of available primary materials should prove irresistibly inspiring.

Literary History of Astronomy: Prehistory through the Victorian Period

The vast majority of "literature and astronomy" studies (especially those examining the late medieval to early Renaissance era) have been produced by literary scholars and critics, often those working from historicist perspectives or in the tradition of intellectual history or the history of ideas. The *literary history* of astronomy reveals a fantastic abundance of primary materials. Throughout human history, countless creative writers sought and achieved some level of understanding of astronomy, astrology, or cosmology, past and contemporary. They crafted their accounts according to the unique formal requirements of their chosen genre: rhyme schemes, rhythms, conventions, tropes, rhetorical traditions, dramatic unities, characterization etc. They expressed both intellectual and emotional responses to the cosmic dilemmas posed by the phenomena in the sky and our mortal condition here below. Although inspired by these challenges, such works often exhibit the tension of rendering the truths of natural philosophy both technically and aesthetically whole. At its best, the artistic interplay of literature and astronomy further elevates the already ennobled investigations of natural philosophy and science by literally embodying and recreating the essence of the quest. Such literature represents the beauty and profundity of our attempts to understand the phenomena, the poignancy and significance of our failure to achieve insights into nature's mysteries as well as the power of our most successful visions of the inner workings of the universe.

The sophistication of the astronomical content of literature varies proportionally or inversely to the aesthetic achievement of the works themselves. Successful poetic adaptation of an astronomical concept or discovery to metaphor is not guaranteed by technical expertise nor necessarily thwarted by inaccuracy or anachronism. "Bad" astronomy does not negate the aesthetic value of a poem or play otherwise well-written and conceived. For example, the poetic effect of John Keats' *On First Looking into Chapman's Homer* is not particularly intensified by his correct allusion to the new planet, Uranus, nor reduced by his erroneous reference to Cortez as the "discoverer" of the Pacific. Only rarely has "good" science saved "poor" verse from obscurity, with perhaps, James Thomson's aesthetically uneven *The Seasons*, a good case in point. Generally, however, the "astronomical" poems that receive the most scholarly attention are those considered canonically sound either by virtue of their individual merits and literary interest, or the standard critical assessment of their authors' oeuvre. Coincidentally, those same works are often the ones that treat issues considered canonically central to the development of astronomy since the Scientific Revolution as well (and thus most mentioned here are in Latin, English, French, Italian, and German).

There is a surprising range of astronomical phenomena and theoretical issues employed in literary works, in all historical periods, although a good deal of this content has gone unrecognized by even the closest literary readers, general or professional. The basic phenomena of earth, sun, moon, planets, and stars, and other "naked-eye" celestial objects are, of course, well-represented in literary imagery. Allusions to the earth as a planet include discussions of the four elements, the nature of the sublunary realm, technical aspects of Aristotelian physics and comparisons of geocentric and Tychonic systems. Magnetism, meteorology, electricity, auroras, and the earth's rotation appear frequently in literary imagery. Myriad references, poetic and prosaic, draw upon solar eclipses, sunspots, the inequality of the seasons, corona, anima motrix, solar retinopathy, heliocentrism, lunar topography, lunar phases and eclipses, the tides, two- and three- body systems and imaginary moon voyages. Literature documents the development of concepts concerning planetary phenomena from the music of the spheres, the nature of solid or crystalline spheres, planetary intelligences, Ptolemaic and Copernican models, through Galilean telescopic discoveries (satellites of Jupiter, rings of Saturn, phases of Venus), to circular and elliptical orbits, Keplerian laws, Newtonian gravitation, retrograde motion, the plurality of worlds, and extraterrestrials. Literary references to stellar observations and theories range from the astrological to the astrophysical, including: the fixed stars, trepidation, constellations, asterisms, stellar "influences," the Milky Way, the infinity of stars, their distances and proper motion, novae, variable stars, the nebular hypothesis, and pulsars. The muse of astronomy, Urania, has inspired plentiful allusions to comets, space, the void, plenum, extension, the infinity of the universe, entropy, and the role of the supernatural in the establishment and maintenance of natural law.

In all periods, writers enlist their astronomical knowledge to discuss such important and recurrent themes as the world in decay, the argument from design, sympathetic nature, the cruelty of nature, and the anthropomorphic fallacy. Astronomical figures illustrate philosophical relations of faith and reason, the role of imagination and fancy in poetic and scientific creativity, problems of the reason–sense dichotomy (including the reliability of sensory perception), and the place of emotion in scientific thought and natural investigation. References to astronomical ideas and discoveries, allusions to the lives and works of historical astronomers as well as the creation of fictional ones, bring important social issues to public notice. Such examples fuel and provide illustrations for the ancients and moderns debate, arguments concerning the utility of astronomical science, the educational value of the mathematical arts, the mathematization of nature, public attitudes toward astronomers as scientists, and astronomy's role in cosmology, especially in relation to evolution and geology.

Prehistory through the Middle Ages

In prehistoric and ancient times, the origins and materials of the *literary history* of astronomy overlap substantially with those informing the literary *history of astronomy*. Ethnographers believe that people of ancient oral cultures throughout the world, like their contemporary counterparts, created myths and narratives to preserve and transmit knowledge of the celestial bodies and beliefs about their origins. Artifacts of archaeoastronomy are encoded with early sophisticated observational astronomy.[5] Solar, lunar and stellar phenomena were recorded by the structure and positioning of lodges and kiva (such those of the Pawnee and Hopi), earthworks and burial mounds (as in North American and Britain), pyramids, temples, and city grids (as in Mexico, Egypt, and Southeast Asia). Archaeological evidence found in many geographical areas suggests that astronomical information was marked upon the ground with stones, stakes, chalk or pigment. Anthropologists, paleontologists, and archaeoastronomers examining evidence in Europe, South America, the American Great Plains and Southwest, Egypt, Sumer, and China have found many examples of early forms of writing – paintings on cave walls, buckskin, and sand; bone and antler markings; decorative art; designs on woven fabric and headdresses; petroglyphs and pictograms – that they believe carry astronomical content. The astronomy in ancient literatures in

---

[5]   See such works as: James Cornell, *The First Stargazers: An Introduction to the Origins of Astronomy* (New York: Scribner's, 1981); Anthony F. Aveni, *Skywatchers*, rev. ed. (Austin: University of Texas Press, 2001), — ed., *World Archaeoastronomy: Selected Papers from the 2nd Oxford International Conference on Archaeoastronomy* (1986; Cambridge: Cambridge University Press, 1989), and — ed., *Native American Astronomy* (Austin: University of Texas Press, 1977).

all forms greatly contributes to our understanding of cultures' religious myths and rituals, cosmological speculations, agriculture, animal husbandry, time-keeping, and social and political organizations (as in Sumer, Egypt, China and Japan). As these cultures framed perceptions of the cosmos, and explanations for its phenomena, the linkage of literature and astronomy was driven by many of the same forces that connected religion and astronomy: necessity, curiosity, wonder, and fear. Successful farming, hunting, and survival itself, were dependent on accurate observation of seasonal patterns, determination of how such patterns were integrated with solar and lunar cycles, and the effective preservation and transmission of this vital information.

As conditions permitted, poets, priests, and astronomers – when their functions were not embodied by a single figure – pondered together questions concerning the nature of human existence and the cosmos. They recorded celestial observations and speculations about the relations of the human and individual to the natural and universal in various preliterate and literary forms. Oral astronomical narratives (often poems or songs) were practical mnemonic devices integral to the enactment and perpetuation of religious rituals and social functions. These narratives fulfilled aesthetic and philosophical goals as they communicated cosmogonic myths and agriculturally useful information. In syllabic and alphabetical literatures, poetry was the genre of choice to inscribe astronomy, astrology, meteorology and cosmology for many centuries, possessing the high seriousness and aesthetic sublimity appropriate to considerations of the astrological and meteorological significance of observed phenomena (as in examples found in Egypt, Sumer, India, China, Greece, Italy and throughout Islam). So rich was the philosophical and astronomical content in these verses (Hesiod, Parmenides, Empedocles, Aratus, Lucretius, Manilius, et al.) that literary critics (both contemporary and recent) questioned whether they should even be classified as poetry. Historians of astronomy who specialize in pre- and early human history and cultures have long depended upon these literary and aesthetic raw materials to provide evidence of technical knowledge of celestial phenomena as well as contextual support for the cultural value of such knowledge.

Many works in the Greek and Roman classical literary traditions have also been integral to the history of astronomy of those cultures. Obviously the dialogs of Plato and the encyclopedic natural philosophy of Aristotle have long been prized as both literary and astronomical treasures. Although the philosophical nature poem was the dominant form of astronomical–astrological, meteorological and cosmological literature in the classical period, significant astronomical images and astrological references are also present in Homeric epic, Greek drama (Aristophanes, Aeschylus), and various forms of Latin verse and prose (Vergil, Ovid, and Varro). Plutarch treated popular astronomical lore in *De Facie in Orbe Lunae*. The earliest extant works of "science fiction," Lucian's *True History* and *Icaromenippus*, exerted strong influence, as did Cicero's "cosmic dream," *Somnium Scipionis*. The visionary cosmologies of Hildegard of Bingen and other early church figures are fascinating variations of this genre.

Drawing as it does upon both ancient classical and biblical originals, the philosophical–cosmological poem is one of the most important forms within medieval literary history of astronomy. Historians of astronomy have long recognized Dante's *Divine Comedy* as an essential reference for understanding medieval verse in this genre, but it has been scholars working from within literary or medieval studies who have produced the most detailed interdisciplinary studies of it.[6] *Image du monde* is an influential descriptive astronomical poem, probably written by the French poet Gossouin in the mid-thirteenth century. Translated as *The Mirror of the World* by William Caxton, this work (drawing upon the same sources as Sacrobosco) is perhaps the most comprehensive account of medieval astronomy available in English until the mid-sixteenth century. Again, it has been literary scholars, such as Francis Johnson, who have brought attention to it as an important resource for both literature and the history of astronomy.[7]

Renaissance and Early Modern

At the point where Renaissance literary and artistic endeavors meet the achievements of the Scientific Revolution, primary source materials for the *literary history* of astronomy are ubiquitous. The concerns and conventions of star-crossed lovers and starry nights predominate in lyric poetry, while increasingly elaborate imagery and themes drawn from astronomy, astrology, and cosmology are commonplace in encyclopedic astronomical–philosophical and astrological–meteorological poems as well as poetic "shepherd's calendars." Appearing in both Latin and the vernacular such works include Vincent de Beauvais' *Speculum naturale*; *Le Compost et Kalendrier des bergiers*, 1493, and its English translations, *Kalendar of Shepherdes*; *De proprietatibus rerum* of Bartholomaeus Anglicus; and the *Zodiacus vitae* of Marcellus Palingenius, 1531. Although the quality of versification and levels of cosmological and philosophical complexity in these poems vary widely, their characterizations of the Aristotelian-Ptolemaic system are immensely useful for tracing contemporary popular and technical understanding of the natural world and celestial phenomena.

Literary accounts of astronomy in the first post-Copernican century, exhibit all of the variety, beauty, and flaws of those written previously. Following the fluxes of literary fashion and criticism, all of the major forms and genres mentioned above – the philosophical or cosmological poem, astrological–meteorological verse, drama, epic,

---

[6] Alison Cornish, *Reading Dante's Stars* (New Haven: Yale University Press, 2000); Richard Kay, *Dante's Christian Astrology* (Philadelphia: University of Pennsylvania Press, 1994); and Mary Acworth Orr, *Dante and the Early Astronomers* (1913; Port Washington, NY: Kennikat Press, 1969).

[7] Francis R. Johnson, *Astronomical Thought in Renaissance England: A Study of the English Scientific Writings from 1500 to 1645* (Baltimore: Johns Hopkins University Press, 1937) 70; hereafter: Johnson.

lyric, popularizations in prose and verse, cosmic voyages – were variously modified and put to new purposes, and all still carried astronomical concepts and content. Some early modern writers continued to draw upon their knowledge of ancient and medieval astronomy. As significant developments occurred in astronomical thought and new observational discoveries were made, they appear virtually concurrently in the writings of interested astronomers and the literary subject matter, themes, and images of non-astronomers. In England, the first vernacular treatments of Copernicanism – popular texts and astrological almanacs – were printed within a dozen years of *De Revolutionibus* (1543). Like astronomical–philosophical poems, these prose works were intended to fulfill the Horatian invocation to delight and instruct (e.g., Robert Recorde, Thomas Digges). Soon after, popular considerations of heliocentrism appeared in encyclopedic cosmological poetry. Of long influence (upon Milton and eighteenth-century writers, especially) was Guillaume de Saluste Du Bartas' *La Sepmaine, ou Création du monde*. This poem, well-known in England from about 1580 (first full English translation: Sylvester's *Bartas: His Devine Weekes*, 1605), countered the nonsensical physics of the Copernican system with Christianized Aristotelian arguments primarily drawn from medieval encyclopedists (Johnson, p.186+). Modeled upon classical and medieval originals, Edmund Spenser's *Shepheardes Calender*, *The Fairie Queene*, and *Epithalamion*, incorporated contemporary astronomical and astrological concepts into conventional tropes and compliments appropriate to Christian values and court verse.

In the classical and medieval periods, great poets composed great philosophical– cosmological or astronomical–philosophical poems. Curiously, then (especially when compared to other Renaissance and early modern writers), William Shakespeare's use of astronomy, astrology, and cosmology has generally been deemed conventional and tangential to the central themes of his drama; although there has been some cross-disciplinary debate recently about whether Shakespeare wrote *Hamlet* as an allegory of the competing cosmological models of Thomas Digges and Tycho Brahe.[8] Much Renaissance drama, however, is rich territory for exploring social and intellectual attitudes toward the natural sciences, including astronomy, as they emerged alongside what would later be called the pseudosciences of alchemy, astrology, and magic.[9] There is no question, for instance, that Christopher Marlowe gave contemporary astronomy serious evaluation. In his complex morality play, *Dr. Faustus*, the title character rejects the flawed and limited knowledge of law, philosophy, rhetoric and theology and aspires, instead, to godlike omniscience and power via demonic

---

[8]   Peter D. Usher, "Shakespeare's Cosmic World View," *Mercury* 26.1 (Jan/Feb 1997): 20–23.

[9]   See the work of: J. C. Eade, *The Forgotten Sky: A Guide to Astrology in English Literature* (Oxford: Clarendon Press, 1984); John Mebane, *Renaissance Magic and the Return of the Golden Age: The Occult Tradition and Marlowe, Jonson and Shakespeare* (Lincoln: University of Nebraska Press, 1989) and Barbara Traister, *Heavenly Necromancers: The Magician in English Renaissance Drama* (Columbia: University of Missouri Press, 1984).

conjuring with damnable results. The cosmic voyage he undertakes as part of this quest propels him from Earth to the spheres of all of the planets, but rather than gaining secret insight into the ways of Heaven (via the heavens), he gains a one-way ticket to Hell – a dramatic condemnation of the dangers of overreaching in all human sciences.

Extending the definition of astronomy to include meteorology and other atmospheric phenomena (as was the case throughout the Renaissance), the imagery and themes of Shakespeare's *The Tempest* offer an interesting contrast to those of Marlowe's play. Powerful magus that he is, Prospero proves a better student of nature and human nature than Faustus. Commanding the forces of nature, he comprehends the need to temper his natural instinct toward retribution with compassion and to exert self-control rather than power. Whether wielding their wands over the spirits of the air, wind and rain or objects at greater altitudes in the sky, the characterizations of Faustus and Prospero provide models for future literary depictions of the magician–scientist "mad" with the quest for knowledge or power. Exchanging wands and conjuring chants for telescopes, observing charts and the calculus, both historic and fictional astronomers will later be described as types of these two figures.[10]

Despite much literary evidence of strong popular interest and admiration, early modern astronomy served as a target for satire as well as one of its vehicles. In fashionable satiric comedies, Ben Jonson equates the novelties disclosed by Galileo's telescope with the trivial "new news" of daily headlines and horoscopes (*News from the New World Discovered in the Moon*, *The Staple of News*). In these two plays, and others, the cosmic scale of his mockery of astronomy and astrology allows him to stage the fantastic spectacles expected by his often courtly audiences (*Love Freed from Folly and Ignorance*). In *The Alchemist*, Jonson satirizes a constellation of dubious sciences (the sister sciences of astrology and astronomy included) through direct contemporary allusions to alchemical language and pseudoscientific practices. The play is particularly useful for its depiction of how ignorance of new science and blind faith in the arcane powers of magic, alchemy and astrology were shared by representatives of many social strata, educational levels, both genders, and those with amorous, economic, political and religious motivations.

Throughout the Scientific Revolution, literary writers subject the quest for natural knowledge to intelligent, healthy critique. Rarely does a poet or playwright grant unquestioning acceptance to early modern science or its practitioners. Astronomy and medicine (with its additional linkage to astrology) all receive dramatic scrutiny in plays by Thomas Shadwell, Aphra Behn, and Molière, among others. In a typical treatment, central characters who crave physick or practice astrological medicine are depicted as selfish hypochondriacs or quacks whose scientific or pseudoscientific involvement diverts them from fulfilling their normative roles in family and society.

---

[10]   For additional tracing of such usages see: Roslynn D. Haynes, *From Faust to Strangelove: Representations of the Scientist in Western Literature* (Baltimore: Johns Hopkins University Press, 1994).

This type of warning, directed primarily at male projectors at the beginning of the seventeenth century, also targets female virtuosa by that century's end.

In the early 1600s though, no one (even among the other Metaphysical poets) matches the versatility and virtuosity of John Donne in his mastery and use of early modern astronomy.[11] Renowned for his inventive extended conceits and analogies, created from all aspects of natural philosophy and wit (sometimes *ad absurdum*), Donne was equally adept at adapting complex astronomical analogies to rakish purposes of seduction or the serious pledging of wedded love and loyalty (*A Lecture Upon A Shadow, The Sunne Rising, Valediction: Forbidding Mourning*). From his first-hand knowledge of contemporary astronomical thought of Copernicus, Clavius, Galileo and Kepler, he constructs unique syntheses of natural philosophy and religious faith (*Good Friday 1613, The Anniversaries*). He ingeniously satirizes the philosophical and political excesses of the Jesuits by modifying the genre of the cosmic voyage (*Ignatius His Conclave*). This mixed genre blends fanciful and scientifically speculative fictions of space travel with social, political and religious allegory and themes. Before mid-century, many other examples of this proto-science fiction genre appear (Kepler's *Somnium*, Savinien Cyrano de Bergerac's *L'autre monde* and *Les états et empires de la Lune et du soleil*, Francis Godwin's *Man in the Moone*). As a result, John Wilkins' thoughtful popularization of the major features of Galilean lunar topography and Keplerian selenography in *Discovery of a World in the Moone* (1638) may have struck his audience as comparatively mundane.

In the latter half of the seventeenth century, literary treatments of astronomy begin to be affected by the presence of the Royal Society, public perceptions of that organization's purposes, and the social value of the "New Science." In his *Ode to the Royal Society* Abraham Cowley so effectively adopts the "plain style" advocated by Thomas Sprat that even an allusion to novae falls well short of the poetic "sublime." The high-flown goals and modest achievements of the Royal Society fare even less well in the verse of Samuel Butler. His burlesque satire, *Hudibras*, lampoons the still-prevalent folly of astrology and astrologers. The delightful *Elephant in the Moon* exposes flaws and foibles of the astronomical observers of the F.R.S.. Butler recognizes the human limitations inherent in natural philosophy, including the unreliability of sensory perceptions (even when aided by instruments) and the mixed motivations of investigators of nature often manifested by their pursuit of personal fame and glory, or their chauvinistic, imperial-minded, claim-staking greed. In the satiric comedy, *The Virtuoso*, Thomas Shadwell also ridicules actual experiments and astronomical work undertaken by Royal Society members, characterizing the natural philosophers as men possessed with their quest for knowledge to the detriment of common sense and the common good.

The tradition of popular philosophical–cosmological and astronomical–philosophical works is represented by widely divergent forms in the late seventeenth

---

[11]   Gossin, "John Donne and the Astronomical Revolution," *Poetic Resolutions of Scientific Revolutions* 30–216.

century. Jean de La Fontaine's homely *Fables* gives accessible accounts of contemporary astronomical concepts while emphasizing the fraud of judicial astrology. Of a "romanticical [sic] . . . philosophical . . . fantastical" type, as designated by the author herself, is Margaret Cavendish's *The Description of a New World, called New Blazing World* in which she combines elements from the cosmic voyage motif with dialogues on natural philosophy and social and political satire (a medley form that will be adapted later by Swift). This work received immediate (and to a certain extent, unfair) scorn from her would-be male peers in the Royal Society, although it is difficult to determine what they found most offensive about it: its flamboyantly female author or its heavily French Cartesian philosophy, equally apparent in her other atomistic cosmological writings. Precise poetical descriptions of the Copernican universe and seventeenth-century natural philosophy are featured in Henry More's Neoplatonic cosmological poems, *Psychathanasia* and *Insomnium Philosophicum*. On a grander scale still, resides John Milton's *Paradise Lost*, the principal example in English of a Christian metaphysical and cosmological poem in classical epic form. Synthesizing what he learned from astronomical and cosmological poetry (Du Bartas) and encyclopedias, neither the ambitions nor inadequacies of the Royal Society seem to exist in Milton's universe. Here, Milton adapts the classical device of the cosmic voyage to Satan's journey through primal chaos (Book 2) and the astrological–meteorological poetics of Aratus and Manilius to his dialogue on astronomy in Books 7 and 8. Two famous passages record the direct influence of Milton's personal contact with Galileo, as the discussion focuses on "two" chief world systems, and ultimately concludes that of the two "books" of knowledge given to mankind, the book of faith and revelation must ultimately prevail over that of nature (and fallible human knowledge of nature). Astronomical knowledge, aspects of solar lore, and the figure of Galileo are prominent, too, in Milton's more earthly prose writings where he enlists them in his call for educational and political reforms (*On Education, Aeropagitica*).

After the publication of the *Principia* (1687), Isaac Newton, his achievements in astronomy, physics and optics, his highly visible involvement with the Royal Society, Newtonianism's social and theological implications, and mechanical philosophy *per se*, all find a place in astronomical literature. Depending on how the authors viewed the man, his work, its theological implications and mechanical philosophy, in general, their literary treatments of Newton praise or try to bury him. Aphra Behn's farcical *Emperor of the Moon* (1687) draws upon Godwin, Wilkins, Jonson and Butler, to satirize mechanical philosophy, hermeticism, enthusiasm, and the "lunatic" antics of a "learned" doctor obsessed with observing the moon. Her translation of Bernard le Bovier de Fontenelle's *Conversations on the Plurality of Worlds* provides a popular critique of contemporary astronomy. Jonathan Swift relentlessly parodies the learned controversies of real-life astrologers and astronomers (John Flamsteed, Edmond Halley and Newton) in a series of pamphlets known as the *Bickerstaff Papers* and the poem *The Progress of Beauty*.[12] In *Gulliver's Travels* (a conflation of the cosmic voyage and travelogue modes earlier used by Cavendish), he ridiculed the peculiarities of theoretical astronomy by characterizing its practitioners as the absent-minded Laputans. His account of the Grand Academy of Lagado satirizes the experimental science of Newton and the Royal Society, especially chastizing their "unnatural" natural investigations and offering a critique of the social and theological implications of Newtonianism (Book 3, see also *Mechanical Operation of the Spirit*).[13] In Book 4, Swift suggests through the normative philosophy of the reasonable Houyhnhnms that human attempts to understand celestial phenomena should be limited to what is necessary for time-keeping and agriculture. In one of the earliest modern novels, *Tristram Shandy*, Laurence Sterne cleverly incorporates aspects of Newtonian physics ("flying off on a tangent") and mechanical philosophy (matter in motion) into the very structure of his rowdy, rambling tale, taking every opportunity to contrast lofty "discoveries" with commoners' views of them.

Alexander Pope's famous two-line epitaph for Newton is emblematic of the literary praises of the natural philosopher in the early eighteenth century ("Nature and Nature's laws lay hid in night: God said, *Let Newton be!* And all was light." 1730). Probably taking inspiration from the themes introduced by Halley's *Ode* (prominently prefacing the *Principia*), writers repeatedly describe Newton, his genius, and his work in terms of the divine. The young R. Glover composed such a "Halleyian" ode for Pemberton's version of Newton's great work. Writers of memorial verses celebrate Newton in florid style (James Thomson's *To the Memory of Sir Isaac Newton*). Physico-theological and "nature" poems exalt his insights into the mysteries of the natural world, especially hailing his "conquering" of the comet and "discovery" of universal law, in terms previously reserved for the powers of Christ (Thomson's *The Seasons*, Richard Blackmore's *Creation*, others by John Ray, William Derham). Essayists, Boyle lecturers, and other popularizers (for "ladies" as well as gentlemen), exercise no greater restraint (e.g., Voltaire, William Whiston, James Ferguson, Richard Steele).

Only a few years later, however, in Pope's *Essay on Man*, the greatest mind of the age serves to illustrate the limitations of human intellect. In *The Dunciad*, Pope describes the final destruction of all intellectual "light" (once symbolized by Newton et al.) by a disordering "vis inertiae" and a universal "gravity" (now reverted to the meaning "dead weight") of mental "dullness." Samuel Johnson's prose and poetry provide a balanced assessment. An admirer of Newton's intellect who was well-versed in his conceptualizations of the plenum, matter, and vacuity, Johnson nonetheless

---

[12]   Gossin, "Jonathan Swift and the Newtonian Revolution," *Poetic Resolutions of Scientific Revolutions* 217–355.

[13]   Marjorie Nicolson and Nora M. Mohler, "The Scientific Background of Swift's *Voyage to Laputa*," *Annuals of Science* 2 (1937): 299–334, reprinted in *Science and Imagination* (Ithaca: Great Seal, 1956) and "Swift's 'Flying Island' in the *Voyage to Laputa*," *Annals of Science* 2 (1937): 405–30.

voices legitimate cultural concerns about the practical applications of mathematical principles of natural philosophy. In a number of essays, Johnson reminds his readers that eternal benevolence and wisdom are behind all extraordinary God-given talents, even the intellectual achievements of a genius such as Newton. He repeatedly stresses the reasonableness and utility of practical science and astronomy, as long as they operate within a moral context, working toward the salvation of the experimenter or observer ("On the Death of Stephen Grey," "The Rambler," "Rasselas").

After Newton: Romantic and Victorian

As the age of revolutions dawned, Pierre-Simon Laplace, Immanuel Kant, and William Herschel introduced their cosmological theories. Sounding dire warnings about the dangers of such systems, William Blake whirled with the vortices of the nebular hypothesis to effect a revolution of his own. Transforming the "limited" bounds of traditional astronomical–philosophical verse with the "physics" of his visionary poetry, he offers the unbounded spaces of his own poetic cosmos as a liberating alternative to the natural world (and world view) he sees as polluted by reason, science and industry (*Vala, Jerusalem, Book of Urizen, Milton*). Blake believes that his "illuminated" poetry counters the imprisoning action of Newtonian reason with the energizing reaction of imagination. Despite the otherworldliness of his ideas and versification, his poetic powers were fired considerably by his extensive reading in contemporary primary works of natural philosophy and eighteenth-century astronomy.   While Blake's shorter verse and the works of the later Romantics rarely draw upon astronomy (describing instead the sensory delights of more down-to-earth scenery), the unresolved (and, to his mind, unresolvable) conflicts that Blake identified in the "oppositions" of imagination and reason, poetry and science echo throughout the literature of the next two centuries. William Wordsworth recounts a disappointing first-hand experience with a public telescope in *Star-Gazers*, yet he was among the first to predict that science would increasingly inspire literary imagery (see his description of Newton and "applied geometry" in *The Prelude*). Other Romantic considerations of science and poetry include Samuel Taylor Coleridge's discussion of science, cosmology and Newton in *Religious Musings*; P. B. Shelley's treatment of the earth–moon system in *Prometheus Unbound*; and John Keats' often misinterpreted allusion to the Newtonian rainbow in *Lamia*. In the United States, Ralph Waldo Emerson's philosophical contemplations of atomistic cosmology finds its way from his prose into verse (*Monadnoc*). While Mark Twain experiments with fictional time travel in *A Connecticut Yankee in King Arthur's Court*, Walt Whitman prefers to encounter the heavens without the interference of astronomical apparatus (*When I Heard the Learn'd Astronomer*), as does Emily Dickinson (*Arcturus*).

      Throughout the Victorian period, popular astronomical information becomes available in a variety of literary forms: essays (William Whewell), popular texts (Richard Proctor, John Herschel), illustrated journals, astronomical histories and encyclopedias (Agnes Clerke), children's books and women's magazines

(Maria Mitchell), public lectures, observatories and exhibitions. These, added to the notice given international astronomical expeditions, the controversial ideas of Robert Chambers, Herbert Spencer, Charles Darwin et al., the formation of interdisciplinary philosophical societies, and the personal "star quality" of William Herschel and family, all foster intellectual interest in astronomy for some of the most important British writers of the age. Essays and novels rival poetry as important forms of popularization of the sciences in the nineteenth century with William Whewell's *Bridgewater Treatise* as arguably the most directly influential.

Queen Victoria's poet laureate, Alfred, Lord Tennyson, was a student of Whewell and an amateur astronomer who maintained a life-long avid interest in the subject. He developed a sound knowledge of cosmology and evolutionary theory, synthesizing them as manifestations of a single process in *In Memoriam*. The feminist university of *The Princess* features astronomical observation and study of the nebular hypothesis as liberating intellectual activities for women. With similar sophistication, "Mark Rutherford" (pseudonym of William Hale White) uses the crafting of an orrery as a symbolic act embodying the union of romantic and scientific imaginations in his novella, *Miriam's Schooling*. The two main characters' mutual emotional response to the geometry and beauty of the planetary system saves their marriage. In the lyric mode, the union of sound and sense, of poetry and cosmology, in Algernon Swinburne's *Hertha* and *Anactoria* is utterly unique. In the latter, Sappho seeks to fuse her grief, her identity and her aesthetic vision into the eternity of an elemental cosmos. George Meredith's *Meditation Under Stars* is an optimistic exploration of ethical and aesthetic responses to the possibility that humanity shares its origin with the inorganic stars. In *A Dead Astronomer*, Francis Thompson describes the spiritual forces that draw a soul toward salvation in terms of planetary dynamics. In science fiction novels, Jules Verne's *From Earth to the Moon* and H. G. Wells' *First Men in the Moon* are important adaptations of the "scientific romance" or cosmic voyage. Wells joins social commentary and the satiric elements introduced by Lucian and Swift with the technical detail and political allegory utilized by Kepler (*In the Days of the Comet*). At the end of the nineteenth century, utopian visions of space travel are countered by a darker literary treatment of the laws of physics (e.g., entropy in Joseph Conrad's *Heart of Darkness*).

By the final years of the nineteenth century, Hardy could look back at the literary history of astronomy and cosmology and find himself in very good company. The influence of these past works, conjoined with his own, continue to be felt into the early twentieth century, when the first generation of modern poets and novelists draws upon the latest developments and ideas in astronomy, astrophysics, and Einsteinian physics (among the latter, Virginia Woolf, who read Hardy's *Two on a Tower*).[14] Astronomical–philosophical poetry, nature and science writing, scientific biographies and autobiographies, drama (for stage, film, radio, and television), music and music

---

[14]   Holly Henry, *Virginia Woolf and the Discourse of Science: The Aesthetics of Astronomy* (Cambridge: Cambridge University Press, 2003) 3, 135.

videos, science fiction novels, comics, toys and video games all carry popular astronomy and space science to extensive twentieth and early twenty-first century readerships.

Scholarly Engagement of the *Literary History* of Astronomy

As even this all-too-brief overview suggests, the *literary history* of astronomy is replete with primary materials in every conceivable form, genre, style and mode. Given such an embarrassment of riches, the relative dearth of secondary studies and critical analyses of literature and astronomy seems somewhat bewildering. Just as historians of astronomy have not fully exploited these materials in their work, literary scholars likewise have not engaged them in their research as frequently, as consistently, or in as much depth as their sheer numbers might predict. A handful of excellent book-length surveys and multi-author treatments are available, as are monographs on single authors such as Chaucer, Dante, and Woolf.[15] While the annual number of interdisciplinary articles treating the astronomy of individual authors and their works probably peaked (along with literary critics' interest in intellectual history) in the 1960s, Marjorie Nicolson's premier work on the sources and interpretation of astronomical imagery is still eminently worth consulting. In fact, she may have done her work too well. Daunted perhaps by her achievement in the analysis and understanding of primary works of astronomy and popular astronomy (which are often highly mathematicized texts), only a handful of scholars among those now working in literature and science studies (LS) specialize in literature and astronomy. The vast majority of LS scholars currently work, instead, with primary texts of the life sciences, medicine, and natural history which are often written in narrative styles more directly accessible via a variety of interdisciplinary, rhetorical, and discursive modes of analyses.

The literature of astronomy may also have fallen through critical gaps in literary methodology. Of the few scholars who extended Nicolson's studies of how literary works reflect, respond to or critique astronomy and cosmology, most focused on how astronomy influenced literary imagery (such as A. J. Meadows' *The High Firmament* published in 1969). As such studies were being produced by the first and second

---

[15] Marjorie Hope Nicolson, *The Breaking of the Circle: Studies in the Effect of the "New Science" on Seventeenth-Century Poetry*, rev. ed. (1950; New York: Columbia University Press, 1960); *Newton Demands the Muse: Newton's Opticks and the Eighteenth-Century Poets* (Princeton: Princeton University Press, 1946); *Science and Imagination* (Ithaca, NY: Great Seal Books, 1962); A. J. Meadows, *The High Firmament: A Survey of Astronomy in English Literature* (Leicester: Leicester University Press, 1969); Walter Clyde Curry, *Chaucer and the Mediaeval Sciences* (1926; London: Allen, 1960) and *Milton's Ontology, Cosmology and Physics* (Lexington: University of Kentucky Press, 1957); Chauncey D. Wood, *Chaucer and the Country of the Stars: Poetic Use of Astrological Imagery*, diss., Princeton University, 1963; and others previously mentioned, such as Cornish and Henry.

generation of Nicolson's students (direct and indirect), critical trends shifted toward questions of how cultural influences run in the *other* direction – asking how *literary* culture may have shaped the development of the *science* by actively participating in its popularization and cultural construction. Nicolsonian style studies of literature and science (especially astronomy) were then categorized as "old" atheoretical historical studies, and found themselves decidedly out of favor, along with their content (which was, perhaps, judged guilty by association). This judgement has just recently begun to reverse itself as theorists within new literary history have strengthened their case that history *is* in fact theoretical and literary critics have become more aware of the presence of theory within historical methods and practice (although theoretical concerns are still not placed as self-reflexively at the center of most historical writing as they might like).[16] Emergent approaches to the study of literature and science question the nature of the audience for scientific literature, the hermeneutics of scientific metaphor, and authors' use of scientific language *per se*, often examining primary scientific texts as literature. Although nothing inherent in the texts of astronomical literature (even the tables, geometry and calculations) really precludes them from such considerations, very few scholars employing the latest linguistic and rhetorical modes of critique include them in their studies.

   The literary *history of astronomy* and the *literary history* of astronomy have much to offer each other and to interdisciplinary LS studies at large. Because literature and astronomy are so inextricably interconnected in human thought and activity, studying them in tandem can illuminate interactions of scientific and nonscientific communities, the popularization of science, aesthetics and science, humanism and science, gender and science, and the histories of literature and science themselves. If Francis Crick is right about "gossip" being the best indicator of where the most innovative research will come from next, then a lot of evidence points toward the interrelations of literature, historical studies and astronomy. In online academic chatrooms, listservs and email exchanges, at conference breaks and in post-conference correspondence, scholars in one field are asking questions that cross over into the other and are actively seeking interdisciplinary collaborators. On hastro-l, the History of Astronomy Discussion Group listserv, recent topics have included *Hamlet's Mill*, Shakespeare and Brahe, astronomy in the Bible, Hebrew and Mormon texts, and requests for assistance compiling lists of astronomical biographies, autobiographies and primary "astronomical" literary works for classroom use. Although print publications are just beginning to reflect the trend, the themes of recent conferences and panel topics clearly indicate that the field is poised for expansion. SLS 2003, held in Austin, Texas, devoted the year's meeting to "Rethinking Space and Time Across Science, Literature and the Arts," featuring a plenary address by science writer, Timothy Ferris, entitled "Dark Energy and the Fate of the Universe(s)" as well as two sessions on "Astronomy

---

[16]   David Perkins, *Is Literary History Possible?* (Baltimore: Johns Hopkins University Press, 1992) and —, ed., *Theoretical Issues in Literary History* (Cambridge, MA: Harvard University Press, 1991.

and Cosmology," one focusing on "Victorian and Modern Literature and Astronomy" and the other on "Maya and Renaissance Art." Historians of archaeoastronomy and astronomy have held a number of recent international conferences exploring the interrelations of culture and astronomy and HSS 2004 included a panel exploring "Astronomy and Representation in the Nineteenth Century."[17]

As the joint literary history of astronomy demonstrates, while the majority of educated people in any one time and place may not have been able to claim mastery of both literature and astronomy, or even a polite interest in both, some at least, always could. Poets, novelists, dramatists, essayists, natural philosophers, astronomers, and physicists, through history, combined literary and astronomical approaches to understanding, and communicating knowledge about, the phenomena of the cosmos and our human relation to it. Hardy lived and worked, of course, at least half a generation before the *bi*-disciplinary scholarly communities of literary studies and the history of science were sufficiently developed to engage in *inter*-disciplinary negotiations over the critical rights to such primary materials. He knew, however, that he was far from alone as a creative writer in consciously building the thematic frameworks of his fiction and poetry upon the foundations of the literary history of astronomy – in both variant meanings of the phrase – that the western world willed to him.

The Origins of Hardy's Literary Cosmology

Hardy made his own study of literature, history, and astronomy unfettered by the disciplinary distinctions that now work to segregate our source materials and interpretative approaches. His eclectic synthesis of archaeology, mythopoetic, classical and Biblical traditions, anthropology and folklore, and "great works" of western literature (past and contemporary) displays a prescient awareness of their important confluence within human consciousness and culture. Drawing upon these resources and contemporary accounts of natural history and popular astronomy, Hardy created his own sense of cosmology – an understanding of the phenomena of the universe, both inorganic and organic, from its earliest moments on.

The Building Blocks of a Personal Philosophy:
  Hardy's Education and Self-study

The humble circumstances of Hardy's formal education are well-known. Small and frail as a child, Hardy was kept home from even the village school until he was eight or nine. At age ten (1850), he was strong enough to walk daily three miles to the

---

[17]   See, for instance: the annual conferences of the European Society for Astronomy in Culture, INSAP's annual "Inspiration of Astronomical Phenomena" conferences, and the biennial History of Astronomy Workshops held at the University of Notre Dame.

Dorchester British [elementary] School. From 1853 to 1856, Hardy attended an independent "commercial academy" begun by his British School's master. There he added Latin and French to his reading, writing and mathematics work which had been directed mostly toward practical and technical applications of the building trades. During this stage of his schooling, Hardy was already demonstrating the desire to augment his schoolwork by learning on his own. He began the habit of keeping a notebook entitled "Miscellaneous Questions" and had chosen as one of his prizes for academic success the three volume work *The Popular Educator* by "that genius in home-education, John Cassell."[18] Hardy's self-motivation would prove valuable as in 1856 at the age of sixteen, his formal education ended.

During his subsequent apprenticeship to a Dorchester architect, Hardy studied several hours each morning before reporting for his training. He improved his Latin and began Greek during this time. After his apprenticeship (1862), Hardy left to work for a London architect and took full advantage of the exhibitions, National Gallery, museums, libraries, and theaters in the city. Reading widely through the years, he followed his own interests unbiased by the growing prejudice within British literary tradition to exclude scientific writings from the canon. On his own, he developed an easy familiarity with many popular journals that frequently published essays on literary history and criticism, natural history, biology and chemistry, and astronomical discoveries and theories.

Hardy's architectural training encouraged him to investigate the artifactual and architectural inscription of astronomical and cosmological knowledge and belief. Later in life, as he worked on plans for his own home, he spent many hours calculating the angles of sunlight for its various elevations, at different seasons. Like many present-day archaeoastronomers, Hardy had a life-long curiosity about the Celtic and Roman ruins in Britain, especially those in and around his local Dorset. Numerous critics have marked the influence on his work of the archaeological speculations and solar myths of Norman Lockyer and Max Müller, especially apparent in the staging of the final Stonehenge scene in *Tess*. The depth and breadth of his interest in geology, archaeology, and anthropology are only now being fully appreciated, as new studies by such scholars as Andrew Radford thoroughly demonstrate. As Radford argues,

> Throughout his literary career, Hardy broods over the landmarks of local topography because they are crusted with ancestral imprints and open up fresh possibilities for his art. He wonders if the resonant meaning these imposing structures possessed for the people who shaped them might be recoverable and so stimulate or enhance late-Victorian life, and he employs occasions of anthropological significance to question the value of and the need for historical continuity.[19]

---

18   Michael Millgate, *Thomas Hardy: A Biography* (Oxford: Oxford University Press, 1982) 53; hereafter: Millgate.
19   Andrew Radford, *Thomas Hardy and the Survivals of Time*, The Nineteenth Century Series (Aldershot, Eng.: Ashgate, 2003) 4.

From his study of antiquities and his reading of contemporary comparative mythology (such as Frazer's *Golden Bough*), Hardy garnered a sense for how primitive humans may have felt living beneath a seemingly capricious sky, how they considered natural phenomena such as the movements of the sun, moon, stars, and planets, meteors and the weather, and how they devised strategies to try to predict and control them. Bit by bit, Hardy accumulated a feel for a prehistoric world view that he could compare to his era's and his own. As Radford suggests, such a sense informed both Hardy's understanding of past cultures and provided him with an explanatory framework for the ongoing presence of their myths.

> When Hardy read Frazer's *The Golden Bough* in the 1890s, the most extended attempt at the time to interpret and relate folk customs to the great myths and legends of the past, he saw that 'survivals' afforded irreplaceable insight into the earliest habits of thought. Andrew Lang spoke for the majority of late-Victorian anthropologists when he announced that 'we explain many peculiarities of myths as survivals from an earlier social and mental condition of humanity.' Freud, an archaeologist of the mind, developed this research to show how the prehistoric impulses of the race were replicated in the unconscious layers of the individual psyche, tracing basic neurotic traits back to a common prehistory. (27)

Hardy's interest in archaeological evidence of human cultures' understanding of natural phenomena was enriched by his reading of primary works in the classical mythopoetic tradition and by his contemporaries' work in ancient history and the history of philosophy. As has been long known, Hardy's self-study included deep reading of the Greek and Roman classics, especially drama, epic, lyric, satire and pastoral. Of the classical authors most alluded to in Hardy's poetry and prose – Aeschylus, Aristophanes, Aristotle, Homer, Lucretius, Ovid, Plato, Sophocles, Vergil – all produced profound dramatic or poetic treatments or philosophical discussions of the relations of the gods to humans and the situation of humanity within nature and society. All made essential contributions to the literary history of ancient astronomy and cosmology, with several giving exceptional intelligibility to tragic and atomistic perspectives on the interactions of human will and fate. We know that Hardy's notion of the classical world view was made more sophisticated by his close reading of Matthew Arnold's critique of Hellenism, from which he adapted much of his philosophy of life, both personally and aesthetically.[20] Hardy's view of the classical "mind" was also influenced by his reading of Edward Gibbon's *History of the Decline and Fall of the Roman Empire* and G. H. Lewes's *History of Philosophy from Thales to Comte*, among other authoritative texts.

Most critics have long agreed that the primary literary influence on Hardy was his deep and abiding first-hand knowledge of the Bible. Nearly fifty different books of the Bible are alluded to or cited by Hardy in his poetry and prose.[21] The Bible also

---

[20] Michael Millgate, *Thomas Hardy: His Career as a Novelist* (New York: Random House, 1971) 174–5.
[21] F. B. Pinion, *A Thomas Hardy Dictionary* (Washington Square, NY: New York University

provided Hardy with his most powerful cosmological influence. The cosmogonical story of Genesis, with its account of a personal artist–sculptor God who creates by a laying-on of His divine hands and a communion of His breath, the Garden and the Wilderness, the valleys and the mounts, the Old Testament's regretful and vengeful Father, the New Testament's care-taking and path-shaping Holy Spirit and the *charitos* and *pathos* of the Son – all worked together to form Hardy's vision of the ancient relation of supernatural to natural, divine to human, before and after Christ. The poetics of church hymns and carols (many of which are alluded to in his works) also contributed to Hardy's sense of how the people around him, close family, friends, villagers and rural workers, related personally to their idea of God and nature. Accompanying his father on the violin at wedding suppers and local dances, Hardy found many opportunities to directly witness how musical rituals were practiced by the Christian faithful (and not-so-faithful) of his local community.

In many ways, Hardy's hometown acted as a living history museum for him as many of the beliefs and practices long-gone from contemporary city life, persisted there virtually unchanged. The past was still very much present in the local language and folkways of the rural environs of Dorset, and Hardy could act as an anthropological participant–observer by visiting and attending to life as it unfolded around him.[22] Hardy's deep and wide reading in philosophy, the history of religions, and theology, past and contemporary, provided him with a complex framework within which to organize his collection of humanity's narratives about the universe and the entities within it. Hardy supplemented his reading of influential philosophers, such as Hegel, Hume, Kant, Mill, Nietzsche, Schelling, Schiller, Schlegel, Schopenhauer, Spinoza, and Voltaire, with contemporary authors treating some of the most controversial topics of the day (Ernest Renan; Carneth Read, *Metaphysics of Nature*; James Ward, *Naturalism and Agnosticism*; Harald Höffding, *Philosophy of Religion*; and Arthur James Balfour, *Theism and Humanism*).

Hardy's eclectic reading of the classics of medieval, Renaissance and Enlightenment literature as well as contemporary works, both verse and prose, exposed him to a wide variety of authors who had created fictional, dramatic or poetic accounts of human life in the cosmos, on minute to magnificent scales. The influence of Dante, Milton and Shakespeare on his conception of the human relation to the natural, social and supernatural can hardly be overemphasized. In many ways, Hardy's novels attempt, in prose, the kind of philosophical–cosmological syntheses that they achieved in verse. Hardy read many works by poets and essayists who followed the development of the Copernican and Newtonian Revolutions and incorporated scientific findings and natural philosophical speculations into their works (Edmund Spenser, Donne, Dryden, Ben Jonson, Samuel Johnson, Pope and Swift). The vast majority of his favorite contemporary poets and novelists as well were among those who maintained above-average interest in and knowledge of the concepts and theories

---

Press, 1989) ix.

[22]   Ruth A. Firor, *Folkways in Thomas Hardy* (New York: Russell and Russell, 1931).

of nineteenth-century astronomy, physics, chemistry, and natural history, as well as astute critical awareness of the risks and benefits of the processes and products of the Industrial Revolution, among them: Balzac, the Brownings, Byron, Carlyle, Coleridge, Dickens, George Eliot, Flaubert, Hugo, Keats, Ruskin, P. B. Shelley, Swinburne, Tennyson, Francis Thompson, Turgenev, Wordsworth and Zola. Many of these writers, as well as others, provided Hardy with close models for his literary analysis of the interrelations of human character and the environment, both in the local and global sense (Burns, Fielding, Gray, Ibsen, Kipling, Samuel Richardson, George Sand, Scott, Shaw, Tolstoy, Trollope, Whitman, Yeats and again, of course, Zola). To an astounding extent, the list of Hardy's most-cited authors coincides with those most prominent in the literary history of astronomy, from both literary and scientific perspectives.

A Cosmological Framework Takes Shape:
 Evidence from Hardy's "Literary Notebooks"

As most students of Hardy know, he kept numerous notebooks in which he recorded reading notes, organized select quotations taken from articles, books and journals, and jotted down his own responses to the ideas he encountered. Although most of his notebooks were destroyed in the years just before his death, the extant notebooks, compiled between 1876 and 1927, contain much evidence of his wide reading in scientific subjects and his collection of scientific ideas. As the front flyleaf of Lennart A. Björk's masterly edition so aptly puts it:

> The span of Hardy's entries in the *Literary Notebooks* is striking both in its chronological and broadly intellectual dimensions: the entries range from the Greek dramatists to George Bernard Shaw; from the radical French utopian Charles Fourier to Cardinal Newman; and from *The Milliner and Dressmaker and Warehouseman's Gazette* to Einstein.
> The *Notebooks* show how Hardy intensifies his determined preparatory studies in the mid-1870s; how keenly he follows the contemporary debate over realism and other aesthetic questions; how he primes himself in philosophical studies at the turn of the century for the metaphysical challenge of *The Dynasts*; and how he gradually becomes more preoccupied with poetic matters while maintaining his lifelong interest in religion and science.[23]

Throughout the notebooks, Hardy makes frequent reference to scientific articles in such popular magazines as *Blackwood's Edinburgh Magazine, Cornhill Magazine, Daily News, Edinburgh Review, Fortnightly Review, Westminster Review, Saturday Review, Continental Review, Examiner,* and *Encyclopaedia Britannica.* Hardy's notes from these journals exhibit an interest in a vast range of scientific fields such as

---

[23] Lennart A. Björk, ed., *The Literary Notebooks of Thomas Hardy*, 2 vols. (London: MacMillan, 1985) front flyleaf; hereafter: *LN*.

astronomy, biology, and Darwinism, as well as details of natural history, and the relations of science with religion, culture, philosophy and history. Many of the historical and scientific concepts that Hardy records in the notebooks he later used in his poems and novels.

Although by no means comprising a systematic account of how Hardy constructed his personal and literary cosmology, the notebooks do offer a montage of the various topics, themes and lines of interest from which Hardy composed his world view. The interconnected histories of science, art and literature, and religion figure strongly throughout. The quality and kind of scientific passages in the notebooks vary widely from brief factual bits of interesting data to long philosophical passages explaining the place of science and scientific thought in human history or in relation to some other aspect of nature or culture. Life, as experienced by all creatures great and small, is a central consideration throughout the notebooks, as is the increasingly apparent belief that the literary eye could observe and record its variations and themes as well as the scientific. Hardy includes such apparently mundane tidbits as the fact that the dodo was a link between still living and extinct animals (*LN* I. 604, 604n), detailed descriptions of primeval vegetation (*LN* I. 880, 880n) and the Canadian snow (*LN* I. 976–9, 976–9n). What seem to be extremely close accounts of the minutiae of entomology are recorded faithfully in the notebooks and include fine descriptions of ants, wing shedding, developmental transformations, beetles, larvae, behaviors of parasites, the nature and functions of compound eyes, the ugliness and beauty of various insects, the apparent happiness of ephemeral insects such as May-flies, and the migratory habits of still others, such as butterflies (*LN* I. 312–13, 316–23, 326–43). As mundane as they may seem, Hardy found a place for each of these passages in the pages of *The Dynasts*, *Return of the Native* and *The Mayor of Casterbridge*. In both *A Pair of Blue Eyes* and *The Mayor of Casterbridge*, he incorporated scenes in which an objective (or at least remote) observer comments upon the activities of human social life and interaction as though he or she were a naturalist studying the microscopic actions of biological specimens.

Other entries of general scientific interest have not been specifically traced to particular usages in his novels or poetry, but nonetheless seem to have become part of the recurrent themes and philosophical assumptions underlying Hardy's work. Hardy paid close attention to articles that reported investigations into the biological basis of life. From Dr. Andrew Wilson's article "Concerning Protoplasma" published in *Gentleman's Magazine* in October of 1879, Hardy noted: "Protoplasm a mystery . . . the one mystery of life. The difference between such protoplasmic specks [as sponges] & the germ which is destined to evolve the human frame [is] of immense extent. . . . Why & wherefore we are ignorant [his emphasis]" (*LN* I. 1130, 1130n). From an *Edinburgh Review* article, "Darwin on the Movements of Plants" (April 1881), Hardy enters the physical description, functions and behavior of amoebae (*LN* I. 1228). He carefully notes the central arguments from Frederic W. H. Myers' discussion of "Human Personality" from the *Fortnightly Review* (November 1885) which included information on the

Lowest form of life = "The single cell of protoplasm, endowed with reflex irritability."– "A more complex organism" = "mere juxtaposition [of cells] attaining to what is styled 'a colonial consciousness,' where the group of organisms is for locomotive purposes a single complexly acting individual, though when united action is not required each polyp in the colony is master of his simple self."

[The drift of the article is that beings have a multiplex nature, human as other; that what we suppose to be choice is reflex action only – that by implanting impulses in hypnotic states they can be made part of the character. There seems reason in this, for physical developments – (e.g., of the hand) – can be produced <in other ways –> (by labour say) – as well as hereditarily] (*LN* I. 1358)

Hardy also makes special note of articles dealing with human abnormality and illness such as the causes of lunacy (*LN* I. 1186), the efficacy and limits of medicine, and the operation of drugs and patients' expectations (*LN* I. 1364).

The connections between protoplasm and human life were obvious to a novelist like Hardy who was consciously styling his craft after the narrative forms and structures of natural history, as his notebooks illustrate. Man, Arthur Schopenhauer told him in *Studies in Pessimism*, was "like infusoria in a drop of water under [a] microscope" (*LN* II. 1789, 1789n). Hardy cites the German naturalist, Christian Ehrenberg "one of the highest authorities on microscopic science," as stating that "Berlin stands upon a stratum composed entirely of living infusoria" (*LN* I. 121, 121n). Such passages helped shape and reinforce Hardy's vision of humankind as a proper object of "scientific" study in the laboratory of a novel.

Hardy further shaped the conditions within which he was to observe and record the behaviors of his novels' characters by adapting concepts he found not only in the results of science but in his reading of the history and philosophy of science. He seems especially to have concentrated on the relations of science and religion and the ways that both helped create the human response to the universal "environment" and influence our perceptions of the basic conditions of human life. In John Addington Symonds' *Studies of the Greek Poets*, Hardy found and noted the following passages.

> Science. – does not annihilate or neutralize what man has gained from Xty. . . . Each [moral] synthesis combines the indestructible elements of the momenta which preceded it, excluding only that in them which was the accident of time & place & circumstance. Thus the Greek conception of life was posed; the Xtian conception was counterposed. . . . Our object is to combine both the Hellenic & Xtian conceptions in a third, which shall be more solid & more rational than either

> God. – The name of a hitherto unapprehended energy, the symbol of that which is the life & motion of the universe (*LN* I. 634, 635; 634n)

Other entries in Hardy's notebooks illustrate how he continued to watch through the years for insights into the problem Symonds introduced. Hardy came to agree with statements that he found in Auguste Comte's *Social Dynamics* that the developments of human science and religion were on a collision course.

Enemies to God. Mathematics & Astronomy – in other words abstract science –were found (by the Gks) "to clash with Theology" . . . "No reconciliation between natural laws & divine wills."

"Narrowest limits of Theology – the combination of a Supreme will with immutable Laws" Aristotle supplied the conception leading to this.

A self-contradiction in the conception of a single God. "For omnipotence, omniscience, & moral perfection are irreconcilable" with a radically imperfect world. (*LN* I. 654, 665, 671; 654n, 665n, 671n)

Hardy himself was to conclude in 1890, "I have been looking for God for 50 years, and I think that if he existed I should have discovered him" (as in *LN* I. 671n).

Other contemporary thinkers echoed Comte's sentiments and they used particular views of science to support their conclusions. Hardy was well acquainted with the works of George Henry Lewes, Leslie Stephen, Ernest Renan, and Herbert Spencer. Some of Lewes's work presented evidence from physiology and biology which he "declared was enough to banish for ever the conception of a Soul, except as a term simply expressing certain functions" (*LN* I. 899). Hardy also noticed when others made use of Lewes's arguments to argue against the existence of a supreme deity by inverting the argument from design: "There is not a single known organism which is not developed out of simpler forms. . . . Nothing could be more unworthy of a supreme intelligence than this inability to construct an organ at once, without making several tentative efforts" (*LN* I.1301 and 1301n). Hardy copied a remark of Leslie Stephen's found in his *English Thought in the Eighteenth Century* (1876): "The deist Collins said, sarcastically, that nobody doubted the existence of the Deity until the Boyle lecturers had undertaken to prove it" (*LN* I. 980). Hardy was greatly influenced by Stephen through his personal relations with him and through his dealings with him in the publishing business. Björk points out that "contrary to his habitual public reticence in such matters," Hardy was "explicit and enthusiastic" in acknowledging that Stephen's philosophy "was to influence his own for many years, indeed, more than that of any other contemporary" (*LN* I. 980n).

Hardy had a similar high regard for the thought of Spencer as his many notes about Spencer's views on agnosticism, his attack on the positivists, ideas on phenomenology and the "ultimate question" in the notebooks attest (*LN* I. 1335). Hardy also read deeply in the works of Renan. As Björk tells us, Hardy owned Renan's *Saint Paul* (1880), *The History of Origins of Christianity*, Bk 2: *The Apostles* (n.d.) and *The Life of Jesus* (1927) (*LN* I. 1278n). Hardy records "M. Renan's remarkable definition of Providence – 'the totality of the fundamental conditions which determine the march of the Universe'" (*LN* I. 1278).

A strong example of how to "apply" such philosophy to social matters is provided by an elaborate passage that Hardy meticulously noted, probably in 1888. The paraphrased excerpts could have served as an extremely rich source for many of the philosophical premises of *Jude* and *Tess*. Hardy apparently admired James Cotter

Morison's book *The Service of Man. An Essay toward the Religion of the Future.* The following selections from the long entry he devoted to Morison indicate how the philosophical bases of certain scientific concepts were being analogically applied to contemporary social and political issues.

> The great problem of population. – As things go now it is the feeblest, the least moral, & most worthless classes of the community wh. multiply the most rapidly. – The human race, in old countries at least, by its reckless propagation, is getting jammed into an <u>impasse</u> from wh. there is no escape. – A and his prolific spouse must be made to realize that few evil doers are more injurious to the world than they are.
>
> Decay & death stamped not only on man & his works, but on all that surrounds him. Nature herself decays – Alps – Sun himself – from the animalcule to the galaxy.
>
> Beliefs more perishable than the temples they wrought – The world has now reached one of the great turning-points in the evolution of thought (from Xty [crossed out] <theology> to positivism) only to be compared to transition from polytheism to Xty – The transition not without jeopardy. –
>
> Systems of thought, &c, have many of the characteristics of organs, ceasing to be useful they become shrunken & meaningless; also noxious. Conflict of faith with science. – At first Theology was queen – now the suppliant.
>
> Creator not so wise as was supposed. It is now known that for one case of successful adaptation of means to ends in nature there are hundreds of failures. Organs serving no end at all, such as teeth in foetal whales, wh. when grown up have none, useless wings in insects &c – ("origin of Species") Rudimentary tail in man, & rudiments of the muscles wh. moved it (Haeckel, Hist. of Creation). (*LN* I. 1464)

Yet from other passages he copied with equal attention, Hardy appears to have realized that science was not a cure-all for society's ills, as the coldness of the logic of this passage from Augustine Birrell *In Obiter Dicta* (1884) may indicate.

> The world is full of doleful creatures who move about demanding our sympathy. I have nothing to offer them but doses of logic, & stern commands to move on or fall back. Catholics in distress about Infallibility; Protestants devoting themselves to the dismal task of paring down the dimensions of this miracle, & reducing the credibility of that one – as if any appreciable relief from the burden of faith could be so obtained; sentimental sceptics who, after labouring to demolish what they call the chimera of superstition, fall to weeping as they remember they have now no lies to teach their children; democrats who are frightened at the rough voice of the people, & aristocrats flirting with democracy. Logic, if it cannot cure, might at least silence these gentry. (*LN* II. 1742)

"Science," as Hardy found in later writings of Symonds, ". . . has prepared the way for the identification of Law with God" (*LN* II. 1802) but what humankind was to do with that identification was not at all clear.

Hardy's notebooks testify to his astuteness as a critical reader. He almost seems to have had a sixth sense that guided him in his autodidactic studies. Whether by luck, purposeful detective work, or outside referral, his notes repeatedly show evidence of his awareness of multiple facets of many of the most significant issues in the history and philosophy of science as they were developing in the mid-nineteenth century. From his exploration of such concerns, Hardy developed a relativistic, rather than positivistic, view of human intellectual achievement in the sciences. Hardy was aware that the contemporary presentation of scientific discoveries skewed the public perceptions of the significance of various achievements in science. He made five separate entries to record notes from Dr. J. H. Bridges' article "Harvey and Vivisection" which appeared in *Fortnightly Review* on 1 July 1876. Bridges commented on how capriciously honor is assigned to figures in the history of science.

> In the deplorable condition of our present historical & scientific training – history leaving out science, & science leaving out history – discoverers of equal or greater intrinsic merit than Harvey remain uncommemorated. Archimedes, Kepler, Huyghens, Lagrange, Lavoisier, Bichat, are names which though known to the many, are appreciated only by the few. (*LN* I. 487)

Hardy made special note of Bridges' description of the nature of the scientific enterprise.

> Every great scientific effort demands . . . the imaginative audacity to soar above the level of routine & prejudice, & to evoke . . . from the unknown chaos unheard-of hypotheses, until one shall appear worthy of being confronted with the facts – capable of informing them with meaning. (*LN* I. 490)

Hardy recognized that the description equally fit other intellectual enterprises, including that to which he applied his own "science"– the invention of novels. Hardy may have been helped to this view by his reading of Thomas Huxley's works and his personal contact with him. From Huxley's "The Coming of Age of 'The Origin of Species'" in *Science and Culture and Other Essays* (London 1881), Hardy noted further remarks on the nature of scientific endeavor and the relativity of its ideas.

> <u>It is the customary fate of new truths</u> to begin as heresies & to end as superstitions.
>
> The scientific spirit is of more value than its products; & irrationally held truths may be more harmful than reasoned errors.
>
> The essence of the scientific spirit is criticism. It tells us that, to whatever doctrine claiming our assent we should reply, Take it if you can compel it.
>
> The struggle for existence holds as much in the intellectual as in the physical world. A theory is a species of thinking, & its right to exist is co-extensive with its power of resisting extinction by its rivals. (*LN* I. 1269–1271)

Early in the next decade, the concept of shifting perspectives in "objective" science still fascinated him. Hardy carefully read Havelock Ellis' *The New Spirit*

(London 1890) in which the author discussed the personalities of several great thinkers. Hardy recorded Ellis' quotation of Diderot.

"When men begin to say that everything has been done, the men come who say that there has yet nothing been done. We have congratulated ourselves that many sciences of nature & of man are in the main settled, but we are always compelled to begin again, & on a larger & perhaps simpler scale." (*LN* II. 1699)

About three years later, Hardy added to his notebooks another variation on the theme of flux in human intellectual "progress." Hardy read with attention Frederic W. H. Myers' "Modern Poets and the Meaning of Life" published in *The Nineteenth Century* (January 1893), noting:

The Meaning of Life. F. W. H. Myers says, concerning modern Poets, that we thrill to the old music of the word Liberty, but that that motif can be worked afresh no more by the poet. Liberty represents the next stage of progress after Peace & Plenty. . . . Before the race can make out for itself a new practical ideal – such as Plenty & Liberty were once to the many, & such as Science is now to the few, we must somehow achieve a profound readjustment of our general views of the meaning of life & of the structure of the universe.
Now . . . we may say that just as Liberty represents the next stage <of human progress> after Peace & Plenty, Love represents the next stage after Liberty. (*LN* II. 1906)

In his early novels, as well as in *Tess* and *Jude*, Hardy seems to have come to the same conclusions independently. Time and again, we see Hardy bring his characters face to face with the "facts" of the universe. He then plays out before the reader possible solutions to the dilemmas these "facts" represent for humankind. In novels that have strong scientific elements, *Far From the Madding Crowd, The Return of the Native,* and *Two on a Tower*, to name a few, science sometimes appears as the new rallying cry of certain characters, a temporary "call" word (such as Myers implies "Liberty" and "Plenty" used to be). In direct contrast to these figures, Hardy shows how other characters successfully deal with the world by relying on inner character, moral strength, and human caring. Similar to Myers' philosophy, Hardy postulated that human love and kindness might offer viable solutions to certain kinds of universal questions. Willing to place much faith in the value of the human heart and spirit in his works, however, he did not expect that humankind would survive by them alone. From his active search among the results and ideas of the new sciences of his age, psychology, anthropology, and sociology, Hardy discovered a rich store of resources from which he could draw additional dilemmas and potential solutions to those dilemmas for use in his novels.

Hardy read and adapted some of Auguste Comte's notions of psychology to *Far From the Madding Crowd*, in which he used them to explain Bathsheba's mental state and to reveal the degree to which her mind was subject to her biological being (*LN* I. 728n, 730n). Hardy's debt to Comte is documented in his note of Comte's discussion of "Biological Dependence" – "The nobler phenomena are everywhere subordinate to those which are grosser, but also simpler & more regular. . . . man is entirely subordinate to the World – each living being to its own environment" (*LN* I. 730). Hardy's notebooks also contain evidence of the extent to which Hardy kept abreast of work in French psychology (*LN* I. 1561) and closely followed William Kingdon Clifford's work. Hardy read Clifford's *Lectures and Essays* (London 1879) noting,

> Clifford's theory of the intellectual growth of mankind: "as the physical senses [e.g. the eyes of the first animals with eyes] have been gradually developed out of confused & uncertain impressions, so a set of intellectual senses or insights are still in course of development, the operation of which may ultimately be expected to be as certain & immediate as our ordinary sense-perceptions." (*LN* I. 1453)

The relations of social progress and scientific progress intrigued Hardy. Björk believes that Hardy's "general scepticism towards the Idea of Progress" may have been "modified" by Comte's analysis of it. Hardy twice drew upon the following note in his writing: "Social Progress – 'like a looped orbit,' sometimes apparently backwards, but really always forwards" (*LN* I. 749, 749n). Next to this remark Hardy sketched a drawing of a looped orbit that marked how a series of temporary backward motions could result in an accumulated forward effect. In some ways Hardy's notebooks indicate that he may have seen social Darwinism as following this pattern of motion. From Leslie Stephen's "An Attempted Philosophy of History" (*Fortnightly Review* April 1880), Hardy recorded:

> Darwinism is as fruitful in its /? po [crossed out]/ bearing upon sociology as in its bearing upon natural history.
>
> [By Darwinism] we are no longer forced to choose between a fixed order imposed by supernatural sanction, & accidental combination capable of instantaneous & arbitrary reconstruction, [but] recognise in society, as in individuals, the development of an organic structure by slow secular processes. (*LN* I. 1193, 1194)

The slow random change of society works its effects upon Hardy's characters, especially in *Jude* and *Tess*. But another new science provided for Hardy a vision of slow change in past human history that gave depth and perspective to that he described as currently acting within the environment of his novels.

The notebooks show Hardy's attention to the contemporary findings of anthropology. Rather than suspecting that the anthropologists' interpretations of past cultures might reflect their own (and his) intellectual and social milieu, Hardy seems to have accepted their evidence as support for some of his own suspicions about modern culture. Comments taken from such diverse sources as James Parton's *Life of Voltaire* and J.G. Frazer's *The Golden Bough* illustrate the extent of Hardy's interest in the subject and indicate some of the applications he found for anthropology in his own studies of human culture. His notation of Voltaire's view may display one of the roots from which Hardy's sentiments sprang to find later expression in such poems as

"God's Funeral": "It is characteristic of barbarians to believe the divinity malevolent. Men make God in their own image" (*LN* I. 1259). Hardy noticed when other writers saw similar messages about modern religion in anthropological work. The many entries Hardy made in his notebooks of details taken from John Addington Symonds' *Essays, Speculative and Suggestive* (London 1890) attest to the similar view of the issues that the two men shared. As Symonds wrote, "Mumbo Jumbo, Indar, Shiva, Jahve, Zeus, Odin, Balder, Christ, Allah – what are these but names for the Inscrutable, adapted to the modes of thought wh. gave them currency?" (*LN* II. 1869).

In his entry on *The Golden Bough - A Study of Comparative Religion*, dated 7 July 1891, Hardy summarizes the book's content making special note of those topics that most interested him.

> This is a work on primitive superstitions & religion. As he fears, the author seems to have pushed the theory of the G. Bough too far.
> In the sacred grove & sanctuary of Diana Nemorensis or Diana of the Wood near the town of Aricia (the modern La Riccia) grew a certain tree round which a strange figure prowled, drawn sword in hand. He was a priest & a murderer. A candidate for the priesthood cd. only succeed by slaying him & having slain him he held office till he was himself slain.
> The book treats of Priestly kings, sympathetic magic, rain making, inspiration by blood drinking (at Argos, blood of a lamb) – India &c) – live human gods (in South Sea islands). also
> Tree-worship. Many tribes ascribe souls to trees. Tree-spirits, May King – queen. Man – god (the Mikado): (*LN* II. 1872)

The other five notes to Frazer's work indicate that Hardy saw immediate connections between stories in *The Golden Bough* and many early Dorset myths and legends with which he was already familiar.

Max Müller's work on solar mythology also intrigued Hardy. Müller's findings seemed to suggest sources for Dorset solar rites and festivals which Hardy himself had observed.

> The Sun [crossed out] <Solar Myths> "Greek, Roman, & Vedic myths; traced back to their source, found always to apply to the sun in his ever varying aspects . . . . Folk-lore of Hottentots Red Indians, Mexicans, Samoyedes, & Andaman Islanders . . . everywhere the same story, the same worship of the sun, myths of the sun, legends of the sun, riddles of the sun . . . We with our modern ways of life are not aware how everything we think or speak or do is dependent on the sun." Max Müller "19th Cent" Dec '85. (*LN* I. 1359)

Hardy's wide-ranging interest in all kinds of nineteenth-century science and the social and cultural implications of those sciences is reminiscent of Donne's in the seventeenth. The scientific endeavors that most influenced Hardy personally and as a writer are Darwinism and astronomy and astrophysics. Hardy's deep reading and application of Darwinian concepts in his work have been explored most recently by

Gillian Beer, Tess Cosslett, and others.[24] Hardy read Darwin's works firsthand, recorded extensive notes to Francis Darwin's *Life and Letters of Charles Darwin* (London 1887) (see *LN* I. 1534–1540), and studied Spencer's *Principles of Biology* with special attention to his definition of determinism (*LN* I. 882–96+; 1485). He also noted miscellaneous instances of Darwinian thought as they occurred in the work of other writers. It is fair to say that Hardy had a more accurate and subtle understanding of evolutionary theory and Darwinism, in particular, than most twentieth and twenty-first century readers who tend to rely on stereotypical notions of "struggle" and "fittedness" rather than the finer points of the survival mechanisms Darwin described, especially those that emphasized the interactions of life forms and their environments.

Theodore Watts's comments on Darwinism in a literary review published in *The Examiner* (6 May 1876) caught Hardy's interest. He immediately recognized the melancholy truth of Watts's statement as it applied to unique and fragile individuals of the human species. "Science," Watts wrote, "tells us that, in the struggles for life, the surviving organism is not necessarily that which is absolutely the best in an ideal sense, though it must be that which is most in harmony with surrounding conditions" (*LN* I. 392). Hardy also put to literary use in *Tess* the striking pessimism he found in a *Spectator* review of Francis Galton's *Inquiries into Human Faculty and Development* (London 1883).

> Galton on the defects, evil, & apparent waste on our globe. –
> "We perceive around us a countless number of abortive seed & germs; we find out of any group of a thousand men selected at random, some who are crippled, insane, idiotic, & otherwise incurably imperfect in body or mind, & it is possible that this world may rank among other worlds as one of these [i.e. 'a blighted planet,' my addition] (*LN* I. 1311)

Darwin's powerful vision of the characteristics and mechanisms of evolution seemed to Hardy to be supported by living evidence all around him. Historical process and social process both seemed to fit the patterns Darwin described. "History," Hardy noted, "depends upon the relation between the organism & the environment" (*LN* I. 1195).

---

[24]   See, for instance: Peter Allan Dale, "Reversing the Positivist Oracle: The Unvisionary Company of Darwin, Maudsley, and Hardy" Chapter 9, in *In Pursuit of a Scientific Culture: Science, Art, and Society in the Victorian Age* (Madison: University of Wisconsin Press, 1989) 219–40; Gillian Beer, "Finding a Scale for the Human: Plot and Writing in Hardy's Novels " in *Darwin's Plots: Evolutionary Narrative in Dickens, George Eliot and Nineteenth Century Fiction* (Boston: Routledge and Kegan Paul, 1983) 229–41; Roger Ebbatson, *The Evolutionary Self: Hardy, Forster, Lawrence* (Brighton, Eng.: Harvester Press, 1982) and Tess Cosslett, "Hardy" in *The Scientific Movement and Victorian Literature* (Brighton, Eng.: Harvester Press, 1982). Although his mention of Hardy is surprisingly meager, readers may also wish to consult George Levine, *Darwin and the Novelists: Patterns of Science in Victorian Fiction* (Chicago: University of Chicago Press, 1988).

Social evolution followed nature's lead, as societies achieved survival and development through slow change not revolution (*LN* I. 1295). Man was an animal like any other and was subject to the same natural laws; but man's response to nature's power need not be one of dejected subjection. In a note dated 21 February 1891, Hardy summarized an article he found in the *National Observer* (February 1891) entitled "The Facility of Life."

> It is not hope inspires the most of us with content; it is rather the immediate & manifest delights of living . . . : Where we thrust our hideous ancestry from our rarer minds, we yet derive from it our greatest blessing, for 'tis only so far as we are of common clay with the brute that we can forget & enjoy. . . . For to forget & to enjoy – these are the capacities that serve us best, & these are of the brute's prerogative . . . [my elision]
>
> Life is very facile to animals; it is facile also to the supreme animal. (*LN* II. 1781)

Yet Hardy was also fully cognizant of how the operation of impersonal natural law could appear sinister to those who suffered randomly by it. Symonds often emphasized in his writings how the subjective powers of the human mind could affect the world view of those observing it. The same anthropomorphic tendency that had led primitive humans to see gods in every natural occurrence could explain the felt presence of evil in the world as well. As Symonds wrote, "the mysteries of sin, pain, disease, . . . are quite as well accounted for by formulas of evolutionary strife & imperfect development as by the old hypothesis of a devil" (*LN* II. 1807). The notion that evolution operated as a modern devil was too good for Hardy to pass up. In several novels, Hardy makes a point of showing how a single unfortunate incident can be interpreted in various ways by characters observing it, depending on the degree to which their individual personalities utilize subjectivity, superstition, and anthropomorphization to form a response. Hardy does not pass judgement upon these points of view, nor does he hint at his own preference for what may be the best approach to a certain phenomenon, he merely allows the range of possibilities to display themselves and play themselves out.

*   *   *

Although it would be fair to say that Darwinism was the most influential set of scientific concepts in the later half of Victorian nineteenth-century culture, evidence from Hardy's varied reading and deep study shows that it did not stand alone in his mind as such. Hardy saw developments in contemporary astronomy, fast becoming astrophysics, as exerting an equally powerful influence upon the human consciousness and imagination. To a certain extent, this may have been so because biological evolution on earth was considered by at least some Victorian thinkers to be a continuation of cosmic evolution in the universe. The inorganic development of the galaxies, stars, and planetary systems gave birth to organic development, so astronomy and Darwinism were naturally linked in the scientific story of the cosmos. The two sciences were also linked by the fundamental contributions their researchers made to the perception of the universal conditions and physical environment in which Hardy and his contemporaries lived. Hardy consciously and extensively drew upon the results and implications of both astronomy and natural history to create literary environments for his characters that included what he believed to be the most profound elements of the universal reality the two sciences were revealing. Hardy's characters live and move and try to preserve their being within the social, physical, and emotional conditions that Hardy thought were laid down for them by the findings of astronomy and geology. There were, as Tennyson had said, *two* "terrible muses" for the age's literature, and Hardy was well aware that the other one was astronomy.

Chapter 3

The *Other* "Terrible Muse"
Astronomy and Cosmology from Prehistory through the Victorian Period

For the vast majority of people on earth, the conditions of life have never been much altered by whether scientific experts viewed the cosmos as Aristotelian, Copernican, Keplerian, Newtonian, Einsteinian, or otherwise. For some astronomers, star-crossed lovers, and poets and novelists such as Hardy, however, it has always mattered – immensely. Wondering "what is out there and why?" has been central to their imaginative construction of aesthetically and philosophically satisfying world views. Despite unprecedented interest in space travel and the possibilities of extraterrestrial life in the late twentieth and early twenty-first centuries, despite fantastic satellite photos of the moon, planets and starship Earth, and computer generated visualizations of the deepest reaches of the universe, in the most direct sense, people of the *past* had a *better* view of the cosmos. Our night sky used to shine much more brightly. Three hundred, two hundred, even one hundred years ago, the smog and light pollution of highly industrialized countries and the fires of burning rainforests had not yet dimmed the brilliance of the spectacle of the vast Milky Way, planets, constellations, and comets. All visible to the naked eye, such objects were equally likely to inspire the contemplation and wonder of shepherds, night riders, and insomniac philosopher-kings.

Throughout his long life, Thomas Hardy was a keen observer of his local night sky and an avid student of contemporary astronomy and cosmology. Although Hardy's literary and philosophical uses of the central tenets of evolutionary theory have attracted the lion's share of scholarly attention, Hardy's astronomy has received some critical mention in the "literature and science" surveys of A. J. Meadows and Tess Cosslett and within brief articles by Harumi James, Jacob Korg, and Paul Ward, among others.[1] To the best of my knowledge, no one has previously attempted a

---

[1] See, for example: Harumi James, "*Two on a Tower*: Science and Religion, Space and Time" *Hardy Review* 2 (Summer 1999): 141–56; Jacob Korg, "Astronomical Imagery in Victorian Poetry" in *Victorian Science and Victorian Values: Literary Perspectives*, eds. James Paradis and Thomas Postlewait (New Brunswick, NJ: Rutgers University Press, 1985) 137–58; Paul Ward, "*Two on a Tower*: A Critical Revaluation" *Thomas Hardy Yearbook* 8 (1978): 29–34; Jim Barloon, "Star-Crossed Love: The Gravity of Science in Hardy's *Two on a Tower*," *The Victorian Newsletter* (Fall 1998): 27–32; and Edward C. Sampson "Telling Time by the Stars in

systematic, critical appraisal of the importance of astronomy and cosmology within his literature and thought.

In many ways, the astrophysical revolution through which Hardy lived was no less significant than the astronomical (Copernican–Keplerian) and Newtonian revolutions of the previous centuries. Yet those two designations are accepted nomenclature of the historiography of science, while the astrophysical revolution (perhaps eclipsed by the roughly contemporary phenomena of the Industrial Revolution), is not. Although historians of science may never agree about the nature or meaning of scientific "revolutions" philosophically, most could probably list with some general agreement certain "revolutionary" moments, achievements, discoveries, and concepts that comprise the first two periods. Such a list would not be so easily agreed upon by those trying to describe the chief developments and significant contributions of the astrophysical revolution. For one, the process of scientific development in astronomy from the mid-eighteenth through nineteenth centuries did not so naturally focus upon the outstanding achievements of individual workers in the field as it seems to have done in the cases of the revolutions brought about by Nicholas Copernicus, Galileo, Johannes Kepler, and Isaac Newton. In fact, historians of science generally describe the period of post-Newtonian science in the nineteenth century as precisely that: a period of fulfillment and elaboration of the Newtonian agenda. Such a description, however, fails to appreciate the unique perspectives of, and problems engaged by, Victorian astronomy and cosmology, both as science *per se* and, more philosophically, as world-view-making bodies of natural knowledge.

Granted a viewpoint atop at least twenty-five hundred years of recorded astronomical observations and accumulated theory (by even the most conservative estimates), Victorian culture was uniquely situated to integrate its knowledge of astronomical and cosmological history – ancient to near-modern – with its own emergent and ever more urgent attempts to understand and explain humanity's place in the cosmos through narratives provided by contemporary natural history, literary history, and social, religious and philosophical thought and ideas. To fully comprehend and value Hardy's achievement in producing texts that creatively express various aspects of that integration through his own synthesis of literary and astronomical cosmologies, it is necessary to balance our account of his engagement with the literary history of astronomy (as given in Chapter 2) with an equally detailed story tracing how the lines of discovery and inquiry in astronomy, physics and cosmology which intertwine only intermittently in ancient times, distinctly separate, then gradually re-converge during his lifetime, developing into the hybrid science of astrophysics. Such a recounting will enable us to accurately envision how Hardy conjoined the two streams of cosmological ideas and texts (the literary and the natural philosophical/scientific) in his own mythic tales of universal truths and consequences.

Far from the Madding Crowd," *Notes and Queries*, ns 14 (1967): 63–4.

A Brief History of Astronomy and Cosmology:
Ancient Times through the Age of Newton

Although its roots are often mistakenly translated as meaning "to name" the stars, the word astronomy comes from the Greek ἄστρον - νέμω (astron - nemo) which signifies the ability "to distribute," "to account for" and "to manage" the stars or constellations, with the verb having a strong association with the duties of herdsmen, "to drive to pasture" or "to shepherd." This etymology, perhaps, reflects the ancient identification of shepherds as the first astronomers and it is easy to imagine them watching over both "flocks" by night – counting the white spots of their wooly charges against the shadowy hillsides and numbering the bright points of starlight within the dark sky. For many centuries, astronomers watched and wondered about celestial objects, primarily the sun, moon, stars, planets, comets, and meteors. They recorded changes in the appearance and motions of the sun and moon, identifying monthly, seasonal, and annual patterns. They observed, measured, and mapped the positions of the "fixed" (stationary-appearing) stars relative to one another and tracked the motions of each known planet (πλανήτης "wanderer") against the background of those stars. They speculated about the origins and nature of the celestial bodies, especially the planets, and imagined mechanisms as well as mathematical and geometrical models to explain and predict their motions.

The central tasks of astronomy – observing, measuring, and recording the positions and motions of the celestial bodies – remained essentially the same from the ancient world through the age of Galileo. For most of those two thousand years, astronomical observations were made by the lens of the human eye, aided by an increasingly sophisticated array of measuring instruments (sun-dials, time-keeping devices, sextants, quadrants, the triquetrum, torquetum, cross-staff, astrolabe, mural quadrant, equatorial armillary, among others), but not magnification.[2] Across those same two millennia, however, cosmology – the conception of the origin, nature, ordering principles, shape and extent of the κόσμος (cosmos) – transformed dramatically. While early astronomy and cosmology both considered the objects of the universe as the subjects of their studies, it is important to realize that the latter was not always directly dependent on, limited by or responsive to the former. Astronomy grew in sophistication as a branch of the practical, observational and theoretical, mathematical sciences; while cosmology evolved more eclectically from mythology, religion, and speculative natural philosophy. There has not always been direct reciprocity or correspondence between the two. The observations of the most skilled early astronomers may have informed educated cosmological speculators about some of the visible, material facts of the universe, but rarely did such observations or discoveries provide patent insight into the nature of celestial objects, their interrelations, and behavior. Through most of human history, as well, astronomical (geometrical and mathematical) models did not function as literal representations of the physical reality

---

[2]   Henry C. King, *The History of the Telescope* (1955; New York: Dover, 1979) 1–24.

of cosmic order. So, for such reasons, and others, the popular, generally accepted cosmologies of the ancient world seldom reflected the most sophisticated views of contemporary astronomical research and theory. Such was surely the case well through the age of Copernicus, and an argument could be made that the gap between the latest astronomy and astrophysics and popular cosmology is, if anything, even vaster today.[3]

Similarly, the general reading public's sense of the history of the interactions of astronomy and cosmology tends to reflect an oversimplified three-fold narrative in which: 1) the primitive classical mind responds with shock and awe to celestial phenomena (made barely intelligible by the erratic behavior of the gods and goddesses of Greco-Roman myth); 2) pagan cosmology is replaced by the less superstitious tenets of medieval and Renaissance Judeo-Christian understanding (*Genesis* to *Revelation*); and 3) religious faith in a cosmic Creator is itself replaced by the Big Bang, evolutionary theory, and scientific rationalism. The history of science tells a far richer story and one which Hardy and the numerous outstanding classicists in nineteenth-century Britain were in a better position to appreciate than perhaps any highly educated group of readers since the Augustans. Victorian poets and critics such as Matthew Arnold, Algernon Swinburne, Robert Browning, Alfred Tennyson, and John Ruskin, had a deep fascination with classical and medieval cosmologies, were highly literate in Greek and Latin, and had access to a multitude of classical literary works and philosophical treatises. They soon learned that they were far from the first to take up the task of fashioning a meaningful life for themselves in a deterministic natural world surrounded by a mechanistic universe. In constructing their understanding of life in the cosmos, many nineteenth-century thinkers drew upon and incorporated responses they first encountered in the original texts and artifacts of earlier cultures. Revisiting the reading of Hardy and his peers, it is fascinating to see how many aspects of early cosmologies resonate with Victorian concerns.

The Greek Cosmos: Ancient to Medieval

The most influential cosmologies in Western intellectual tradition, from the ancient Greek world through the Scientific Revolution, and beyond, were those of Plato and Aristotle.[4] Several hundred years previous to either, however, Greek nature

---

[3]		As Richard P. Brennan reports, a poll taken in 1989 by Northern Illinois and Oxford Universities found that "only one-third of British adults and one-half of Americans knew that the Earth revolves around the Sun and takes one year to do so" (*Dictionary of Scientific Literacy* (New York: John Wiley and Sons, 1992) 58). Copernicus proposed that model for the Earth–Sun system nearly 450 years previous and it is generally believed that his ideas achieved professional acceptance between 300–375 years ago. Given such a state of affairs, it is hard to imagine what minute percentage of the world's current populace might, with understanding, consider themselves to be living in a Newtonian or Einsteinian cosmos, let alone the "elegant universe" postulated by current string theorists.

[4]		I am deeply indebted for much of the following discussion to the masterful synthesis of

philosophers had already proposed cosmic systems that differed significantly from the familiar mythopoetic world view of Homer and Hesiod in which the universe was imagined to be under the control – or at the mercy – of a pantheon of emotionally labile gods and goddesses. Although the Olympians lived and ruled in popular consciousness and religious belief and practice for many centuries into Roman times, by the sixth century B.C.E. the pre-Socratics had removed divine whims, fancies, and passionate vengeance from their views of the behavior of natural phenomena. Because of their preference for non-supernatural explanations of φύσις (phusis, "physics"), nature and the nature of things, Aristotle labeled them the φύσιολογοι (physiologoi, "nature-studiers") or φύσικοι (physikoi, "the naturists," or "the physicists"). These pre-Socratic thinkers offered materialistic and rationalistic philosophies of nature. Among the materialists, the Milesians (Thales, Anaximenes, Anaximander), all proposed naturalistic explanations for the origins, material nature, underlying reality, order, and diversity of the cosmos. Radical materialists, Leucippus and Democritus (fl. 440, 410 B.C.E., respectively) were atomists who envisioned the cosmos as an infinite space filled with an infinite number of inert minute particles (ἄτομος, atomos, the "uncut") moving and interacting at random, devoid of divine will or purpose. Other early Greek philosophers proposed cosmologies that were the result of a combination of material and immaterial explanations. Empedocles's cosmos came into being as four material elements (earth, air, fire, water) and their qualities were acted upon by the immaterial forces of "love" and "strife." The rationalist Pythagoreans originated the still-current scientific notion that the underlying reality of nature is inherently numerical and harmonious and that mathematics is the necessary key to its understanding. The Eleatics, Parmenides and Zeno, treated the evidence of the senses with high skepticism, rejecting entirely the illusions of physical being and the natural world they provided, preferring instead, to rely upon reason as the sole path to truth and understanding. The central questions and epistemological dilemmas underlying early Greek natural philosophy – What is the universe made of? What is real? How can we know it? Should we trust our sensory experience of nature or our rational and logical analyses of it? Should we believe in the invisible and doubt the visible? Can chance and matter alone explain all of the order we see in the universe? – all resurface in nineteenth-century scientific philosophical debates.

Greek natural philosophical thought achieved by David C. Lindberg of the University of Wisconsin-Madison's History of Science Department (now emeritus), in lectures given between 1984 and 1986. Much of this material has been published in his *The Beginnings of Western Science: The European Scientific Tradition in Philosophical, Religious, and Institutional Context, 600 B.C. to A.D. 1450* (Chicago: University of Chicago Press, 1992). For additional perspectives on ancient to medieval astronomy and cosmology, see also: Edward Grant, *Planets, Stars and Orbs: The Medieval Cosmos, 1200-1687* (Cambridge: Cambridge University Press, 1994); McCluskey, *Astronomies*; Sabetai Unguru, *Physics, Cosmology and Astronomy, 1300–1700*, Boston Studies in the Philosophy of Science, 126 (Dordrecht: Kluwer Academic, 1991) and relevant essays in Norriss S. Hetherington, ed., *Cosmology: Historical, Literary, Philosophical, Religious, and Scientific Perspectives* (New York: Garland Publishing, 1993).

Plato's natural philosophy included both astronomical and cosmological elements that were of long influence within the early medieval Christian world view and later, in Renaissance Neoplatonism. Although he apparently visualized the cosmos as a two-sphere system – a spherical Earth surrounded by a celestial sphere upon which all of the other heavenly bodies inscribed their motions – the philosophical underpinnings of Plato's cosmology were more influential than the technical details of his astronomy. Influenced by Pythagorean philosophy, Plato discouraged observational astronomy (since it involved using the inferior physical senses to observe mere material things in nature), but commended theoretical astronomy as among the most exalted of the sciences, given that those dedicated to it made abstract consideration of the highest and finest things of the cosmos with the highest and finest tools of the human intellect – geometry and mathematics. In theoretical astronomy, Plato has traditionally received credit for posing the query that challenged and confounded astronomers and their mathematics for the next two millennia: how to account for the motions of the planets using only uniform circular motions.[5]

In cosmology, many elements of Plato's natural philosophy endured because they were so amenable to assimilation into Christian thought. He rejected the purely mechanistic explanations of many of the pre-Socratics, believing that order (κόσμος, cosmos) could not be accounted for by the disorderly random action of inert particles of matter alone (χάος, chaos). For Plato, there were two levels of reality: the invisible eternal realm of perfect, ideal immaterial forms and the visible world which contains imperfect temporal material copies of those forms, with the highest or truest reality residing in the realm of forms. He believed that the design and pattern of universal nature had been chosen and created by a rational, highly orderly soul or spirit (ψυχή, psyche) which he personified as the Demiurge (δημιουργός, demiurgos) an eternal, benevolent, divine craftsman. In Plato's story of creation, the Demiurge is not omnipotent and does not create *ex nihilo* (out of nothing), but instead makes the imperfect, visible realm of reality that we perceive ourselves to be in by shaping and molding primitive chaotic matter according to the ideas or forms, making the best and most beautiful world possible, within the limits of that inherently flawed raw material. In his creative efforts, the Demiurge is guided by design principles that are moral, aesthetic, and mathematical. Although expressing a geometric atomism in which the "triangular" nature of essential matter combines and recombines to form the objects in the universe, the final created cosmos for Plato is animate, alive with soul and reason which motivate it, just as the human soul/mind moves the body.

Although there are many important distinctions between the basic components of Christian and Platonic cosmology, Plato's concepts of an eternal, benevolent, rational, divine creator, an eternal realm of perfection, a flawed world of imperfection, and a world-soul were close enough to Christian ideas of a Creator-God, Heaven, the sinful

---

[5]	Lindberg cites D. R. Dicks, *Early Greek Astronomy to Aristotle* (Ithaca: Cornell University Press, 1970), chapter 5, as casting doubt as to whether Plato should be so credited; see: *The Beginnings of Western Science* 92–3 and fn. 9.

earth and Holy Spirit, that he was christened a pagan Christian prophet, one who must have received partial revelation of God's truth. His cosmology was interwoven with Christian teachings until the early twelfth century when they were displaced in the medieval scholastic world view by those of his student, Aristotle.

University students in the British Empire were no strangers to Aristotle, as his works formed an essential part of the core curriculum through the nineteenth century, well into the twentieth. Aristotle rejected Plato's notion that the universal, ideal types of things are the ultimate reality. Instead, he made a more down-to-earth proposal that individual material objects are reality, with the forms or ideas of those things having no existence independent of them. Aristotle proposed learning about nature by using both reason and the senses to observe those individual things and discover their general (and essential) characteristics. He acknowledged that there is design, purpose, and order in the cosmos, and he sought through his philosophy to discover the cause of that order (whether material, formal, efficient or final). Aristotle's concern with observing, recording, and inquiring into the causal mechanisms of nature was greatly influential on the development of the scientific enterprise.

Aristotle posited a cosmos that was both materialistic and deterministic. He conceived of φύσις – the physical nature of the universe – as made up of four material elements (earth, air, fire, water) and their four more fundamental qualities (hot, cold, wet, dry). These qualities, mixed with *prima materia* (prime matter), produce all of the substances we observe in the world. The essential differences between the qualities explain the changes of state that we see occurring in nature (from solid to liquid to vapor, etc.). Aristotle's cosmos is divided into two material realms: the temporal sublunary realm of the four elements "below the moon" and the eternal superlunary realm of quintessence (the fifth essence) "above the moon." The physical order of Aristotle's cosmos is determined by the nature of those elements which arrange themselves according to their relative weights, with the heaviest finding its natural place in the center (the Earth), the lightest (fire) rising to the upper edge of the sublunary realm. Stasis, in the sublunary realm, is never achieved, as all material things there remain in constant flux, changing, admixing, moving, growing, decaying. By contrast, the superlunary region, the celestial realm of the purest fifth element, exists in unchanging eternal perfection, in perpetual circular motion.

Aristotle accounted for the appearances of the stars and planets with a complex system of interacting nested crystalline spheres (several for each planet, with sets of three counteracting spheres in between, usually totaling 55, with one additional for the sphere of fixed stars), with the Earth (as the heaviest material object) at rest in the center.[6] He postulated the existence of a deity, an "Unmoved Mover," whose perfect rest inspires the "intelligence" of the planetary spheres to imitate him, thus motivating them into uniform circular motion, the most perfect motion that the most refined

---

[6]   As in John North, *The Norton History of Astronomy and Cosmology* (New York: W. W. Norton, 1995) 83; Anton Pannekoek, *A History of Astronomy* (New York: Dover, 1961) 116 and Lindberg, *The Beginnings of Western Science* 96.

matter can achieve. This deity, however, is not a creator as both he and the cosmos have existed coeternally, without beginning or end. He does not care for the cosmos or intervene in the lives of those within it. As the souls (forms) of all cosmic individuals cease to exist when the individual ceases to exist, Aristotle posits no afterlife. All of the causes of things are determined by the nature of nature itself; there is no divine intention or interaction.

Read outside of the scholastic tradition of Christianized Aristotelianism, it is not difficult to see that many of Aristotle's cosmological ideas were in direct conflict with some of the most basic tenets of Christian belief. However, the explanatory power of Aristotle's physics and the descriptive power of his natural philosophy were reconciled to and deeply integrated within Christian theology and teaching for many centuries.[7] While practical and predictive medieval and early Renaissance astronomy was based upon the mathematical and geometrical models of Ptolemy (complex, eclectic systems for each planet utilizing, in various combinations, the eccentric, equant, epicycle, and deferent), the general conception of the physical reality of the universe was essentially based on Aristotelian physics (natural things behave according to their essential material natures and seek their natural places) and his cosmology – a geocentric (Earth-centered) system of nested spheres, each conveying one of the seven "planets" (Saturn, Jupiter, Mars, Venus, Mercury, the sun and moon) along in its circular motion, all enclosed by the outermost sphere of fixed stars. Although medieval Christian philosophers did closely identify Aristotle's Prime Mover with the Christian care-taking God, that did not mean that they viewed their universe as a safe and cozy, tight-knit cosmos as old histories of science and religion once taught. They thought their universe to be closed and finite, but their estimates of its size made the scale of God's creation seem unfathomable enough (with the fixed stars located nearly 73.4 million miles from Earth, in fact, according to Campanus of Novara at the end of the thirteenth century).[8] For those few aware of the best contemporary estimates for the size of the cosmos, the space between their medieval earthly home and the gates of Heaven loomed large. Rather than engendering a crisis of faith, such vastness was quickly pressed into service both as an object lesson in proper human humility and additional evidence of the even greater vastness of its Maker.

---

[7]   See: David C. Lindberg, "Science and the Early Church" and Edward Grant, "Science and Theology in the Middle Ages" in *God and Nature: Historical Essays on the Encounter between Christianity and Science*, eds. David C. Lindberg and Ronald L. Numbers (Berkeley: University of California Press, 1986) 19–48, 49–75; various references in David C. Lindberg and Ronald L. Numbers, eds., *When Science and Christianity Meet* (Chicago: University of Chicago Press, 2003) and David C. Lindberg, ed., *Science in the Middle Ages* (Chicago: University of Chicago Press, 1978); as well as relevant essays in Hetherington, ed., *Cosmology*, 69–224.

[8]   See: Lindberg, *The Beginnings of Western Science* 252; Albert Van Helden, *Measuring the Universe: Cosmic Dimensions from Aristarchus to Halley* (Chicago: University of Chicago Press, 1985) 34–7; and Hetherington, ed., *Cosmology* 195–7.

The basic astronomical facts of the known universe did not change through the long centuries of the middle ages. Late medieval and early Renaissance astronomers sought to explain the appearances of the same visible celestial phenomena that had puzzled ancient astronomers: the motions of the five heavenly bodies that we call the planets (Mercury, Venus, Mars, Jupiter and Saturn), plus the sun and moon. Indeed if, as Aristotle had postulated, the heavenly bodies were unchanging and unchangeable (and no one had serious grounds to doubt him), there was no practical motivation for constantly making new observations. Consequently, when Copernicus offered his reformation of mathematical astronomy (revising the astronomical tables that were used to establish the dates of the Church calendar), he had no qualms about utilizing observational data that had been collected hundreds of years earlier and employing, by some estimates, only twenty-seven new observations in his *De Revolutionibus*).[9]

Copernican Astronomy and Cosmology

Like all of the central figures of the Scientific Revolution, Copernicus's astronomy and cosmology were deeply influenced by the details and principles of Greek natural philosophy.[10] As an astronomer, Copernicus worked in the Platonic–Pythagorean tradition, committing himself aesthetically and philosophically to seeking in the motions of the heavens the mathematical unity, coherence, and harmony that he believed his Demiurge-like Christian geometer God had created there. His "revolutionary" conceptual scheme – a moving Earth within a heliocentric system – was adapted from ideas introduced by several ancient authorities, including Heraclides and Ecphantus who proposed the diurnal rotation of the Earth on its axis, the sun-centered system of Aristarchus of Samos, and the Pythagoreans' notion of a "central fire" (and perhaps, their tendency toward sun-worship as well). He devised his mathematical models for planetary motions by refining those of Ptolemy according to a rigorous Platonic–Pythagorean ideal of uniform circular motion. Copernicus shifted the order of the celestial bodies and proposed planetary models that required an "immense" interstellar universe to contain them (far greater than any medieval model), yet he retained far more of the ancient system than he changed, actually shrinking the planetary system to one-half of its medieval size, and maintaining the basic cosmological idea of a central body and a sphere of fixed stars in a closed, finite cosmos, as well as many of the technical complexities of Ptolemy's geometrical predictive models.

---

[9] North believes that Copernicus distilled these from a much larger number of new observations that he made, *The Norton History of Astronomy and Cosmology* 287.
[10] See: Kuhn, *The Copernican Revolution*; Richard S. Westfall, *The Construction of Modern Science: Mechanisms and Mechanics*, The Cambridge History of Science Series (1971; Cambridge: Cambridge University Press, 1992); North, *The Norton History of Astronomy and Cosmology*; Pannekoek, *A History of Astronomy*; Hetheringon, ed., *Cosmology*; and Van Helden, *Measuring the Universe*.

Among his fellow astronomers his proposal of a truly "solar" system represented an earth-shifting revision of previous models, its most earth-shaking consequences being, for them, the adjustments that a sun-centered perspective required of their mathematical calculations. Such was not the case when philosophers began to seriously consider whether Copernicus's mathematical astronomy might be taken as an expression of cosmological reality. Unlike many of his predecessors, Copernicus was dissatisfied with Ptolemaic astronomy not only because of its predictive inaccuracies, but also because of its inaccurate description of physical phenomena. Although Andreas Osiander's notorious anonymous preface claimed that Copernicus viewed his work as a hypothesis only (and fooled many readers into believing that was the author's position), Copernicus's own text reveals his deep concern that the predictive models he was attempting to reform did not adequately account for the real appearances of the heavenly bodies as observed in the sky. Ptolemy's geometrical model of the moon's orbit, for example, was an especially egregious case. While it was useful for predicting lunar positions over time, Ptolemy's lunar model described the moon's distance from earth as greatly variable, enough so that it seemed to predict that the diameter of the moon should appear twice as large at the quarters than at full; yet the apparent size of the moon, as real-life observations tell us, does not change.[11] By suggesting that mathematical astronomers should strive for a physical correspondence between their geometric models and physical observables, Copernicus proposed a deeper degree of interaction between astronomy and cosmology – in some respects more reflective of ancient goals for astronomy than medieval ones.[12] While his proposed change of perspective required a relatively simple geometrical maneuver for his mathematical peers in astronomy, under the "laws" of Aristotelian physics and cosmology, he would find the Earth less easy to move.

Uniting astronomy and cosmology within a heliocentric system created conflict with various aspects of common-sense physics, religious belief, and poetics. Taken as cosmology, the heliocentrism of *De Revolutionibus* (1543) violates commonsense and Aristotelian physics in several ways. It proposes moving the heavy Earth from its "natural" place at the center of the cosmos and lifting it "unnaturally" into orbit around the Sun. It proposes bringing "down" the light and fiery sun from its natural tendency to rise. It proposes three motions for the "obviously" motionless Earth (diurnal, annual

---

[11] Pannekoek, *A History of Astronomy* 196–7.

[12] It is important to note at this point in our discussion that astrologers had long assumed a physical connection and a cause–effect "correspondence" between the stars, planets and earthly beings. The subjects and methods of astronomy and astrology were often interwoven in complex ways during ancient, medieval, and early modern times, but for reasons of space and simplicity of narrative, I have separated out the astrological enterprise (interpreting "the stars" in order to forecast personal, political, and social events) from my discussion of how astrophysics developed out of the concerns of mathematical and observational astronomy and cosmology. Although now generally regarded as a pseudoscience, the concern of astrology with physical causation and interaction of celestial and terrestrial bodies did nevertheless influence the development of astrophysics, as we shall see.

and axial), when we all "know" and can "see" and can "feel" from our "stationary" position, that the sun moves across our sky while we remain still. It suggests no adequate replacement for Aristotle's explanation of why we (and all other earth-y "heavy" things) "stick" to the Earth, rather than flying off of its surface – an especially difficult point, if the Earth is spinning, wobbling, and orbiting all at once and all the time. It offers no reason why the body of the Earth itself does not fly apart under the stresses of such rapid and violent motions. Copernicus's proposal also disrupts religious cosmology based on scriptural evidence, as it seems to demote the Earth from its Biblically honored place as God's "footstool" and flout the truth of Joshua's account that he commanded the sun (not the Earth) to stand still when he needed more hours in his day to do battle against his enemies. Given that Aristotelian natural philosophy and Christian theology were so intertwined in Copernicus's lifetime, all of the above consequences seemed equally blasphemous, equally absurd, and equally easy to reject in the absence of very good evidence to the contrary; and while Copernicus had his reasons, he did not have (and, technically, astronomy would not have for several hundred more years) definitive *evidence*.[13]

Although the predictive power of his mathematical models was only slightly better than Ptolemy's, Copernicus's system provided intelligible explanations for many of the phenomena (celestial appearances) that Ptolemy's could not. For instance, by assigning three motions to the Earth, Copernicus could explain why the sun, moon, and stars "appeared" to rise, travel across the sky, and set and why there were seasons and seasonal changes in the sun's path. In a heliocentric system, the retrograde motion of the planets (when they appear temporarily to slow down, stop, and then reverse their direction in the sky) is revealed as an optical illusion created by the relative orbits of the earth and those planets.[14] While Copernicus's explanations for these relatively remote phenomena were intriguing and innovative, they called into doubt the relative reliability of the senses and human reason – seemingly suggesting that through the long centuries since Creation our God-given senses had fooled us all into believing in optical illusions. Many preferred to doubt that God would present us with such deceptive gifts. However clever the explanatory consequences of Copernicus's change of perspective, such cleverness was not reason enough to discard a natural philosophy as sensible and testable by direct human experience as Aristotle's or one as integrated with the articles of faith.

---

[13]   Such as that offered by stellar parallax which is defined as the apparent change in position of a relatively close star against the background of very distant stars due to the change in our viewing angle as the earth moves from one side of its orbit around the sun to the other (a distance of approximately 186 million miles). The first telescopic discovery of stellar parallax was made by Friedrich W. Bessel who measured it in the star 61 Cygni in 1838.

[14]   For those curious about the technical details of this phenomenon, helpful diagrams illustrating the appearance of retrograde motion and its geometry as an optical illusion, respectively, are readily available in Lindberg, *The Beginnings of Western Science* 91 and Kuhn, *Copernican Revolution* 166.

In many ways, the beauty of the system was Copernicus's best argument for its truth. Recognizing that his new conception of the structure of the universe required adjustment of religious and symbolic associations and meanings, Copernicus undertook some of this aesthetic and poetic (not to mention proto-psychological) work himself, suggesting that the beauty and harmony of the heliocentric system – with all planets (including, now, the Earth) arranged in the order of their known orbital periods, was itself an expression of God's creative design and plan. He further speculated that something innate to the geometry of the planetary spheres themselves may cause them to move "naturally" in circles, and that our humble abode, Earth, was never intended by its Maker to occupy the exalted center of things, but rather a more apt, but still special, place, moving worshipfully around the metaphoric image of His throne, the Sun.

Heliocentric Astronomy and Cosmology:
  Accommodated, Defended, Revolutionized

In Copernicus's wake, it was left to Tycho Brahe, Galileo, and Kepler to strengthen the case for uniting astronomy and cosmology. Like many before him Tycho noticed that the astronomical tables were poor predictors of celestial phenomena, such as planetary conjunctions and eclipses. Unlike many of his predecessors, however, Tycho did not assume that the discrepancy between the mathematical models and reality was entirely due to the inadequacy of human geometry to match heavenly perfections. Instead, he doubted the accuracy of the data and set out to reform observational astronomy.[15] A Lutheran and Danish nobleman, Tycho had the religious freedom to doubt the infallibility of Aristotle and access to the resources necessary to effect the astronomical reformation he desired. In 1572 he discovered a supernova, a new star, visible to the naked eye, that changed color and size over time. This discovery offered visual proof that Aristotle's notion of the unchangeable celestial heavens was incorrect. Aristotle did not know it all and he could be wrong. After Tycho published his findings, the Danish king rewarded him with land, funding, and serfs enough to construct and run a large island observatory complex. By the early 1590s, he was recognized as Europe's greatest observational astronomer, inventing and building observational instruments, gathering immense quantities of observations and measurements for the fixed stars and planets, and achieving vast improvements in accuracy.

For Tycho, astronomy was not an exclusively mathematical science; he believed that it should offer a description of physical reality. Although he knew that Aristotle's natural philosophy *in toto* was not inerrant, he had confidence in its physics which

---

[15]   North refers to this emphasis on data gathering as part of a "new empiricism" that emerged in early modern astronomy. It is worthwhile to note, however, that it also represents a return to the ancient Greek emphasis on astronomical observation and the creation of models that attempted to represent physical reality.

supported a literal interpretation of the Bible and its references to a stationary Earth. He reconciled these philosophical constraints by developing a geoheliocentric system that incorporated the mathematical advantages of the Copernican model, maintained Aristotelian physics, and honored revelation. The Tychonic cosmological "compromise" model features a central Earth, with the sun in orbit around it, Venus and Mercury orbiting the sun, and all of the other more distant planets orbiting around the entire double-centered Earth-sun system.[16] Given his observation of the path of the comet of 1577, most historians of science believe that Tycho had discarded Aristotle's notion of crystalline spheres as the vehicles for planetary motion, and instead, was the first astronomer to propose true geometrical circles as orbits in his model for the cosmos (although, significantly, he offered no replacement for the mechanical function they served).

Galileo's contributions to the union of astronomy and cosmology were even more dramatic. From very early in his career, he seems to have understood that a successful reconciliation of Copernican astronomy and Roman Catholic cosmology would require new arguments and evidence on three fronts: physics, faith, and vision. As Copernicus had suspected, an unwillingness to disengage the Aristotelian perspective was at the center of the problem. Galileo had faith that Copernican heliocentrism revealed a hidden truth behind the sensory appearances of our situation here on Earth: the phenomena of the heavens look the same whether we imagine that the Earth turns on its axis or the heavens revolve around us. In a parallel argument, Galileo responded to Aristotelian objections to a moving Earth by suggesting that a similar relativity of perspective affects our sense of motion. In essence, we mistakenly feel ourselves to be unmoving, relative to the Earth, because of the phenomenon of shared motion: i.e., because we are moved along with it, the Earth's motion feels like nonmotion to us. Moreover, in his studies of projectile motion, Galileo offered a reconceptualization of the nature of inertia, arguing that the tendency of things to remain in motion once put in motion is just as "natural" as Aristotle's notion that all things tend (by their essential natures) toward rest. Once set into motion, then, the celestial bodies can remain in motion without constant force being applied (and the imagination of complex mechanisms à la crystalline spheres etc. being required). Although none of these concepts offered proof that a heliocentric system corresponded to physical reality, they were conceptual building blocks that made a solar system and mere geometrical planetary orbits more imaginatively cogent, and laid the groundwork for a new mechanical view of the dynamics of the universe.[17]

---

[16] For a clear and easily comprehensible illustration of Tycho's geoheliocentric system, see: North, *The Norton History of Astronomy and Cosmology* 304.

[17] It is important to emphasize here that the simplified heliocentric model that Galileo was defending as "Copernican" was inspired by the familiar illustration of Copernicus's relatively simple concentric ordering of the planets, rather than the detailed and complex geometrical (and ad hoc) models he developed for each planet's orbit.

Regarding matters of faith, Galileo offered an equally ingenious new perspective: that God had given humankind two "books" for learning about His creation: the Bible and the "book" of nature. The Bible, he asserted, was not intended to address every natural phenomenon through all time and we should not look to it to do so. Instead, we should supplement our Biblical understanding of our Creator and His creations by using our God-given powers of observing and reasoning to "read" the book of nature and discover God's hand in its design. He argued that priests were called to interpret the former, and natural philosophers the latter; and, that just as natural philosophers deferred to their priests as the authoritative readers of the revealed word, priests should defer to natural philosophers' interpretations of the revealed world. Although, as we know, Galileo was convinced to surrender his position in this debate, his view of how to reconcile matters of reason to faith and scientific knowledge to theology gradually became the norm among believers and, eventually, with Church authorities as well.[18]

While reasoning might or might not lead to believing, Galileo felt certain that seeing had the potential to do so. He firmly believed that his "perspective glass" had the power to transform the cosmological perspectives of those around him. Like Tycho, he offered observational evidence of previously undiscovered celestial objects and phenomena. The first to fully exploit the telescope as an astronomical observing device, Galileo published his findings in *Sidereus Nuncius* in 1610 and *Letters on Sunspots* in 1613. Through the telescope, Galileo saw: 1 and 2) the imperfect surface of the moon and sunspots (disproving Aristotelian sub- and superlunary divisions between heavenly perfection and earthly decay); 3) the Milky Way resolved into its myriad individual stars (evidence that our "common" sense of sight was not enough to discover all of God's glory); 4 and 5) the rings of Saturn and the moons of Jupiter (adding additional plausibility to the idea that Earth was not uniquely chosen by God to have an orbital companion); and 6) the phases of Venus (which Galileo interpreted as supporting the idea that we lived in a helio- not geo-centric system, as such phases would not be visible in the latter).

Unfortunately, not all of those who looked through Galileo's telescopes instantly "saw" the same things he saw, in exactly the same ways (an experience for which anyone of us who has ever attended a public viewing night at an observatory can surely vouch). The light-gathering power of the lenses he used was not great, the viewing area was small, the optical distortion significant, and inexperienced observers did not know what to look for or how to look for it. Some astronomers reported

---

[18]   As Pannekoek relates, even past the middle of the eighteenth century, Catholic astronomy texts referred to heliocentrism as a "hypothesis." The ban against the teaching of heliocentrism was lifted in 1822 and the texts of Copernicus, Kepler and Galileo were removed from the index of banned books in 1835 (interestingly, three years *before* stellar parallax was telescopically observed and measured), see: *History of Astronomy* 234. The Vatican issued a formal apology for the Galileo affair in 1992, stating that the astronomer's insights into the true structure of the heavens must have been divinely guided.

tremendous difficulty even holding the instrument steady.[19] Even he admitted that the effects of spherical and chromatic aberration created "appearances" that were deceiving – blurry shapes and colors that might or might not really be "up there." Additionally, even had his peers been able to perfectly replicate his observations, none of these new visual phenomena provided unequivocal evidence of the truth of Copernicanism (for instance, the phases of Venus are equally accounted for by Tycho's compromise system). All of these astounding new astronomical discoveries only made Galileo's argument in favor of the cosmological possibility of a heliocentric system more plausible, not certain; and his experience attempting to bridge the gap between scientific evidence, argument, demonstration, and public understanding and belief has stood ever since as the history of science's most telling example of the difficulty of changing a culture's world view.

As Galileo argued for a new perspective in physics, faith, and vision, Johannes Kepler was taking a different approach to the same set of problems. Rather than devise ways to change other people's minds and points of view, Kepler worked on changing *his own* mind by attempting to see the cosmos from *God's* point of view. An unorthodox Lutheran mathematician whose eclectic beliefs about the nature of the triune God were too radical to support a pastoral vocation, Kepler felt himself called to reveal God's glory through Copernican astronomy. Deeply devout, Kepler was also, like Copernicus, motivated by ancient Platonic–Pythagorean aesthetic and mathematical values, and sought insight into the beauty and harmony of God's geometrically created cosmos. Kepler genuinely wanted to understand the design and engineering principles his Maker had used in forming creation and he believed that he could best do so through a combination of religious faith, mathematics, ancient philosophical and astronomical concepts, and fresh empirical data.[20] He published his first attempt at such insight in the *Mysterium Cosmographicum* (1596) in which he revealed his discovery of a geometrical reason for the number, order, and spacing between the planets: a nested system of the five regular "Platonic" solids. Kepler was so convinced that geometry held the key to God's nature that when his model did not match the observations perfectly, he did not doubt the truth of his model, but assumed that he needed better data; and he knew that the best observational data in the world were Tycho's.

His first major assignment as Tycho's assistant was to find a mathematical model for the orbit of Mars that would match the master-observer's new measurements of that planet's positions. In taking on that challenge, Kepler assumed that his

---

[19]   Albert Van Helden and M. G. Winkler, "Representing the Heavens: Galileo and Visual Astronomy," *Isis* 83 (1992):195–217; Albert Van Helden, "The Telescope and Authority from Galileo to Cassini," in *Instruments*, eds. Thomas L. Hankins and Albert Van Helden, *Osiris* 9 (1994): 9–29; and Pannekoek, *A History of Astronomy* 228–9.

[20]   As mentioned in footnote 12, Kepler may be a figure whose thinking about the causes of celestial phenomena and whose interest in physics proper was directly influenced by his early and life-long interest and belief in astrology (Pannekoek, *A History of Astronomy* 235).

mathematical astronomy would describe and account for physical reality. Since he was not able to imagine that his geometer-God would use such an unwieldy device in the perfect workings of His universe, Kepler rejected the use of epicycles (as the predictive models of both Ptolemy and Copernicus had used), although he retained the ancient requirement that all planetary motion must be uniform circular motion. Unlike so many previous generations of mathematical astronomers, Kepler wondered about the kind of force God might use to drive the machinery of the heavens and asked what geometry that force might most naturally generate by its motion. He imagined that God moved the solar system by a special spirit, the *anima motrix* (which he later conceived of as a quasi-magnetic solar "vis" or force), which radiates out from the central sun as it turns on its axis, sweeping all of the planets along in circular orbits. Although Kepler's inquiry was as much a mystical or spiritual quest for him as a mathematical one (an attempt to behold the glory of God's thought in its details), his curiosity about the physical forces at work in the heavens – the dynamics of celestial physics – established one of the central lines of inquiry in early modern science.

Initially motivated to seek the geometrical secret to the architecture of the cosmos, Kepler's dual commitment to the question of forces and the accuracy of Tycho's data led him to transform astronomy far more than Copernicus's "revolutionary" work which had essentially retooled Ptolemy's technical apparatus. Failing to match Tycho's data for Mars to a circular orbit to a degree of accuracy that satisfied him, Kepler then chose to approach the problem from several unprecedented directions. Seeking other kinds of order in other kinds of mathematical relations, Kepler studied the physical proportions of the planetary orbits, their sizes and periods. One new relation he saw: that the areas swept out by a planet's line of motion in one month's time were equal (although the distances they traced out across the sky were not). Unfortunately, two years' worth of calculations proved to him that this generalization (known later as his "area law") did not hold for Mars on a circular orbit. Still not doubting Tycho's data, Kepler again departed from past astronomical tradition and for the first time since the ancient world raised questions about the essential "truth" of Platonic assumptions that had become so integrated into mathematical astronomy over the centuries: that circles were the ideal shape for celestial bodies' motion. Perhaps God had a reason to value a different geometry. Kepler then opened up his imagination to the possibility of various ovoid shapes, and found that his area law fit Tycho's data when Mars was assumed to move on an elliptical orbit. [21]

In his *Astronomia Nova αιτιολογητος [aitiologetos] seu physica coelestis tradita commentariis de motibus stellae Martis* (*New Astronomy, the causes spoken to, or Celestial Physics, related from notes concerning the Motions of the Star, Mars*, 1609), Kepler shared his belief that God had blessed him with the discovery of the mathematical harmonies of His cosmos. In the Copernican model, the sun was "central" as the important source of heat and light for our world, but it occupied a cosmologically indefensible position slightly off-center from the geometric center of

---

[21]   The fact that the planets move on elliptical orbits is known as Kepler's "first law."

each planets' orbit, with no two orbits sharing the same exact center-point. In the *Epitome of Copernican Astronomy* (1618), Kepler presented his model as a truly unified and harmonious solar *system*, as all of the planets' motions were governed by the same force (*anima motrix*) which originated from the same physical body (the sun) and the sun itself occupied the same geometrically and physically significant point in all of the planets' orbits (at one focus of each planetary ellipse, with all of the orbits sharing that one focus). Kepler's sun offered central heat, light *and* power. Moreover, the astronomical predictions made by his system were far more accurate than previous models, and the overall symbolic beauty of the system seemed to speak to its poetic and theological truth. He had previously described the correspondence between the tripartite cosmos and the triune God in the *Mysterium*:

> ... The Sun in the center, which was the image of the Father, the Sphere of the fixed Stars, or the Mosaic waters, at the circumference, which was the image of the Son, and the heavenly air which fills all parts, or the space and firmament, which was the image of the Spirit – then, except for these, I say, nothing would exist in this cosmic structure ... (95)

Kepler's new astronomy was really *new*, in the sense that hardly any of the assumptions of ancient astronomy remained. No one had previously proposed a heliocentric system of ellipses, as no one before had thought them "natural," particularly beautiful, or worthy of the motions of celestial bodies. Kepler had discovered that the seemingly chaotic irregularities of planetary motion, their changing velocity and variable distances from the sun, were actually not chaotic at all. Rather, the *appearance* of irregularities and inequalities had arisen due to past astronomers' insistence that the data satisfy the ancient aesthetic and philosophical constraint of perfect circular motion. The true reality of God's harmonious geometric choice had eluded them all because of their commitment to the circle. Once Kepler recognized that planetary orbits were elliptical, the data fit, the motions were accounted for, and the hidden orderliness of the planets' motions was revealed in the area law and the harmonic law ($T^2 \propto R^3$: the ratio of the periods of the orbits T squared is equal to that of the radii R of their orbits cubed). In more ways than one, then, the limitations of human ways of seeing had obscured their vision of heaven, and Kepler responded with sheer joy and a humbly worshipful gratitude that God had blessed him with these insights.

Kepler's new astronomy, divinely motivated (or inspired) as it was, simultaneously presented a new cosmology, uniting the considerations and aims of religious faith, mathematical astronomy, and physics. As Gerald Holton explains,

> ... it is noteworthy that prior to Kepler's discovery the "place" for God, both in Aristotelian and in neo-Platonic astronomical metaphysics, had to be either all of space or, more commonly, outside the last celestial sphere; for only those alternatives provided a "place" for the Deity from which all the celestial motions in the pre-Keplerian universe were equivalent. Now Kepler saw the great third possibility: in a truly heliocentric system God would be brought back into the solar system itself, so to speak, enthroned at the fixed

and common point of reference, the source of light, and the origin of the physical forces holding the system together. In the *De Revolutionibus*, Copernicus had glimpsed part of this vision when he wrote, after describing the planetary arrangement, "In the midst of all, the sun reposes, unmoving. Who, indeed, in this most beautiful temple would place the light-giver in any other part than that whence it can illumine all other parts?" But it remained for Kepler to implement the vision.[22]

Unfortunately, virtually no one during his lifetime fully understood or appreciated Kepler's achievement.[23] While the predictions made by Kepler's system were much more accurate than those of other systems, it was not other professional mathematical astronomers, but popular astrologers and almanac makers who were the first to use Kepler's work for their calculations. Although he tried to court important astronomers and solicit their recognition, many historians of science believe that their bias in favor of circular orbits was too great to allow them to fairly evaluate Kepler's elliptical system. Galileo, for instance, may have believed that Kepler's ellipses were the products of undetected math errors that fooled Kepler into believing that the planet's orbits were slightly out of round. Ironically, Kepler's elliptical system offered a transcendent replacement for the simple homocentric model of the cosmos at just the time that Galileo risked excommunication to defend it, and as the man who created arguably the most spiritually imaginative of the early modern systems, Kepler simultaneously (through his concern for mathematical description and physical forces), prepared the way for modern mechanism. It remained for Newton to fully implement Kepler's vision.

During Kepler's lifetime (1571–1630), the instrumentalist tradition in professional astronomy was so ingrained that few practitioners seriously expected mathematical models of celestial behavior to offer descriptions of reality. The accuracy of such models' predictions might be useful, but it was not thought to "prove" anything about the physical nature of things. Kepler's predecessors and peers "knew" that some sort of circular motions were "up there" because ancient authorities closer to the *prisca sapientia* (the original, pure knowledge of things) than they were told them that the circle was the most appropriate geometric shape for celestial bodies to move in. Seeing the demonstrative power of mathematical descriptions of nature (so astronomy could be seen as cosmology) required disbelieving in certain aspects and assumptions of the natural philosophy of the ancients and the many since who had worked under their influence. Such transformations do not occur over night.

Kepler's new astronomy articulated a new cosmology, physically and spiritually, offering a replacement for the cosmological allegory of medieval Christianized

---

[22] Gerald Holton, "Johannes Kepler: A Case Study on the Interaction of Science, Metaphysics, and Theology" *The Philosophical Forum* 14 (1956): 30.

[23] Significant exceptions were the English "Keplerians," including, as I argue, John Donne. See: Wilbur Applebaum, *Kepler in England: The Reception of Keplerian Astronomy in England 1599–1687*, diss. (University of New York-Buffalo, 1969) and Gossin, "John Donne and the Astronomical Revolution," *Poetic Resolutions of Scientific Revolutions* 30–216.

Aristotelianism, with the Father, Son and Holy Spirit figuratively represented within and by the architecture of the universe. He firmly believed that he had been called by God, the divine geometer, to discover and reveal through his geometrical astronomy the hidden order directing planetary motion through His cosmos. Each of what we now call Kepler's three "laws" expressed, for him, a revelation of providential pattern and orderly regularity to the motions of the planets, not previously suspected or imagined. Although most of Kepler's contemporaries did not (perhaps *could* not) see his system in the mathematically demonstrative glory he had intended, seventy years later, Isaac Newton's mind was prepared to do so.

Newton's Mathematical Principles of Natural Philosophy

Like Kepler, Newton held his mathematical principles and analyses in high esteem, believing that his mathematical astronomy discovered (literally "revealed") truths about the reality of God's cosmos. In his view, astronomy and cosmology were united as one enterprise, both through his faith in God and his faith in mathematics. Building on Kepler's laws, Newton divined a mathematical description of universal gravitation that made intelligible the motions of all earthly things (falling bodies, projectiles, tides) as well as the motions of the heavenly bodies (including comets) in relation to the sun and to each other. While other natural philosophers had offered imaginative speculations as to why objects and creatures on Earth did not fly off its surface, they offered different explanations for why the planets were carried along by their spheres or moved in their orbits. Newton offered the same explanation for both terrestrial and celestial physics, with mathematical demonstrations of its veracity.

Newton's mathematical natural philosophy developed from diverse influences. Working in the heart of Cambridge Neoplatonism, he was personally motivated by theological concerns, interaction with Kepler's mathematical descriptive astronomy, and reaction against the fanciful, unverifiable, elements of Cartesian mechanical philosophy. Descartes, working in the heat of the Skeptical Crisis, conducted his own search for truth among the philosophies of the ancients and moderns. Reacting against animism and the magical world view, Descartes' view of nature was strongly influenced by Greek materialism, especially atomism, while his epistemology was modeled after Pythagorean–Platonic mathematical philosophy. In his famous dualism, he divided the cosmos into two realms: mind and matter. Nature, for Descartes, was fundamentally mathematical (matter = extension through space) and all of his explanations for natural phenomena are material explanations, with all effects being caused by matter in motion. Although he did not contribute directly to the development of astronomy *per se* (except, perhaps, through his invention of the geometrical coordinate system), his imaginative vortex theory offered a plausible explanation for the motions of the planets that contributed a vital element to Newton's thought. Thinking about matter in motion, Descartes discerned that "natural" motion would be rectilinear (in straight lines) and all other forms of motion must be caused by the interaction of straight-line motions. Thus, in his vortical theory, he imagined that the planets' natural tendency to move in straight lines away from the center of the solar system (their centrifugal tendency) is "bent" into circular motion by contact with the surrounding particles whirling around them. Although Newton would not be satisfied with Descartes' vortical explanation for planetary motion, Descartes' line of reasoning and his conception of centrifugal force and rectilinear motion would prove essential to his theory of gravitation. Descartes' mechanistic view significantly informed modern cosmology by providing a basic framework for our thinking about nature: by reducing nature to its smallest particles, we can understand the "machinery" (the inner workings) of the universe.

Newton's thought was also influenced by some elements of contemporary French epistemology. Descartes doubted the evidence of the senses and thought that all secondary qualities that we perceive to exist in nature are illusions, however regular and predictable they may seem. His fellow countryman, Pierre Gassendi, a Christian atomist, argued that the function of natural philosophy should be to explain observable evidence, not just offer plausible explanations or imaginative mechanisms. Although recognizing the value of mathematical descriptions, Gassendi did not agree that nature was essentially mathematical itself, nor did he offer speculations as to what the ultimate reality might be. He accepted that the nature of nature might be unknowable and that we might never see more or be able to describe more than the superficial appearances of things, their behaviors, and characteristics. Newton's phenomenological conception of scientific knowledge was influenced by the ideas of both men, Gassendi especially, and it continues to influence our notion of the purpose of science today: the description and correlation of perceived phenomena, a quest for probabilities, not certainty.

When Newton pondered the problem of how and why the planets moved, he saw it from astronomical *and* cosmological perspectives, offering both a mathematical description of the planets' motions over time, as well as a mechanical explanation of the force that causes them to do so. His thinking about planetary motion combined Kepler's speculation that some sort of magnetic attraction between celestial bodies might hold them in their orbits, with Descartes' conception of centrifugal force. If the body of a planet were simultaneously acted upon by an inertial tendency outward with some sort of pull of attraction inward, the two kinds of rectilinear motion might combine to produce its orbit. Mathematically, Newton demonstrated that an inverse square law ($F \propto 1/R^2$) would yield the type of orbits that Kepler believed to be there. Then, solving his equations according to the best observational data available (those of John Flamsteed), he was able to demonstrate that an inverse square law accurately described the motions of the moon, the planets, and even comets. Indeed, the same force that pulled the moon into its orbit around the Earth, was the same force that pulled apples down to it as well.

Although Newton believed that providing a mathematical analysis of the interaction of forces in nature was sufficient for natural philosophical inquiries (and he often evaded the pressure to speculate about causes), he did attempt to test various theories about the possible cause of gravitation. He considered that gravitational force might exert itself as "action at a distance" but discarded that notion because of its animistic and magical implications. He studied mechanical causation (transference of motion between heavenly bodies through very fine material particles or "ether") as a strong possibility, but after many years of experiments, he could not prove the existence of such an ether. Finally, he considered that the effects of gravitation might be caused by the direct, divine action of God ordering the planets to move through continuous interaction with His invisible hand.

Throughout the Christian era, natural philosophers and theologians had worked continuously to reconcile matters of faith to the discoveries and ideas of natural science. The insights offered by Newton's mathematical, mechanistic, and deterministic natural philosophy were similarly accommodated, in fact, were taken in much the same light in which Newton himself viewed them: as special revelation of the divine laws governing nature from the moment of its creation. Although a number of astronomers and cosmologists through the ages had proposed that the universe might be infinite in extent (suggesting that the abode of the Creator might be infinitely far away), most astronomy and cosmology through the age of Newton effectively served to bring humanity nearer to Him, through a closer understanding of His creation. However distant He might be (William Whiston estimated the distance from the sun to Saturn as 777 million miles and Newton calculated that a bright star was at least 100,000 times more distant than Saturn),[24] Newton's mathematical insights into the order of the universe revealed how the power and vision of our watchmaker-God's engineering skills provided care-taking action across that distance for His creatures and creation, past, present, and future.

For most general readers in the post-Newtonian era, natural theology offered a cosmology that comfortably accounted for then-current astronomical discoveries and theories. It did not hurt the local reception of his world view that Newton's genius was generally accepted as a national treasure that was a direct gift from God. Although Newton's cosmology did strongly depend upon observational astronomy, general acceptance of it as reality still *preceded* definitive observational "proof" by over one hundred and fifty years. Flamsteed, the foremost observational astronomer of Newton's time, had provided (not always willingly) the data that had enabled verification of Newton's theory. Flamsteed's life's work – a catalog of nearly 3,000 "fixed" stars – offered the most detailed map of the celestial heavens then achieved, with unprecedented accuracy, but even he had not yet detected stellar parallax.[25] In succeeding decades, astronomical observations became indispensable to new

---

[24] Van Helden, *Measuring the Universe* 155–9.

[25] It is a commonplace within the history of astronomy to compare the relative accuracy of astronomical observations in this way: Copernicus had been satisfied with measurements accurate to within 10 minutes of arc, equivalent to measuring the diameter of a quarter at a distance of 30 feet; Tycho achieved observational accuracies of 2–5 minutes of arc (the appearance of a quarter at 300 feet); while Flamsteed increased accuracy to 10 *seconds* of arc (the ability to accurately measure the diameter of a quarter at a distance of 3 and 1/4 *miles*).

astronomical–cosmological endeavors to test Newton's predictions against the reality of cosmic phenomena (the predicted return of "Halley's" comet in 1758 being the most salient case in point). Newton's mathematics not only offered an accurate description of the celestial bodies as they were observed in the present, but provided an accurate *preview* of the universe as it would be observed *in the future* as well. Just as Kepler's spiritually imagined cosmos carried with it the makings of modern celestial mechanics and dynamics, so Newton's work, so strongly motivated by theological concerns and so apparently blessed with divine insight, set the stage for a renewed apprehension of the mathematical, mechanistic, and deterministic world view first glimpsed by the ancient Greeks.

After the publication of the *Principia*, the mathematical principles and basic details of Newton's astronomy and physics were disseminated, discussed and popularized through diverse avenues: through Halley's proselytizing, Richard Bentley and the Boyle lectures, Samuel Clarke's correspondence with Leibnitz, the lectures and publications of William Whiston, numerous poems and plays, and the multifarious sermons and texts of astrotheology and natural theology, such as those by William Durham and William Paley (the latter still required reading at Cambridge during the years Darwin and Tennyson attended; North, 379). In the popular mind, Newton's mathematical justifications of God's astronomical ways to man were taken on faith well before the best evidence was available that his mathematics "worked" by making accurate predictions and before its significant anomalies were resolved. Few early Newtonians, for instance, quelled their praises because Newton's reformation of physics – however mathematically verified – substituted one abstract concept for another, although many offered speculations about the possible nature of that "force." Other questions remained about the insolubility of the three-body problem (especially regarding the moon's motions) and the stability of the solar system – whether the observed inequalities of the planetary orbits would "run down" into eventual collapse, or whether God intermittently sent the mass of comets to "fine tune" the system and maintain its equilibrium, thus benevolently preventing such disasters (as Newton and Whiston had proposed).

Jonathan Swift seems to have been one of a very select few in Newton's lifetime who foresaw the potential social and philosophical consequences of the "inequalities" in Newton's work and the popular perception of his world view. To Swift, Newton's abstract mathematical demonstrations seemed to inspire credulity with the same magical speed as astrological prognostications, pseudo-medicinal potions, political pamphlets, and fanatical prophecies. Did people need reminding that the proper focus of their faith and praise should be their omnipotent Creator and the wonders of His revelation, and not the vain-glorious achievements of an all-too-human mathematician's attractive power of gravitation? Arguing in *Gulliver's Travels* (and elsewhere) for a broader historical perspective that considered the ultimate limitations and relative vanity of all human knowledge, Swift's characterization of the Laputans satirically chastized a society that would work itself into hysterics over such distant (in time and space) possibilities as the death of the sun and the collision courses of comets. If we all really believed our world to be in God's hands, the value of such human predictions – whether made by the disciples of scientific geniuses or equally vociferous religious doomsayers – should be negligible. Swift seems to have concluded that the fate of humanity would be better served if we devoted the powers of our minds to *moral* rather than mathematical principles of our collective philosophies, and expended less energy reconciling the irregularities in lunar motions and more correcting the soul-endangering errors of our own all-too-earthly lunatic behavior as sinners.[26] However well-intentioned and well-reasoned Swift's caveat, astronomical and cosmological momentum was against it.

In the first few decades following Newton's death, several gifted mathematical astronomers, including Leonhard Euler, Alexis Clairaut, Jean Le Rond d'Alembert and Joseph Louis Lagrange, all contributed their analytical skills to Newtonian problems such as the determination of planetary and cometary orbits and lunar theory. In 1773, Pierre Simon Laplace was able to prove mathematically that the apparent instabilities of the orbits of Saturn and Jupiter oscillate over time, effectively cancelling each other out, and as a consequence, the solar system has an inherent stability – no heaven-sent comets need be applied. The unique irony here is that it was Laplace's deep understanding of mathematical astronomy (which so *confirmed* Kepler's and Newton's belief in the active presence of God's design in the universe) that led him to *decline* the services of the divine Architect of Newtonian cosmology.

Nearly twenty years previous, Immanuel Kant, working within the tradition of speculative natural philosophy, had arrived at a similar cosmological conclusion. Influenced by a sketchy review of Thomas Wright's *An Original Theory or New Hypothesis of the Universe* (1750), Kant published his imaginative conception of our Milky Way as one of many, perhaps an infinite number, of self-created "island universes," systems of stars or galaxies, which had formed spontaneously over time from "nebulae" – luminous clouds of gaseous vapor (*Universal Natural History and Theory of the Heavens*, 1755). Laplace presented his popular cosmology, known as the "nebular hypothesis" (later the Kant–Laplacian hypothesis), in *Exposition du système du monde (Exposition of the System of the World)* published in 1796. While the point of Wright's speculations had been to propose "supernatural centers" for the star systems as well as to map the cosmic locations of heaven and hell, both Kant's philosophical cosmology and Laplace's popular one dispensed entirely with the unnecessary "hypothesis" of a comet-sender, watchmaker, caretaker God. As J. D. North so quietly understates it,

> This conflict of intellectual and religious interests was one of the less obvious legacies of centuries of discussion of the cosmic harmonies, a discussion to which Plato, Kepler, Newton, Leibniz and scores of lesser scholars had contributed. (379)

---

[26]   Gossin, "Jonathan Swift and the Newtonian Revolution," *Poetic Resolutions of Scientific Revolutions* 217–355.

Victorian Astronomy and Cosmology:
"What the Greeks only suspected we know well; what their Aeschylus imagined our nursery children feel." —*The Return of the Native*, 132

When Alfred Tennyson dubbed the sciences of geology and astronomy "terrible muses" he may well have had in mind the existential consequences for human individuals that their findings seemed to present: our solar system having condensed from formless masses of swirling gases, we exist on this planet as chance organisms doomed to live-out short brutish lives before joining our fossilized forebears amidst the countless nameless layers of cast-off remnants of other life-forms, ultimately to be mixed back into a multitude of chaotic chemical transformations in the inorganic cosmos at large. And, really, when you put it that way, who can blame him? Looking up into the deep of the night sky, it is hard *not* to experience the same fear and awe with which human beings have responded to atmospheric and astronomical phenomena from time immemorial. Whether encountering of an evening, the sudden blaze of a meteor, a specter of swamp gas, lightning bolts, auroras, or comets, all who valued their lives were wise to react to such unidentified flying objects with fear first, and awe-filled questions later. As leisure permitted, and we found time to study the sky in some stillness, the contrast of scale and the extent of the unknown worked upon our minds. As human explanations for celestial phenomena grew in sophistication, primitive responses of fight or flight were moderated – and replaced – with more sophisticated fear and awe.

In an insightful conference presentation, Anna Henchman identifies "four forms of astronomical terror" in the Victorian era: 1) numerical loneliness, owing to "the discovery that the sun is only one in a galaxy of an estimated 300 million stars"; 2) fear of emptiness, because the universe seems to be "both devoid of a divine presence and literally made up of 'deep wells of nothingness,'" as Hardy put it; 3) fear of universal decay, as the sun and all "fixed" stars will one day, in Hardy's words, "burn out like candles" and, 4) epistemological fear, as "astronomy forces its practitioners to confront irresolvable conflicts between sensory perception and abstract knowledge."[27] Although I very much agree with Henchman that each of these concepts held deep philosophical importance for many Victorians, Tennyson and Hardy chief among them, I disagree with her implication that such realizations were somehow unique, or particularly owing to, the astronomy and cosmology of the Victorian period.

As we have seen in the first portion of this chapter, the cosmos has been continuously conceived of as unimaginably vast and our world insignificantly minute

---

[27]   "Cinders of Stars, Solar Catastrophes: The Terror of Victorian Astronomy," presentation abstract, in *Rethinking Space + Time Across Science, Literature + the Arts*, conference booklet, 17th Annual Conference of the Society for Literature and Science (October 23–6, 2003) 24. See also: Anna Alexandra Henchman, *Astronomy and the Problem of Perception in British Literature, 1830–1910* (Thomas De Quincey, Alfred, Lord Tennyson, George Eliot and Thomas Hardy), diss., Harvard University, 2004.

since ancient times. Both pagan and medieval Christian thinkers considered Earth to be but as a single grain of sand upon an infinite, or nearly infinite, cosmic beach.[28] Many natural philosophers (ancient through Victorian) pondered the possibility of a plurality of worlds.[29] Likewise, while some philosophers maintained that the cosmos was a plenum, most recognized its *apparent* emptiness, noting the measureless distances and "wasted" space between objects within it. Through much of human history it seems we could have the luxury of thinking of our cosmos as eternal, or God-filled, but rarely both. Ancient cosmologists considered the universe to be an eternal realm of unchanging quintessence (often without beginning or end), but either a bit too full of gods and goddesses who needed banishing from it or, alternatively, inattentively attended by an aloof divinity who resided just outside its confines. Christian cosmologists, by contrast, viewed the heavens as filled with God's presence, but all material creation – having "fallen" with sinful humanity – well-along in the process of decay, and all together moving toward a final end that was divinely planned (although the extent of the coming cosmic renovation was left open to debate).

The themes of mutability and decay were ubiquitous in religious and creative literature throughout the Christian era and were well-integrated into daily meditations and contemplations of life on earth, inspiring both humility and gratitude. Galileo himself argued that celestial decay such as that he had found in the sun's spots should be no more alarming than the terrestrial variety: "If the earth's small mutations do not threaten its existence (if, indeed, they are ornaments rather than imperfections in it), why deprive the other planets of them? Why fear so much for the dissolution of the sky as a result of alterations no more inimical than these?"[30] Likewise, a multitude of natural philosophers, astronomers, and cosmologists including the Pythagoreans, Zeno, Parmenides, Plato and Aristotle, the medieval scholastics, Copernicus, Galileo, Kepler, Descartes, Gassendi, Newton, Kant and Laplace, had all struggled with epistemological problems of the Reason-Sense and Reason-Faith dichotomies, rejecting, accepting, assimilating, and accommodating logic and sensory evidence, personal belief and theology, in various combinations. Copernicus, Galileo, and Kepler, in particular, had all been acutely aware of how their heliocentric reasoning clashed with both commonsense appearances and theological and natural philosophical traditions. Each found profound ways to resolve the "irresolvables" and beckoned others to follow.

So while astronomical concepts and cosmological conflicts certainly had (and have) the potential for fueling philosophical doubts and personal fears, such

---

[28] For a discussion of ancient cosmic measurements, including Aristarchus's *Sand Reckoner*, see: Van Helden, *Measuring the Universe* 4–14.

[29] See: Steven J. Dick, *Plurality of Worlds: The Extraterrestrial Life Debate from Democritus to Kant* (Cambridge: Cambridge University Press, 1984) and Crowe, *The Extraterrestrial Life Debate: 1750–1900*.

[30] Richard Panek, *Seeing is Believing: How the Telescope Opened Our Eyes and Minds to the Heavens* (New York: Penguin Books, 1998) 61.

quandaries had long been recognized as part and parcel of larger epistemological dilemmas central to both natural philosophy and theology since the Greek sages: Why doubt the visible and believe in the invisible? and, Can chance alone account for all of the "order" we observe in the cosmos? If one were prone to theological doubts, one would have no problem finding "evidence" in astronomy, or other aspects of natural philosophy, to support them. On the other hand, the same celestial or natural phenomena served the faithful equally well in magnifying the glory of their Creator. In an intrepid soul, such as John Donne, new astronomical discoveries and ideas did both in turn, testing, then tempering, his faith – a poetic and religious model that Tennyson and many of his peers (both scientific and literary) seem to have emulated. Although specific astronomical discoveries and cosmological speculations made just before and during Victoria's reign may well have sparked a novel *experience* of such fears for those living through them, there was nothing *newly* "terrible" or freshly fear-inducing about Victorian astronomy and cosmology *per se* – the individual's readiness for the encounter was all. As we shall see in the chapters that follow, Hardy was uniquely ready to experience, process and express the astronomy and cosmology of his time.

From the mid-eighteenth century through Hardy's long life, astronomy and cosmology transformed dramatically enough to deserve the designation "astrophysical revolution."[31] Astronomical work directly benefitted from technical advances made during the Industrial Revolution and as a result, astronomy made rapid progress in three distinct, but interrelated, branches: historically traditional practical and observational astronomy; mathematical and gravitational (Newtonian or theoretical) astronomy; and physical and descriptive astronomy. In this last category, practitioners of the "new astronomy" (as George Hale called it) followed the lead of early Greek natural philosophers by posing questions that focused on φύσις, literally, the "physics" (the nature or natural order) of the heavens. No longer were astronomers' central tasks limited to measuring, mapping, and mathematically describing the positions and motions of remote points of light; their studies could now consider the *physical nature* of those luminous objects themselves. "Astrophysics" (as these collective endeavors would become known) included investigations in three main areas: 1) the physical causes and origins of celestial entities and their structures; 2) the physical basis, elements, and building-blocks of celestial bodies and stellar systems; and, 3) the physical configuration, interaction, and distribution of those entities throughout space. Only intermittently reciprocal through the previous centuries, astronomy and cosmology now really began to converge in astrophysics as innovations in telescope-building ushered in a new age of observational power in astronomy, bringing about the possibility of what J. D. North calls "observational cosmology" (North 398+).

---

[31]   Agnes Clerke believed such to be the case as the premier historian of the subject for the times; see her *A Popular History of Astronomy during the Nineteenth Century* (four editions between 1885–1902; the fourth edition facsimile reprinted in 2003 by Sattre Press, Decorah, Iowa). Her biographer, Mary Brück agrees in her *Agnes Mary Clerke and the Rise of Astrophysics* (Cambridge: Cambridge University Press, 2002) 1.

Improved optics gave observers the ability to directly *see* celestial phenomena (literally, "the appearances"), but just as importantly, enabled them to gauge with greater degrees of accuracy that what they were seeing bore some direct relation to cosmic "reality."[32]

Much of the astronomy and cosmology that "the Greeks suspected" (but had few ways to confirm or verify) and the Victorians "[knew] well," was owing to the highly popularized telescopic astronomy and cosmological theories of William Herschel (1738–1822), his sister, Caroline (1750–1848), and his son, John (1792–1871). Together their work literally expanded the extent of the Newtonian world view. The "universe" that had caught and held the attention of Newton's dynamical and mechanical mind was essentially limited to what was then becoming known as our "solar system": the sun, the planets, their moons (also known as their "satellites"), and the comets. The stars and outer reaches of space rarely concerned him except as a background against which to track the orbital motions of the other celestial bodies. The Herschels' emphasis on stellar astronomy changed that.

For a little over one hundred years (from the publication of the *Principia* in 1687 to the end of the eighteenth century), the lion's share of astronomical attention had focused on highly mathematicized gravitational and theoretical problems, with the hopes of verifying and confirming the operations of Newton's "laws" within the solar system. Most of these efforts were undertaken by socially prominent, highly educated mathematicians working on the Continent, especially in France. The general public had little direct access to the problems of celestial mechanics or their solutions, with the predicted return of Halley's comet, perhaps, the most widely publicized exception. Halley's return was considered to simultaneously provide: 1) definite proof of the power of applying mathematics to problems of physics; and, 2) compelling evidence that the erratic visits of those ominous heavenly bodies should no longer be regarded superstitiously as signs of heavenly displeasure or impending doom, but rather as predictable and regular, though distant, members of our solar system family, moving under the control of the same gravitational laws as the planets and their moons. The extent to which Newtonian mathematics were successful in assuaging public fears of such phenomena, however, remains an open question, since Newton's own cosmology

---

[32] Richard Panek argues throughout *Seeing is Believing* that public belief in the universe as revealed by the New Philosophy and New Astronomy was directly owing to technical improvements in the telescope. As I have been arguing in this chapter, I do not think that the history of the popularization of astronomy supports as strong, as direct, or as early, a cause–effect relationship between observational astronomy and cosmological thinking, as he suggests. Indeed, it is my contention that popular narrative accounts by the Herschels and Hardy et al. (like scores of those produced by popular astronomical-cosmological writers before them) may well have contributed more effectively to contemporary changes in world view by offering their audiences real-life and life-like representations of how human beings might process astronomical information and integrate cosmological perspectives into their minds and hearts.

persisted in associating the intermittent presence of comets with large-scale disasters such as global drought, orbital instabilities, and solar dissipation or demise.[33]

What the general public may have had in mind, then, when they thought of the "big picture" of the Newtonian universe (if they ever thought of it) is open to surmise. While it has generally been accepted that the physics of light in Newton's *Opticks*, including descriptions of the prism and rainbow, was relatively accessible to the visual imagination of contemporary readers, Newton's achievement in describing the astronomy and physics of the cosmos in the *Principia* necessitated reading – and comprehending – abstruse mathematical discussions.[34] Even the skills of many professional mathematicians fell short of that challenge. General readers, curious about Newton's work, could turn to popular, even poetic, accounts that omitted the abstract details, but these encouraged appreciation for, and acceptance of, the descriptive and demonstrative power of his geometry on the strength of his God-given authority alone.[35] Given the technical nature of Newton's contribution to celestial dynamics and mechanics, it is reasonable to wonder to what extent a *non*mathematical understanding of Newton gleaned from such texts really constituted a *meaningful* understanding at all. The universe according to the Herschels, however, was entirely a different story, one almost immediately engaging – a dramatic narrative, profusely illustrated.

The Victorian Cosmos According to the Herschels

Just as Tycho's supernovae and Galileo's resolution of the Milky Way and the discovery of the satellites of Jupiter offered popularly accessible proof that the traditional Aristotelian cosmos was not all-inclusive or infallible, so William Herschel provided his age with direct observational evidence that there was more "out there" than what had been previously seen and believed. Adding to his popular appeal was the fact that he did not emerge from the educated or social elite, but was a self-taught amateur whose personal charm and enthusiasm attracted much attention to his subject. One of six children born into a musical German family, Herschel emigrated as a young adult to England in 1757. He initially made his living as a music teacher, composer and conductor. Later, he played oboe, harpsichord, violin and organ at Bath, where he was appointed in 1766 to the prestigious position of organist of the Octagon Chapel. There, his multiple talents soon elevated him to the center of the town's fashionable cultural scene, where he directed, conducted, performed, composed, arranged, and gave weekly private music lessons by the dozens. Despite his activity-filled schedule,

---

[33] For a thorough historical discussion of the complex relationship between cometary catastrophism and popular perceptions, see Genuth, *Comets, Popular Culture, and the Birth of Modern Cosmology*.

[34] See the discussion of Marjorie Nicolson in *Newton Demands the Muse*.

[35] As the poet James Thomson seems to have been content to do in both his "A Poem Sacred to the Memory of Sir Isaac Newton" and *The Seasons*.

he did not feel that professional music sufficiently challenged his intellect, so he spent his free time in intensive self-study, learning ancient and modern languages, calculus, optics and reading astronomical texts. His early attempts at astronomical observing frustrated by the unwieldiness and chromatic aberration of his rented refracting telescopes, Herschel turned his musical dexterity to the problem of making reflecting telescopes.[36] He cast the metal, ground the lenses, and polished the mirrors himself – all in preparation to obtain, as he put it, "a knowledge of the construction of the heavens" (as in Clerke, 12). In 1772, he brought his sister, Caroline, to England, ostensibly to assist her in establishing a musical career; but soon, she became instead his indispensable astronomical secretary and assistant, recording notes and calculations, and quickly developing her own skills as an observational astronomer. It is through her accounts that we catch glimpses of the musician–astronomer at work. As Agnes Clerke charmingly relates (aided by Caroline Herschel's memoir), "Overwhelmed with professional engagements, [William Herschel] still contrived to snatch some / moments for the stars; and between the acts at the theatre was often seen running from the harpsichord to his telescope, no doubt with that 'uncommon precipitancy which accompanied all his actions'" (Clerke, 12–13).

After gaining a decade's worth of trial-and-error experience in instrument-building, Herschel's improvements to the reflecting telescope made his far superior to others available. Soon, and for many years thereafter, Herschel substantially supplemented his musical income with the money he made selling his telescopes and mirrors. Almost unbelievably, given his daylight commitments, he also found time (and had the energy) to make his own observations. Perhaps owing to Newton's dismissive and condescending treatment of the first Astronomer Royal, John Flamsteed, observational astronomers for some time had been "looked upon with a certain contempt" by gravitational theorists (Clerke 2). The patient taking of precise

---

[36]   The problem of chromatic aberration in refracting telescopes (those predominately used during the previous century for precise measurements) could be reduced by increasing the focal length – thus the monstrously long tubes that were often satirized by critics. Difficult to position and move, such instruments were of little use to observers who wished to scan large expanses of the sky. By reintroducing and improving the reflecting telescope, Herschel eliminated these difficulties and simultaneously increased the light-gathering and magnification power. The precise optics of his eyepieces was unsurpassed. So vastly superior was the magnification power of his telescopes compared to the best available elsewhere, that Herschel himself was skeptical of his estimations of their abilities. Pannekoek reports that very fine telescopes of the day could magnify between 200 and 460x, while Herschel's achieved "unheard-of values of 2,000, 3,168 and 6,450 times" (312). For more details on Herschel's instruments, see: Michael A. Hoskin, *William Herschel and the Construction of the Heavens* (London: Oldbourne, 1963). According to Astronomics (one of today's top suppliers of astronomical equipment), moderately sized reflectors are still the instrument of choice for amateur astronomers today who are most interested in obtaining bright images of deep space objects, see: "How to pick a telescope/Why buy a reflector?" on the Astronomics website <www.astronomics.com>.

measurements and repetitive positional calculations of celestial objects' two dimensional coordinates ("right ascension" and "declination") were regarded as journeymen's work compared to the applications of higher mathematics to planetary dynamics.[37] Amateur observers who sketched and studied the surface features of the moon, sun, and planets were held in even lower esteem, "regarded as irregular practitioners, to be tolerated perhaps, but not encouraged" (Clerke 2). That Herschel – an astronomical *observer* and an *amateur* who used instruments of his own making – should set the research program for the development of astronomy in the next century was, to say the least, as Clerke phrased it, a "conspicuous anomaly" in the history of astronomy (4).

Intrigued by the fact that the greater the light-gathering power of one's instrument, the deeper into space an observer could see, Herschel almost immediately devoted his observational efforts toward gathering new visual evidence about the universe beyond the known solar system, including nebulae and double stars, initiating his first full-scale "review of the heavens" in 1775. So thoroughly did Herschel acquaint himself with every source of light in the sky, that, as Timothy Ferris insightfully notes, "the most significant northern hemisphere star map of the later eighteenth century may well have existed not on the pages of a celestial atlas but in Herschel's mind" (155). This ready familiarity enabled Herschel to discover in 1781 the first new planet in historical times, Uranus (although he initially misidentified the moving fuzzy bright spot as a comet). This discovery, at first named for George III, immediately made Herschel famous, and resulted in an appointment to the Royal Society, an annual pension, and a generous royal grant for building an even bigger telescope.[38] The discovery of Uranus caused a public sensation, at one blow doubling the dimensions of the previously known solar system, and offering unequivocal evidence that even the genius of Newton was not coextensive with the mind of God. There *were* new things under – and above – the sun. As an explorer of the heavens, Herschel discovered not only a planet, but two new moons each for Saturn and Uranus, the polar caps of Mars, over eight hundred double or multiple stars, many thousand nebulae, added many details to astronomical knowledge of lunar and planetary topography, and made at least four full "star counts" of the whole night sky in thirty-four hundred "gauge-fields" (Clerke 13). Such discoveries were significant for the history and study of astronomy as they literally opened up our visual imagination of the universe. They were also of political and national importance, as during the age of empire-building, the British imagination and ego quickly seized on such discoveries as indications that Britain had retaken the lead in the mythical race of science that she had lost during the previous century to French mathematicians, much disgracing the legacy of her native son, Newton.

---

[37] "Right ascension" is a determination of celestial "longitude" eastward, measured in hours, minutes, seconds, along the celestial equator. "Declination" is the angular distance north or south of the celestial equator, measured in degrees.

[38] Although Herschel continued to prefer, for ease of use, his 20 foot reflector (with 18.5 inch mirror) to the 40 foot instrument with 48 inch mirror built with the King's grant.

Before Herschel, little was known about the objects of deep space except that they were too remote to permit the detection of stellar parallax (and were therefore thought to be at least 400,000 AUs distant),[39] that some exhibited "proper motion," that others appeared "variable" (fluctuating in brightness), while still others were "nebulous" (cloudy or misty). Herschel longed to add to this knowledge and saw himself as working within the long respected tradition of natural history, counting and cataloging, collecting and categorizing astronomical observations by the hundreds and thousands, like so many stellar seashells, or cosmic fossils – all the better to show and tell the story of the universe with. Like the view of nature that other naturalists were discovering in their "fields" (albeit much closer to home for botanists, biologists, and geologists), Herschel compiled a compelling "natural history of the heavens" – a tale of epic proportions, dramatic development and change, and all told from an eye-witness perspective.

Unlike the cosmologies of Wright, Kant, or Lambert which offered imaginative speculations about the "grindstone" or "island" universe(s), respectively, Herschel attempted to determine observationally the shape of the sidereal universe for himself by charting the Milky Way. Although a number of the assumptions he had to make in order to carry out his program proved erroneous (especially his equation of star brightness to star distance, his assumption of the uniform distribution of stars and his estimates of stellar magnitude), his attempt brought cosmology for the first time into the realm of scientific investigation. What Herschel undertook was no less than the first large-scale statistical study of stellar motion and distribution throughout the galaxy – an almost unimaginably immense endeavor. Herschel's "star-gauging" resulted in a depiction of the Milky Way as a lens-shaped star system, of uneven density, containing two branching structures, with apparently empty space in between them [FIG. 3.1]. In his own words: "That the Milky Way is a most extensive stratum of stars of various sizes admits no longer of the least doubt; and that our sun is actually one of the heavenly bodies belonging to it is as evident" and "the stupendous sidereal system we inhabit . . . consisting of many millions of stars, is, in all probability, a detached Nebula". . . . "We inhabit the planet of a star belonging to a Compound Nebula of the third form" (all, as in Pannekoek, 317). In other words, not only are we on Earth (third rock from the sun) not central to our solar system, our solar system is not central within our galaxy, and our galaxy is not particularly central among the many such galaxies that Herschel had observed "out there." As Agnes Clerke's response many years later in her historical account of nineteenth-century astronomy indicates, the effect of such a hierarchy of systems on the cosmological imagination could be powerful indeed: "and so onwards and upwards until the mind reels and sinks before the immensity of the contemplated creations" and (Clerke now quoting Lambert), "'thus everything revolves – the earth round the sun; the sun round

---

[39] AU = "astronomical unit," the distance from the earth to the sun, or approximately 93 million miles. Thus, eighteenth-century estimates of *minimal* stellar distances were 400,000 x 93 million miles, or 37,200,000,000,000 miles (Clerke, 10).

the centre of his system; this system round a centre common to it with other systems; this group, this assemblage of systems, round a centre which is common to it with other groups of the same kind; and where shall we have done?'"(Clerke 14).

Unlike Lambert, Herschel was not just imagining things such as the motion of something as gigantic as an entire stellar system. While it had been observed by Halley in 1718 (and confirmed by several observers since) that some individual stars were not "fixed," but rather had a proper motion of their own, Herschel's mapping of the Milky Way offered the first experimental attempt not only to establish the three-dimensional shape and extent of our star system, but also the *direction and speed* of the whole galaxy *as it moves through space*. Perhaps inspired by the captains of other voyages of discovery who relied on telescopes to guide them, Herschel employed scientifically and poetically apt nautical terms to describe his work. He saw himself as navigating the ocean of stars to "sound" or "fathom" it, so that he could map it in three dimensions, not only plotting the positions of stars along the horizon and their altitude above it, but their "profundity" as well – their distances from us in the depths of space. While occasionally (and forgivably) star-struck by his marvelous discoveries, Herschel presented his findings with appropriate awe and an enthusiasm tempered by rational deliberation: what could be more natural an endeavor than to seek and find new things in nature, making the unknown more knowable?

The values, methods, and reporting style of the natural historian served Herschel well throughout his long astronomical life. He seems to have had a singular ability to keep his classification system plastic and hold his theories provisionally, adjusting them adroitly as anomalous or unexpected objects and evidence came into his ken. As is often the case in natural history, practitioners must be prepared to find something *other* than what they are looking for. Herschel's mind was uniquely open to such opportunities, well into old age, and he frequently adjusted his cosmological interpretations to better fit his astronomical observations. Herschel's studies of double stars and nebulae are good illustrations of how deeply he insisted upon, and maintained, a dynamic reciprocity between theory and observation, each, by turns, constraining and motivating the other, together leading toward truly original discoveries and conclusions.

In his quest to plumb the depths of stellar space, Herschel hoped to determine stellar distances by employing a method for detecting parallax first proposed by Galileo. Toward this end, he took a large-scale inventory of visual (or "optical") double stars – two stars that appear to be so close together in the sky that they seem as one to the naked eye. Hoping to find pairs of stars in which one was especially bright and the other very dim (which might indicate, for parallactic purposes that the former was nearer, and the latter more distant), Herschel measured their angular distance apart from each other and recorded their positions and appearance, noting contrasts in their brightness and color. He collected such information for hundreds of star-couples (and triples and multiples) over several decades. In 1803 and 1804, Herschel published his discovery that in comparing recent observations to his original data, he found that a number of the visual "doubles" (most notably, those in Castor) had changed their positions relative to each other, but not in the way that he had expected or hoped. He correctly concluded that what he had found was evidence of *physical* doubles or "true binaries," each star orbiting the other around a common center of gravity – a new kind of star system. Unfortunately, this fact rendered such pairs useless for Herschel's intended purpose (since both stars must obviously reside at about the same distance from us in the sky). More than adequate compensation, however, was the fact that this discovery stood as the first direct *observational* evidence that Newton's force of gravitation is truly "universal" – extending out and beyond the relatively local confines of our solar system, further suggesting that the terrestrial and celestial are not ontologically distinct realms, but truly moving as one (uni-verse) under the same set of physical "laws."

This discovery also meant that even with the best telescopes in history, with the greatest light-gathering power, magnification, and clarity then achieved by the finest technology, the detection of stellar parallax remained beyond human reach. Herschel knew that whatever the distances involved, they must be *far greater* than the estimates of previous generations of astronomers. While stellar parallax and the first scientific measurements of stellar distances were not achieved until sixteen years after his death, what he knew of stellar "profundity" affected Herschel profoundly. He knew that his vision into the depths of space was also a journey into the depths of "time past." As he remarked in old age, "I have observed stars of which the light, it can be proved, must take two million years to reach the earth."[40] In the last years of his life, few visitors to Herschel left his company without hearing this message from the ancient mariner of the stars.

In addition to his extensive cataloging of the stars, mapping of the Milky Way, and double-star studies, Herschel also paid special attention to nebulae, bright "cloudy" spots in space. 103 such objects had been catalogued by the comet-hunter, Charles Messier, in order to distinguish their apparently stationary positions from the *motions* of the bright spots he sought. Asking the basic questions of natural history, "Where are they?" "How do they look?" and "What are they?" Herschel carefully noted their positions, visual appearance, brightness, and overall structure, grouping them into eight basic classifications. Publishing his results in three separate volumes (1786, 1789, 1802), Herschel's catalog contained information on 2,500 nebulae, many "resolvable" with the high magnification of his telescopes into "star clusters," others remaining "unresolvable." At first, working under the influence of the "island universe" theory, he assumed that all nebulae, given high enough magnification, would prove to be clusters of individual stars, like our Milky Way, some contained within it, some beyond. Over time, however, he adjusted this view, becoming increasingly convinced that some of the nebulae he was seeing were essentially different – "unstarry" in nature – and appeared to be made of a luminous "shining fluid." In 1811 and 1814, he published his theory in which he proposed that his

---

[40] William Beattie, M.D., ed., *Life and Letters of Thomas Campbell*, vol. 2 (London, 1849) 234.

observations of the differences in nebulae revealed not differences among the end-products of creation, but a creative *process* in progress; i.e., the extraordinary variety of forms he observed represented nebulae at various developmental stages in their evolution into stars and star systems, a process he described as an ongoing "condensation" of luminous "fluid" under gravitation with the younger nebulae appearing less condensed and less spherical, the older, more so.

Herschel employed both the professional understatement and taxonomic language of natural history to describe his theory of the evolution of the heavens.

> This method of viewing the heavens seems to throw them into a new kind of light. They are now seen to resemble a luxuriant garden, which contains the greatest variety of productions, in different flourishing beds; and one advantage we may at least reap from it is, that we can, as it were, extend the range of our experience to an immense duration. For, to continue the simile I have borrowed from the vegetable kingdom, is it not almost the same thing, whether we live successively to witness the germination, blooming, foliage, fecundity, fading, withering and corruption of a plant, or whether a vast number of specimens, selected from every stage through which the plant passes in the course of its existence, be brought at once to our view?[41]

Whether Herschel was conscious of the rhetorically mitigating potential of his "simile" for traditional Christian believers, or not, what more naturally appealing and nonthreatening a trope than the homey imagery of a backyard garden to carry to the British public his theory of the life-cycle of the universe – including its final "fading" and "corruption"? The trope had the additional advantage of being true to both Herschel's professional perception of himself and the presentation-style of his work. Like so many collectors of natural history before him (botanists, geologists et al.), in his publications Herschel carefully arranged images of actual specimens he had observed to illustrate every "stage" of growth in his star gardens, assuming that most nebulae would first condense into denser nebulae, then tightly compressed clusters, and finally into a single star or group of stars. While his story of stellar formation did not describe a one-time creative act in which all of the stars appeared, full-grown *ex nihilo*, his borrowing from the "vegetable kingdom" seems to reassure readers that the new perspective he is offering is philosophically mundane. The gradual transformations of growth are at work in the world all around us. We see them for ourselves during the course of every planting season, when we look out upon our gardens using no more powerful a lense than our own kitchen windows.[42] Herschel

---

[41]   As in Arthur Berry, *A Short History of Astronomy: From Earliest Times Through the Nineteenth Century* (1898; New York: Dover, 1961) 340.

[42]   This rhetorical device strikes me as so effective a solution to the problem of presenting the "good news/bad news" of the evolution of the heavens that I have to wonder if Charles Darwin took a page out of Herschel's book in choosing to use the example of domestic pigeons in his discussion of natural selection. Perhaps Erasmus Darwin's work exerted a mutual influence on both men?

just happened to have a very powerful window through which to look out onto his stellar plot.

Herschel's theories of the origins and nature of the universe offered a different story from that imagined by literal readers of the Bible. What Herschel saw of the cosmos did not lead him to believe it was the result of a single set of relatively recent creative acts, although the visual evidence for development strongly indicated that it *had* had some sort of beginning and had not existed from all time. To his telescopically trained eye, the universe appeared to still be in the process of becoming, changing, growing, and decaying. Given the distances of the stars and nebulae and the speed of light, its first moments must have taken place many many millions of years ago, rather than a few thousand.[43] Herschel's own granddaughter was convinced that his cosmogonical views hampered full appreciation of and recognition for his astronomical achievements among some Royal Society members (Pannekoek, 318). Others believe that Herschel's theories regarding the plurality of worlds, especially his belief that there were "lunarians" and inhabitants of the sun who had adapted to its heat, may have been the more likely culprit in impairing his credibility among the F.R.S. Also contributing, may have been his elaborate theories of sunspots and their possible correlation with earthly weather (and wheat prices!) which led to his characterization as a "weather prophet," inspiring some rather merciless satire along the way. Additionally, some historians of science have speculated that Herschel's status as an amateur and his lack of social graces and connections may have played a role, although just as many seem convinced that it was his very position as "outside" traditional, and increasingly professional, astronomy, that essentially enabled his innovations and achievements.

Whatever the cumulative effect of such influences, positive or negative, Herschel acted as his own best advocate, providing numerous opportunities for people to see for themselves, generously and tirelessly treating visitors ("star-gawkers") to impromptu sky shows, even vacationing with his seven-foot reflector so he could give fellow-travelers an hour or two of observing time. By the end of his lifetime, it was clear that no other contemporary observer came close to rivaling his prodigious work. His 40 foot reflector with 48 inch mirror was declared the "eighth wonder of the world," and it, he and Caroline, became international tourist attractions [FIGS. 3.2, 3.3, 3.4]. By their indefatigable graciousness and accessibility, their neighbors and visitors (learned or otherwise) could see them as living examples of how to assimilate and accommodate personal cosmology to new astronomy – whatever new "facts" of the universe their adventures led them to, they flexibly adjusted their thinking, keeping their commitment to science and their devotion to family equally strong. In his written accounts, as in his life, Herschel preached what he practiced. He did not employ

---

[43]   The question of how Herschel's apprehension of "deep time" was received by the popular mind and by various religious communities has not received adequate study; see: Michael J. Crowe, "Age of the Universe in ca.1800 Thought," online posting to History of Astronomy Discussion Group, 28 November, 2003 <http://listserv.wvu.edu/archives/hastro-l.html>

argumentative rhetoric to advance entrenched positions, to convince or compel. Instead, the form of his writing mirrors its content, offering a first-hand account and record of his observations and a personal chronicle of how his interpretation of those observations underwent change and development over time, tracing a steady line of matter-of-fact adaptation of old ideas to new evidence.

Although Herschel died in 1822, his discoveries and theories continued to exert a strong influence throughout the nineteenth century, essentially forming the basis for Victorian cosmology. His astronomical work was directly carried on by his sister, Caroline and his son, John. Although Caroline's central contribution to the history of science may well have been her Aaron-like support of her brother's endeavors, her independent work did earn her independent recognition.[44] For her work as Herschel's assistant, she was awarded an annual stipend from the King – a significant achievement for a woman at the time. She was the discoverer (or co-discoverer) of eight comets between 1786–1797, most observed in those rare moments when William's work did not require her presence. She greatly aided her brother's calculations and those of other future astronomers by preparing an extensive index of Flamsteed's star catalog, correcting it, and adding cross-references and 560 new stars to it. After William's death, she completed his catalog of nebulae, receiving the gold medal of the Royal Astronomical Society in 1828 and honorary membership in the Royal Society (along with Mary Somerville) in 1835. Suffering the loss of William terribly, she moved back to Hanover (Germany) where she became a human mecca for many famous writers, philosophers, and scientists (including Gauss and Von Humboldt). She continued to provide active support and guidance for the career of her nephew, John, and lived on into her 98th year, dying in 1848. Remaining amazingly active into her nineties, she provided to dozens of young female visitors with interests in science living-proof of the erroneousness of the persistent contemporary medical myth that active investigations of nature and deep intellectual engagement would damage women's weaker natures and shorten their lives. Her example (along with that of Maria Mitchell in the United States) did much to promote astronomy as a scientific pursuit suitable "for ladies," second only, perhaps, to botany.

John maintained diverse interests throughout his life, ranging from biology, chemistry and geology, to law, history and poetry. An accomplished mathematician, he, along with his friends George Peacock and Charles Babbage, was instrumental in bringing Continental style calculus (as opposed to Newtonian) into British science and education. As his father's observational powers declined with advancing age, John extended his studies of the Milky Way and nebulae. After his father's death, he continued William's collaboration with James South, producing a much-admired catalog of double stars. In these studies, he attempted to determine the orbital periods of binaries, most notably those in γ Virginis. He took his father's exploration of deep

---

[44] For new detail on Caroline's contributions, see: Michael Hoskin, *The Herschel Partnership: As Viewed by Caroline* (Cambridge: Science History Publications, 2003) and —, ed., *Caroline Herschel's Autobiographies* (Cambridge: Science History Publications, 2003).

space one step farther as well. Becoming a literal "explorer" of the universe, John set out upon and successfully completed a celebrated astronomical expedition to the Cape of Good Hope, where he spent four years charting the heavens of the southern hemisphere, as his father had those of the northern.[45] As previous records of this region's sky contained scant data, John's undertaking resulted in a voluminous collection of observations which took him nine years to assemble and publish. At the Cape, John's mapping of the southern sky included catalogs of over 1,700 nebulae and star clusters, over 2,100 binaries, and over 70,000 stars. He made important observations of the 1835 return of Halley's Comet, including early recognition that it was evaporating gaseous vapor and was repelled by a force that would later be identified as the solar wind. He drew detailed sketches of many unique regions within the southern heavens, including the Magellanic Clouds. He improved upon his father's techniques of star cataloging by inventing the "astrometer," an instrument that allowed him to make comparative measurements of star brightness, a significant advance toward stellar photometry.

After his return, John published his *Results of Astronomical Observations Made During the Years 1834–38 at the Cape of Good Hope* (1847) and *Outlines of Astronomy* (1849) which became the definitive textbook for the rest of the century. His *General Catalogue of Nebulae and Clusters* was later incorporated by J. L. E. Dreyer into the *New General Catalogue* (NGC), which remains a standard work for astronomers today. Both before and after his expedition, he was admired as a popularizer of astronomy, regularly publishing essays and books intended for general audiences, including articles in the *Cabinet Cyclopaedia* and *Encyclopaedia Britannica*, *A Preliminary Discourse on the Study of Natural Philosophy* (1830), and *A Treatise on Astronomy* (1833). His ideas on the history and philosophy of science directly shaped public attitudes toward the sciences and influenced the views of scientists as well, including those of Michael Faraday and Charles Darwin. A poet, and a translator of the verse of Homer, Dante and others, John produced powerful, technically precise, yet accessible, descriptions of cosmic phenomena in his popular astronomy. The poetic sensibility of his prose worked together to achieve a kind of scientific "sublime" that Richard Proctor, for one, felt approached that of Milton in *Paradise Lost*. His death in 1871 was mourned on a national scale and became the occasion for many thoughtful retrospectives on humanity's progress in astronomy and cosmology. In his *Essays on Astronomy* (1872), a text that we know influenced Hardy, Proctor devoted an entire section to an appraisal of John Herschel's life in astronomy and its meaning for contemporary knowledge of the cosmos. The only person in human history to observe the whole universe, John was regarded by the Victorian public as embodying the spirit of high scientific adventure. As a hero of science, he

---

[45] Although this study appeared too late to enhance my discussion here, interested readers may wish to consult: Steve Ruskin, *John Herschel's Cape Voyage: Private Science, Public Imagination and the Ambitions of Empire,* Science, Technology and Culture, 1700–1945 Series (Aldershot, Eng.: Ashgate, 2004).

enjoyed a degree of popular recognition and status that was matched only by Newton in the previous century and by that of Einstein in the next [FIG. 3.5].

Looking back on the astronomical achievements of William Herschel from a distance of eighty years, Clerke remarked that he "opened a channel for the widespread public interest which was gathering towards astronomical subjects to flow in" (4). That channel was substantially widened into the middle and high Victorian periods by his sister's and son's lives and work. At just the time when astronomy was transforming from an elite, private enterprise to one underwritten by governmental and public support, the Herschels offered proof-positive of the potential contributions to astronomy that could be made *by anyone*, formally educated or not, socially well-placed or not, as long as they had the personal persistence, and the vision and desire to undertake the work.[46] An essential part of astronomy's popular appeal throughout the Victorian era, no doubt, was the fact that it was then (and to some extent still remains), a science in which amateurs can (and do) make "real" contributions, as Clerke remarked,

> It is, in a special manner, the science of amateurs. It welcomes the most unpretending cooperation. There is no one "with a true eye and a faithful hand" but can do good work in watching the heavens. And not unfrequently, prizes of discovery which the most perfect appliances failed to grasp, have fallen to the share of ignorant or ill-provided assiduity. (5)

Individually and collectively, the Herschels' discoveries inspired a new age of observatory building world-wide (Clerke 5–7) and encouraged scientific networking via telegraph, by which individual astronomers (amateurs and professionals) could contribute valuable information as they participated in the "collection" of data toward the "natural history" of the cosmos. Hardy's own affinity for the subject may well have been bolstered by its long-established and continuing accessibility to amateurs.

Clerke also gives due credit to William Herschel as the one responsible for widening the scope of the cosmos, by being the first to show "the sidereal universe as accessible to investigations" and "offer[ing] to science new worlds – number, variety, and extent – for future conquest" (7). At just the time that Auguste Comte concluded that knowledge of the chemical or geophysical nature of the stars would remain out of reach, the Herschels' work had already made pioneering inroads toward that end.[47] While many of Herschel's discoveries and ideas stretched his contemporaries' imagination of the extent of the cosmos, they also simultaneously brought astronomy down to earth, so to speak, made it more immediately relevant, by emphasizing the linkage of the celestial and terrestrial, and providing increasing evidence about the

---

[46]   Allan Chapman, *The Victorian Amateur Astronomer: Independent Astronomical Research in Britain 1820–1920* (Chichester, Eng.: Wiley-Praxis, 1998).

[47]   Of investigating the nature of celestial bodies, Comte wrote (circa 1830): "We conceive the possibility of determining their forms, their distances, their magnitudes, and their movements, but we can never by any means investigate their chemical composition or mineralogical structure" (Pannekoek 135).

physical nature of celestial bodies "up there" and their real physical (gravitational, magnetic, electrical, chemical) connection to bodies "down here," opening up the possibility that astrophysical knowledge of the solar spectrum, for example, might help us predict drought, famine, and cyclones. Spurred by the Herschels' success in inventing new technology for observational astronomy, others (as we shall see) quickly followed suit, developing new instruments and investigational techniques for the study of astrophysics.

The Herschels's astronomy and cosmology made deep and lasting impressions upon the visual imagination of the Victorian public. William's descriptive language and enthusiastic example, Caroline's journals and devoted person, John's poetic prose and his filial faithfulness in taking up his father's quest to map all of the heavens were all important factors in disseminating and popularizing their astronomy. In addition, the Herschels realized the value of utilizing pictorial images in their texts. William used astronomical images as specimens in the tradition of natural history. John, who was an especially gifted artist, produced amazingly detailed astronomical sketches of the objects he observed in deep space, taking such imagery to new levels of information preservation and transfer [FIG. 3.6]. In his youthful travels across Europe, he had experimented with making images of interesting geological formations with the *camera lucida* and developed an eye for framing such objects which served him well as he made celestial drawings for posterity. He had experimented with optics and photography as early as 1819, later inventing his own camera, photosensitive paper, and a chemical process for fixing his images.[48] One of the first photographs he made was of his father's 40 foot reflector in 1839, just weeks after the first photograph of a celestial object – the moon – was taken by Pierre Daguerre. The application of photography to astronomical observations contributed immediately to the rapid transformation of astronomy into astrophysics. Not only was the "seeing" of the solitary astronomer made available to multiple viewers, but photographic plates could gather more light over time than the human eye, capturing fainter objects deeper in space, and those images could be preserved for comparisons with past and future observations – bringing new possibilities for the replication, confirmation, and interpretation of astronomical data gathering. Truly the Herschels' vision of the expanded universe – as profound and astoundingly beautiful as it was – provided their audience with but a Pisgah view of a new promised land, a cosmos deep in space and time.

In rapid succession, developments in observational astronomy, gravitational–theoretical astronomy and astrophysics enriched the cosmological picture sketched out by the Herschels. With the confirmation of stellar parallax in 1838, the determination of stellar distances became possible. Measurements of the radial velocity of stars were taken as early as 1842, with the "red shift" detected in 1868. Such techniques led to

---

[48] He is credited, in fact, with coining the word "photography" as well as "positive," "negative" and "snap-shot." Some historians of photography have remarked that had he been less skilled as an artist, he might have felt greater urgency to focus on his early investigations and might now be known as the inventor of photography.

Thomas Hardy's Novel Universe

the necessity for a new nomenclature for stellar distances, the "light year" (the distance light can travel in a year, approximately 6 trillion miles) and the "parsec" (the distance of a star that displays a *par*allax of one *sec*ond of arc, approximately 19 trillion miles). By the mid 1840s, Lord Rosse's 72 inch reflector resolved many more nebulae and revealed the spiral structure of M51, providing visual evidence to support Herschel's notion of the ongoing evolution of star clusters via a process of rotational condensing [FIG. 3.7]. In 1846, another new planet, Neptune, was discovered – this time using mathematical calculations that predicted its location and observational astronomy to confirm its existence. In 1849, just ten years after the first photograph of a celestial object was taken, the camera was fitted to the telescope and became a real tool of observational astronomy. Photographic evidence of new stars and nebulae by the hundreds of thousands soon became available. Over night (as it were), astronomical photography exponentially improved the number, quality, and verifiability of astronomers' observations. Within another ten years (1859), spectroscopy provided the means (that Comte, thirty years earlier was so certain would never exist) to investigate the chemical composition of the stars and nebulae. By the early 1860s, William Huggins obtained spectroscopic evidence to confirm William Herschel's suspicion that unresolvable nebulae were luminous gas, not fully formed occluded stars. In combination, spectroscopy and photography yielded images that recorded not only the visual appearance of celestial things, but their physical chemical natures as well. Astronomers were able to determine that distant stars and our sun were composed of the same chemical elements. What astrophysicists discovered was that there was no "quintessential" difference between the two realms. We were all made of the same star stuff – hydrogen, iron, sodium, etc. Astrophysical investigations of the spectral emission lines of our nearest star, the sun, by investigators such as J. Norman Lockyer and P. Jules C. Janssen only reinforced this kinship.

*   *   *

The nineteenth century was especially active astronomically, both in terms of its historical development scientifically (as we have discussed above) and in the number and variety of phenomena observable during that one hundred-year span. There were dozens of comets. Several of these were of short period which kept excited comet-hunters in eager anticipation by returning every few years; while others (like the "great" comet) were quite visually spectacular, exhibiting bright nuclei and streaming tails, even as seen with the naked eye, with at least one clearly visible during daylight hours [FIG. 3.8]. There were several solar and lunar eclipses and two transits of Venus, all of which inspired international "watches" and adventurous observational expeditions to exotic locations. What phenomena people of various classes could not see for themselves in private garden observatories or through "pay-per-view" telescopes in public parks, were described for them by the accounts of astronomers themselves, as well as in various popular texts, magazines, newspapers, and journals. The cosmological implications of such astronomical events were interpreted by numerous commentators. The grand schemes of natural history that Thomas Burnet, Georges-Louis Buffon and so many others had provided to previous generations were offered to the Victorians by William Whewell in his *Bridgewater Treatise: Astronomy and General Physics with Reference to Natural Theology* (1833) and Robert Chambers in the anonymously published, and amazingly popular, *Vestiges of the Natural History of Creation* (1844). Much of what Tennyson, Darwin, and a host of Victorian readers (literary, scientific and otherwise) knew of the conjoined stories of geology and astronomy was received through the filter of the long intertwined traditions of natural history and natural theology.

Whewell's treatise emphasizes the interaction between natural philosophy and natural theology, while maintaining a transcendent place for Revealed Religion which, he stresses, is "untouched by either" of the other two. Recounting the natural history of the cosmos according to Laplace, Lagrange, and Herschel, Whewell describes God's creation as working through the means of the nebular hypothesis – the vapor clouds may "create" island universes, but God made the vapor clouds and their motions. Using the rhetoric of religious skepticism and doubt, Whewell compiles a long catalog of questions, complications, and paradoxes that cannot be answered by mechanical evolution alone. New evidence for the expanded scale of the universe is but material reinforcement for what we knew spiritually all along – that God is vast and infinite. Whewell concludes that we need only look into the universe, or into our own hearts, for equally reassuring evidence of God's existence.

In *Vestiges*, Chambers emphasizes the continuity and "progress" of the history of nature from its beginnings in nebulous spiral clouds to geological development to biological evolution, from the simplest to the most complex – man. With humanity and human culture as the culmination of Chambers' narrative, there was, as Tennyson concluded, "nothing degrading in the theory."[49] Indeed, Chambers carefully maintains that however random and cruel God's actions through natural law may seem on the global scale, there was "a compensating, a repairing and a consoling effect" locally, in fact, "a system of Mercy and Grace behind the screen of nature."[50] For Chambers, the vastness and incomprehensibility of the Creator's purposes should becalm, rather than cause, humans' fears, "Thinking of all the contingencies of this world as to be in time melted into or lost in the greater system, to which the present is only subsidiary, let us wait the end with patience, and be of good cheer"(386). Perhaps more aware than the author of the Stoic echoes implicit in this remark, one reviewer, amidst an otherwise effusively positive essay discussing *Vestiges*, included the criticism that the author had not adequately recognized the originators of many of these ideas – the Greeks.[51]

---

[49]   As quoted in James Secord, *Victorian Sensation: The Extraordinary Publication, Reception and Secret Authorship of Vestiges of the Natural History of Creation* (Chicago: University of Chicago Press, 2001) 10.
[50]   See the final chapter and especially pages 377 and 384 in Robert Chambers, *Vestiges of the Natural History of Creation* (London: John Churchill, 1844).
[51]   *Examiner*, 9 November 1844, 707–9.

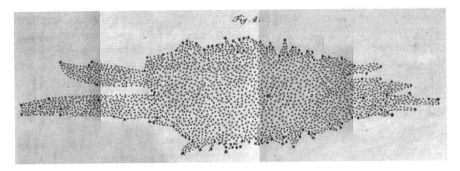

FIGURE 3.1: Star distribution pattern in the Milky Way, from William Herschel, *Uber den Bau des Himmels. Drey Abhandlungen aud dem Englischen ubers . . .* (Konigsberg, 1791). Image copyright History of Science Collections, University of Oklahoma Libraries.

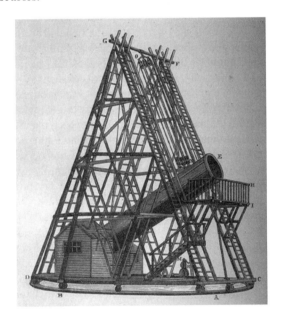

FIGURE 3.2: "Sir William Herschel's Forty-foot Telescope at Slough," as in *Memoir and Correspondence of Caroline Herschel* by Mrs. John Herschel, 2nd ed. (London: John Murray, 1879) 29. Image copyright History of Science Collections, University of Oklahoma Libraries.

FIGURE 3.3: William Herschel by Pirhas. Small Portrait Collection, History of Science Collections, University of Oklahoma Libraries. Image copyright History of Science Collections, University of Oklahoma Libraries.

FIGURE 3.4: Caroline Lucretia Herschel, "From a portrait by Tielemann in 1829," as in Agnes M. Clerke, *The Herschels and Modern Astronomy*. The Century Science Series (London, Paris and Melbourne: Cassell and Co., Ltd., 1895) 114. Image copyright History of Science Collections, University of Oklahoma Libraries.

FIGURE 3.5: John Frederick William Herschel, "From a portrait by Pickersgill for St. John's College, Cambridge," as in Agnes M. Clerke, *The Herschels and Modern Astronomy*. The Century Science Series (London, Paris and Melbourne: Cassell and Co., Ltd., 1895) 142. Image copyright History of Science Collections, University of Oklahoma Libraries.

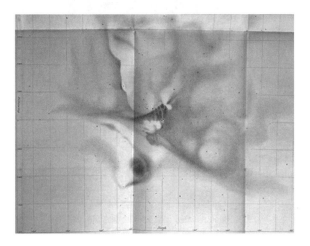

FIGURE 3.6: Detail of John Herschel's large fold-out sketch of "The Great Nebula in the Sword-handle of Orion as seen in the Twenty-feet Reflector at Feldhausen, C. G. H.," from his *Results of Astronomical Observations made during the years 1834, 5, 6, 7, 8 at the Cape of Good Hope . . .* (London: Smith, Elder and Co., 1847) plate 8. Image copyright History of Science Collections, University of Oklahoma Libraries.

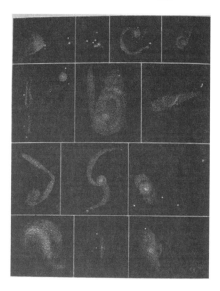

FIGURE 3.7: "Nebulae observed with Lord Rosse's great telescope," as in Robert Stawell Ball, *The Story of the Heavens*, New and Revised edition (London, Paris and Melbourne: Cassell and Co., Ltd, 1897) plate 16, 465. Image copyright History of Science Collections, University of Oklahoma Libraries.

FIGURE 3.8: Detail of the Great Comet of 1882, as in Robert Stawell Ball, *The Story of the Heavens*, New and Revised edition (London, Paris and Melbourne: Cassell and Co., Ltd, 1897), plate 17, 322. Image copyright History of Science Collections, University of Oklahoma Libraries.

FIGURE 4.1: "Saturn and His Rings," tri-fold front flyleaf from Richard A. Proctor, *Essays on Astronomy* (London: Longman's, Green and Co., 1872). Image copyright History of Science Collections, University of Oklahoma Libraries.

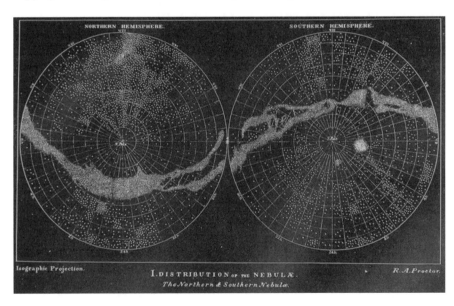

FIGURE 4.2: Example of white-on-black astronomical illustration, from Richard A. Proctor, *Essays on Astronomy* (London: Longman's, Green and Co., 1872). Plate III, 316. Image copyright History of Science Collections, University of Oklahoma Libraries.

PART II
READING HARDY'S NOVEL
UNIVERSE

Chapter 4

Hardy's Personal Construct Cosmology
Astronomy and Literature Converge

Long before the ancient Greeks, and pervasively across cultures ever since, cosmology has been understood as *both* that branch of astronomy concerned with the origins, properties, structure and evolution of the physical universe *and* as the narrative description of such a world view, in Dennis Danielson's words: "discourse concerned with the cosmos and with cosmic questions."[1] Throughout human history, cosmology has been produced by many different creative and intellectual endeavors and has been made manifest in many different forms: mythopoetic stories and legends, magico-superstitious beliefs and rituals, art and artifacts, architectural designs and buildings, religious revelation; metaphysical and natural philosophical speculation; natural history, poetic and literary description, geometric and mechanical modeling; mathematical, dynamical and psychological analysis; naked-eye and telescopic observation, pictorial depiction, photographic and scientific instrumental imaging and animation. Hardy was born into a culture in which virtually all of these forms contributed to and counted *as* cosmology – a space and time where poets, philosophers, and novelists *as well as* astronomers, geologists, and naturalists read and composed cosmological narratives.

As I have tried to establish in the previous two chapters, well-known details of Hardy's life, interests and literary notebooks provide ample evidence that he consciously and deeply engaged the diverse streams of both literary and scientific cosmological texts and narratives. From the primary materials of western civilization made available to him through the vagaries of an eclectic Victorian education, he fashioned his personal philosophy and outlook, in turn, expressing that world view within his own creative literary works. In the past, Hardy's readers have reviewed some of these same materials and evidence of influence, along with his poems and fiction and concluded that he was, essentially – and variously – a pessimist, an optimist, a nihilist, a meliorist, a realist, a regionalist, misogynist, feminist, atheist, moralist, a-moralist, Marxist, Darwinist, disciple of Schopenhauer and Devil's advocate (the last four of which – at least – may be different names for the same thing), as well as, primarily, a satirist, poet, ironist, dramatist, novelist or Modernist.

---

[1] As per, for example, the *Oxford English Dictionary*, *Websters* 10th; Jacqueline Mitton, *Concise Dictionary of Astronomy* (Oxford: Oxford University Press, 1991); and Dennis Danielson, *The Book of the Cosmos: Imagining the Universe from Heraclitus to Hawking* (Cambridge, MA: Helix/Perseus, 2000) xxvi.

To the best of my knowledge, I am the first to review Hardy's extensive reading of literature, history and science and come to the conclusion that he was a cosmologist.

Along with his immediate predecessors and his friends and colleagues in literature, philosophy and the natural sciences, Hardy developed a keen awareness that ancient Greek myth and drama, natural philosophy and astronomy were integrated into the very forms and practices of both mythopoetic/literary and scientific/philosophical tributaries to the growing current of contemporary cosmological ideas. Whether through self-direction or formal schooling, Victorian culture produced in Hardy and his peers a critical mass of highly educated, broadly read, and *classically trained* minds, many of which actively sought out and attempted to make sense of contemporary natural knowledge, especially new discoveries and ideas in geology and astronomy. Given a ready familiarity and ease with original Greek and Roman literatures of all kinds and a profound appreciation for the richness of their influence on many forms of written knowledge throughout the development of Western culture, this special group of readers was uniquely prepared to take on the task of synthesizing contemporary observational discoveries and lines of inquiry within the natural sciences with the received history of related human ideas and narrative forms. Among the various social, political and philosophical problems that they contemplated in common with their classical forebears: how to reconcile the always dramatic and occasionally epic human quest for the meaning of life within the increasingly apparent materialism, determinism and mechanism of the cosmos.

Arnold, Swinburne, Browning, Tennyson, Ruskin, Lewes, and Stephen, were but a few of the nineteenth-century poets and critics who joined Hardy in facing the "facts" of life in a neo-Greek universe. Their efforts built upon important contributions of the previous generation or two of natural historians (Thomas Burnet, Buffon, Erasmus Darwin et al.) who had maintained a close kinship with the literary forms used by classical nature writers such as Lucretius and Pliny, the classically influenced works of Dante and Milton, as well as a plethora of Christian nature poets. As they all knew well, poetic, dramatic, descriptive and encyclopedic impulses had long worked in close harmony to produce accounts of nature's origins and development. Together, Hardy and a number of other mid-Victorian writers and thinkers became conscious of diverse sorts of cultural pressures to converge and merge these various narratives into a single, coherent "universal" story, either through a process of elimination via struggle and competition, or through unification via some grand synthesis – the essential tension being felt most acutely by those who formulated and held physico-theological world views and those who preferred strictly naturalistic natural history and astronomical cosmology, devoid of the divine hypothesis.

Hardy's Knowledge of Contemporary Astronomy and Cosmology

Hardy was attracted to and haunted by the findings of the astrophysical revolution through which he lived. Although it is not possible to identify the direct motivations behind his deep personal interest in astronomy, we can identify some of the sources in which he first encountered the concepts of astrophysics that were to have the greatest effect upon him and trace the ways he used them in his work. Hardy achieved a sophisticated level of astronomical understanding from his active reading in popular sources of scientific information, popular texts and journals, and his attendance at popular scientific lectures. He used his own self-taught, popular knowledge of nineteenth-century astronomy to inform both the content and form of many of his major and minor novels.

Hardy does not respond to the astronomical or geological findings of the history of the heavens and earth, their origins, development, and predicted demise with fear, aversion or "cosmic despair."[2] Instead, along with other Victorian readers who were able to access classical philosophy and literature outside of, or alongside, foundational theological frameworks, Hardy takes a long view of contemporary natural history, humanity included. In the context of the development of human history and culture, Hardy is aware of the remarkable similarities between the Greek and Victorian understanding of the cosmos and the human condition within it. From the "cradle of civilization," humans have contemplated the unknown and their place within it. The nature of the universe as revealed by such observations, including, in his time, the evolution and decay of celestial objects, was not completely unsuspected. Rather, what seems to have made the greatest impression upon Hardy's mind, was the awful irreversibility of the evolutionary accident that had led human beings to develop awareness of *their own* biological natures and mortality, beneath the stars and the planets that they had so long observed.

The presence of astronomy in Hardy's literary notebooks displays a range similar to that of the other sciences. Hardy jots down factual tidbits of astronomical information and records key moments in the history of astronomy. He notes discussions that reveal astronomy's place in the philosophy of science and its relation to cosmology and religion. Most of these details Hardy owes to his reading of various articles and works by Richard Proctor, the nineteenth century's most prolific popularizer of astronomy and a practicing astronomer. Hardy is known to have owned and read Proctor's *Essays on Astronomy* (London, 1872) and the notebooks reveal Hardy's familiarity with other texts in which Proctor explicated his science for a general audience.

One probable source of some of the astronomical points of fact Hardy records in his notebooks is Proctor's *Other Worlds Than Ours* (London 1870); although as Björk is wise to remark, Proctor was "rather repetitive . . . in his . . . writing . . . and Hardy

---

[2] As John Kucich has recently suggested. While I agree with Kucich that Hardy incorporated contemporary sciences into his literary works with unusual philosophical sophistication, I disagree with his assessment that Hardy's response to the meaning of those sciences was essentially hopeless. See his comments, especially pages 130–134, in "Scientific Ascendency" *A Companion to the Victorian Novel*, eds. Patrick Brantlinger and William B. Thesing (Oxford: Blackwell, 2002) 119–36; hereafter: Brantlinger and Thesing.

may well have come across the information elsewhere" (*LN* I.122n). Among other possibilities that Björk suggests are two of Proctor's articles in *Cornhill,* "The Sun's Surroundings and the Coming Eclipse" (March 1875) and "The Planets put in Leverrier's Balance" (September 1875). Hardy recorded physical descriptions of planetary appearances citing Proctor on several occasions. "The planet Mercury is always seen on the bright background of a full twilight sky & does not make a striking appearance even if the most brilliant of the planets" (*LN* I. 122). Under the subheading "Unknown Something," Hardy noted that "Neptune was the unknown something which made the motions of Uranus irregular – so that astronomers felt him before they saw him – After Proctor" (*LN* I. 125). The next entry is equally matter-of-fact in stating that "Uranus's circuit = 84 years [so that a man three-score & ten w[ould] be only 10 months there – or a man at the ripe old age of 84 w[ould] be just 1 year old in Uranus]"(*LN* I. 126).

Besides descriptive and technical aspects of astronomy, Hardy also was aware of its importance historically as the "Queen" of the sciences. He charted, from Comte's account in *Social Dynamics*, the constituent parts of the "'Second or Protestant Phase' (1500–1685) of the Positive movement" noting only the "'Dogmatic' views of Encyclopaedic Hierarchy" (Björk, *LN* I. 769n). Within this hierarchy, cosmology ranks first with its abstract elements (mathematics, then astronomy) placed above its concrete branches (those related to physics, then chemistry). After this group of sciences fall various manifestations of sociology, divided into first biology, then sociology "proper" and finally morals. Some years later, Hardy devised a diagram showing Comte's theory of Modern History from pre-1100 up to about 1900 in which he makes two special notes of significant moments in that development. One note points out the "Introduction of the sciences into Europe by the arabs;" the other marks circa 1500 as the era in which "Open conflict between the two systems [feudal or military vs. spiritual, my note] begins: accelerated by discovery of Printing, & of the true Astronomical Theory by Copernicus & Galileo" (*LN* I. 1201).

Hardy was equally aware of how astronomical findings and ideas were shaping his own culture. Hardy recognized that one of astronomy's greatest gifts was insight into the relativity of time and the human construction of history. From a review of Henri Frederic Amiel's *Journal* (March 1885), Hardy noted that "To look on our own time from the point [of view] of universal history, on history from the point of view of geologic periods, on geology from the point of view of astronomy – this is to enfranchise thought" (*LN* I. 1340). Yet Hardy was ambivalent about what the effects on the human psyche of such a clear vision of geology and astronomy might be. From an article in *Athenaeum* (18 November 1882), Hardy copied the following quotation.

"In certain temperaments the eternal incongruities between man's mind & the scheme of the universe produce, no doubt, the pessimism of Schopenhauer and Novalis; but to other temperaments – to a Rabelais or Sterne for instance – the apprehension of them turns the cosmos into disorder, turns it into something like [a] boisterous joke." (*LN* I. 1289)

Hardy noted Symonds' remark that for some sensitive writers, for instance Wordsworth, "the cosmic em[otion] [was already] a reality & a religion"(*LN* I. 1150). He later carefully noted a passage from Karl Pearson's "The Ethic of Free Thought" (*Spectator* 21 January 1888) in which Pearson attempted to show the inherent rationality of the cosmos and its development through history.

> Suppose the highly developed reason of some future man to start, say, with clear conceptions of the lifeless chaotic mass of 60,000,000 years ago, wh[ich] now forms our planetary system, then from those conceptions alone he will be able to think out the 60,000,000 years' history of the world, with every finite phase wh(ich] it had passed through; each will have its necessary place, its necessary course in this thought-system. . . . This total history he has thought out . . . will be identical with the actual history of the world; for that history has evolved in the one sole way conceivable. The universe is what it is because that is the only conceivable fashion in which it could be – in wh[ich] it could be thought. Every finite thing in it is what it is because that is the only possible way in wh[ich] it could be. It is absurd to ask why things are not other than they are, because were our ideas sufficiently clear we sh[ould] see that they exist in the only way in wh[ich] they are thinkable. (*LN* I. 1499)

Whether Hardy personally accepted such a conclusion is not clear, but he did seem to believe that others perceived the world as governed by such conditions and that the sphere of human action was limited by such conditions.

Hardy paid close heed to the ideas of his friend Symonds on how the world view that astronomy and other sciences were creating had direct effects on human systems of thought and belief. He noted Symonds' remarks (May 1891) that "All things are in process . . . the whole universe is literally in perpetual Becoming, it . . . is impossible for us to believe that any one creed or set of opinions possesses finality" (*LN* II. 1801). After reading Sir Arthur Helps' *Organization in Daily Life: An Essay* (London 1862), Hardy wondered along with the author how it was that "our knowledge of astronomy, . . . [my elision] only gained in comparatively modern times, has not dwarfed & crushed ambition" (*LN* I. 1007). The same author direly predicted that "If scientific . . . [my elision] men really give their minds to the destruction of their fellow-creatures they will invent something which will throw all your Armstrong guns into the shade. . . . Some day there will come the knowledge of the means of creating a pestilence". . . "some vapour" (*LN* I. 1006).

On more abstract terms, Hardy was curious about the extent to which natural laws might control mind as well as matter. He wondered, with Myers,

> Does the law of the conservation of energy condemn man's consciousness to extinction when the measurable energies which build up his chemical texture pass back into the inorganic world, or may his conscious life be a form of activity which, just because it is not included in our cycle of mutually transformable energies, is itself in its own proper form as imperishable as they? What does evolution mean when we get below the . . . . Does it apply to the moral, or only to the material world?" ("Modern Poets and the Meaning of Life" *Nineteenth Century* January 1893; *LN* II. 1907)

From *Studies in Pessimism* (London 1891), Hardy noted Schopenhauer's reference to Kant's view that:

> A man finds himself, to his great astonishment, suddenly existing, after thousands & thousands of years of non-existence: he lives for a little while; & then, again, comes an equally long period when he must exist no more. The heart rebels against this, & feels that it cannot be true. The crudest intellect cannot speculate on such a subject without having a presentiment that Time is something ideal in its nature (*LN* II. 1787).

Yet for all of their difficulty, Hardy did not see the complex conceptualizations of time and space that nineteenth-century astronomy pressed upon the human mind to be the sole concern of the astronomers themselves or philosophers alone. Hardy joined other poets of his time, several equally well-versed in the developments of astronomy and the other sciences, in the attempt to make sense of and grasp the significance of the cosmos unfolding before them. He recorded in his notebook verses in which Robert Browning tried to encapsulate one response to astrophysics: "Life in the star Rephan, – "No change . . . nowhere deficiency nor excess. / . . . No hope, nor fear: as to day, shall be / To-morrow . . . . / . . . In that uniform universe" (*LN* II. 1765). Several years later as Hardy read Hallam Tennyson's memoir of his father (London 1897), he copied one of the great laureate's suggestions on how one might deal with the same subject: "Annihilate within yourself these two dreams of Space & Time" (*LN* II. 1937).

Like Donne, Milton, Swift, and others before him, Hardy took seriously his poetic mission to justify the ways of seemingly godlike scientists to other men. Hardy shared with Symonds a vision of poetry and literature as mediators "between rationality and religion" and as possessing the "power . . . to humanize Nature's truths" (Björk, *LN* I. 1151n). Symonds saw some of these attributes realized in Wordsworth's poetry.

> In proportion as the sciences make us more intimately acquainted with Man's relation to the universe, while the sources of life & thought remain still inscrutable, Words[worth] must take stronger & firmer hold on minds which recognize a mystery in Nature far beyond our ken. What Science is not called upon to supply, the fervour & the piety that humanize her truths, & bring them into harmony with permanent emotions of the soul, may be found in all that W[ordsworth] wrote:–
>
> > For I have learned
> > To look on nature, not as in the hour
> > Of thoughtless youth; but hearing oftentimes
> > The still sad music of humanity, &c (*LN* I. 1151)

Leslie Stephen may have influenced, even more directly than Symonds, Hardy's use of his literary gifts to incorporate and interpret science. Hardy meticulously recorded a long passage from Stephen's *The Moral Element in Literature* which outlines the high role, subject matter, and approach he believes authors should take in modern times.

> The novelist, as Fielding often tells us, is the true historian of the time. He tries to show us . . . the real moving forces in the great tragi-comedy of human life. He has to make the world intelligible to us, & the deeper & truer his insight, the greater his permanent power. So far his attitude is the same as that of the scientific observer or the philosophic reasoner. And this is enough to condemn the disguised pamphlets which are called novels with a purpose [my elision]. . .
>
> A poet is great so far as he has set before us some impressive ideal of life, or found utterance for the deepest emotions of his contemporaries. . . . Nobody can appreciate the great issues of the time or sympathise with the great currents of thought, who has not been more or less at home with the writings of such men as Mr. Carlyle, or Cardinal Newman, or J. S. Mill, or Mr. Darwin, of Mr. Tennyson, or Mr. Browning – I will mention no one whose name could excite a controversy.
>
> . . . All then that is to be said is this: that to get from literature the best that can be got from it, to use books as instruments for developing our whole natures, the true secret is to select our friends judiciously; to become as intimate as possible with some of the greatest thinkers of mankind, & to study the works of some great minds until we have been saturated with their influence, & have assimilated & made part of ourselves the sentiments which they express most vigorously. (*Cornhill* January 1881; *LN* I. 1217)

Hardy, taking to heart Stephen's advice about how to make himself a great reader, seems also to have aspired to enroll his name in the list Stephen presented of great thinkers and great writers. What made such writers great, was the greatness of their subject matter, and Hardy noted, in June of 1890, Augustine Birrell's opinion of how to determine such greatness.

> In considering a poet:– . . . How are we the better for him? Has he quickened any passion, lightened any burden, purified any taste? Does he play any real part in our lives? Has he had anything to say, which wasn't twaddle, on those subjects which are alone of perennial interest –
>
> "On man, on nature, & on human life"
>
> on the pathos of our situation, looking back on to the irrevocable & forward to the unknown. (*LN* II. 1737)

The capacities of individual poets to understand the "situation" of the universe (as various sciences were defining it) were being severely taxed by the influx of new scientific findings and the proliferation of concepts of an increasingly specialized kind. Some doubted that nineteenth-century writers would be up to the task, either in terms of their scientific expertise or their versification. In about 1890, Hardy noted Symonds' opinion of the matter.

The time is not yet ripe for poetry to resume the results of science with imaginative grasp. What has been called the cosmic enthusiasm is too undefined as yet, too unmanageable, too pregnant with anxious and agitating surmise, to find free utterance in emotional literature . . . /
Yet signs are not wanting . . . shorter poems of Tennyson . . . in the great neglected work of Roden Noel. (LN II. 1867 and 1868)[3]

Another reason that Symonds may not have found what he was looking for in the way of literary synthesis of the results of contemporary science with human feeling is that he was looking primarily at contemporary *poetry*, not novels. By the time of his remark, Hardy had already drawn upon his own "cosmic enthusiasm" to develop many sophisticated stories "'On man, on nature, & on human life' . . . on the pathos of our situation, looking back on to the irrevocable & forward to the unknown," successfully relating the cumulative interactions of scientific, social, political, psychological, emotional, and personal forces that comprise the complex environment in which the fictional humans that populate his novel universe live.

*

As we have seen, Hardy's literary notebooks suggest the origin, depth, and richness of the stream of science running through his consciousness. Hardy was hardly unique in directing this stream into his poetry and fiction. Many aspects of nineteenth-century science found their way into the literary works of the time. The latest developments in cell biology, medicine, psychology, sociology, geology, and Darwinism all received literary treatment by various authors. Such works stand as evidence of the degree to which particular sciences had been popularized and made accessible to the generally educated but non-scientific public. The literary popularization of these sciences also indicates the extent to which scientific discoveries, ideas, and theories were of interest to lay people outside of the communities of scientists most directly involved with them.

What is unique, however, is the fact that although many popular textbooks of astronomy were produced during the nineteenth century, it has retained the reputation of being the one science least popularized through literary means. Why this should be so is a puzzle. The concepts of Darwinism were not inherently more accessible to nineteenth-century minds than, say, John Herschel's descriptions of double stars. Determining the accessibility of nineteenth-century science to nineteenth-century minds, however, may not be the most important factor in estimating the prevalence of

---

[3] Noel's works, unlike Tennyson's, are still neglected, see: Margaret Smith's "Lord Roden and Horace Noel," *Thomas Hardy Journal* 15.3 (Oct.1999): 99–102 and Desmond Heath's "Roden Noel and Thomas Hardy: Correspondence, 1892," *Thomas Hardy Journal* 15.1 (Feb. 1999): 71–6.

astronomical concepts in the literary works of the period. The apparent dearth of astronomy in Victorian literature may well owe more to the fact that nineteenth-century astronomy is less accessible than Darwinism to the minds of *twentieth and twenty-first-century* readers and critics, whose interpretations have, as a result, collectively produced that misperception.

Hardy, Proctor and Victorian Popular Astronomy

Hardy's desire to express his conception of the relationship of humanity to the Victorian "facts" of the universe grew out of his own deep personal interest in astronomy. His notebooks reveal some of the popular texts from which Hardy learned about astronomy. Among these, the works of Richard Proctor were, by far, for Hardy, the most important sources of astronomical detail, descriptions, and up-to-date information on theories and discoveries in the field. Proctor's *Essays on Astronomy* appeared in 1872, the year before Hardy published *A Pair of Blue Eyes*.[4] We know that Hardy owned the book and, as we have already seen, had read other astronomical articles by Proctor by this time. By taking a closer look at what Proctor communicated about contemporary astronomy in this text and how he communicated it, we may gain some insight into how popular knowledge of astronomy and cosmology was transmitted to and received by Hardy and his Victorian compeers.

At first glance, the table of contents to Proctor's *Essays* seems of a sort unlikely to attract immediate popular interest. However, the title page and fold-out illustration opposite indicate how self-consciously and finely Proctor crafted his popular text for his intended audience. The tri-fold illustration invites opening and depicts three views of the bright body and rings of Saturn (always one of the most attention-grabbing of celestial objects for amateur observers) dramatically shown against a black background, much as it would appear through a telescope [FIG. 4.1]. The full title of Proctor's book reads: *Essays on Astronomy-A Series of Papers on Planets and Meteors, the Sun and Sun-surrounding Space, Stars and Star Cloudlets; and A Dissertation on the Approaching Transits of Venus. Preceded by A Sketch of the Life and Work of Sir John Herschel.* All of the topics are introduced in plain English without recourse to astronomically technical terms. Both his inclusion of the memoir of John Herschel and mention of the transits of Venus would have attracted the reader's attention for their immediate topicality, as well as for their evocation of Britain's proud and continuous contributions to astronomy, near past and near future. The long title and series of subtitles is followed by Proctor's name, degree, Cambridge affiliation, post as the "Honorary Secretary of the Royal Astronomical Society," and a brief list of some of his other works. But that is not all.

---

[4]   Richard Proctor, *Essays on Astronomy* (London: Longmans, Green and Company, 1872); hereafter: Proctor.

After the information about the author, Proctor includes on the title page of this popular science text, a thirteen line quotation – verses from an early version (later excised) of Tennyson's "The Palace of Art."

'Hither, when all the deep unsounded skies
Shudder with silent stars, she clomb,
And as with optic glasses her keen eyes
Pierced through the mystic dome,
Regions of lucid matter taking forms,
Brushes of fire, hazy gleams,
Clusters and beds of worlds,
and bee-like swarms of suns, and starry streams.
She saw the snowy poles of moonless Mars,
That marvellous round of milky light
Below Orion, and those double stars
Whereof the one more bright
is circled by the other.'

The poetic lines accomplish several things for Proctor. They, too, introduce the astronomical topics he will cover in the essays that follow (from stellar astronomy, the nebulae to double stars); but they do so in a *literary* way, one that illustrates that such topics *can* be understood by non-scientists, in fact, *are already* deeply meaningful to their country's poet laureate! Fortunately for Proctor, of course, few members of Tennyson's extensive audience as the most popular author in British history were aware that he was an accomplished amateur astronomer and that his quick and deep apprehension of the subject was hardly a good predictor of the experience of true lay readers.

Proctor reinforces his confidence that a popular understanding of astronomy can be grasped by his readers in the dedication. There, he thanks his teacher George Airy for the way in which Airy made "the abstruse clear" for him, implying that Proctor will teach his public just as successfully. As a whole, the volume also has immediate visual appeal. It is profusely and richly illustrated with prints and woodcuts which attractively present various celestial objects as white on black negative images in imitation of their true appearances in the night sky, lending a "you are there, looking up" feeling to the text [FIG. 4.2].

Although Hardy's personal copy of Proctor's book bears "almost no markings," Michael Crowe believes that Proctor's "overall philosophy of astronomy" and "perspective" on the subject were "appealing" to Hardy.[5] In addition, many of Proctor's descriptions found their way into Hardy's writing. Proctor's account of John Herschel's accomplishments, his completion of his father's research, his testing of his father's theories, his original observational work at the Cape, and Proctor's analysis of Herschel's justly admired prose descriptions of celestial objects, may all have played a

---

[5]   Michael J. Crowe, letter to author, 25 April, 1988.

part in developing the character of Swithin St. Cleeve in *Two on a Tower*. Further, Proctor's volume includes essays on the planets Mars and Saturn, several on shooting stars and meteors (that may be drawn upon in *The Return of the Native* and other places), one on "zodiacal light," and a half dozen on the solar corona (that may have inspired allusions in *Tess*). Proctor writes especially descriptive accounts of "coloured suns" and Sirius in which he details the variety and range of stellar coloration and explains the appearances and behavior of double and multiple star systems. In addition, the volume includes an appendix on the up-coming transits of Venus, with final essays dealing with complex stellar astronomy, an account of the distribution of nebulae, "A New Theory of the Milky Way," and two updates on William and John Herschel's work entitled: "On the Resolvability of Star-groups regarded as a test of distance" and "A proposal for a Series of Systematic Surveys of the Star Depths." All of these descriptions and illustrations had such a strong effect on Hardy's mind's eye that he imaginatively transformed them into his own visual and symbolic images within his own literary depictions of the universe and the creatures and objects within it. One of the closing sections of Proctor's text deals with new developments in astrophysics, including "A Novel Way of Studying the Stars" and one cannot resist wondering if Hardy detected a pun in this title and decided, then and there, to conduct his own study of the stars in his own "novel" way.

The popular knowledge of astronomical matters that Hardy gained from Proctor and other popular sources was supplemented by his personal acquaintances who had similar interests: Alfred, Lord Tennyson, a "scientific poet" and avid amateur astronomer; and his friendships with members of the Royal Society, Francis Martin, an amateur scientist and meteorologist, and Sir Henry Thompson who owned a private observatory. Hardy's family owned a telescope during his childhood but the only specific use Hardy is known to have made of it is the observation of a local public hanging (Millgate 63). Hardy did observe celestial phenomena as an adult and wrote two poems, "The Comet at Yell'ham" (ca.1858) and "At a Lunar Eclipse" (ca.1867) which record his impressions of the experiences. He and his wife watched the June 1881 apparition of a comet from their garden at Wimborne just three months before Hardy created the outline for *Two on a Tower*.[6] During the same period, Hardy followed the plentiful publicity concerning the upcoming transit of Venus expected in December 1882.

The best evidence of Hardy's personal knowledge of astronomical discoveries and cosmological ideas, however, rests within the pages of his novels themselves. Astronomy is everywhere in Hardy's work. Astronomical ideas and imagery are so ubiquitous in so many of Hardy's novels, that it is nothing short of amazing that no one has previously conducted a thorough study of them and their relationship to other literary treatments of science by Hardy and others. By attending to the ways in which Hardy uses astronomy and cosmology within the plot, structure, characterizations,

---

[6]   Thomas Hardy, *The Life and Work of Thomas Hardy*, ed. Michael Millgate (Athens, GA: University of Georgia Press, 1985) 154; hereafter: *Life and Works*.

themes, and symbols of his works, we can appreciate the sophistication of Hardy's knowledge of the field and begin to delineate the various purposes toward which he puts it. To a certain extent, the presence of *Two on a Tower* in the Hardy oeuvre – a purposefully "astronomical" novel – may itself have caused some readers and critics to assume that he put all of his astronomical concerns into the pages of that work. Instead, close reading of even his earliest works reveals that Hardy, as he entered his career as a writer, already had a deep drive to conduct literary thought-experiments in which he took great care to create novelistic environments for his characters that took into account the reality of the universe as contemporary astronomy was describing it.

Hardy's Personal Construction of an Astronomical–Literary Cosmology

Hardy's knowledge of the literary history of astronomy and his awareness of historical and contemporary astronomy and cosmology converge in his desire to articulate a world view that at once engages the long tradition of mythopoetic cosmological narrative and recognizes that new discoveries and developments in nineteenth-century astronomy were causing and calling for concomitant changes in popular cosmological understanding. That such an undertaking might not be appropriate work for poets and literary writers is a thought that seems never to have crossed his mind since so much of his reading in both classical and modern authors manifestly affirmed otherwise. During Hardy's lifetime, the popularization of natural knowledge was still a relatively open domain – priests and parsons, amateurs, academics, and emergent scientific professionals alike could, and did, participate in the process of producing popular talks and texts. While he may at times have had concerns about his own training and talents as a writer, Hardy expresses no doubts that the poetry and prose of his time could (and should) convey literary "natural history" and that he could use either to express a world view both crafted within, and contributing to, the tradition of cosmological narratives and cultural mythology.

Having built up his personal world view bit by bit, layer upon layer, by accruing and drawing together "truths" he found in mythopoetic, classical and Biblical traditions, folklore, anthropology, comparative religion, and archaeology, literary works of drama, poetry, and prose – ancient through contemporary – that engage astronomical phenomena, cosmogony and cosmology, Hardy conjoined them with popular contemporary accounts of natural history, biology, chemistry and psychology to construct his own cosmological narrative – a descriptive story of the apparent nature of things, how the physical phenomena of the universe, inorganic and organic – human life included – act, react and interact. For Hardy, the accumulated "truths" of Victorian natural sciences, especially those of astronomy, are not "terrible" in and of themselves; instead, they help him formulate what will remain a crucial question throughout his life and career: how can anyone cope with the truly frightening fatal flaw in nature's unintended consequences, namely, that beneath an *astronomical* sky, filled with evolving and decaying stars, upon this actively *geological* planet, *biological* beings should ever have evolved *consciousness* of our own evolution and mortality? This cosmic dilemma produced by the interaction of astronomy, geology, biology and psychology is central to Hardy's vision of the complex interrelations of character and environment, local and universal forces, regional and cosmic scales of being, male and female, natural and supernatural, all within "lost" or fast-disappearing rural settings. Indeed, Hardy's apprehension of the complexities of this quandary situates his novels as virtual sequels to one of Western civilization's greatest cosmological narratives: Milton's *Paradise Lost*.[7] That epic closes with the most awful of beginnings: "The World was all before them, where to choose / Thir place of rest, and Providence thir guide: / They hand in hand with wand'ring steps and slow, / Through Eden took thir solitary way."[8] And *then*, what happens? Human history happens. That Hardy overtly evokes Milton's epic conclusion in the ending of *Tess*, has been recognized for many years, of course, but that same conclusion is implicitly integral to recurrent themes and situations throughout Hardy's poetry and fiction. The dilemma these final lines pose is realized by every conscious life that Hardy imagines: Given the perceived conditions of the universe, what resources can (and will) individual human beings bring to bear upon the problem of their own survival? With what consequences? With what meaning?

Paradise Lost may well have struck Hardy as the ultimate model for cosmological storytelling. For one (perhaps, as Blake thought, being of the Devil's party without knowing it), Milton narrated the mythic moment at which humanity came into consciousness of our "universal" situation. All human stories flow from that kind of moment, whether realized within Biblical history, within other spiritual or historical frameworks, or without, as a turning point in the development of an individual's psychosocial self or education. All of Hardy's stories flow from that moment too. In recognizing (or failing to recognize) their situation within that dilemma, the central characters in Hardy's novels each embody a unique cosmology – a particular set of ontological and epistemological beliefs and theories about what is "out there," and what is and is not possible *within* the sphere of human feeling, will, and action. His characters' world views are comprised of various scientific and religious ideas about the origin, evolution and structure of the universe and the nature of the natural world, as well as more personally and locally internalized maps of how the familial, social, educational, and political "worlds" around them work. Whatever their fictional locale, in most of Hardy's novels there are as many cosmologies as there are characters, with

---

[7] Hardy's extensive knowledge and use of Milton have long been recognized. For one perspective, see: Joan Grundy, "Hardy and Milton" in *John Milton: Twentieth-Century Perspectives, Volume 1: The Man and the Author*, ed. J. Martin Evans (New York, NY: Routledge, 2003) 329–40, reprinted from *Thomas Hardy Annual* 3 (1985): 3–14.

[8] Book XII, lines 646-649 in John Milton, *Paradise Lost*, ed. Merritt Y. Hughes, New Edition (New York: Odyssey Press, 1962) 307–8.

each novel in and of itself expressing on a larger scale, a vision of Hardy's own cosmology as well.

Besides addressing the problem of cosmology in mythological, proto-psychological, and proto-anthropological terms, Milton's epic also provides what may be the ultimate solution for the literary problem of setting a story that is intended to be at once both cosmic and local: one couple, in a garden, somewhere in the universe. Like his fellow "regional" and "pastoral" novelist, Willa Cather (who was also influenced by Milton), Hardy chafed under the critical confinement of such designations, adamantly resisting the notion that their provincial location should inhibit his stories' relevance for readers who happened to live in more densely populated urban or industrial centers. Adam and Eve were of the Garden *and* of the Universe; wasn't that true of us all? Also, like Cather, Hardy sensed the larger possibilities of the regional and pastoral as exemplified by the unity of the local/universal and microcosmic/macrocosmic achieved within the settings of Greek drama. If the comedies and tragedies of a handful of Greeks inhabiting the environs around Athens, Corinth, and Thebes could speak to all times and all places, stories about human life in Nebraska or Wessex could do the same.[9]

Hardy's critical experience anticipated Cather's in another way as well. Some of her critics misconstrued the archetypal simplicity of her descriptions of farm life in Nebraska as simple, seriously underestimating the sophisticated way her narratives relate the interactions of the human individual with the natural, social, and technological. Mistaking her stories as local in place – and time – such critics also missed Cather's evocation of a profound sense of human narrative tradition, as carried on by and within oral and written literatures, to be sure, but also within the "song" of human life itself. Such a sense is central, for example, to *O Pioneers!*, as in one seemingly "simple" scene. The two main characters are sitting together under the moonlight within the flower and vegetable garden – the Eden – that Alexandra's vision, will, and understanding of the land has realized. Addressing Alexandra, Carl Linstrum (one of Cather's autobiographically drawn characters) registers his response to the changes that the latest influx of human inhabitants has effected upon the rural realm around them.

---

[9]   The philosophical and political complexity potential within pastoral poetry and prose has been well-explored since at least the time of Vergil's *Georgics*. For a useful overview of how such complexity is treated within nineteenth-century novels, see: Ian Duncan's "The Provincial or Regional Novel" in Brantlinger and Thesing 318–35. Of particular relevance to my discussion is Duncan's description of Hardy's "rhetorical insistence on the recurrence of primordial, mythic events, embedded in the structure of the cosmos" (334). For more general related studies see works by these authors listed in this volume's *Bibliography*: Ralph Pite, Michael Irwin, Roberto Maria Dainotto, Richard W. Bevis, Zoe Veater, William R. Siebenschuh, Jonathan Bate, Jeremy Hooker, Robert Langbaum, Kevin Z. Moore, Owen Schur, Jo Draper, Shelagh Hunter, Denys Kay-Robinson, John Lucas, Michael Squires, Ian Gregor, and Merryn Williams.

"I . . . think I liked the old country better. This is all very splendid in its way, but there was something about this country when it was a wild old beast that has haunted me all these years. Now, when I come back to all this milk and honey, I feel like the old German song, 'Wo bist du, wo bist du, mein geliebtest Land?' Do you ever feel like that, I wonder?"

"Yes, sometimes, when I think about father and mother and those who are gone; so many of our old neighbors." Alexandra paused and looked up thoughtfully at the stars. "We can remember the graveyard when it was wild prairie, Carl, and now— "

"And now the old story has begun to write itself over there," said Carl softly. "Isn't it queer: there are only two or three human stories, and they go on repeating themselves as fiercely as if they had never happened before; like the larks in this country, that have been singing the same five notes over for thousands of years."[10]

From the simplest of settings – two people, in a garden, under the stars – and with the "same five notes" and "only two or three human stories," life fashions unity and infinite variety, shared experiences and original individual ones. Hardy's thrush and Cather's lark have more in common than their biological classification. Their songs are anything but simple, they are implicate echoes of the songs of their genetic ancestors, as well as their authors' "singing" which corresponds, in turn, to that of Homer and all other bards of the human past.

Although Hardy and Cather both substantially integrated the continuity of the human and natural past into the settings of their fiction, that past is preparatory to a present that they imagine in vastly different ways. In *O Pioneers!*, Cather's Alexandra is at home on the land and in the universe. She perceives herself and her world as residing in a cosmos where through empathetic understanding, the human and natural can, and do, work together through trials and tragedies to promote growth and create harmonic order. Her relationship to the stars is one equally rare in Naturalist and Romantic literature: when she contemplates the "vastness and distance" and "ordered march" of the stars and reflects "upon the great operations of nature . . . and of the law that lay behind them" she feels "a sense of personal security" (70–71). Few of Hardy's characters, male or female, will conceive of the possibility of such a sense of peace and place, either in the world they see around them or beneath the heavens they see above them.

The fictional world that Hardy creates for his characters to live in is a whole universe, built from the top down. Although the social, political, and philosophical elements of his fiction have received more critical notice, the settings of his early and later novels are simultaneously cosmological, physical, geological, biological, and psychological. Like a scientific great chain of being, all of those aspects – from the universal scale down to the individual sphere of a single mind – together comprise the initial conditions of the fictional environments within which his characters seek to survive. Different aspects receive more focus than others in various narratives, varying in direct correspondence to their importance within individual characters' cosmologies. As his literary notebooks show, Hardy's multifarious reading in astronomy, cosmology, geology, evolutionary theory, antiquities, anthropology,

---

[10]   Cather, *O Pioneers!* 118–19.

mythology, and the classics all seemed to reinforce, for him, the same set of strong messages about the human condition: the past is present, biologically and historically; evolution and adaptation are ongoing processes; adaptation and change do not imply progress; chance and will do not imply providence or grace. Perhaps recapitulating the convergence of his own learning from diverse sources, Hardy's characters are led to the same lessons from many different directions.

For many decades, Hardy scholars have sensed that he was doing some interesting and unique things with the characters and environment in his work, although they have differed widely about what exactly those things are and how they work.[11] In *Thomas Hardy: Landscapes of the Mind* (1979), Andrew Enstice analyzes how Hardy utilizes the various sorts of landscapes that he creates in his fiction, with some more, some less closely identifiable with "real" geographical locations. He argues that Hardy's use of landscape changes over the course of his career from the "enclosed" landscapes of town, village, farm, heath, and woodland (where characters exist as "of the place," as a part of the landscape), to "landscapes of the mind," literary settings which exist only in the mind of the author, readers, and characters, as a "perceived amalgam of many ways of looking at the same thing."[12] Enstice builds a fascinating and detailed case for his thesis, describing Hardy's career as a novelist within a developmental model in which he argues for a progressive shift, from the simple, concrete, and realistic settings of the early works, to complex, abstract, and perceptual psychological and mental worlds of *Tess* and, especially, *Jude*.

As careful and detailed as his argument is, however, Enstice's apparent predisposition for making a case for developmental change causes him to under-appreciate evidence in the texts that indicates that even in his earliest fiction, Hardy carefully establishes the epistemological frameworks, problem-solving tools, and habits of thinking and feeling that his central characters employ to interpret and interact with the natural and social worlds around them. Indeed, an extended passage from *The Mayor of Casterbridge* that Enstice cites in the course of his argument, serves as an apt example of my differing view.

> To learn to take the universe seriously there is no quicker way than to watch – to be a 'waker' as the country-people call it. Between the hours at which the last toss-pot went by and the first sparrow shook himself, the silence in Casterbridge – barring the rare sound of

---

[11]　See, for instance: Rosemary Sumner, *Thomas Hardy, Psychological Novelist* (New York: St. Martin's Press, 1981); Geoffrey Thurley, *The Psychology of Hardy's Novels: The Nervous and the Statuesque* (St. Lucia, Australia: University of Queensland Press, 1975); Herbert Borthwick Grimsditch, *Character and Environment in the Novels of Thomas Hardy* (New York: Russell & Russell, 1962); several relevant essays in Helen Small and Trudi Tate, eds., *Literature, Science, Psychoanalysis, 1830–1970: Essays in Honour of Gillian Beer* (Oxford: Oxford University Press, 2003); and Vincent Newey, ed., *Centring the Self: Subjectivity, Society, and Reading from Thomas Gray to Thomas Hardy* (Aldershot, Eng.: Scolar Press; Brookfield, VT: Ashgate, 1995).

[12]　Andrew Enstice, *Thomas Hardy: Landscapes of the Mind* (New York: St. Martin's Press, 1979) xi.

the watchman – was broken in Elizabeth's ear only by the timepiece in the bedroom ticking frantically against the clock on the stairs; ticking harder and harder till it seemed to clang like a gong; and all this while the subtle-souled girl asking herself why she was born, why sitting in a room, and blinking at the candle; why things around her had taken the shape they wore in preference to every other possible shape. Why they stared at her so helplessly, as if waiting for the touch of some wand that should release them from terrestrial constraint; what that chaos called consciousness, which spun in her at this moment like a top, tended to, and began in. (as in Enstice 27)

This quotation appears in the first chapter of Enstice's book in which he lays the foundation for his view that the most concrete of relationships between the settings and the characters occur in Hardy's early fiction. Yet, as Enstice himself admits, the passage is a *tour de force* evocation of the relation between the universal and the personal as experienced through the internal "world" of a single character.

> Concrete and abstract seem to mingle and dissolve into one overwhelming perception, and in this brief passage the startling awareness that has characterised our view of the town and its people is distilled into a feeling of the immensity of simply being alive. This and not religion, characterises Hardy's perception of human existence. (27)

Indeed, this passage contains the essence of what I call Hardy's "personal construct cosmology." Hardy depicts his central characters as experiencing the world as a psychological phenomenon, an environment that exists for them because, and as, they perceive it. Each of his fictional men and women "lives" in a universe of their own making, of their own made-meaning, within sets of personal constructs that function at once as archive and framework, containing all of their interdependent experiences and interpretations, as filtered through, and processed by, their individual biological natures.[13] The profundity of this passage is achieved not by describing Elizabeth's primitive fear of the night or her sophisticated awe of the stellar universe, but rather through her apprehension of her own being, within the context of her future mortality. It is Hardy's description of her simultaneous consciousness of consciousness, vitality, and mortality – life *as* a death watch – that makes the reader gasp in recognition of our shared fate.

---

[13]   For background on the history and development of personal construct psychology, see: Kelly, *The Psychology of Personal Constructs* and Robert A. Neimeyer, *The Development of Personal Construct Psychology* (Lincoln: University of Nebraska Press, 1985). The accuracy and power of Hardy's literary descriptions of human psychology attracted the attention of at least one contemporary psychiatric practitioner who cited his work in a medical address, see pages 68–69 of Athena Vrettos's discussion of "Victorian Psychology" in Brantlinger and Thesing. I am aware of only one other reader of Hardy who has drawn directly on Kelly's ideas: Cintra Whitehead, "Construct, Image, and Prediction: A View of Hardy's *Jude the Obscure* through George Kelly's Psychology of Personal Constructs," *Constructive Criticism: A Journal of Construct Psychology and the Arts* 1.2 (June 1991): 129–49.

Although, I agree with Enstice that the settings of Hardy's novels grow in intricacy as he grows as a writer, such early passages indicate that he does not reserve the complexity of mental perception for the character of Jude alone. The elemental presentation of the ways that the psychology of an early character like Elizabeth gives shape and meaning to her life and her fictional world should not be confused with a lack of writerly skill on Hardy's part or a lack of complexity in his early vision. In such passages, Hardy's synthesis of the individual and the universal, the local and cosmic, are expressed by his parallel synthesis of the literary pathos achieved within the pastoral, dramatic, and epic.

*   *   *

As I hope to demonstrate in the chapters that follow, throughout his fiction, Hardy employs literary conventions and expectations, carefully matching the fictional landscape to the forces and circumstances that will be most at play upon and within his characters's lives and minds. In his imagination of possible postlapsarian natural worlds, Hardy may depict the human relationship to the cosmos as idealistic, horrific, harmonic or discordant; yet always, *genre conveys cosmology*, establishing the natural setting and initial environmental conditions and social constraints within which his characters must struggle to survive and seek love, happiness, meaning and a future. As in *Paradise Lost*, in Hardy's novel universes, cosmic nature may provide the setting for wars between the forces of good and evil, survival or demise, on an almost unimaginably titanic scale, but the truly epic battle occurs within the drama of the individual minds and souls of the living beings who eke out their existence within the "garden" of such a battlefield; and each one of them does battle for us all.

The perceptions of the human mind and its conceptions of the nature of nature, the nature of life, essentially constitute the cosmos for Hardy's characters. From the earliest to the latest of Hardy's works, his characters' various understandings of the world and their own minds do not comprise a linear cosmological narrative from primitive to modern. Instead, in any one time and place, within any one community, within any one character, there are multiple – even competing – cosmologies at work. His characters' minds make meaning out of any number of possible belief and thought systems, depending on the stimuli of the forces operating upon them in both their immediate and remote environments: superstition, myth and ritual, pagan and orthodox religion, the biological and instinctual, sex, gender, class, the familial, economic, social, and political. Part of the very real beauty of Hardy's stories is the degree to which he is able to express and empathize with the exquisitely painful pathways by which human individuals make their way through life in the universe. So many potential paradises, so many ways to lose them.

Chapter 5

Celestial Selection and the Cosmic Environment
A Pair of Blue Eyes, Far From the Madding Crowd, and *The Return of the Native*

Hardy's interest in astronomy and cosmology and his attempts to incorporate their concepts into the milieux of his fiction was a life-long concern that only increased in its sophistication, grace, and profundity as Hardy grew as a writer. As I hope to demonstrate here and in the remaining chapters, Hardy's "literary history of astronomy" integrates the history of human understanding of, and response to astronomy, including the prehistoric and primitive, agrarian, early industrial and near modern. Within each novel's universe, Hardy depicts with sensitivity and appreciation, with compassion and sorrow, the hope and loss, the confusion and tension that may be experienced by any particular set of individuals, living at any one time and in any one place – indeed, beneath the very same sky – but with vastly different cosmologies in mind.

A Pair of Blue Eyes (1873)

Astronomy and geology play equally important roles in constituting the fictional universe of *A Pair of Blue Eyes*.[1] Both Richard Proctor's *Essays on Astronomy* and Charles Darwin's *Descent of Man* were published the year before Hardy's third novel appeared. Paul Ward convincingly argues that the problems of natural selection and human sexual selection figure strongly in the storyline.[2] Hardy consistently maintained

---

[1] Among those relatively few readers who notice the sciences in *A Pair of Blue Eyes* at all, critical attention has overwhelmingly focused upon the latter, as in recent studies by Andrew Radford, "The Victorian Dilettante and the Discoveries of Time in *A Pair of Blue Eyes*," *Thomas Hardy Yearbook* 33 (2002): 5–19 and pages 46–65 in his *Thomas Hardy and the Survivals of Time*; and Edward Neill's chapter, "Fogeys and Fossils: *A Pair of Blue Eyes*" in *The Secret Life of Thomas Hardy: 'Retaliatory Fiction'* (Aldershot, Eng.: Ashgate; 2004) 20–30.

[2] Paul Ward, "*A Pair of Blue Eyes* and the *Descent of Man*," *Thomas Hardy Yearbook* 5 (1975): 47–55.

that he did not mean to forward "a scientific system of philosophy" in his works, insisting, instead, that his depictions of science within them are "provisional impressions only, used for artistic purposes because they represent approximately the impressions of the age, and are plausible, till somebody produces better theories of the universe" (as in Ward 48). Yet as Ward recognizes

> the effect of major scientific discoveries is nowhere better registered than in the literature of the age concerned, because the polemical debates following close on the heels of a discovery are usually heated and frequently characterised by distortions and exaggerations inevitable when people's intellectual and moral positions are exposed to a very basic threat or challenge. Literature has the great advantage of being able to absorb and interpret the implications of scientific discovery in a fully human context. (47)

While some readers may detect in Ward's comment an implication that scientific forums of debate fail to interpret the implications of discoveries in "fully human contexts," I think, rather, that he means simply to emphasize the unique ways that *literature* raises and explores such questions. Both creative and critical forms of literature certainly played such a role in Victorian England. Read against that context, Hardy's denial that he is forwarding a "scientific system of philosophy" in his literary works should in no way be construed as a denial that he was forwarding a *literary* philosophy of scientific systems.

In *A Pair of Blue Eyes*, according to Ward, Hardy asks not whether certain human specimens will survive by natural selection in certain environments, but rather: "what sort of humans will survive and how?" Are those "fittest" to survive the best morally and spiritually? What implications will such a mechanism have on the continuity of culture? As Ward points out, Hardy realized that the human species is not just concerned with physical survival and biological perpetuation like other animals, but our reproductive choices and activities have social, moral, intellectual and emotional qualities at stake as well (51). In Ward's view, the "moral" of *A Pair of Blue Eyes* is that the various possible male–female pairings in the novel are doomed to failure for reasons related to the flawed operation of natural selection. Reliance on physical attraction alone can lead to a coupling that is doomed in spiritual, moral, intellectual and social ways and such is the case with Elfride's attraction to Stephen Smith which is thwarted by social convention and class standards (52). Elfride's attraction to Henry Knight, Ward demonstrates, has intellectual respect as its basis, yet the "instinct for joy" and procreation that Elfride might realize with him is thwarted by other factors, namely Knight's unreasonable and dogmatic philosophical ideals (53–4). Elfride agrees to her final match, with Lord Luxellian, out of a sense of fatalistic self-sacrifice and to make peace in her family, thus demonstrating her ability to rise above animal attraction and base her selections on moral and ethical standards. As Ward concludes, in this novel Hardy tests out ways in which natural selection can occur in human matches and reveals how his characters' inability to assess accurately the full possibilities of selection and their failure to predict the consequences of their choices, ultimately leads to tragedy, with the least fit (morally) surviving, not much the wiser for their experience.

An All-Natural Setting: Natural History and Natural Knowledge

In *A Pair of Blue Eyes*, Hardy creates a fictionally controlled environment in which the pastoral natural world and his characters' knowledge of nature serve as the essential variables. The interactions of nature and human nature combine to generate the narrative action in which all of the male characters are morally unfit survivors (as Ward describes them) who, by teaching Elfride what they know about nature – including male nature – contribute to her death. In Hardy's narrative, the differences in what each character knows about nature (including what they do and do not know about natural history, natural and sexual selection, the workings of the greater universe) and how they synthesize and apply that knowledge – their personal cosmologies – correlates closely with their ultimate fates.

Hardy represents each central character as having some popular knowledge of nature and natural history gained variously by direct experience of nature, formal or informal education, or scientific activity. Elfride, a naive but curious country girl, is an unanalytical collector of flora and fauna who picks up moss, sticks, shells and seaweed along her country rides on horseback.[3] Her uncritical attitude will typify her approach to learning of all kinds. Stephen, her first serious beau (with whom she shares a natural compatibility), is a self-made architect and autodidact who betters himself through immersion in the popular knowledge of science available through the British Museum and learned friends. Elfride's father, the Reverend Swancourt, keeps collections of stuffed wildlife, plants, and an aquarium. Alongside the "stuffed specimens" (and roughly equivalent in status) are artifacts of his daughter's existence.

> The rector's background was at present what a rector's background should be, his study. Here the consistency ends. All along the chimney piece were ranged bottles of horse, pig, and cow medicines, and against the wall was a high table, made up of the fragments of an old oak lych-gate. Upon this stood stuffed specimens of owls, divers, and gulls, and over them bunches of wheat and barley ears, labelled with the date of the year that produced them. Some cases and shelves, more or less laden with books, the prominent titles of which were Dr Brown's 'Notes on the Romans,' Dr Smith's 'Notes on the Corinthians,' and Dr Robinson's 'Notes on the Galatians, Ephesians and Philippians,' just saved the character of the place, in spite of a girl's doll's-house standing above them, a marine aquarium in the window, and Elfride's hat hanging on its corner. (59)

---

[3]   Thomas Hardy, *A Pair of Blue Eyes*, New Wessex Edition (New York: St. Martin's Press, 1985) 140; hereafter cited by page number within the text.

Indeed, the Reverend treats his daughter as his social possession, a collectible among other collectibles, refusing to marry her to Stephen. Her rash response to his arbitrary decision damages her reputation and narrows the possibilities of her life.

Henry Knight is obviously a sophisticated member of the all-male social "club" of mid-Victorian amateur scientists: he meets his friends for dinner beside a table "spread with a few scientific periodicals and art reviews" (378). For all of his sophistication, however, Knight is primarily attracted to what he perceives to be Elfride's inexperienced purity. He takes pleasure in introducing her to nature and the nature of men – explaining in Hardyan set-pieces aspects of geology, meteorology, astronomy and his own unrealistic double-standard, by which she will ultimately be condemned. Personifying the most modern manifestation of the British mania for specimen collecting, Knight keeps an aquarium of "zoophytes" in the window of his London home. When the sun lights up the aquarium, it is brought to life, with the "timid communitie's" actions seeming to express "gladness" for the warmth and light. Here, Hardy alludes to the Darwinian "instinct for joy" that many of his human characters possess. Yet Knight keeps himself clearly aloof from such "joy" and coldly draws a parallel between the life of the aquarium and the "Humanity Show" of the streets of London visible on just the other side of his glass windowpane. There, a new "volume of light," not from the life-giving sun, but from an artificial source – gas street lamps – illuminates a "spectacle" for this objective observer of nature and human nature (160, 163–164).

> Crowds – mostly of women – were surging, bustling, and pacing up and down. Gaslight glared from butchers' stalls, illuminating the lumps of flesh to splotches of orange and vermilion, like the wild colouring of Turner's later pictures, whilst the purl and babble of tongues of every pitch and mood was to this human wild-wood what the ripple of a brook is to the natural forest. (164)

Hardy does not allow Knight to remain haughtily superior to the "spectacle" for long. Even as Knight directs the attention of his visitor (Stephen Smith) to the scene, he excuses himself to dress for the evening. The chapter ends: "Knight was now ready. Turning off the gas, and slamming together the door, they went downstairs and into the street" (165). With this remark, Hardy makes his readers acutely aware of the fact that they may be, like Knight, aloof observers, peering into the aquarium of the novel at the characters Hardy has placed there; but they are also part of the crowded masses of life that Hardy is observing.

Hardy sets the Darwinian sexual selection of the novel's action squarely within geological and meteorological reality. When the characters undertake geological excursions to the cliffs in the area, they are exposed to layers of the past. Hardy mentions specific formations of igneous and metamorphic rock, slate and fossils that are found in the region (133, 240), establishing that part of the story's place is also its time. Hardy ironically associates changes in the weather with changes in his characters' emotional states or changes in the dramatic action. As Elfride sets out to join Stephen in carrying out plans for an elopement, she rides out into one of late summers' "brightest mornings." Soon, however, an impending storm threatens, the mercury drops, and a cloud places itself "between her and the sun." She correspondingly falls into sadness.

> One of the brightest mornings of late summer shone upon her. The heather was at its purplest, the furze at its yellowest, the grasshoppers chirped loud enough for birds, the snakes hissed like little engines, and Elfride at first felt lively. Sitting at ease upon Pansy, in her orthodox riding-habit and nondescript hat, she looked what she felt. But the mercury of those days had a trick of falling unexpectedly. First, only for one minute in ten had she a sense of depression. Then a large cloud, that had been hanging in the north like a black fleece, came and placed itself between her and the sun. It helped on what was already inevitable, and she sank into a uniformity of sadness. (140)

Here, Hardy uses meteorology to invert the pathetic fallacy. He shows that nature is more likely to affect the moods of human beings than reflect or sympathize with them. Perhaps alluding to Plato's parable of the Horse and Rider, he also uses the scene to indicate the indecisiveness of Elfride's personality. Further on in the passage, Elfride leaves the decision of whether to proceed on to the next town (and secret marriage) or to turn back home up to her horse's instincts. She half-counts on Pansy to go back, but the horse defeats the expectations of the rider. Throughout the novel, Elfride continually places herself at the disposal of nature and fate, leaving herself open to the will of others and vulnerable to the consequences of others' actions.

From the earliest pages of *A Pair of Blue Eyes*, Hardy establishes close associations between his characters' inner lives and the realities of natural history, amateur science, geology and meteorology that surround them. Although the microcosmic atmosphere of this fictional world is suffused with varying degrees of natural knowledge and scientific awareness, Hardy himself tells us in the preface to the 1895 edition that the central analogy he had in mind for the story and the interrelationships of its characters was primarily drawn from the world of architecture.

> The following chapters were written at a time when the craze for indiscriminate church-restoration had just reached the remotest nooks of western England, where the wild and tragic features of the coast had long combined in perfect harmony with the crude Gothic Art of the ecclesiastical buildings scattered along it, throwing into extraordinary discord all architectural attempts at newness there. To restore the grey carcases of a mediaevalism whose spirit had fled seemed a not less incongruous act than to set about renovating the adjoining crags themselves.
>
> Hence it happened that an imaginary history of three human hearts, whose emotions were not without correspondence with these material circumstances, found in the ordinary incidents of such church-renovations a fitting frame for its presentation. (35)

Hardy uses the phrase "not without correspondence" in an analogical, almost mathematical sense. He consciously sets up correspondences between the three central characters and the three central forces at work in the historical and social moment of the 1860s in England: those spirits desiring to preserve the medieval, those wishing to build the modern, and the forces of nature indifferent to them both.

A Pastoral Gothic Cosmos

The pastoral setting and Gothic mode of the story are so closely intertwined as carriers of significance and meaning within *A Pair of Blue Eyes* that Hardy himself had difficulty categorizing the novel as one emphasizing "Character and Environment" or "Romances and Fantasys," although he ultimately decided upon the latter. The trajectory of the storyline may well have tipped the scales for him. Within the plot of the novel, the young Elfride is courted by three men.[4] Two of these men play prominent roles within the story and they, along with Elfride herself, represent in different ways various interactions of the three forces – the medieval, modern and natural – that Hardy introduces in the preface. The young "self-made" architect, Stephen Smith (risen from his lowly birth to a master-mason), arrives in Elfride's town to make drawings of the old and crumbling Gothic village church in order to preserve images of its structure and decorations before nature reclaims the stones out of which they are made. Stephen's character and career combine the best of the old with the best of the new. He appreciates the value and beauty of the past, and is doing his best to "better" himself and his social position by the education and professional opportunities made available to him by the modern age. Elfride's second love, the essayist and reviewer, Henry Knight, is a mature educated gentlemen, "modern" in his philosophy, his London lifestyle, his objectivity, his interest in geology and astronomy and his cynicism, but strangely antiquated (even regressive Hardy hints) in his ideas about male–female relationships.

The third male figure of the story (he barely appears on the "stage" of the novel, and is not a fully developed character) is Lord Spenser Hugo Luxellian, Gothic in family position and heritage, and Gothic in local legend. The Luxellian line is apparently cursed, as several female members of the family have been doomed by misfortune in love to live entombed in unsatisfying marriages. They are freed only by sudden and early deaths. Elfride is related by blood to this line and will be bound to Luxellian in marriage by the story's end. The misfortunes of her life, loves, marriage, and death apparently follow the pattern of the family "curse," but as Hardy will make explicit, her fate can also be explained without recourse to the supernatural. What happens to Elfride may be interpreted as a natural function of the interaction of natural phenomena, her own inexperienced personality, chance, circumstances, misunderstandings, and the actions and choices of others. For critical and ironic purposes, Hardy creates Gothic undertones to this story that are so strong that some

---

[4]   Four, if you count the young farmer, Jethway, whose funeral has just taken place as the story begins. His death indicates that an agrarian "match" (and a completely satisfactory pastoral life story) is unavailable to Elfride.

readers (those inclined to superstition or particularly susceptible to the conventions of Gothic novels), might view Elfride's fate as the product of a curse. Yet Hardy undercuts this line of interpretation by carefully revealing, through rational explanation, the reality behind the Gothic appearances. The tragic waste of Elfride's life and loving heart can be blamed on nothing but the random indifferent action of the natural universe and the actions of the men within it who so poorly predict what consequences their own choices and desires will have upon the innocents of the world such as she. It is tempting to conclude that Elfride is the hapless victim of the laws of nature and the laws of human nature, but Hardy provides a deeper analysis.

The system of correspondence through which Hardy relates his characters to the forces of medievalism, modernism and nature is but the essential foundation upon which he builds a full understanding of the novel's individual personae. Hardy shows how each character's behavior, speech, actions and thoughts are influenced by a multiplicity of complex factors. He carefully reveals how each person's own psychological make-up, philosophical bent, political opinions, social class, personal prejudices and predilections, jadedness or naivete, ideals, professions, vocations, and avocations affect and motivate her/his actions. To this picture of the internal machinations of human nature, Hardy adds a background out of which the external forces of nature, society, and twists of fate and coincidence emerge as the hidden controlling powers behind the human drama. Rather than a *deus ex machina*, Hardy, as stage-manager, calls in *fatum ex machina*.

Building upon the long association of fate with the "stars," Hardy creates an astronomically correct universe in *A Pair of Blue Eyes*, gauging the sophistication of cosmic phenomena to the level of understanding and learning of the individual characters who perceive them. Like the central character, Elfride, most of the story's astronomy is basic, simple, and direct. The solar, stellar, and lunar phenomena that Hardy mentions would have been known to even casual urban observers of the nighttime and seasonal skies, and as a matter of course by rural folks or village dwellers. Besides plain references to the sun, moon, and stars (collectively), Hardy mentions by name only one planet (Jupiter), one star (Sirius), and one particular constellation (Ursa Major or the Great Bear). Yet Hardy is able to achieve subtle cosmological effects with this relatively simple palette of astronomical images.

In *A Pair of Blue Eyes*, astronomical allusions work within the pastoral tradition to establish the place, scenery, seasons, time of day or night, and the weather. Hardy uses astronomy descriptively to "type" certain minor characters and as a foreshadowing and mood-setting device (romantic, tragic and otherwise). The visage of the Reverend Swancourt, for instance, is described as handsome in the same "sense in which the moon is bright: the ravines and valleys which on a close inspection are seen to diversify its surface being left out of the argument" (59). Hardy alludes to the moonlight as possessing a quality that should encourage meditation and peace, but notes that Stephen was "hardly philosopher enough to avail himself of Nature's offer" (124). Hardy often uses the sun to set the mood for certain action and to comment ironically upon it. As Stephen and Elfride journey to London to elope, "the few tattered clouds of the morning enlarged and united, the sun withdrew behind them to emerge no more that day, and the evening drew to a close in drifts of rain" (144). When they must return unwed, the "weather cleared, and the stars shone in upon them," – then – "day began to break . . . the sun rose and sent penetrating shafts of light in upon their weary faces" (146). What should be a joyful journey to a wedding is marred by sullen weather. What should be a defeated ride home is brightened by the glare of sunshine. Hardy uses the contrast to evoke for the reader the indifference of nature to the lovers' situations.

Hardy uses astronomical allusions to critique the "objectification" and blindness of scientific perceptions and observation and to sharpen the contrast between readers and observers of "natural" signs and the language of the rural environment and those who develop and live by the elaborate systems of artificial "signs" of high society. In a section that he drastically cut down to reduce its cynicism, Hardy presents the social philosophy of Elfride's new stepmother. Mrs. Swancourt compares her skills as a social "face-reader" and interpreter of the superficial appearances and "surface phenomena" of high society to the skills of rural folk who, without clocks, can tell the time. Reverend Swancourt describes the rustic observers' abilities.

> by means of shadows, winds, clouds, the movements of sheep and oxen, the singing of birds, the crowing of cocks, and a hundred other sights and sounds which people with watches in their pockets never know / the existence of, they are able to pronounce within ten minutes of the hour almost at any required instant. (167–8)

Mrs. Swancourt describes her own.

> Exactly . . . . And in just the way that those learnt the signs of nature, I have learnt the language of her illegitimate sister – artificiality; and the fibbing of eyes, the contempt of nose-tips, the indignation of back hair, the laughter of clothes, the cynicism of footsteps, and the various emotions lying in walkingstick twirls, hat-liftings, the elevation of parasols, the carriage of umbrellas, become as A B C to me. (168)

Early in the novel Hardy establishes that members of different classes possess different levels of astronomical knowledge. In chapter two, Stephen arrives back home. Silhouetted against the dusken winter sky, the cart in which the young man is riding pushes across the "summit of a wild lone hill" into the west country.

> Scarcely a solitary house or man had been visible along the whole dreary distance of open country they were traversing; and now that night had begun to fall, the faint twilight, which still gave an idea of the landscape to their observation, was enlivened by the quiet appearance of the planet Jupiter, momentarily gleaming in intenser brilliancy in front of them, and by Sirius shedding his rays in rivalry from his position over their shoulders. The only lights apparent on earth were some spots of dull red glowing here and there upon the distant hills, which, as the driver of the vehicle

gratuitously remarked to the hirer, were smouldering fires for the consumption of peat and gorse-roots, where the common was being broken up for agricultural purposes. (43)

Besides placing Jupiter and Sirius correctly, in the west and south respectively, of the winter sky, Hardy has given important clues about Stephen's origins in this descriptive passage. As the eyes of the traveler and his driver are attracted to the only lights visible to them, the driver "gratuitously" explains the nature of the rural fires to his rider. Such drivers often chat "gratuitously" whether one wants them to or not, but in this case, the explanation is also gratuitous in the sense of being superfluous and unnecessary, as Stephen is returning to an area whose character and rural activity he knows well. Although he has been educated and "improved" beyond his origins as the son of the local master mason, he is more than capable of identifying two of the most important kinds of country-style "navigation" lights: Jupiter and Sirius, and the peat fires.

The lowliness of Stephen's origins will come back to haunt him as he courts the local parson's daughter, Elfride. The Reverend will reject his suit on the grounds of social incompatibility. That fact, and the resultant unhappiness of the couple, will both be associated with simple astronomy: "Stephen lay watching the Great Bear; Elfride was regarding a monotonous parallelogram of window blind. Neither slept that night" (131). Although their emotional states are similar (they have just concluded a secret meeting in which they have agreed to elope) and both are resting in the same house, their approaches to a nightlong watch are distinctly different. Stephen, practical-minded and optimistic, charts the progress of a circumpolar constellation that never sets. Elfride, a *tabula rasa* psychologically, does not look beyond the modern window covering of her own room.

That Stephen has chosen an apt celestial object on which to fix his attention through the night, and Elfride stares at blank nothingness, is not without significance. The differences in the two young peoples' outlooks will be represented by such associations with astronomy throughout the rest of the story. Stephen later designates Elfride as his "own particular bright star" to whom he swears to remain true (and does). At the point in the story when Stephen has reached a new height of professional reward for his talent, Hardy describes with quaint charm how Stephen's parents have decked themselves out in their country finest to receive him. His father wears his "second best suit" and his mother wears a dark blue print dress "covered broadcast with a multitude of new and full moons, stars and planets, with an occasional dash of comet-like aspect to diversify the scene" (252). The fabric, doubtless a product of the Industrial Revolution's new fabric-printing techniques, handily symbolizes how the Smith family's lucky stars are shining brightly as they rise in social position, due in part, to their son's acclaim and success. Later, Hardy will make the association explicitly when he describes Stephen himself as a "rising star" of the "Every-Man-His-Own-Maker Club" after he achieves international recognition for his architecture.

Elfride's associations with astronomy are as negative as Stephen's are positive. Her stars do not bode well for her family now in decline financially and socially.

Emerging from her sheltered rural youth, Elfride's encounters with the world of men and the natural world bewilder and confuse her. Her demeanor as a student of nature and men continually places her at the disposal of nature and fate, leaving her open to the will of the male characters and vulnerable to the consequences of their actions. Her exposure and submission to cosmic forces are especially revealed in two telling scenes in which truths about her are exposed by sunlight and by starlight. In a typical social critique, Hardy unequivocally demonstrates that such truths, and whether they count as exposures or not, rest squarely in the eye of the male beholder and the social values or traditional standards he chooses to uphold.

In Chapter 30, Hardy sets Elfride and Knight upon the same rocks where, exactly one year earlier, Elfride and Stephen shared a first kiss. Just as Knight wonders whether "'any lovers in past years ever sat here with arms locked, as we do now'" (332), Hardy creates a Stonehenge-type effect with the rays of the sun angling across crevices in the stones until they light up an earring Elfride lost during her first innocent embrace.

> Her recollection of a well-known pair who had, and the much-talked-of-loss which had ensued therefrom, and how the young man had been sent back to look for the missing article, led Elfride to glance down to her side, and behind her back. Many people who lose a trinket involuntarily give a momentary look for it in passing the spot ever so long afterwards. They do not often find it. Elfride, in turning her head, saw something shine weakly from a crevice in the rocky sedile. Only for a few minutes during the day did the sun / light the alcove to its innermost rifts and slits, but these were the minutes now, and its level rays did Elfride the good or evil turn of revealing the lost ornament. (332–3)

Hardy's description holds the sun blameless for randomly bringing to light Elfride's experience and prompting Knight's dismay and disgust. Knight is responsible for his response. He fell in love with Elfride at "first blush" because of the particular angle in which the sun shown upon her: "Knight could not help looking at her. The sun was within ten degrees of the horizon, and its warm light flooded her face and heightened the bright rose color of her cheeks to a vermilion red, their moderate pink hue being only seen in its natural tone where the cheek curved round into a shadow" (189). Now, as the rosy tones of the sunlight heighten her embarrassment, he will fall out of love with her instead.

Our closest star – the sun – simultaneously exposes Elfride's first fall into a relationship with Stephen and signals her fall from Knight's graces. Hardy uses images of more distant stars to suggest the consequences she will suffer for gaining knowledge of the world and the world of men. The blank slate of Elfride's self-awareness and her ignorance of her personal relation to the stars ironically reveals her blindness to the potential dangers of the awkward love triangle in which is she is quickly becoming entangled. One evening Elfride and Knight are talking. Knight, unknown to Elfride, is Stephen's much-admired teacher, and is on the verge of becoming his rival. As the evening draws on, the stars begin to appear. The dialogue that follows plays off of the triangulation of Stephen's geographical location under the stars in relation to that of Elfride and Knight.

> Their conversation detained them on the lawn and in the portico till the stars blinked out. Elfride flung back her head, and said idly –
> "There's a bright star exactly over me."
> "Each bright star is overhead somewhere"
> "Is it? 0 yes, of course. Where is that one?" and she pointed with her finger.
> "That is poised like a white hawk probably over one of the Cape Verde Islands or thereabouts."
> "And that?"
> "Looking down upon the source of the Nile."
> "And that lonely quiet-looking one?"
> "He watches the North Pole, and has no less than the whole / equator for his horizon. And that idle one low down upon the ground, that we have almost rolled round to, is in India – over the head of a young friend of mine, who very possibly looks at the star in our zenith, as it hangs low upon his horizon, and thinks of it as marking where his true love dwells."
> Elfride glanced at Knight with misgiving. Did he mean her? She could not see his features; but his attitude seemed to show unconsciousness.
> "The star is over *my* head," she said with hesitation.
> "Or anybody else's in England."
> "O yes, I see." She breathed her relief.
> "His parents, I believe, are natives of this country. I don't known them, though I have been in correspondence with him for many years till lately. Fortunately or unfortunately for him he fell in love, and then went to Bombay. Since that time I have heard very little of him." (213–14)

The scene reflects Hardy's knowledge of elementary celestial projection and the basic techniques of astronomical triangulation. It also quite likely reflects his familiarity with the solicitous tone of the male teacher to his female student in Fontenelle's *Conversations on the Plurality of Worlds* (1686). Although she is given an astronomy lesson, Elfride fails to act upon the message of the stars (triangulation is risky business) and how the stars will out. The next time she and Knight are star-gazing together, she unconsciously reveals (murmuring through a nightmare) her former engagement to Stephen, and her fate is sealed.

> Knight said no more on the words of her dream. They watched the sky till Elfride grew calm, and the dawn appeared. It was mere wan lightness first. Then the wind blew in a changed spirit, and died away to a zephyr. The star dissolved into the day.
> "That's how I should like to die," said Elfride, rising from her seat and leaning over the bulwark to watch the star's last expiring gleam. (319)

Here, just before she is finally rejected by Knight, she fatefully identifies herself with the stars. Her wish for a death of dissolution will be fulfilled.

The strongest use of imagery with cosmological significance in *A Pair of Blue Eyes* occurs in a *tour de force* scene in Chapter 22 also involving Knight and Elfride. She has hiked up to the cliff tops with a telescope to watch for Stephen's ship to come in from India. Knight, who had been busying himself in the area with geological excursions in the wake of Elfride's refusal of him, unexpectedly joins her. The situation is already emotionally uncomfortable enough for the two when they observe through the telescope a young male figure on board the approaching vessel simultaneously observing them through a telescope (232). Elfride suspects the figure is Stephen's and suggests that they move out of sight of the sea. While resting from their climb up the cliff's slope, Knight makes one of his typical scientific observations, this time about interesting inverted air currents he has noticed in the area. He launches into a lengthy lecture as Elfride listens attentively.

> "Over that edge," said Knight, "where nothing but vacancy appears, is a moving compact mass. The wind strikes the face of the rock, runs up it, rises like a fountain to a height far above our heads, curls over us in an arch, and disperses behind us. In fact, an inverted cascade is there – as perfect as the Niagara Falls – but rising instead of falling, and air instead of water. Now look here."
> Knight threw a scrap of shale over the bank, aiming it as if to go onward over the cliff. Reaching the verge, it towered into the air like a bird, turned back, and alighted on the ground behind them. They themselves were in a dead calm. (233)

Knight predicts that directly behind them the atmospheric cataract will cause a brisk backward current. He leans over the bank to test his supposition and his hat is blown off, proving his hypothesis. He, half-embarrassed to find his scientific theory proved in so personal a way, climbs down the slope to fetch it and does not return. Momentarily Elfride discovers him hanging from the cliff's edge propped only "by a bracket of quartz rock." With her first instinctive motion to help him, she only endangers herself. After being convinced that she must climb back up over Knight's body, Elfride must find a way to help while he holds on. Telling Elfride that "This is not a time for superstition," he calmly and rationally guides her in her upward climb. After she disappears safely over the ledge, Knight finds that superstition is not so easily banished. "Knight felt himself in the presence of a personalized loneliness" (238).

This scene has been singled out for special mention by almost every critic of *A Pair of Blue Eyes*. The description of Knight's "literal cliff-hanger" (as Ronald Blythe puts it), is one of the most powerful passages to be found in any of Hardy's work.[5] Hardy does a masterful job of contrasting the pride Knight has just been exhibiting in his intellectual knowledge of the cliffs, with the cliffs' overpowering presence that so immediately humbles him once he has fallen. Within the episode, Hardy compresses

---

[5]   Ronald Blythe, "Introduction," *A Pair of Blue Eyes* 29.

time for Knight, and for the reader, and takes both sequentially through several stages of existential fear.

Hardy opens his account with ironic understatement as he relates Knight's real "discovery" about the cliffs, namely, that "Their summits are not safe places for scientific experiment on the principles of air-currents, as Knight had now found, to his dismay" (239). Yet initially, Knight does not panic; instead, he holds on to the "face of the escarpment . . . with a dogged determination to make the most of his every jot of endurance." Yet as he assesses the chances that a mere girl will be able to run far enough, fast enough, and find sufficient help in time, he begins to "judge" that "there existed but a doubtful hope for him." Hardy sums up Knight's first response to his dilemma: "He could only look sternly at Nature's treacherous attempt to put an end to him, and strive to thwart her" (239).

As Knight surveys his surroundings, however, "grimness" begins to appear in "every feature" (240). In a passage that introduces what will become a personal convention in his works, Hardy uses coincidence to juxtapose humankind and nature.

> By one of those familiar conjunctions of things wherewith the inanimate world baits the mind of man when he pauses in moments of suspense, opposite Knight's eyes was an imbedded fossil, standing forth in low relief from the rock. It was a creature with eyes. The eyes, dead and turned to stone, were even now regarding him. It was one of the early crustaceans called Trilobites. Separated by millions of years in their lives, Knight and this underling seemed to have met in their place of death . . .
>
> The creature represented but a low type of animal existence, for never in their vernal years had the plains indicated by those numberless slaty layers been traversed by an intelligence worthy of the name. Zoophytes, molluscan shell-fish, were the highest developments of those ancient dates. The immense lapses of time each formation represented had known nothing of the dignity of man. They were grand times, but they were mean times too, and mean were their relics. He was to be with the small in his death. (240)

Yet Knight's training as an intellectual and a scientist helps him through this stage of daunting dread.

> Knight was a fair geologist; and such is the supremacy of habit over occasion, as a pioneer of the thought of men, that at this dreadful juncture his mind found time to take in, by a momentary sweep, the varied scenes that had had their day between this creature's epoch and his own. There is no place like a cleft landscape for bringing home such imaginings as these. (240)

At the literal (and literary) moment of truth, Knight sees the evolution of all life flash before his eyes.

> Time closed up like a fan before him. He saw himself at one extremity of the years, face to face with the beginning and all the intermediate centuries simultaneously. Fierce men, clothed in the hides of beasts, and carrying, for defence and attack, huge

clubs and pointed spears, rose from the rock, like the phantoms before the doomed Macbeth. They lived in hollows, woods, and mud huts – perhaps in caves of the neighbouring rocks. Behind them stood an earlier band. No man was there. Huge elephantine forms, the mastodon, the hippopotamus, the tapir, antelopes of monstrous size, the megatherium, and the myledon – all, for the moment, in / juxtaposition. Further back, and overlapped by these, were perched huge-billed birds and swinish creatures as large as horses. Still more shadowy were the sinister crocodilian outlines – alligators and other uncouth shapes, culminating in the colossal lizard, the iguanodon. Folded behind were dragon forms and clouds of flying reptiles: still underneath were fishy beings of lower development; and so on, till the lifetime scenes of the fossil confronting him were a present and modern condition of things. These images passed before Knight's inner eye in less than half a minute, and he was again considering the actual present. Was he to die? . . . The previous sensation, that it was improbable he would die, was fainter now. (240–41)

At this point Hardy steps aside to comment that "those musing weather-beaten West-country folk who pass the greater part of their days and nights out of doors" have learned to regard Nature as moody, "read" her "as a person" (as though the term "anthropomorphize" might need translation for his readers), who "scatters heartless severities and overwhelming generosities in lawless caprice" like a cat playing with her prey before devouring it (241). In the same spirit of cat and mouse, he then cuttingly remarks that because of all of Knight's objectivity, native and learned, "Such a way of thinking had been absurd to [him], but he began to adopt it now" (241).

Soon, Knight can not help but take Nature's tortures personally. Because of the atmospheric cataract he so expertly pointed out to Elfride, it begins to rain upwards upon him, nearly forcing his fingers from their grasp. He can no longer regard the wind as neutrally "indifferent" but instead it becomes for him "a cosmic agency, active, lashing, eager for conquest" (242). He is sure he has been hanging on for at least ten minutes, but Hardy points out that Elfride "had been gone but three." Knight laments that the rain has never been so heavy or so cold. Hardy corrects the misperception: "He was again mistaken. The rain was quite ordinary in quantity; the air in temperature. It was, as is usual, the menacing attitude in which they approached him that magnified their powers" (242). Knight, who had always resisted any superstition or belief in the supernatural, suddenly cannot believe the sun would dare to shine at such a moment and sees it as "a red face looking on with a drunken leer" (243).

For a moment, Knight lapses into hubristic denial: "the thought – he could not help thinking – that his death would be a deliberate loss to earth of good material; that such an experiment in killing might have been practised upon some less developed life" (243). Hardy then interjects: "A fancy some people hold, when in a bitter mood, is that inexorable circumstance only tries to prevent what intelligence attempts. Renounce a desire for a long-contested position, and go on another tack, and after a while the prize is thrown at you, seemingly in disappointment that no more tantalizing is possible" (243). Hardy has Nature, apparently, play such a game with Knight now. Just when he falls into despair and has given "up thoughts of life utterly and entirely," Elfride arrives to save him.

~

Although *A Pair of Blue Eyes* is one of Hardy's first novels, the genius of this scene gives clear indication of Hardy's position on many of the philosophical themes that he will return to frequently throughout his career: the interrelationship of humankind and nature; Darwinism and the fossil record; science, religion, and superstition as responses to natural phenomena; the anthropomorphization of an indifferent cosmos; the hubristic error of human learning; the complexity of male–female relationships. Astronomy and geology both have lessons to teach in this story, and neither Elfride or Knight really learns all that they could have. If Elfride could have learned to read the signs of nature as predictors and taken appropriate action, she could have saved herself. What Knight should have gained from his brush with death was the humbling recognition that his education and pride are ultimately powerless and meaningless. For all of his powers of natural observation, critical discernment, and scientific perception, Knight allows his over-rational visionary idealism to blind him to the reality that Elfride's loving kindness and personal sacrifice has life-saving power no matter what the circumstances of the universe. Even after he has gotten first-hand experience of her ability to save him from a fall, he does not see this truth and cannot value it. As Elfride's life force is wasted in the novel's sad ending, Hardy expresses more sympathy for her emotionally fatalistic resignation to the power that abstract forces exert upon her than to Knight's callous idealism which denies that Elfride's heart is the purest thing he will encounter on this earth.

Hardy's evocation of the pastoral Gothic in *A Pair of Blue Eyes* – where his characters interact upon a rural geological terrain under open astronomical skies – is an appropriate mode for carrying a story in which he demonstrates that country or city, local or global, some of the deepest human miseries result from mistakes in our own meaning-making. Throughout his career, Hardy engages in an extended thought-experiment with these essential elements, altering the quantities and qualities of the variables, and relating the multifarious results.

Far From the Madding Crowd (1874)

In *Far From the Madding Crowd*, Hardy again explores the central cosmic themes that he introduced in *A Pair of Blue Eyes*. This time, however, he de-emphasizes the Gothic consequences of the struggle among modern, medieval and natural forces being played out upon and within the rural environment and culture, so the story need not end unhappily. Redefining and refining his conception of fate and the role it may play in humankind's "predicament," Hardy re-focuses upon the dramatic potential for tragedy or joy inherent within the pastoral mode itself, with the time line following the natural rhythms of the shepherd's calendar. Situating his narrative in a fictional time and space that seem to represent the lingering last bastion of pastoral possibilities, Hardy's description of seasonal and astronomical cycles underscores the equalizing interplay of the comic, ironic and tragic in the daily lives and yearly rhythms experienced by his minor and major characters. Again, Hardy juxtaposes natural and artificial approaches to human life and work to suggest how the power of human love – as manifested by caring and nurturing each other, planting and harvesting the land, and human procreation – can be a potent creative force, exerting universal influence.

Gabriel's Cosmological Character

In the opening pages of *Far From the Madding Crowd*, the reader is immediately struck by the startlingly increased sophistication of Hardy's use of astronomical imagery. The story begins with Hardy's introductory description of Gabriel Oak, a self-employed shepherd. Among Gabriel's peculiarities is the fact that although he has his grandfather's watch, it is not reliable and he must remedy this by "constant comparisons with and observations of the sun and stars."[6] In the next few pages, Hardy describes Gabriel keeping watch over his flock on a clear December night.

> The sky was clear – remarkably clear – and the twinkling of all the stars seemed to be but throbs of one body, timed by a common pulse. The North Star was directly in the wind's eye, and since evening the Bear had swung round it outwardly to the east, till he was now at a right angle with the meridian. A difference of color in the stars – oftener read of than seen in England – was really perceptible here. The sovereign brilliancy of Sirius pierced the eye with a steely glitter, the star called Capella was yellow, Aldebaran and Betelgueux shone with a fiery red. (12)

Hardy's association of the stars twinkling with organic "pulsing" may have had its source in William Herschel's developmental theories regarding nebulae. The notion that the stars were not "fixed" either in space or uniform in their stage of physical evolution was intriguing to many nineteenth-century writers, and Hardy's comparison is later echoed by George Meredith in his poem, "Meditation under Stars." As Hardy's inclusion of the phrase "oftener read of than seen" seems to indicate, his description of stellar colors may be directly owing to a section from Richard Proctor's *Essays* entitled "Coloured Suns."[7]

---

[6]   Thomas Hardy, *Far from the Madding Crowd*, ed. Robert C. Schweik (New York: W. W. Norton and Company, 1986), 8; hereafter cited by page number within the text.

[7]   Although, the possibility also exists that Hardy was detailing the celestial scene as he himself observed it in the rural night sky far enough removed from industrial pollution to permit "good seeing." As Pete Richards relates from his own amateur astronomical experience, the view from the Canary Islands, March, 1994, was so remarkably similar that he was inspired to quote Hardy's passage to describe it: "Then we looked upwards . . . '*The sky was clear - remarkably clear . . . A difference of colour in the stars - oftener read of than seen in England -*

In tropical countries the colours of the stars form a very obvious and a very beautiful phenomenon. The whole heaven seems set with variously coloured gems. In our latitudes, none but the brightest stars exhibit distinctly marked colours to the naked eye. Sirius, Regulus, and Spica are white stars; Betelgeux, Aldebaran, Arcturus, and Antares are red; Procyon, Capella and the Pole-star are yellow; Castor exhibits a slightly green tint; where Vega and Altair are bluish. (257)

Hardy employs the specific details of his popular knowledge of astronomy to establish from the outset that Gabriel is especially empowered to observe the natural universe. As a shepherd, he would have more opportunity than most to study the night sky and observe its motions, of course; but Hardy indicates that there is something else at work as well. Hardy gives Gabriel a special sensitivity to the natural world. He can *feel* the earth turn beneath him. Hardy's patient, poetic, prose description of the phenomenon of the earth's rotation is not only lovely scene- and mood-setting, it establishes the essential conditions of the universe as the special nature of his character, Gabriel, perceives them.

To persons standing alone on a hill during a clear midnight such as this, the roll of the world eastward is almost a palpable movement. The sensation may be caused by the panoramic glide of the stars past earthly objects, which is perceptible in a few minutes of stillness, or by the better outlook upon space that a hill affords, or by the wind or by the solitude; but whatever be its origin the impression of riding along is vivid and abiding. The poetry of motion is a phrase much in use, and to enjoy the epic form of that gratification it is necessary to stand on a hill at a small hour of the night, and, having first expanded with a sense of difference from the mass of civilized mankind, who are dreamwrapt and disregardful of all such proceedings at this time, long and quietly watch your stately progress through the stars. After such a nocturnal reconnoitre it is hard to get back to earth, and to believe that the consciousness of such majestic speeding is derived from a tiny human frame. (12)

Gabriel Oak, by his very name (celestial, yet rooted), is in tune with the heavens and the earth. He is a hero who represents the best approach to the "human dilemma": how to live with life, not against it; how to love life and not fear it. By careful juxtaposition, Hardy relays that this "down to earth" approach to life is amenable within the context of the greater stellar universe. After warming a newborn lamb

---

was really perceptible here. The sovereign brilliancy of Sirius pierced the eye with a steely glitter, the star Capella was yellow, Aldebaran and Betelgueux [sic] shone with a fiery red.' The italicised text is not mine, it's Thomas Hardy's . . . in *Far From the Madding Crowd*, but it is the perfect description of the night sky we saw from the edge of the caldera on Tenerife. [. . .] The star Canopus, which is below the horizon from the British Isles, was high in the sky. Another immediate impression was the great number of naked eye stars which made many of the constellations difficult to recognise . . ." as posted on the website of the University of Cambridge's Institute of Astronomy <http://www.ast.cam.ac.uk/~ipswich/Events/Excursions/Excursion_Reports.htm>

within his house, Oak returns the "little creature" to its mother, then "carefully" examines the sky "to ascertain the time of night from the altitudes of the stars" (14). Hardy's account accurately depicts the prominent features of the late night winter sky in England.

> The Dog-star and Aldebaran, pointing to the restless Pleiades, were half-way up the southern sky, and between them hung Orion, which gorgeous constellation never burnt more vividly than now, as it soared forth above the rim of the landscape. Castor and Pollux with their gloomy square of Pegasus was creeping round to the north-west; far away through the plantation Vega sparkled like a lamp suspended amid the leafless trees, and Cassiopeia's chair stood daintily poised on the uppermost boughs.
> "One o'clock" said Gabriel.
> Being a man not without a frequent consciousness that there was some charm in this life he led, he stood still after looking at the sky as a useful instrument, and regarded it in an appreciative spirit as a work of art superlatively beautiful. . . . Human shapes, interferences, troubles, and joys were all as if they were not, and there seemed to be on the shaded hemisphere of the globe no sentient being save himself; he could fancy them all gone round to the sunny side. (15)

By nature, Gabriel has a truly cosmic perspective on his life. He perceives himself to be carried around on a planet in a solar system in interstellar space. He relates to his cosmic life via the utility of the information he can glean from the patterns and behavior of natural phenomena, his appreciation for their beauty, and the sense he has of being one among many, yet completely content in the company of his own consciousness.

Although Hardy could have relied on pastoral conventions as easy literary justification for attributing special natural abilities to his main character, instead, he further sets Gabriel apart from the crowd – even his country neighbors – by revealing that his star-reading skills are far from the norm for rural folk and urban dwellers alike. Although such techniques had been part of a long tradition of rural knowledge that Gabriel has kept alive – along with calligraphy and sundial-making (one of Hardy's own special crafts) – Hardy is careful to depict his time-telling as a contemporary rarity, no longer a country commonplace. Gabriel is widely admired for it by the farm workers around him; but this harmonious relation to the stars serves as an outward manifestation of an inner state of being that truly marks him as unique. Even in the greatest adversity, after he has lost everything he has worked his life to earn, Gabriel has about him a "dignified calm," an "indifference to fate which, though it often makes a villain of a man, is the basis of his sublimity when it does not" (34). Hardy would later find a philosophical twin to this statement in Schopenhauer's *Studies in Pessimism*. About 1890, Hardy entered the passage in his literary notebook: "A man is great or small according as he leans to one or the other of these views of life [that it is not worth any great anxiety, or that it is momentous]" (*LN* II. 1794).

In the climactic storm scene, Gabriel's skill as a reader of nature's "signs" will designate him once and for all as the "natural" hero, who lives in attentive accordance with nature as the angel in *Paradise Lost* told Adam mankind should. *Paradise Lost* is one of the few books Gabriel owns and he takes its message to heart. He willingly risks his own life to save the property of the woman he loves. As Gabriel and Bathsheba work together to save the farm, they are bonded by their common purpose, as were Adam and Eve. "[L]ove, life, everything human, seemed small and trifling in such close juxtaposition with an infuriated universe" (194).

Cosmology and Consciousness

Although Gabriel is the one character in this story for whom astronomical and cosmological nature is most closely aligned to his inner nature, Hardy has liberally interwoven astronomical imagery with his characters' psychologies throughout *Far From the Madding Crowd*. The reader learns from Hardy that although material causes and emotional effects are "not to be arranged in a regular equation" (103), astronomy and geometry both serve well as comparisons for doing so. Farmer Boldwood thinks of women as comets and can only see them poorly in terms of unfocused optics.

> To Boldwood women had been remote phenomena . . . comets of such uncertain aspect, movement and permanence, that whether their orbits were as geometrical, unchangeable, and as subject to laws as his own, or absolutely erratic as they superficially appeared, he had not deemed it his duty to consider. (93)

Apparently aware of professional astronomers' technique for making naked-eye observations of comets and other nebulous bodies by looking slightly to one side of them, Hardy relates that Boldwood "had never inspected a woman with the very centre and focus of his glance; they had struck upon all his senses at wide angles" (93). Throughout the novel, Boldwood's vision will stay off-center and Hardy will describe his private cogitations in terms of optical allusions emphasizing how the wrongly angled, and unnatural reflections of indirect natural light misguide his insight into the nature of things. At one point Boldwood will look at Bathsheba and see that his misperceptions of her are reflected back at him like "sorry gleams from a broken mirror" (156). Hardy uses these images from optics to indicate the inner state of mental processes and conceptual frameworks by which his characters interpret their worlds and each other. Boldwood's unfocused and irregular vision (as seen in scenes illuminated with oddly cast moonlight and sunlight) indicate that Boldwood and Bathsheba are an unnatural pair and a marriage between them would not be one "made in heaven."

In addition to direct references to the sun, moon, stars, comets and optics, Hardy associates his characters' inner lives with more abstract cosmological theories and ideas, such as the nebular hypothesis. As Bathsheba follows its progress, a swarm of bees settles in a nearby tree.

A process somewhat analogous to that of alleged formations of the universe, time and times ago, was observable. The bustling swarm had swept the sky in a scattered and unified haze, which now thickened to a nebulous centre: this glided on to a bough and grew still denser, till it formed a solid spot upon the light. (140)

Hardy may have learned about the nebular hypothesis directly from many accounts of the highly popularized works of Laplace, or from William Herschel's similar theory described in his own much popularized texts. According to Herschel, the life cycle of nebulae begins when the largest star within nebulous clouds attracts others to it to form a cluster, or island universe, through the joint action of inward attraction and projectile forces operating within the cluster. The greater the sphericity of the nebula, the longer the "conglobing" effects of stellar evolution have been at work. Herschel's work directly influenced Tennyson, and Hardy may well have noticed this bee-swarm comparison as it appeared in the verses quoted on the title page of Proctor's *Essays*. More importantly for this point in Hardy's story, however, is the association of nebular development that Herschel himself insisted on, namely, that it provided evidence of the essential *unity* of celestial and terrestrial processes of creation. Just so, Bathsheba has been in the dark about nature, including her own human nature; she has been oblivious to her proper social sphere, and has had to learn to read the signs through social error, shame and hardship. She further needs to learn that organic, chemical and biological forces in the world are working in concert with the abstract, inorganic and physical to effect change, growth and continuity. Later in the narrative, Hardy will show her gaining awareness and appreciation for the fact that her own small self is participating in this grand process of survival and renewal in operation throughout the cosmos.

Hardy extends this vision of the unity of organic and inorganic to the agricultural environment and community surrounding Bathsheba. Hardy casually describes rural folk in terms of astronomy: a circle of farm workers passing the cup becomes a cup making "a gradual revolution" around those of the lower sphere who "revolve in the same orbit" (47, 48). Two drinkers facing each other across a three-legged circular-table "might have been said to resemble the setting sun and the full moon shining vis-a-vis across the globe" (218). The old maltster bent with age "seemed to approach the grave as a hyperbolic curve approaches a straight line – less directly as he got nearer, till it was doubtful if he would ever reach it at all" (83). Fanny, a fallen woman, weak with illness and heavy with child, struggles down a country road on a moonless, starless night toward the Casterbridge lights which shine before her like a "halo," an "aurora," and finally, "like fallen Pleiads" (207).

As in *A Pair of Blue Eyes,* Hardy again offers pointed contrasts between natural and artificial light. Hardy's critique of the artificial centers on the character and personality of Troy. Hardy describes the flashes of reflected light during Troy's "sacrifice" of Bathsheba within the center of his sword exercise as an "aurora militaris." Troy's red uniform is often mistaken for the brightness of the sun and temporarily distracts the eye of Bathsheba away from the natural (and celestial) light represented by Gabriel. Near the end of the story, Troy finally recognizes that he is like an ephemeral atmospheric phenomenon, not the solid hero he expected himself to be.

> He had not minded the peculiarities of his birth, the vicissitudes of his life, the meteor-like uncertainty of all that related to him, because these appertained to the hero of his story, without whom there would have been no story at all for him; and it seemed to be only in the nature of things that matters would right themselves at some proper date and / wind up well. This very morning the illusion completed its disappearance, and, as it were, all of a sudden, Troy hated himself. (243–4)

Pastoral Potential in a Darwinian Cosmos

Although astronomical understanding is linked essentially throughout *Far From the Madding Crowd* to Gabriel's character, Hardy intimately conjoins such knowledge with the imagery of Darwinism to show the richness and fertility of life on earth and to emphasize how all lives must be in harmony with their surroundings – on all scales of being, earthly to celestial – to survive. Bathsheba must learn lessons from both astronomy and Darwinian evolution in order to appreciate Gabriel and to develop and appropriately apply her own natural skills and talents. Working side-by-side with Gabriel against the storm, she recognizes the value of attending to the natural signs of the heavens. After spending the night in a marsh to escape the reality of her failed marriage to Troy, she emerges into a new dawn and begins to value anew the life within her and around her.

> There was an opening towards the east, and the glow from the as yet unrisen sun attracted her eyes thither. From her feet, and between the beautiful yellowing ferns with their feathery arms, the ground sloped downwards to a hollow, in which was a species of swamp, dotted with fungi. A morning mist hung over it now – a noisome yet magnificent / silvery veil, full of light from the sun, yet semi-opaque – the hedge behind it being in some measure hidden by its hazy luminousness. Up the sides of this depression grew sheaves of the common rush, and here and there a peculiar species of flag, the blades of which glistened in the emerging sun, like scythes. But the general aspect of the swamp was malignant. From its moist and poisonous coat seemed to be exhaled the essences of evil things in the earth, and in the waters under the earth. The fungi grew in all manner of positions from rotting leaves and tree stumps, some exhibiting to her listless gaze their clammy tops, others their oozing gills. Some were marked with great splotches, red as arterial blood, others were saffron yellow, and others tall and attenuated, with stems like macaroni. Some were leathery and of richest browns. The hollow seemed a nursery of pestilences small and great, in the immediate neighbourhood of comfort and health, and Bathsheba arose with a tremor at the thought of having passed the night on the brink of so dismal a place. (232–3)

Here, at last, Bathsheba comes to understand that survival through struggle is not a pretty sight. Nature, left to herself, produces mutant unhealthful plants, neither lovely nor beneficial. Gabriel offers her a model of survival through cooperation and by the novel's end she will realize that by working together they can make the controlled environment of their farms productive and beautiful.

As the novel closes, the calendar has come full-circle and it is Christmas time again. Like the star of Bethlehem in the Christmas story, celestial light will lead Bathsheba to the right choice of mate and way of life.

> So desolate was Bathsheba this evening, that in an absolute hunger for pity and sympathy, and miserable in that she appeared to have outlived the only true friendship she had ever owned, she put on her bonnet and cloak and went down to Oak's house just after sunset, guided on her way by the pale primrose rays of a crescent moon a few days old.
>
> A lively firelight shone from the window, but nobody was visible in the room. She tapped nervously, and then thought it doubtful if it were right for a single woman to call upon a bachelor who lived alone, although he was her manager, and she might be supposed to call on business without any real impropriety. Gabriel opened the door, and the moon shone upon his forehead. (301)

When Gabriel and Bathsheba marry, the essential rightness of the bond is celebrated by the workfolk who joyfully remark upon how "wonderful naterel" the pair is (307). Hardy allows them to make this final choral comment on the necessity and value of a companionable male–female relationship, following the sentiments of his own earlier narration:

> This good fellowship – camaraderie – usually occurring through similarity of pursuits, is unfortunately seldom superadded to love between the sexes, because men and women associate, not in their labours, but in their pleasures merely. Where, however, happy circumstance permits its development, the compounded feeling proves itself to be the only love which is as strong as death – that love which many waters cannot / quench, nor the floods drown, beside which the passion usually called by the name is evanescent as steam. (303–4)

~

Bathsheba's reception of Gabriel's tutelage in natural knowledge is the only wholly successful and life-affirming account of such a male–female information exchange in Hardy's fiction and even so, she must tame her inner nature in order to achieve harmony with the external conditions of life. In subsequent works, Hardy continues to evaluate the possibilities of various love pairings within a variety of cosmic circumstances. How men and women utilize and respond to knowledge of natural forces will become a powerful recurrent theme. In his later novels, the pastoral potential for joy has played itself out and the emplotment of women's education into natural knowledge most often leads to ambivalent or tragic consequences (Grace, Eustacia, Sue). In the cases of other heroines (Elfride, Viviette, and Tess), astronomical knowledge of the cosmic situation will be directly connected to a fall into sexuality and an extinguishing of life itself. No other characters beneath Hardy's stars will join Bathsheba and Gabriel in achieving a love "as strong as death."

The Return of the Native (1878)

The Return of the Native is often considered Hardy's most representative work and his first major novel. The maturity of Hardy's writing style and its technical mastery set this novel on a level above *A Pair of Blue Eyes* and *Far From the Madding Crowd*, although it is misleading to consider Hardy's development of literary skills as progressing along a linear path. In some of his later work, he will treat scientific concepts and their implications with greater sophistication than in the three early works discussed in this chapter, yet, those same "mature" works will show a marked decline in subtlety of natural description, dialogue, and characterization. Michael Millgate, in *Thomas Hardy: His Career as a Novelist*, marvelously encapsulates Hardy's achievement in this work.

> The new novel opened with a piece of scene setting and natural description far more ambitious than anything Hardy had previously attempted, and the early chapters made it abundantly clear that he was not only drawing more heavily upon more sources of imagery than ever before but deploying those images in a deliberate search for expressionistic and broadly symbolic effects. Hardy had by this time learned that there was much more to novels than characters and plots. He now realised that narrative and thematic statements could be made through setting structure, symbolism, the conscious exploitation of pastoral and other conventions, and in *The Return of the Native* he set out to turn his discoveries to the fullest possible artistic advantage. Coming to the novel in the chronological sequence of Hardy's work, one senses that he felt the time had now come for him to aim beyond mere handiness at a serial, and to concern himself with 'the proper artistic balance of the complete work.'[8]

As in previous novels, Hardy is primarily concerned in this narrative with investigating human relationships before a universal background. This time geology and geography provide central symbolic force as they are embodied in the physical presence of the heath – the setting and literal "environment" of the novel's story. The heath, as many critics have noticed, is representative of impersonal forces at work in the universe, eternal truths about the relationship of humankind and the land, a repository of the human past, and a carrier of meaning for the human lives existing upon it. In the impressive opening pages, Hardy leaves no doubt about the importance of this environment, its physical presence, and shape, to the human players who live upon it. Time makes little impression upon it. The heath controls the effects of

---

[8]   Millgate, *Thomas Hardy: His Career as a Novelist* 130; hereafter: *Career.*

astronomical time, can delay dawn, "sadden" noon, rush the fall of dusk. The heath has the power to intensify fears caused by darkness on moonless nights. It is proof that the world and firmament are divided by time no less than by matter. This particular environment is as "unaltered "as the stars overhead. Upon the heath, the large barrow is the very "pole and axis" of the local universe, the highest point in the area, so that above it there was "nothing that could be mapped elsewhere than on a celestial globe."[9]

The Neo-Greek Cosmos of the Heath

In the fictional cosmos of *The Return*, Hardy's conceptualization of fate becomes increasingly classical, and in particular, Greek. In this novel, Hardy uses fate, in various manifestations, to create a sense of an elemental, Empedoclean universe in which matter (even living matter) is put into motion by the immaterial forces of Love and Strife. This mechanistic world view generates a mechanical plot for the novel that is fatalistic in outlook and tone. To underscore the effect of the Greek dramatic elements, at significant turns in the plot, Hardy interjects sardonic choral pronouncements: "Providence is nothing if not coquettish" (94); such are the "cruel satires that Fate loves to indulge in" (163); or Clym's bitter: "I am getting used to the horror of my existence" (294). To keep before the reader the deterministic nature of nature, Hardy draws upon astronomy to depict cycles of time intervals – hours, days, nights, months and seasons – that whirl like fate's spindle. The relation of Greek fatalism to the modern variety is made more pointed as Eustacia herself is compared directly to the Goddess of Fate, and the character of Clym is made to embody the effects of the "new" fatalism.

> In Clym Yeobright's face could be dimly seen the typical countenance of the future. Should there be a classic period to art hereafter, its Pheidias may produce such faces. The view of life as a thing / to be put up with, replacing that zest for existence which was so intense in early civilizations, must ultimately enter so thoroughly into the constitution of the advanced races that its facial expression will become accepted as a new artistic departure. . . .
>
> The truth seems to be that a long line of disillusive centuries has permanently displaced the Hellenic idea of life, or whatever it may be called. What the Greeks only suspected we know well; what their Aeschylus imagined our nursery children feel. That old-fashioned revelling in the general situation grows less and less possible as we uncover the defects of natural laws, and see the quandary that man is in by their operation. (131–2)

That our increasingly sophisticated knowledge of nature should have the ironic consequence of cutting us off from what pleasure we may once have felt in being a

---

[9]   Thomas Hardy, *The Return of the Native*, ed. James Gindin (New York: W. W. Norton and Company, 1969) 2–9; hereafter cited by page number within the text.

part of it – and might otherwise still have been free to feel – was not lost on Hardy. In *The Return*, the fast-fading pastoral realm of *Far From the Madding Crowd* has retreated even farther and only the most rural of rural folk are still able to participate in traditional revels, dances and seasonal rites. Such rites hold no joy for the others.

Astronomy, in fact or lore, is central to many of the workfolk's superstitions and rituals in *The Return of the Native* and Hardy's descriptions of them allow him to allude to the many levels upon which natural laws operate and the wide range of human response to their operation. There is no precisely and particularly "nineteenth-century" astronomy and cosmology in the storyline. Instead, some characters live and move and have their being in a perceived cosmos that seems frozen in a timeless pre-Christian pastoral culture, while others feel themselves to exist within an almost skyless cosmos comprised of the actions and reactions generated by modern social, political and economic forces. Hardy uses astronomical images to allude to his main characters' highly individual conceptions of time and space. While the countryfolk carry on age-old rituals of seasonal time-telling and rural chores, Eustacia carries a telescope and hourglass with her as personal symbols to remind her of the material nature of time and her desire to transcend the immediate space around her, if only in the abstract, as far as her field of vision will allow her to imagine.

Cosmology and Character

As Hardy's management of the geography of his fictional space becomes more complex in *The Return*, so too does his use of particular astronomical phenomena become more "expressionistic and broadly symbolic" (in Millgate's phrase) than in previous works. As in the other novels, there are many seemingly incidental, but meaningful, comparisons of characters with astronomical images. Mrs. Yeobright appears on the barrow in a "superior" manner carrying "her weight of character . . . like planets [carry] their atmospheres along with them in their orbits" (26). As she falls victim to sun stroke and an adder bite, her final thoughts and dying soul will be compared to a falling meteor as her body escapes its earthly orbit.

> While she looked a heron arose on that side of the sky and flew on with his face towards the sun. He had come dripping wet from some pool in the valleys, and as he flew the edges and lining of his wings, his thighs, and his breast were so caught by the bright sunbeams that he appeared as if formed of burnished silver. Up in the zenith where he was seemed a free and happy place, away from all contact with the earthly ball to which she was pinioned; and she wished that she could rise uncrushed from its surface and fly as he flew then.
>
> But being a mother, it was inevitable that she should soon cease to ruminate upon her own condition. Had the track of her next thought been marked by a streak in the air, like the path of a meteor, it would have shown a direction contrary to the heron's and have descended to the eastward upon the roof of Clym's house. (226)

Indeed, the interrelations of many of the characters can be mapped in correspondence to each other according to the astronomical phenomena with which they are associated. Hardy employs the orbital motions of planets to relate the relative positions of minor characters. When a little boy approaches Mrs. Yeobright, as she rests during her fatal visit to Clym's, his motion is described as that "tendency of a minute body to gravitate towards a greater" (223).[10] In another case, a hired hand's relation to Eustacia is captured by an astronomical comparison: "she had been a lovely wonder, predestined to an orbit in which the whole of his own was but a point" (258).

Hardy's description of the character of Eustacia grows in complexity as it accumulates astronomical associations. She is considered by moonlit revelers to be "as deep as the North Star" (40). At another moonlit country dance with Wildeve, she is described "like the planet Mercury surrounded by the lustre of sunset, her permanent brillancy passed without much notice in the temporary glory of the situation" (205). She is transfixed, caught, within the contradictory influences of the celestial lights that dance upon her: the pagan "lunacy" and lust of the moon; the unfathomable remoteness of Polaris; Mercurial elusiveness. When Clym comes into her life, Eustacia's lover, Wildeve, is described as an eclipsed sun, resembling "at present the rayless outlines of the sun through smoked glass" (116). Thomasin will be associated with the wholesome, nurturing warmth of the sun as an "oblique band of sunlight which follow[s] her through the door became [her] well" and it "illuminate[s] her·as she illuminate[s] the heath" (167). By contrast, the sun's connections to Clym are more evocative of the mythical experience of Icarus. Hardy makes it clear that Clym's disabling photophobia has direct material causes. His eyes were overexposed to sunlight and that exposure was the direct result of his wrong-headed choice to work as a rural day-laborer, work for which he is not "fit" by nature. The immaterial cause of Clym's blindness, however, which Hardy makes equally clear, is a psychological one, which now, ironically, like his physical condition, causes him to avoid seeing the reality of things in anywhere near their true light (194). Dreading insight, he is psychologically photophobic, literally fearing how things might appear were light shed upon them.

---

[10]   Interestingly, there are at least three novels in which Hardy uses this description. In *A Pair of Blue Eyes* a little boy follows Knight "by that natural law of physics which causes lesser bodies to gravitate toward the greater" (183). In *Far From the Madding Crowd*, Oak notices the way that Bathsheba unconsciously adjusts herself to Boldwood's speech patterns and mannerisms. He sees "she was far from having a wish to appear mysteriously connected with him; but woman at the impressionable age gravitates to the larger body not only in her choice of words, which is apparent every day, but even in her shades of tone and humour when the influence is great" (116).

Astronomical Tropes and Tropism

The most significant usage of a single astronomical phenomenon in *The Return* prefigures the type of extended metaphors that Hardy will develop further in *Two on a Tower*. Hardy devotes a whole chapter of one of the novel's five books to a detailed description of a lunar eclipse. Through a complex analogy, Hardy compares the human observers of the celestial event to it and foreshadows the development of their relationship by his description of the stages of the eclipse. Evening falls and Clym leaves his mother to go up to the Rainbarrow to watch the eclipse. As the heath was dry "he flung himself down upon the barrow, his face towards the moon, which depicted a small image of herself in each of his eyes" (153). He feels slightly guilty about the circumstances under which he has departed, knowing that "this was the first time that he had been ostensibly frank as to his purpose while really concealing it" (154). Soon, however, he becomes lost in contemplation of the features of the moonscape. He considers the reasons why he has returned to the heath and the kind of life he longs for.

> In returning to labour in this sequestered spot he had anticipated an escape from the chafing of social necessities; yet behold they were here also. More than ever he longed to be in some world where personal ambition was not the only recognized form of progress – such, perhaps, as might have been the case at some time or other in the silvery globe then shining upon him. His eye travelled over the length and breadth of that distant country – over the Bay of Rainbows, the sombre Sea of Crises, the Ocean of Storms, the Lake of Dreams, the vast Walled Plains, and the wondrous Ring Mountains – till he almost felt himself to be voyaging bodily through its wild scenes, standing on its hollow hills, traversing its deserts, descending its vales and old sea bottoms, or mounting to the edges of its craters.
>
> While he watched the far-removed landscape a tawny stain grew into being on the lower verge: the eclipse had begun. This marked a preconcerted moment: for the remote celestial phenomenon had been pressed into sublunary service as a lover's signal. (154)

At this signal, Clym's mind "flew back to earth." Anxiously he anticipates the arrival of Eustacia. "Minute after minute passed by, perhaps ten minutes passed, and the shadow on the moon perceptively widened" (154). Suddenly, he hears a rustling and "in a moment the figure was in his arms, and his lips upon hers. "My Eustacia!" "Clym dearest!" (154). To which, Hardy comments ironically: "Such a situation had less than three months brought forth" (154). This last comment will be echoed in *Two on a Tower* in a similar meeting of lovers during astronomical observations.

As the eclipse progresses, the lovers hold hands, watching it. They speak of how long it has been since they have seen one another. Clym studies Eustacia's face by moonlight as he has just studied that of the moon itself. What Clym should see by reading her face is evidence that the terrain of Eustacia's psyche is composed of the same contradictory elements as that of the lunar surface he has just so accurately surveyed. Their subsequent conversation ranges across a dizzyingly random array of hopes, beliefs, fantasies, and feelings, not unlike the moon's topography which consists of the "Bay of Rainbows, the sombre Sea of Crises, the Ocean of Storms, the Lake of Dreams," mountains, valleys, and deserts. A less stable or hospitable environment would be hard to imagine, but Clym remains blind to the potential meaning he should get out of this celestial analogy. Eustacia, however, has no trouble reading a lot into the phenomenon. She expresses fears that Clym's mother might "eclipse" their relationship and tries to convince him that her shadow may fall between them. As Clym asks Eustacia to marry him, she sees that the moon is half-eclipsed and that their time together is "slipping, slipping, slipping." Eustacia then interprets the "eclipsed moonlight" as it shines in a golden glow upon Clym's face as an indication that he should be doing better things in a better place. As they prepare to part, Eustacia sees the eclipse as an hour-glass: "Yes, the sand has nearly slipped away, I see, and the eclipse is creeping on more and more." Feeling panicky at the visible passing of time, she will not let Clym go until the moon is in full eclipse. Insisting that he speak of remote and exotic places that he has been, Eustacia imaginatively escapes the here and now of the scene, and psychologically escapes, as well, having to contemplate Clym's all-too-real and down-to-earth marriage proposal.

Neither Clym or Eustacia sees that their entire natures are at cross-purposes, but after they part, Clym realizes the constituent factors of the basic dilemma that he now faces as a result of his marriage proposal. He is caught in the middle of a three-body problem like the one that produced the eclipse: "Three antagonistic growths had to be kept alive: his mother's trust in him, his plan for becoming a teacher, and Eustacia's happiness. His fervid nature could not afford to relinquish one of these, though two of the three were as many as he could hope to preserve" (159). Clym will not find a solution to this insoluble problem. In the end, blinded by the sun and his own high-flown ideals, Clym will lose his mother, Eustacia, and his dreams.

Significantly, throughout this important scene, Hardy draws upon traditional lunar myth and lore as well as contemporary scientific lunar science and nomenclature to build up a history of the associations and meanings that human beings attach to that celestial body. The moon has governed chastity and fertility, caused lunacy and lust, lit lovers' trysts and symbolized their inconstancy. Even the scientific names attached to its topographical features carry human hopes and fears. During the Victorian era, eclipses (both solar and lunar) were the objects of popular watch parties as well as daring scientific expeditions. As such, they were associated with the romance of discovery and exploration, as well as the dominance of empire. In theoretical and gravitational astronomy, eclipses represented the most famous of insoluble problems: how to apply math and physics to calculate the complex influences of mass and gravitation among three or more bodies in space and predict their motions. The problem had daunted Newton and had challenged some of the best mathematical minds in the century since. It should come as no surprise that whatever emotional calculus or forms of rational analysis Clym possesses, these qualities of heart and mind will not be sufficient to resolve the inequalities of the system in which he finds himself. In point of fact, given the nature of the forces and the closeness of the bodies involved, he should feel the consequences of their conjunction that much *more* intensely, as the gravitational force between him and Eustacia is far stronger than that operating between masses separated by vast distances. Indeed Eustacia's "mass" exerts a greater force upon Clym than any "influence" (mythological, astrological, astrophysical) that might be emanating from the moon. While it was already a commonplace in Victorian humor (as it is in our own) to substitute gravitational attraction as a trope for sexual attraction, here Hardy takes the physics seriously.

To foreshadow the tragedies to come, immediately after Clym and Eustacia marry, Hardy shifts the physics of the astronomical metaphor he uses to describe them. As a couple, away from Clym's mother, in their own little house, as husband and wife, they now represent a living *two*-body problem.

> They were enclosed in a luminous mist, which hid from them surroundings of any inharmonious colour, and gave to all things the character of light. When it rained they were charmed, because they could remain indoors together all day with such a show of reason; when it was fine they were charmed, because they could sit together on the hills. *They were like those double stars which revolve round and round each other, and from a distance appear to be one.* The absolute solitude in which they lived intensified their reciprocal thoughts; yet some might have said that it had the disadvantage of consuming their mutual affections at a fearfully prodigal rate. (emphasis added, 187)

Several months thereafter, husband and wife have grown apart; they have in fact changed places in respect to one another: "The feelings of husband and wife varied, in some measure, inversely with their positions. Clym, the afflicted man, was cheerful; and he even tried to comfort her, who had never felt a moment of physical suffering in her whole life" (200). Clym realizes that his wife's illusions about his "brilliance" have disappeared and have been replaced with an image of him "in brown leather." They, as double stars, have revolved around each other so that Clym's "light" is now eclipsed by Eustacia's. Soon, their orbits around each other will break apart entirely. At her death, Eustacia becomes a dead "light" and her beauty then: "eclipsed all her living phases. Pallor did not include all the quality of her complexion, which seemed more than whiteness; it was almost light" (293). In grief, Clym loses all grip on his ideals and dreams and blames himself for his losses. He is wrong to do so, Hardy thinks: "Human beings, in their generous endeavors to construct a hypothesis that shall not degrade a First Cause, have always hesitated to conceive a dominate power of lower moral quality than their own; and, even while they sit down and weep by the / waters of Babylon, invent excuses for the oppression which prompts their tears" (295–6).

~

Hardy's account of the changing dynamics between Clym and Eustacia is astronomically true to the physics of binary star systems, as William and John

Herschel and Richard Proctor had all described them. Whether or not a "First Cause" created the nebulous cloud from which such systems eventually formed, in the natural order of cosmological change, no one is to blame for the decay of the system, it is simply a consequence of the interactions of bodies in motion. Given Victorian readers' resistance to narratives that classified them biologically as "monkey's uncles," it is doubtful that Hardy imagined them embracing his new myth of the astrophysics of their time: that their relations to each other were subject to the same laws as any other matter in the universe. However ready he may have been to posit such a cosmology, he was cognizant that many other explanatory models were operating in the minds of his readers.

Throughout *The Return of the Native*, Hardy uses the concept of cosmic "influences" in a way that literally conjures their significance within the magical thinking of the primitive mind. Depending upon the lore in which a character has been educated, he or she interprets the celestial phenomena of nature in an astrological/superstitious or astronomical/rational fashion. The only real difference between the most primitive and the most scientific of responses, however, as Hardy seems to indicate, is that the former interpret such influences as raining down upon the terrestrial realm and its occupants, while the latter project their thoughts, feelings, and inner natures out upon the celestial objects instead. So, while the sources of the old and new symbolic meanings and associations are imagined to differ, their actual consequences remain remarkably the same. Working within the fatalistic conventions of Greek tragedy and atomistic natural philosophy, Hardy makes it clear that both traditional folklore and modern physics are capable of making equally accurate predictions about the nature of this story's end.

*   *   *

In each of these three early novels, Hardy employs literary conventions and expectations to establish the cosmological contexts, the setting, and initial environmental conditions within which his characters live. Although these works relate three very different kinds of human stories, Hardy is careful to show that each form represents and participates in its own literary history, containing within itself a full range of interpretative frameworks from the most ancient of mythological associations, to the most modern of explanatory models. The cosmological is present in these novels, then, as narrative and as imagined environment, with the biological and psychological natures of the characters' recapitulating on the microcosmic level the interrelations of things as they are defined at the macrolevel.

In *A Pair of Blue Eyes*, Hardy plays off the conventions and expectations of medieval romance and the Gothic novel, in part to underscore ironically that it is precisely the conventions and expectations of the medieval-minded still among us which constitute the most intractable obstacles for those hoping to realize a new kind of potential. Knight is far from a shining example of ideal manhood as he misapplies the letter of his Arthurian law of chastity – and not its spirit – to Elfride and thus proves himself unworthy of her love. Elfride's youthful idealistic cosmology may be most obviously symbolized by the "romance" novel she is writing. Like her own fictional heroine, any number of decisive choices may have led to this imagined narrative becoming the "story of her life." Instead, her choices, indecision and errors, and the choices, indecision and errors of others, and her apparent belief that there were no other choices – a staple of all Gothic horror – results in her accepting the lead role in another kind of narrative: the family curse. If she could have read the world within a different mythological and cosmological framework, or others around her could have, Elfride may have been able to write a different fate for herself, one in which she might not have met her end as a "dying star."

In *Far From the Madding Crowd*, the pastoral mode provides Hardy's narrative with a cosmological framework built up of the myths and mores of agrarian harmony reminiscent of stories of the Golden Age and the biblical and Miltonic Eden. In Gabriel's cosmos, these pasts are present and his cosmology *works*. With patience and compassion he teaches his future mate to make her view of life and nature accord with his. Together – cosmologically, psychologically and biologically – they stand a real chance at recreating an Edenic garden in which they will not only survive, but thrive.

In *The Return of the Native*, the conventions of Greek tragedy reproduce the conditions of Greek cosmology, a mechanistic and deterministic universe of matter in motion, causes and effects. As in the Greek originals, seeing too much too soon and seeing too little too late, have equally tragic consequences. In *The Return*, the central characters' personal cosmologies write their own self-fulfilling prophecies.

In all three of these works, astronomical and cosmological selection recapitulates natural and sexual selection as how the characters' view their relationship to "the stars" dramatically correlates with their survival and reproductive futures. What Hardy accomplishes in the lunar eclipse scene and with the image of double stars in *The Return of the Native* – a thematic union of astronomy, cosmology, biology and psychology; foreshadowing; the introduction of plot complications; the philosophical management of the interrelations of humankind and the universe – will all be adopted on a grander scale within the complex structural metaphors he employs in *Two on a Tower*. The astronomical and cosmological subject matter that has helped him form the background of these three early works and helped him to establish the basic conditions of living and thinking for his characters' outer and inner lives, Hardy will now bring into the foreground and make explicit.

The shift of perspective will not be without sacrifice. The intense concentration of the rural environment, so beautifully handled in *Far From the Madding Crowd* and *The Return of the Native* will become but sketched-in details in *Two on a Tower*. Yet important aspects of each of these early works will be refined and reassembled in *Two on a Tower*, including: the close emotional human bonding brought about by observing the universe together, the simultaneous embodiment of old and new cosmologies, the drama of the possible range of human response to the apparent indifference of nature and our mortal place within it. Drawing upon the Gothic, romantic, pastoral, and tragic, Hardy creates a melodramatic medley in *Two on a Tower* in which the two main characters interact as double stars. As their story unfolds, Hardy explores the potentials and limitations of the personal cosmologies variously informed and formed by science, religion, superstition and loving kindness. Although the novel may fail to achieve the artistic coherence and integrity of Hardy's best work, in it he expresses clearly to his readers a full range of possible solutions to the universal "quandary" he believed nineteenth-century astrophysics revealed to him.

Chapter 6

The Stellar Dynamics of Star-Crossed Love in *Two on a Tower*

Two on a Tower is probably Hardy's least known and least appreciated novel. Written in haste, the story first appeared in serial form before being published as a book in 1882 (Millgate 197). In September 1881, Hardy was recovering from what he believed had been a near-fatal illness and was anxious about the small size of the estate he would have left his wife had he died. Looking forward to the additional income, Hardy eagerly accepted the request from the editor of *Atlantic Monthly* for a serial to be published the following year and, in reply, quickly sent an outline for *Two on a Tower*. The serial ran in *Atlantic Monthly* from May to December 1882. The book was first published in three volumes in October 1882 and in one volume in December of the same year. It was not a critical success. The novel was chastised on moral grounds for certain elements of sexual innuendo and as an unfair satire on the Established Church of England. *Saturday Review* used the phrase "extremely repulsive" (Millgate 229) to describe the plot twist whereby Viviette, pregnant by Swithin who has left England for the Cape of Good Hope, accepts a marriage proposal from the Bishop of Melchester. The *St. James Gazette* (January 1883) emphasized how the incident "shocked" the reader and "insulted" the Church. Some reviewers admitted that they admired the "astronomical aspects" of the novel, although most thought that they were not "integrated sufficiently into the central story" (Millgate 229) and assessed the plot as improbably Gothic and overly melodramatic.[1] Hardy expressed disappointment at the novel's reception and stated in the preface to the second edition (1895) that he felt the greater purpose he had intended the story to fulfill had been overlooked. Namely, he had wished "to set the emotional history of two infinitesimal lives against the stupendous background of the stellar universe, and to impart to readers the sentiment that of the contrasting magnitudes the smaller might be the greater to them as men."[2]

Now, over one hundred and twenty years since Hardy wrote it, the significance of astronomy and cosmology within *Two on a Tower* has still not received systematic evaluation.[3] As far as I am aware, there is not another novel in the whole of English

---

[1] See Mark Lencho, "Autobiography in *Two on a Tower*," unpublished paper (Central (Oklahoma) State University, 1980) 5.

[2] Thomas Hardy, *Two on a Tower* (New York: Harper and Brothers, 1895) vii; hereafter cited by page number within the text.

[3] *Two on a Tower*'s marginalization as a "minor" novel has no doubt contributed to the lack

literature that has so much of its form and content focused upon astronomy.[4] The vocation of Swithin St. Cleeve, the central male character of the novel, is astronomy. Astronomy becomes the avocation of the central female character, Lady Viviette Constantine. Throughout the book, Hardy skillfully details astronomical pursuits, observations, events, instruments, discoveries, and theories. He views astronomy and science from various thematic perspectives in their relation to religion, art, emotion, love, intuition, history and prehistory, society, and other realms of knowledge and ways of knowing. Hardy uses astronomical images in poetic devices that underscore and heighten the interrelation of themes in the novel and link elements of the novel's structure. He echoes astronomical allusions of past literature that inform the tradition out of which *Two on a Tower* evolved. Drawing deeply upon the knowledge of astronomy that he had gained from his own reading in popular sources, he incorporates his understanding of astronomical discoveries and theories and the implications he sees in them into another form of popular expression – the serial novel. It is more than high time to take Hardy at his word and consider the sidereal message of his most astronomical story.

Hardy's Cosmological Mythos

For the contemporary readers who read the book despite its poor reviews, the deeper significance of the astronomical aspects of *Two on a Tower* may have been overshadowed by the distracting "immoral" elements of the plot line and the racy intricacies of the love story. The complex astronomical structure of the novel may also have gone unnoticed or been misunderstood because the complexity of Hardy's astrophysical analogies surpassed the level of popular knowledge of astronomy generally held by the Victorian reading public. If any members of Hardy's audience received his message about the importance of astronomy to philosophy, religion or culture, they likely already possessed a working familiarity with the scientific phenomena and concepts that Hardy incorporated. Without at least a popular understanding of the "stupendous background of the stellar universe," it might well have been difficult for general readers and reviewers alike to realize how fully this novel fits the philosophical scheme and purposes of the rest of Hardy's oeuvre. Written at the height of the busiest astronomical age of discovery to-date, *Two on a Tower* offered insight into the consequences of humanity's new view of the heavens, essentially proposing a new cosmological myth by which late Victorian readers might understand their relation to the universe and to each other.

---

of attention critical scholars have paid to its science. Substantial close readings of the text as a whole are rare, and only a limited number of brief studies have appeared that focus on some aspect of the novel's astronomy; see this volume's chapter 3: fn 1.

[4]   Mark Rutherford's [William Hale White's] novella, *Miriam's Schooling*, has considerable astronomical content, but the technical detail is nowhere as accurately expressed or significantly symbolic as in Hardy's work.

In *A Pair of Blue Eyes, Far From the Madding Crowd*, and *The Return of the Native*, Hardy used astronomy as an important means by which to relate his views about humanity's relationship to "the stars" – whether through traditional associations of celestial phenomena with cosmological myth, pagan or orthodox religious beliefs and rituals, or modern scientific and rational investigations. While the heavens provide a complex cosmic "background" for *Two on a Tower*, they also provide an intricately interlaced fore- and mid-ground for the narrative. Hardy depicts both of his central characters as having their "heads in the clouds" (although in distinctly different ways). Both Swithin's and Viviette's personalities and characters are defined by the essential relation they believe to be operating between themselves and the heavens (his scientific, hers religious). The differences in their cosmologies will provide much of the dramatic tension for the story, reflecting a scenario that was playing itself out among many traditionally believing wives and increasingly agnostic rising men of science in middle and upper-middle class marriages across England (including Hardy's own). Hardy richly contextualizes the inner and interpersonal cosmological struggle of his main characters by depicting their interpretative frameworks as two among many possible ways to make sense of "the heavens." The minor characters in *Two on a Tower*, occupying the various social and economic strata of the town and countryside, embody a full range of contemporary world views and the many ways that those perspectives may be applied to the problems of everyday life and love.

In *Two on a Tower*, Hardy uses his popular knowledge of astronomy to portray the personality and career of a Victorian amateur astronomer as he progresses from novice to professional. Swithin typifies his mid-Victorian generation's experience with the sciences as gentlemanly amateur pursuits transformed to salaried positions in formally established institutional settings. Hardy sketches around his main character the ways in which the other characters and social classes view the scientific personality and astronomy, *per se*, as an occupation. Hardy had a keen eye for how astronomical information and cosmological concepts were being disseminated through his own culture and he draws upon this insight to recreate their reception at the microcosmic level of his fictional locale. More impressively, Hardy creates elaborate astronomical metaphors which work not only heuristically to further a general understanding of astronomy through their accuracy, but hermeneutically, to express the story's deepest assumptions and meaning. The detailed astronomical descriptions and extended structural metaphors that Hardy creates for *Two on a Tower* express the kinds of epistemological and existential dilemmas that astronomical concepts represented for Hardy personally. Yet, here, such images allow Hardy to envision a broad range of possible solutions for those dilemmas which he then displays, or plays out, for his readers within the action of the novel.

In specific preparation for writing *Two on a Tower*, Hardy wrote an astronomical engineer for information on lens grinding and telescope construction. He requested permission to visit the Royal Observatory at Greenwich in order to make inquiries into the feasibility of adapting a "hollow memorial pillar, with a staircase inside" into a small observatory and wondered "how it can be roofed so as not to interfere with observations."[5] When asked by the Observatory to fill-out a form asking him to state "whether you have an Observatory of your own or are forming one, or are in the habit of making astronomical, magnetical, or meteorological observations," Hardy answered:

> Have no Observatory of my own; am not forming one; but am sketching plans for one:– am not in the habit of making observations, but have written astronomical passages which are quoted both in England and America. (*Collected Letters* 96)

The fact that "sketching" was meant in a purely literary sense and not an architectural one, Hardy omitted clarifying. Nonetheless he gained permission to visit the Observatory, and although direct evidence documenting the actual visit seems lacking,[6] the details of what he learned (there or elsewhere) regarding the building of a domed observatory tower appear in *Two on a Tower*:

> The top of the column was quite changed. The tub-shaped space within the parapet, formerly open to the air and sun, was now arched over by a light dome of lath-work covered with felt. But this dome was not fixed. At the line where its base descended to the parapet there were half a dozen iron balls, precisely like cannon-shot, standing loosely in a groove, and on these the dome rested its whole weight. In the side of the dome was a slit, through which the wind blew and the North Star beamed, and towards it the end of the great telescope was directed. This latter magnificent object, with its circles, axes, and handles complete, was securely fixed in the middle of the floor.
> "But you can only see one part of the sky through that slit," said she.
> The astronomer stretched out his arm, and the whole dome turned horizontally round, running on the balls with a rumble like thunder. Instead of the star Polaris, which had first been peeping in through the slit, there now appeared the countenances of Castor and Pollux. Swithin then manipulated the equatorial and put it through its capabilities in like manner. (66)

In *Two on a Tower*, Hardy not only tries to present an accurate picture of the technical equipment required for astronomy, but he also tries to represent authentically the personality of an astronomer and the development of his career as an upwardly mobile man of science. As Hardy describes Swithin's astronomical life as progressing through three distinct stages, he draws upon aspects of real-life astronomy in mid-Victorian Britain, including the role of gentleman amateurs, the importance of inheritances (one's own or that of one's wife) to the funding of private astronomical research, the astronomical observatories of the great country houses, the call of

---

[5]   Richard L. Purdy and Michael Millgate, eds., *The Collected Letters of Thomas Hardy*, 1: 1840–1892 (Oxford: Clarendon Press, 1978) 96; hereafter: *Collected Letters*.

[6]   F. B. Pinion and Martin Beech disagree as to whether Hardy actually made this visit. See: Pinion, *Thomas Hardy: His Life and Friends* (1992) and Beech, "Thomas Hardy: Far from the Royal Observatory, Greenwich," *The Observatory* 110 (December 1990) 185–7, as cited in Chapman, *The Victorian Amateur Astronomer*, Chapter 12: fn 78.

astronomical expeditions of discovery, and the growth of international networking.[7] First, Hardy details a period during which Swithin diligently works in essential isolation, with a small personal stipend, but under the increasing patronage of Viviette. This stage is presented by a narrative which concentrates attention on the interaction between the two main characters. Second, Hardy depicts a period during which Swithin is distracted from his observational work by his love for Viviette. Here, the narrative shifts towards an account of the couple's courtship and marriage, with only brief mention of Swithin's productivity. Third, Hardy turns the story toward a four-year span in which Swithin pursues professional career goals on an international basis after leaving Viviette at her request. During this stage, Hardy's narrative concentrates primarily upon Swithin and his work, and returns to an account of Viviette only to describe her macabre demise.

As Swithin grows up from late adolescence to mature manhood, his response toward astronomy and cosmology evolve from a blindered enthusiasm for the technical details and competitive chase of astronomical discovery (complete with an agnostic view of cosmogony) to an open-eyed appreciation for the philosophical and moral perspective that a cosmic point of view can give to the importance of life around us. The fact that Swithin learns to integrate the greater lessons of his astronomy into his personal cosmology as he makes his educational and professional journey around the globe and returns to Viviette's arms provides a powerful object lesson for Hardy's Victorian readers as they were experiencing the same "progress" of astrophysics in the scientific realm around them. If they learned to appreciate the universe and care for one another as Swithin and Viviette did, there was a chance that humanity might successfully adapt a compassionate value system to a scientific world view. As Hardy cautions, however, it is unlikely that such ambitious journeys of discovery through uncharted territories will be carried to completion without casualties.

The Scientist as a Young Man: Astronomy in Social and Spiritual Spheres

When the reader first meets Swithin, he is a youth not quite twenty years old, of high aspirations but low origins, who has just completed the curriculum at Warbonne Grammar School and has returned home. He has trespassed onto the land of the Lady of the county, appropriated without permission a commemorative tower in her husband's family cemetery and has been using it as astronomical observatory for several months. At this stage, Hardy carefully establishes that Swithin's personality traits are owing equally to his personal as well as professional immaturity. The quirks of his behavior are due to his youth and personal character, not his stereotypical "scientific" nature. Swithin's emotional qualities are presented in different lights depending on whether they are judged in scientific, intellectual, social, or moral

---

[7] For a full historical discussion of each of these aspects of astronomical research during the nineteenth century, see: Chapman, *The Victorian Amateur Astronomer.*

contexts. For instance, Swithin's natural impatience is described as a scientific virtue when he displays it as the "young scientist" to make the best use of his short observing time (5). The same impatience appears when Swithin, as a spoiled, insensitive child, reacts nastily to his frail grandmother's confession that she nibbled away at his dinner while he was observing at the tower (15).

Yet some of the intellectual characteristics of a scientist which Swithin displays are stereotypical according to mid- to late nineteenth-century views already widespread in the caricatures of *Punch* and present nearly two hundred years earlier, as noticed by Archibald Geikie in his study, *English Science and its Caricaturists in the Seventeenth and Eighteenth Centuries*. Swithin is oblivious to the attractions of feminine beauty (6); exhibits a "scientific earnestness and melancholy mistrust of all things human" (i.e. emotional) (9); is mathematically accurate even in walking (13); is rational in comparing relative values (35); is a believer in chance and probability, but not religion or God (41, 43); is "selfish" and "ungallant" in his ignorance of social etiquette; prefers the truth to social tact (58); is obtuse to mundane and "sublunary thought" (41); is "married to science" (67); transcends the flesh and its desires via telescopic journeys to the cold unknown (69); reads as he walks long distances, even in the rain (74); risks his health by overwork and devotion to study (71); displays the most emotion over the success or failure of his scientific pursuits (49, 76); is matter-of-fact, taking statements literally without looking for deeper meaning or irony (92); completely separates the love of astronomy from the love of a woman and refuses to "ordinate two such dissimilars" (93).

Hardy attributes much of Swithin's exaggerated, stereotypically scientific behavior to his schoolboy affectation and newness to his pursuit. He also shows Swithin's actions to be defensive against what he believes to be unapproving attitudes toward science as an occupation by his grandmother and the local "work-folk." When Swithin is looking forward to an evening of calculating in his upstairs room, he is distressed to learn that the work-folk's choir will be coming to practice below him. He nervously bursts out to his grandmother, "not a word about astronomy to any of them whatever you do. I should be called a visionary and all sorts." To this his grandmother replies, "So thou beest, child. Why can't you do something that's of use?" (16). After her comment, Swithin retreats to his study and lays paper over the knot-holes in his floor so that no light from his room will give away his presence to those downstairs.

Swithin's paranoia about the villagers' views of his work is not justified. Some of his defensiveness may be explained by the fact that his grandmother's pragmatic criticism against astronomy is true (he is not directly helping to support his eighty-year-old only living relative). Yet the male field-workers' and serving woman's attitudes toward Swithin and his astronomy range from decided disinterest to awestruck wonder. Haymoss, the chief spokesman for the work-folk, tells Viviette early on in the book that the community rather pities Swithin because he is parentless and without direction, but in general "nobody troubles about 'en [him]" (12).

When Swithin is taken ill and asks the aged woman who is caring for him "What news to-day?" the following exchange occurs:

"O, nothing, sir," Hannah replied, looking out of the window with sad apathy, "only that there's a comet, *they* say."

"A WHAT?" said the dying astronomer, starting up on his elbow.

"A *comet – that's all*, Master Swithin," repeated Hannah, in a lower voice, fearing she had done harm in some way.

"Well, tell me, tell me!" cried Swithin. "Is it Gambart's? Is it Charles the Fifth's, or Halley's, or Faye's or whose?"

"Hush!" said she, thinking St. Cleeve slightly delirious again.

"'Tis God Almighty's, of course. *I haven't seed* en myself; but they say he's getting bigger every night, and that he'll be the biggest one known for fifty years when he's full growed." (79, my emphasis)

Hardy contrasts Hannah's disinterest to the attitude of Haymoss and his co-workers who eagerly watch the comet's progress and ask Swithin to allow them a chance at viewing the display through his telescope. While waiting for Swithin to open the observatory one night, the group of workmen sit back for a smoke and exchange speculations about the comet's meaning.

"He's sure to come rathe or late," resounded . . . Hezzy Biles. "He wouldn't let such a fine show as the comet makes to-night go by without peeping at it,– not Master Cleeve! . . . Why, his spyglass will stretch out that there comet as long as Welland lane!"

"I'd as soon miss the great peep-show that comes every year to Greenhill Fair as a sight of such a immortal spectacle as this!" said Amos Fry.

"'Immortal spectacle,' – where did ye get that choice mossel, Haymoss?" inquired Sammy Blore . . .

"And what do this comet mean?" asked Haymoss.

"That some great tumult is going to happen, or that we shall die of a famine?"

"Famine – no!" said Nat Chapman. "That only touches such as we, and the Lord only concerns himself with born gentlemen. It isn't to be supposed that a strange fiery lantern like that would be lighted up for folks with ten or a dozen shillings a week and their gristing, and a load o'thorn faggots when we can get 'em. If 'tis a token that he's getting hot about the ways of anybody in this parish, 'tis about my Lady Constantine's, since she is the only one of a figure worth such a hint." (95–6)

Haymoss, who has earlier in the novel expressed an anti-superstitious attitude that he does not believe in any "such trumpery about folks in the sky" (12), tempers his friends' astrological interpretation of the comet with a more down-to-earth explanation of the planet's effect on human life:

If they [Swithin and Viviette] get up this tower ruling plannards [planets] together much longer, their plannards will soon rule them together, in my way o' thinking. If she've a disposition towards the knot [marriage], she can soon teach him. (97)

The upper classes' views toward astronomy exhibit a similar range. The highest ranking members of the county's society are represented by Lady Constantine, the parish parson, Reverend Torkingham, and the visiting Bishop of Melchester. Viviette, the wife of the highest ranking gentleman in the county, initially displays an educated ignorance about the subject of astronomy. She assumes because she "learned" astronomy as a schoolgirl that she "knows" astronomy and can discuss with Swithin the objects of his observation. Swithin begins:

> "I observe from seven or eight till about two in the morning, with a view to my great work on variable stars. But with such a telescope as this – well, I must put up with it!"
> "Can you see Saturn's ring and Jupiter's moon?" He said drily that he could manage to do that, not without some contempt for the state of her knowledge.
> "I have never seen any planet or star through a telescope."
> "If you will come the first clear night, Lady Constantine, I will show you any number. I mean, at your express wish; not otherwise."
> "I should like to come, and possibly may at sometime. These stars that vary so much – sometimes evening stars, sometimes morning stars, sometimes in the east, and sometimes in the west – have always interested me."
> "Ah – now there is a reason for you not coming. Your ignorance of the realities of astronomy is so satisfactory that I will not disturb it except at your serious request."
> "But I wish to be enlightened." (9–10)

Viviette expresses sincere interest in learning more about astronomy and in a spirit of intellectual exchange, she offers the use of her library to Swithin. Swithin truthfully – and tactlessly – divests her of the notion that old rare books are more valuable than new, cheap pamphlets and journals as far as modern science is concerned (58). Although Viviette eventually becomes proficient at making notes on astronomical observations, the first time she is entrusted by Swithin to watch a star for him her failure to consider the laws of probability as they apply to variable star periodicity causes her to seriously blunder.

> "Did you watch the star? . . . Did you watch every night, – not missing one?"
> "I forgot to go – twice," she murmured contritely. "O, Lady Constantine!" he cried in dismay. "How could you serve me so! What shall I do?"
> "Please forgive me! Indeed, I could not help it. I had watched and watched, and nothing happened; and somehow my vigilance relaxed when I found nothing was likely to take place in the star."
> "But the very circumstance of it not having happened makes it all the more likely every day." (41)

When Viviette decides to become Swithin's patroness she considers the undertaking as a diversion ("I lack a hobby and I shall choose astronomy" 56) which will alleviate the ennui she has imposed upon herself by honoring her vow to her husband to remain secluded from society during his absence. She recognizes that assuming the role of benefactress emphasizes her higher social position, and she hesitates to complete the analogy when she tells Swithin that he will be her Astronomer Royal and she will be "his Queen" (56). Nonetheless, her social skills suit the role. She realizes the importance of publishing results in order to "insure ownership" of a discovery, and she warns Swithin about avoiding an "Adams and Leverrier" controversy (71). She uses her social rank to order telescope parts and observatory equipment and receives, delivered at home within days, materials for which Swithin had to wait nine months and travel miles to pick up.

Under Swithin's tutelage, Viviette does become "enlightened" about the significance of the depths of space. Her newly gained understanding synthesizes Western culture's three most powerful approaches to explaining the universe: science, religion and magic.

> "And to think," said Lady Constantine, "that the whole race of shepherds, since the beginning of the world,– even those immortal shepherds who watched near Bethlehem, – should have gone into their graves without knowing that for one star that lighted them in their labours, there were a hundred as good behind trying to do so! . . . I have a feeling for this instrument not unlike the awe I should feel in the presence of a great magician in whom I really believed. Its powers are so enormous, and weird, and fantastical, that I should have a personal fear in being with it alone. Music drew an angel down, said the poet: but what is that to drawing down worlds!" (68)

As Swithin and Viviette take turns at the telescope scanning the night sky, the narrator comments,

> Thus the interest of their sidereal observations led them on, till the knowledge that scarce any other human vision was travelling within a hundred million miles of their own gave them such a sense of the isolation of that faculty as almost to be a sense of isolation in respect of their whole personality, causing a shudder at its absoluteness. . . . Having got closer to immensity than their fellow-creatures, they saw at once its beauty and its frightfulness. They more and more felt the contrast between their own tiny magnitudes and those among which they had recklessly plunged, till they were oppressed with the presence of a vastness they could not cope with even as an idea, and which hung about them like a nightmare. (68–9)

Hardy was well aware that in this passage, and others like it, he was departing significantly from traditional literary descriptions of star-crossed lovers beneath the evening sky. Romance is not the only mode potential in such a setting. Building upon the star-gazing scene in *A Pair of Blue Eyes,* Hardy once again draws correspondences between the human observers and their cosmic objects. This time, however, the state of the universe is not a Gothic romance and the last melancholy moments of the night's final "dying star" will not convey his message about his heroine's fate. Rather, in this elevated medley of a cosmic melodrama, with the constant admixture of things high and low, young and old, tragic and romantic, light-hearted and black-humored, pointedly purposeful and accidentally askew, his two main characters stand in for the postlapsarian Adam and Eve, bonding emotionally as they face together the exquisite and terrific truths of the universe. Their shared experience of cosmic awe – fear *and* beauty together – will prove the tie that binds them. Whatever Viviette's personal romantic interest in Swithin might have been without his astronomy, she proves a successful recipient of his attempts to popularize the most profound aspects of his scientific pursuit. Surely such passages must have had the same effect on at least some of Hardy's more sensitive readers (whether ladies or not), as similar passages by Proctor and the Herschels had first affected him.

In fact, by dramatizing the findings of astronomy in this way, Hardy was essentially following Proctor's suggestion for how to popularize successfully the subject matter of his science. Proctor's prescription for the process is evident in his account of John Herschel's greatness as a writer of descriptive astronomy:

> But how few have there been who have had, like Herschel, a real insight into the grandeur of astronomical truths! how few who, like him, could so touch the dry bones of fact that they became clothed at once with life and beauty! It may be said of some of the most skilful of Herschel's astronomical contemporaries, that they have scarcely even perceived the essential truths of astronomy; and not many can be truly said to have felt the full import of those / truths. But to Herschel astronomy was not a matter of right ascension and declination; of poising, clamping, and reading off; of cataloguing and correcting. He saw the real value of the technical and instrumental details; *but he did not mistake these details for astronomy*, as some have done. When he read the wondrous lessons taught by the heavens, *it was for their meaning that he cared*, not for the outward symbols by which they are expressed. (*Essays* 1–2, emphasis added)

When Hardy went to write "astronomical passages" for *Two on a Tower* and other works, he already had similar passages by John Herschel and Proctor available to him to use as sources of astronomical details, but, perhaps even more importantly, to serve him as literary models. Herschel and Proctor both clearly provided precedents for Hardy that emphasized the "meaning" and "essential truths" of astronomical work as the "true astronomy" worthy of popular treatment. Further, Proctor heralded the imaginative creativity of Herschel's mind as the *sine qua non* of both his power as an astronomical theorist and writer. "Another faculty which the theorist should possess in a high degree is a certain liveliness of imagination, whereby analogies may be traced between the relations of the subject on which he is theorizing and those of objects not obviously associated with that subject" (*Essays* 21). This description of Herschel's *modus operandi* is, of course, equally applicable to Hardy's analogical approach to astronomy in *Two on a Tower*.

Moreover, Proctor supported his claims that Herschel's writing captured the sublimity of the subject with an example that treats the relativity of scale in the universal frame with a drama similar to that with which Hardy treats it in the above passage.

Sir John Herschel, indeed, entertained a singularly strong belief in the existence of analogies throughout the whole range of created matter. . . . "An opinion," he wrote, "which the structure of the Magellanic Clouds has often suggested to me, has been strongly recalled by what you say of the inclusion of every variety of nebulous or clustering form within the galaxy – viz., that if such be the case, that is, if these forms belong to and form part and parcel of the galactic system, then, that system *includes within itself miniatures of itself* on an almost infinitely reduced scale; and what evidence then have we that there exists a universe beyond? – unless a sort of argument from analogy that the galaxy, with all its contents, may be *but one* of these miniatures of that vast universe, and so on *ad infinitum*; and that in *that* universe there may exist multitudes of other systems on a scale as vast as *our* galaxy, the analogues of those other nebulous and clustering forms which are *not* miniatures of our galaxy." (*Essays* 23)

"This," concludes Proctor, "perhaps, is the grandest picture of the universe that has ever been conceived by man" (23). Yet, as Hardy's literary treatment of similar astronomical concepts indicates, there was still room for improvement in this conception. Herschel had not found a place in his description for human emotion and being; Hardy melds universal truths to human ones. It may not be too far-fetched to speculate that Hardy may have written *Two on a Tower* to redress just such omissions.

Besides describing the effect of Swithin's astronomy lessons upon Viviette, Hardy shows how other prominent residents of the county utilize opportunities to learn about the science. The views of astronomy held by members of organized religion in the novel's local society are symbolized by the parson, Torkingham, and the Bishop of Melchester who has honored the parish with a visit. The parson and the Bishop represent two ways in which men of religion reconciled contemporary science to their faith. The parson views astronomy as a way to increase his knowledge of the glories of God's creation. The Bishop epistemologically subjugates scientific inquiry to moral imperatives. He is blind to the insight a more "objective" gathering of information might give him into the reality of his parishioners' spiritual state, let alone any vision into the reality of the universe.

Parson Torkingham is an open-minded man who has often visited Swithin's observatory. He comments to the Bishop that he has "looked through [Swithin's] telescope with great benefit to my ideas of celestial phenomena" (170). Just before the Bishop's arrival, the parson brought a group of work-folk to the observatory to view a lunar eclipse (170), and he knows enough of Swithin's nightly routine to be able to predict when Swithin will be present at the tower (186). The Bishop, on the other hand, highly educated, highly principled, and dogmatic, expresses a reluctant willingness to visit the tower "if the distance is not too great" and admits that he has "never seen the inside of an observatory in [his] life" (187).[8]

---

[8] This scene may owe something to a similar visit made by King George III and the Archbishop of Canterbury. As the usual anecdote tells it, in leading the Archbishop toward William Herschel's large reflector, he offered him his arm, with these words: "Come, my Lord,

At first the Bishop is politely interested in Swithin's "precise processes" until he discovers evidence that appears to indicate that Swithin is hiding a lover in the observatory cabin. From that point on in the observations, Swithin notices that the Bishop has his eyes "fixed hard on him" and not the stars (192). The Bishop's view of Swithin as "fallen" cancels, in his mind, the "beauties" and "glories" of the heavenly heights Swithin traverses with his telescope. In a private meeting the next day, the Bishop asserts his authority over Swithin as his "spiritual head" and refuses to accept Swithin's attempt to "save the appearances" of his moral indiscretion with the same determination he refused to attend to Swithin's astronomical descriptions.

Although Swithin *was* hiding Viviette the previous night, he and she are legally and spiritually sanctioned by marriage. Swithin, who has sworn to keep their union secret, cannot convince the Bishop that there may be an alternative explanation for the phenomena he believes to be damning. Hardy intentionally contrasts his sympathetic portrayal of the Parson's pragmatic natural theology with his disapproval of the Bishop's abuse of reason, theology and power. As the melodramatic plot thickens, the Bishop's tendency to interpret evidence in the light most flattering to his own ego, will be turned against him, as he never questions that Viviette's child – the spitting image of Swithin – may not be his.

The opinions of men of religion toward astronomy are especially important to an interpretation of *Two on a Tower* because the narrator designates astronomers as the "new priesthood" for the modern age. At the early moment in the novel when Swithin is covering the knot-holes in his floor to shield himself from the view of the choir below, they are singing "The Lord look'd down from Heaven's high tower / The sons of men to view" (20). The parallel between Swithin and the Lord is obvious; however, the narrator later inverts the analogy. Swithin, as one of the "sons of men" is using his own "high tower" to look up at heaven. Swithin is described as "drawing down worlds" (68) and as a light-bearer: "He brought a little lantern from the cabin, and lighted [Viviette's way] up the winding staircase to the temple of the sublime mystery on whose threshold he stood as priest" (65). Viviette compares his scientific zeal to Christ's protection of the sanctity of his Church: "You were once so devoted to your science that the thought of an intruder into your temple would have driven you wild" (106). Swithin himself recognizes that his scientific views have caused him to depend on secular endeavors and human relationships instead of the Church and knows that by doing so he is "inverting the established order of spiritual things" (157).

Hardy purposefully considers the possibility that Swithin's education into astronomy and cosmology may be preparing him for a "calling" as a modern mediator between the heavens and the earth. With obvious symbolism reflecting Hardy's opinion of the state of orthodox Victorian religion, Swithin's father, a clergyman, has died and left him orphaned in the world. Unlike Hardy's "natural" astronomer, Gabriel Oak, Swithin seems to have retained few, if any, ancient or instinctual connections with the natural world, above or below. Without primitive or traditional religious

---

let me show you the way to heaven."

frameworks to draw upon, Swithin, instead, builds upon the history of human scientific investigations of nature, relying upon his own devices of sensory experience and reason to figure out the universe and his place within it. Fortunately, he proves to be a good learner. As he gains experience within his profession, he is also rapidly acquiring knowledge about the world of men – and women. Swithin's fictional life runs precisely parallel to those moments in British history when educational and professional opportunities for amateur astronomers were at their greatest potential.

As the character with the most direct access to the broadest perspective on the cosmos, Swithin is a good model for a modern student of the universe. Unfettered by the weight of obsolete beliefs, Swithin does not have to unlearn the old cosmology before opening his mind to the new. Although Viviette's Christian *charitos* is clearly able to accommodate newly discovered facts of the universe, it is Swithin, Hardy suggests, who is in the strongest position to develop and implement a value system that integrates loyalty, trust, and love with rational and pragmatic realism. Together their mutual catechism – he teaching her the vastness of stellar astronomy, she teaching him the depth of feeling in the human heart – comprises a bildungsroman for all Victorians who faced coming-of-age in William Herschel's Milky Way.

Although the narrator implies the seriousness of the degree of cultural change that a replacement of religious cosmology by science would indicate, he also considers that the current popular obsession with science may be a fad. In a moment of playful jealousy, Viviette remarks to Swithin,

> Suppose you become a popular physicist (popularity seems cooling towards art and coquetting with science now-a-days), and a better chance offers, and one who would make you a newer and brighter wife than I am comes in your way. (156)

As Hardy will show, however, to whatever extent Swithin's highly technical reading of the stars has the potential to one day transform the cosmology of his age, Viviette's sensitivity about emotional and social "signs" has enduring – as well as locally applicable – predictive power the value of which should not be disregarded or dismissed.

The Astronomer and His Profession

Hardy's presentation of a full range of possible views toward the significance of astronomy (the social and spiritual aspects of which we have just reviewed) is augmented by his representation of astronomy *qua* science. Hardy meticulously details the enthusiastic beginnings, distracted interlude, and professional achievements that occur as Swithin practices his astronomical occupation. Through Hardy's descriptions of Swithin's work, Victorian readers gained an observational window into the astronomer's observatory. The startling discoveries of the Herschels et al. – the vastness, change and decay, the beauty and "horror" of the stellar universe – were, after all, but the result of mundane human processes, the reasonable findings of the same natural curiosity and persistent pursuit that fueled so many other triumphant endeavors ongoing throughout Victoria's empire. Hardy's nonthreatening portrayal of Swithin's work-a-day nightlife makes his astronomy seem equally understandable, approachable, and desirable.

Swithin begins his career as an astronomer innocently enough, spending a year of evenings working six or seven hours each night in order to gain a practical familiarity with the heavens (9). He uses a homemade telescope with a lens "altogether inferior, cheap and bad" (13) which he has rigged to a crude swivel base of his own construction (38). Swithin observes sunspots. He possesses practical ambitions and believes himself to be on the verge of a "great work on variable stars" which will account for their irregular orbits and the intensity and periodicity of their color change (37, 39, 40). In his youthful daydreams, he envisions himself as Astronomer Royal (9) and as the "new Copernicus . . . what he was to the solar system, I aim to be to the systems beyond" (32). Many of Hardy's late Victorian middle-class readership could identify with, and approve of, the general nature of Swithin's aspirations, if not their particulars.

The details of Hardy's account of Swithin's incipient endeavors into amateur astronomy were not made up out of whole cloth. A close reading of *Essays in Astronomy* again shows that Hardy seems to have followed Proctor's lead in describing the enthusiasm of a young astronomy "bug," choosing an area of research for his young astronomer, and in setting his goals. In the third chapter of his *Essays*, "The Study of Astronomy," Proctor launches himself into a lengthy complaint about the waste of good telescope power by amateur users (or abusers!). After viewing the "various objects of which his books have informed him . . . the spots of Venus or Mars, the more delicate details of lunar scenery or of the sun's surface, the belts of Jupiter, the features of the Saturnian rings, the duplicity of the closer double stars, and the characteristics of those exceedingly difficult objects of study, the nebulae," Proctor laments that most amateurs stop their work here, or worse continue in the same vein "year after year without aim or purpose" (43). Proctor's obvious frustration at the level at which British amateur astronomers were working is apparent in his biting characterization of their labors.

> Yet in one or other of these ways, not merely the hundreds of cheap telescopes at this moment in the hands of *amateur* observers, but numbers of the finest telescopes which our Cookes, and Brownings, and Dallmeyers had turned out from their manufactories, are simply lost to the cause of astronomy. A fine instrument is purchased, and erected in a well-fitted and costly observatory; and during the first weeks after its erection the purchaser turns it on some of the objects he has read about. Then presently his enthusiasm is exhausted, and the telescope is no more used, save perhaps to amuse visitors. Or, else, the telescopist's enthusiasm waxes fiercer; he passes night after night in his observatory making his life a burden by unceasing efforts to just see with his telescope what one a little larger would show him easily; he sets his clocks and watches and all his neighbours' clocks and watches by transit observations; he notes down (to

the second or third decimal place of seconds) the epochs when the moon occults stars or when Jupiter's satellites are eclipsed or occulted; and he seemingly remains / all the while unconscious of the fact that twenty times his misplaced energy devoted for twenty lives to such work as I have described would produced results simply worth *Nothing*. (43–4)

Hardy goes to some pains to show that Swithin does wax fierce in his amateur enthusiasm for astronomy, but he is careful to point out that Swithin's zeal for observational work is not misplaced nor is he neglectful of his instrument's potential. Proctor himself had stated explicitly in his *Essays* one particular area toward which amateur talents could profitably be directed. Hardy readily took the hint to make Swithin an authentic amateur and one who was making the right kind of decisions in the field. In the chapter entitled "Coloured Suns," Proctor endorsed John Herschel's opinion of the study of variable stars, stating that: "there is no field of labour open to the *amateur* telescopist which affords a better promise of original discoveries than the search for such variations as we have described" (268). Variable stars are, in fact, the main objects of Swithin's painstaking observations. Moreover, the way in which Hardy has Swithin describe his career goals make it sound as though Swithin read Proctor as closely as he did. In "News From Sirius," Proctor forecasts the richness of stellar astronomy and concludes that:

> There now really seems a promise that one / day something may come to be learned respecting the movements of the sidereal mechanism. The constellations which now seem to be scattered without discernible law over the vault of heaven may be forced, perhaps, to reveal to us their secrets, the law of Organisation which binds them into a system, the paths along which their component stars have been travelling before they reached their present position, and those along which they are to travel for many future ages. Meantime long processes of patient labour and systematic observation lie before the astronomer. Not in our day, nor perchance for many generations, will the Copernicus of the stellar system appear; and for him astronomers will have to lay up during those long years a rich store of materials. (*Essays* 280–81)

Hardy indicates that Swithin is willing to undertake patient and slow observational data-gathering, but he also allows the reader to see how Swithin's youthful perspective on the work of long years causes him to misjudge the possibility of becoming the "new Copernicus" in a single lifetime. Similarly, Hardy's gentle use of scientific stereotypes puts a humorous face on Swithin's ambition to "know" the universe, making his high-flown goal-setting seem more a result of overly optimistic inexperience than overreaching hubris.

Unlike some of the amateurs Proctor deplored, Swithin is skilled enough in observation to know when he has reached the technological limits of his equipment. To confirm his variable star theory he will need an eight inch lens and an equatorial mount. He sells all he possesses and borrows an additional sum from his grandmother in order to purchase the large first-quality "object-glass." He spends six weeks laboring to build a tube for the new telescope (42). But even at this stage, equipment-building and observation are only a part of his work. His workspace at home is a clutter of reference books, maps, calculating sheets, globes, and cardboard mock-ups of telescope designs (16). The walls and ceiling of his room are smudged with astronomical diagrams (277). True to the scientific spirit of the age, Swithin stays abreast of both the British and American astronomical communities by subscribing to professional journals, newsletters, and pamphlets which he receives regularly and reads voraciously (44).

When Swithin is distraught to discover that his newly completed large telescope will not focus properly without an equatorial, Viviette sympathetically decides to become his patroness and buy him the mount. Although taken aback at the purchase price ("equal to two grand pianos"),[9] Viviette keeps her promise. Moreover she orders a moveable dome to be constructed to house the telescope and equatorial. A cabin for note-taking, research, and sleeping-quarters completes Swithin's observatory. The new equipment allows Swithin to see double stars in Leo and Virgo which had until then appeared single (63). Like Swithin, many Victorian astronomers working in the "Grand Amateur" tradition were able to do so because of the inherited wealth of their wives and mothers, William and John Herschel foremost among them. Allan Chapman emphasizes the importance of this source of support for amateur astronomical research, as well as the proliferation of private observatory building upon the estates of the great country houses (many of which, no doubt, were homes to those second-rate amateurs who underappreciated their first-rate equipment, so frustrating to Proctor). Also true to contemporary astronomical life, as in the cases of the gigantic telescopes of William Herschel and Lord Rosse, Hardy immediately reports the new phenomena that Swithin is able to observe with his new technology. Quite in another sense, from this point on in the story, Swithin is able to "see double," and will now include Viviette within his ken, where he had not done so before.

Hardy is equally true to life in relating the professional publication strategies of his amateur astronomer. Because of the equatorial, Swithin finds proof of his variable star idea and begins to prepare his "great theory" for publication (69). He promises to share his fame with Viviette, who has made his discovery possible (67). Swithin sends-off three sealed copies of his article, "A New Astronomical Discovery," by registered mail (not post), one each to the Royal Observatory, the Royal Society, and a "prominent astronomer." At the same time, Swithin submits an abstract to the leading daily paper. For all of Swithin's attention to professional detail and protocol, Hardy mentions in an aside that Swithin's article is written in "too glowing a rhetoric for the true scientific tone" (73). This remark is similar to a comment Proctor made in his *Essays* about John Herschel's writing. The great flaw and great beauty of Herschel's popularization of his astronomical discoveries and theories, according to Proctor, was

---

[9]   Chapman doubts whether even this amount of largesse would really have covered the cost of a fine mount from "Hilton & Pimms" (probably "Troughton and Simms"); see: *Victorian Amateur Astronomers* 240 and Chapter 12: fn 77.

that he did not popularize the scientific concepts by making them clear, but rather "by a happy turn of expression, now by some strikingly poetical conception, anon by a grand array of noble thoughts, he [forced] his readers to share his own enthusiasm" (7). Proctor firmly believed "that it is only by presenting astronomical facts in this striking and graphic manner that they can be made acceptable to the generality of readers" (36); yet, in some cases, he felt that the technique could be taken too far.

> Yet let me in this place note that there is a fault of a different nature than want of earnestness, which equally requires to be avoided in scientific treatises. I refer to the undue familiarity of tone by which sometimes even our ablest expositors attempt to descend to the presumed level of their readers' comprehension. Even Sir John Herschel, it must be admitted, has sometimes condescended to express himself in too familiar terms when dealing with subjects which require grandeur of treatment . . . which does not seem suited to the nature of the subject-matter. (36)

To make matters worse, Proctor noticed that other lesser lights who were trying to popularize astronomy and science in their own writing, seemed to have been "led to follow [Herschel's] example in precisely that matter in which it was least desirable that he should be imitated. . . . [they copied one of his particularly poor expressions] as carefully as if it were an ornament rather than a blemish of his style" (37). Hardy allows Swithin to blunder in the same way in his first article. Although Hardy explicitly states in several places that the youthful Swithin is patterning his career after that of the young John Herschel, the additional parallel between the astronomical writing style of Hardy's character and Herschel has not, to my knowledge, been drawn before. Hardy legitimizes Swithin's work and writing by linking it so directly to that of *the* scientific hero of the Victorian age. That linkage provides him with an automatically authoritative grounding for the technical aspects of contemporary astronomy as well as a rhetorical foothold upon which to introduce their cosmological implications.

As the events of the novel unfold, true to the slings and arrows of outrageous scientific fortunes – so full of priority disputes and chauvinistic controversies in the nineteenth century – what could have been Swithin's first professional and public success proves to be his first set-back. As he returns from sending his article, he sorts through his mail only to find a review of a pamphlet by an American astronomer which scooped his discovery by six weeks. Shattered by the melodramatic intervention of such an accident, Swithin (melodramatically) falls dangerously ill. His recovery is uncertain until the comet appears and gives him (and the rest of the novel) a *raison d' être* (79). Within minutes of the news, the novel takes an equally sudden melodramatic upturn, and Swithin has set-up a telescope upon his bed, begun taking notes on the comet's appearance and is once again hoping to make the unknown known.

While observing the comet low on the horizon, the chance circumstance of melodrama again places a new object of observation within Swithin's line of sight: Lady Constantine. Swithin recognizes his feelings for her, and, as his love grows, he finds himself increasingly distracted from his astronomical studies. Neither one of the two wants Swithin to give up his work, so the couple considers two options. One, a good Newtonian resolution, is to decrease the attraction between them by increasing their distance from each other. Swithin proposes to join an expedition to the Cape of Good Hope to observe the southern hemisphere of heaven which appeals to him as a "less exhausted" field of study (114). The other suggestion (the one they adopt) is to take the distracting uncertainty out of their relationship and marry (yet continue to live apart) in order to "restore regularity to [Swithin's] work" (151). As we will see, the shifting dynamics in the romantic plot line here will be mirrored within the professional story as well as at the level of the novel's metaphorical physics.

Just as Swithin has been doggedly determined to stick with astronomy, he now applies that same determination to staying with Viviette; indeed, out of loyalty to her, he rejects an offer that would allow him to realize his most grandiose professional goals. When his great uncle sends a letter offering him a large annuity, inheritance, and financing for a Cape expedition with the strongly worded admonition that he must not marry until age twenty-five (136–7), Swithin ignores it completely. Of course his uncle's words ("Your wide heaven of study, young man, will soon reduce itself to the miserable expanse of her face, and your myriad stars to her two trumpery eyes" (138)) come true. Although Swithin observes occasionally, he finds himself directing his telescope more often toward Viviette's window to watch for a signal to rendezvous (167). Hardy juxtaposes Swithin's resigned acceptance of his decision to remain in England (symbolized by his new study of "fixed" stars) with Swithin's anxiety about missing professional opportunities, especially the upcoming Transit of Venus. Since his marriage, Swithin has been invited by leading astronomers at Greenwich (including the Astronomer Royal) to join an expedition to the Caribbean to observe the transit and has been offered subsequent use, for his own studies, of the Cape Observatory (251, 264). That he might miss the Transit of Venus because of the "love" that is "crossing" his own path, would not be lost on those readers alert to the wordplay.[10]

Whatever his marital state, Hardy's narrative makes it clear that Swithin's skill as an astronomer (and no doubt the renown of his state-of-the-art equipment) have enabled him to enter the circle of advanced amateur and professional British astronomers. It is the intervention of chance again, however, that allows Swithin to pursue astronomy on a full-time international level. Swithin's marriage to Viviette is invalidated when it is learned that the death of Viviette's husband in Africa was misreported and actually occurred after their marriage and not before it. The

---

[10] Transits of Venus were literally "in the air" as Hardy wrote *Two on a Tower* and Richard Proctor had published a popular astronomical account less than ten years earlier on the subject to prepare the popular Victorian mind for the upcoming phenomena (*Transits of Venus*, 1874). Current authors are still exploiting the double meaning of the phrase, using it as the title for drama, volumes of poems, travelogues and novels. Among such works, Shirley Hazzard's novel, *The Transits of Venus* (New York: Penguin, 1980), is probably best known.

consequences of this chance error seem easily rectifiable to Swithin, but Viviette considers the occurrence as a message from God to stop holding Swithin back from his true love – astronomy. She urges him to take the opportunity to accept his uncle's proposal, and Swithin obeys her, promising to return when he is twenty-five.

Unfettered by love or monetary restrictions, Swithin embarks upon a grand astronomical tour, visiting the world's best observatories at Marseilles, Vienna, Poulkowa, Harvard, Yale, and Chicago, followed by the Transit Expedition, and several year's research at the Cape. Swithin arranges to ship his equatorial to the Cape and journeys there first to set up his personal observatory, which he plans to use to supplement his use of the Royal Observatory at Capetown. Swithin then takes the steamer to the United States, where his letters of introduction from Greenwich gain him observing time with the "gigantic refractor" at Yale and many hours of pleasurable intellectual exchange with the "scientific group" there (294). After accompanying the U.S. astronomers on the Transit Expedition to the Pacific, Swithin returns to South Africa to extend and improve upon the charting of the southern hemisphere begun by John Herschel. Swithin is immediately struck by the relative bounty of clear observing nights compared to England. With a "child's delight" (298) he spends his first few months there widely surveying the "new Horizon."

At this point, Hardy openly indicates to his readers that he is in a hurry. Those who had any special interest in the day-to-day activities of a professional astronomer must have felt a certain disappointment to find that Hardy, rushing to meet the deadline for the manuscript's serial publication, decided not to include a complete account of Swithin's four year's of observational work at the Cape. About the details and results of such observations, he has the narrator ask, "Is not all written in the chronicles of the Astronomical Society?" (294).

Although Hardy glosses over the technical aspects of cutting-edge observational astronomy, he pauses long enough to allow his readers to contemplate the "rest" of the heavens as his fictional observer is now beholding them for the first time. Part of Swithin's intellectual excitement about the southern sky stems not only from the sense of discovery at observing its uncharted territory, but from the fact that no long tradition of his Western culture's anthropomorphic mythology makes this unknown region seem as familiar to him as the northern sky: "This was an even more unknown tract of the unknown" (300). All of the grandeur, magnificence, and horror Swithin felt observing the void spaces of the northern hemisphere are magnified by those of the south: "Space here, being less the historic haunt of human thought than overhead at home, seemed to be pervaded with a more lonely loneliness" (300).[11]

Swithin's sense of isolation as a solitary observer in the universe increases when he is surrounded by previously unmet celestial forms: "hybrid suns, fire-fogs, floating

---

[11] I recall with gratitude that the late William Coleman, University of Wisconsin-Madison, pointed out to me several years ago that this passage seems to indicate that Hardy was unaware, or had forgotten, that other peoples, besides the British, had observed and had created myths about the celestial objects they saw in the southern hemisphere's sky.

nuclei, globes that flew in groups like swarms of bees" (299). At such times, Swithin thinks of his distant observing partner, Viviette, but, as the narrator points out, while Swithin is learning a great deal about the external, intellectually perceived universe, what he is learning about the internal, emotional world of himself is less clear.

> Were there given on paper to these astronomical exercitations of St. Cleeve a space proportionable to that occupied by his year with Viviette at Welland, this narrative would treble its length; but not a single additional glimpse would be afforded of Swithin in his relations with old emotions. In these experiments with tubes and glasses, important as they were to human intellect, there was little food for the sympathetic instincts which create the changes in a life. That which is the foreground and measuring base of one perspective draught, may be the vanishing-point of another perspective draught, where yet they are both draughts of the same thing. Swithin's doings and discoveries in the southern sidereal system were, no doubt, incidents of the highest importance to him; and yet from an intersocial point of view they served but the humble purpose of killing time, while other doings, more nearly allied to his heart than to his understanding, developed themselves at home. (300)

At the end of more than three years of "professional occupations," Swithin (again, like John Herschel) has accumulated a "wheel-barrow load" of observations from which he will write a "treatise of scientific utility" (299). His observing work done, Swithin knows it is necessary to return to England to publish his findings. The equatorial is shipped back along with his documents, memoranda, and "rolls upon rolls of diagrams" (302). As soon as he arrives home he hires a local girl to serve as his secretarial assistant in compiling his notes (302), an arrangement increasingly typical in local astronomical societies and clubs of the time.[12] After arranging his professional life, Swithin looks for Viviette, intending to keep his promise to her and offer remarriage. The look of disappointment on his face when he sees how unattractively she has aged causes Viviette to excuse Swithin from his obligation to her, and he turns to leave. Unexpectedly, Swithin changes his mind, realizing that his love for her exceeds matters of physical attraction, and rushes back to her. The joy of this revelation kills Viviette and she dies immediately in his arms. Melancholily surveying his surroundings, holding his dead love tenderly, Swithin's eye catches a glimpse of Tabitha Lark, "the single bright spot of colour and animation" on the "wide Horizon" (313). She is his newly hired astronomical assistant, the one with whom, Hardy implies, Swithin will spend his future.

~

Reviewing the details of the astronomical plot line in this way gives a misleading impression of the amount of narrative space Hardy actually devotes to Swithin's work

---

[12]   See: Chapter 14: "Now ladies as well as gentlemen" in Chapman, *The Victorian Amateur Astronomer* 273–93.

in *Two on a Tower*. The amateur stage of Swithin's career is covered in seventy-five pages of text, fully half of which also introduces Viviette's life and activities. The years Swithin spends abroad, when Hardy does concentrate exclusively on the astronomer, are compressed into forty-five pages; while by far the most page space is lent to Hardy's account of the relationship between Swithin and Viviette (180 pages). But, as Hardy's narrator has already made clear, "the foreground and measuring base of one perspective draught may be the vanishing-point of another," and just so, he dovetails the cosmological significance of his story onto the details of the astronomical narrative.

As in *A Pair of Blue Eyes*, *Far From the Madding Crowd* and *The Return of the Native*, Hardy carries out in *Two on a Tower* a type of thought-experiment in which he tests how his human characters will act once given knowledge of the conditions of an infinite, randomly generated, and probably godless universe. As we have seen in the preceding synopsis, Hardy creates characters who embody the central philosophical and cultural issues that astronomy was raising in his society, and has them act out and voice the range of nineteenth-century responses to new scientific information and conceptualizations of the universe. To underscore these basic conditions and responses, Hardy relates humanity to the cosmos via complex astronomical analogies by which he illustrates the significance and dignity of human love, even relative to the far greater size of the universe. Human kindness can be an influential force in the cosmos, he suggests, for by it we may help each other cope with the knowledge of our own mortality and smallness.

The major governing image of *Two on a Tower* is that of variable stars. Hardy describes Swithin and Viviette as exhibiting behavior similar to that of eclipsing binaries changing over time their relative positions on personal, social, even geographical planes. Their orbits around each other are functions of their mutual attraction, relative distances, brightness and age. Hardy reinforces his suggestion that his main characters (and we) are star stuff, by extending the symbolic presence of astronomy in their world. In one case, Hardy draws upon contemporary cometary theory, still extant astrological associations with comets, and the importance of comets in the history of astronomy, to create the fullest meaning for one of the novel's most significant moments. In another case, Hardy returns to the device of a lunar eclipse. In all three tropes, the astronomical phenomena metaphorically model the dynamics of the physical and emotional relationships in which the story's human characters find themselves.

Stellar Dynamics and Astronomical Tropes in *Two on a Tower*

Variable Stars and a Multiple Star System

Throughout his novels, Hardy commonly pairs characters of opposite genders, personality types, social ranks, and roles. Likewise, he characteristically selects the natural setting for each story, carefully matching the elements of the fictional landscape to the forces and circumstances that will be most at play upon his characters. Whereas in *The Return of the Native* the imposing presence of the heath dominates the physical space in which the story takes place, in *Two on a Tower*, astrophysics *is* the environment of the novel; the stellar universe is not "above" the main characters, they (and we) are inescapably *in* it, at all times and places, whatever their local or social positions on earth.

In this story, the juxtaposition of Hardy's central male and female characters is described in terms of a strong structural astronomical metaphor, that of variable stars. When Viviette and Swithin first come within each other's ken, Hardy contrasts their physical appearance, personality, social position, age, and motivations. She is dark-haired, pale, emotional, wealthy, near thirty and romantically inclined. He is fair-haired, rosy in complexion (with "Rafael's coloring"), rational, of poor stock, near twenty and scientifically oriented. During the progress of the story, Swithin's and Viviette's relative positions are reversed. Swithin, from a poor country family, rises in the professional astronomical world. Viviette's position, conversely, is reduced to naught by her husband's death and debts. After Swithin and Viviette have become a couple, she is required by circumstance (and by Swithin's suggestion) to take on the traditionally male role of obtaining their marriage license where he remains behind to tend to the domestic repairs of his grandmother's house. Viviette, for love of Swithin, benevolently sacrifices her own desire to marry him so that he may be saved from losing his inheritance. At book's end, Swithin offers to marry Viviette and sacrifice his own career, freedom, and opportunities in order to save her from loneliness in middle age.

When Swithin is introduced in Chapter 1, he is engaged in the study of variable stars and believes himself to be on the verge of formulating a new theory to explain their changing color and intensity. His hypothesis is confirmed with the aid of the larger telescope and equatorial Viviette purchases for him. The theory Swithin probably put forth (but which Hardy leaves implicit) is that the visible effect of changing appearance in variable stars is not the result of a single star varying in hue and brightness, but the phenomena created by one of two binary combinations: i) two stars of different colors revolve around each other with the stars alternatively observable from Earth so that the object occupying a single position on a star map would appear, for instance, sometimes red, sometimes white; or, ii) a single star could be eclipsed periodically by a non-luminous, dark body revolving around it and passing between the star and the Earth thus causing the star's brightness to be "shut on or off" or waver in intensity.

Astronomers had long had a general awareness of the existence of double stars although there was some disagreement over whether the appearance of double stars was simply a visual phenomenon or a physical reality. William Herschel had catalogued thousands of double stars. The notion of "eclipsing" binaries also had long been familiar. For instance, the "eclipse" theory had been suggested as an explanation for the variation of Algol by John Goodricke who published his discovery of the periodicity of the variation in 1783 (Clerke 390). As Agnes Clerke points out, however, "the conditions involved by the explanation were first seriously investigated by an American astronomer E. C. Pickering in 1880" (Clerke 390). Pickering's research into the hypothesis received wide publication in England and was probably the one that would have been the best publicized at the time Hardy was writing *Two on a Tower* (Clerke 427).[13]

Classifications of different star colors (the range including white, blue, yellow and red) had been published by Angelo Secchi (ca. 1863–67) and theories regarding the cause of the difference soon followed. H. C. Vogel's theory (ca. 1874) that star color represented star age was pervasive in nineteenth-century England, though by no means completely accepted. Vogel tagged white stars as the youngest (because the hottest), yellow stars as advancing toward middle age, and red stars as "hastening rapidly down the road to final extinction" (Clerke 424). Clerke, however, qualified her account (ca. 1887) of Vogel's theory by saying that it was just as likely that "red may after all be 'younger' than white stars," as the pattern of stellar development and decline in relation to star color is simply "not known."[14] Nonetheless, the state of double star or variable star theory at the time Hardy was writing *Two on a Tower* favored Pickering's and Vogel's ideas.

Swithin and Viviette are consistently and constantly described in their relationship as a stellar binary pair. Swithin is light, luminous. Viviette is dark, pale. Swithin is young; Viviette is approaching middle age. Hardy foreshadows the final result of their age difference in Swithin's reference to the decline of a star in Ursa Major (possibly the binary Mizar-Alcor, the easiest binary to visualize in the northern hemisphere).

> And to add a new weirdness to what the sky possesses in its size and formlessness, there is involved the quality of decay. For all the wonder of these everlasting stars, eternal spheres, and what not, they are not everlasting, they are not eternal; they burn out like candles. You see that dying one in the body of the greater Bear? Two centuries ago it was as bright as the others.[15] (34)

At the end of the same chapter, Hardy compares Swithin and Viviette to two stars in Gemini (very likely the spectroscopic binary alpha Geminorum β and Castor β which Swithin mentions again in Chapter 9): "where two stars in the Twins looked down upon their persons through the trees, as if those two persons could bear some sort of comparison with them" (39). "As if," indeed.

Ironically, Proctor may have inadvertently suggested the double stars/human couple analogy to Hardy by lapsing into the overly "familiar" and slightly anthropomorphic kind of description for which he often chided Herschel. Double stars

---

[13] I have been unable to find a young British astronomer who was "scooped" by Pickering.
[14] Current theory regarding correlation of star color and age has tended to support Vogel's suggestions that cooler (redder) stars are older than hotter (blue/white) stars.
[15] Mizar-Alcor is not in the body proper of the constellation Ursa Major but appears at the base of the tail, or near the bend in the handle of the Big Dipper.

were one of John Herschel's major research interests and he provided visual evidence to prove that binaries were physically related. As Proctor prepares to describe Herschel's contribution to this field of study, he writes:

> [Herschel's] first [field of study] related to those double stars which now form so favourite a subject of study with the amateur astronomer. His father, commencing the investigation of these objects under the impression that the two stars which seemed to form each pair were but accidentally seen nearly in the same direction, had been led after long labours to the conclusion that the double stars are for the most part real star-couples, physically associated by the mighty bond of their common attraction. (14)

In the chapter of the *Essays* that Proctor devotes to "Coloured Suns," he describes the beautiful color combinations of many double and multiple star systems in detail. He singles out for special mention the case of "complementary doubles," noting that "there is one very charming instance" in the star Albireo: "The components of this star are orange and blue, the tints being well pronounced. It has been found that when one of the components is hidden the other still preserves its colour, though not quite so distinctly as when both are seen together" (260). As I have pointed out, Hardy's astronomical "star-couple" complement each other in a similar way, playing off of the well-known cliché in human pairings that "opposites attract."

Hardy describes the love of Swithin and Viviette for each other as the mutual gravitational attraction between two heavenly bodies. They revolve around each other, moving in paths and tracing patterns which border on each other's usual "promenades," "channels," "habitual paths," and territory boundaries. As Swithin begins to recognize his feelings for Lady Constantine, he feels drawn to her and "approaches" her home,

> lingering about uncertainly, in the hope of intercepting her on her return from a drive, occasionally walking with an indifferent lounge across glades commanded by the windows, that if she were indoors she might know he was near. But she did not show herself during the daylight. Still impressed by her playful secrecy he carried on the same idea after dark, by returning to the house and passing through the garden door onto the lawn front, where he sat on the parapet that breasted the terrace.
>
> Now she frequently came out here for a melancholy saunter after dinner, and to-night was such an occasion. Swithin went forward, and met her at nearly the spot where he had dropped the lens some nights earlier. (48–9)

The meeting ends with a statement by Swithin that summarizes the Venn diagram of their orbits in relation to each other (and echoes a similar statement by a lesser "body" to a "greater" in *The Return of the Native*).[16]

---

[16] The Venn diagram of two interlocking circles is similar to the orbital pattern of binary star pairs.

But you will never realize that an incident which filled but a degree in the circle of your thoughts covered the whole circumference of mine. No person can see exactly what and where another's horizon is. (49)

Viviette is attracted in a similar way to Swithin in Chapter 9. When Swithin has fallen dangerously ill after failing to be the originator of the variable star hypothesis and fails to appear at the tower for some time, Viviette makes repeated trips to the column to find him. Her failure to meet him there makes "it seem as if the whole science of astronomy had never been real, and that the heavenly bodies, with their motions, were as theoretical as the lines and circles of a bygone mathematical problem" (73). She then changes course and walks to the nearest hamlet to see if she can learn anything of Swithin's whereabouts. Upon learning that he is ill, she is drawn on toward Swithin's grandmother's home. She reaches the house, is shown in, and is at first content to wait downstairs. "No longer under the control of judgement," she asks to be let up to see Swithin and is guided through his astronomical workroom back into his bedroom. As she is visiting Swithin, the doctor arrives and she withdraws back into the workroom. Hearing from the doctor that Swithin has changed for the worse, she rushes in "[flings] herself upon the bed and [kisses] him" (77).

The mutual attraction of Swithin and Viviette is also placed in an astronomical context (albeit homespun) by Tabitha Lark, a country girl employed to read to Viviette, who realizes that Viviette's interest in astronomy and Swithin has pulled her into an uncharacteristic orbit unbecoming her social position.

> "They say that it isn't the moon, and it isn't the stars and it isn't the plannards, that my lady cares for, but for the pretty lad who draws 'em down from the sky to please her; and being a married example, and what with sin and shame knocking at every poor maid's door afore you can say 'Hands off, my dear,' to the civilest young man, she ought to set a better pattern." (59–60)

Viviette, who has overheard this comment, quickly rushes to Swithin to undo the visible ties of their partnership and takes pains to appear invisible in her influence on and involvement with his research.

> "Astronomy is not my hobby any longer. And you are not my Astronomer Royal. Of course astronomy is my hobby privately and you are to be my Astronomer Royal, and I still furnish the observatory; but not to the outer world. There is a reason against my indulgence in such scientific fancies openly; and the project must by arranged in this wise. The whole enterprise is yours; you rent the tower of me; you build the cabin; you get the equatorial. I simply give permission, since you desire it. The path that was to be made from the hill to the park is not to be thought of. There is to be no communication between the house and the column. The equatorial will arrive addressed to you, and its cost I will pay through you. My name must not appear, and I vanish entirely from the undertaking . . . This blind is necessary." (60–61)

As a binary pair, Swithin and Viviette are each cognizant of and influenced by the place of the other in space and time. Their awareness of the other's position and the strength of their attraction for each other vary in direct proportion to the distance or proximity of their positions. When Swithin is away touring the Greenwich Observatory, Viviette discovers that the date of her first husband's death was in error. She contemplates a remarriage with Swithin and looks forward to their second "conjuncture" and his return to her from his trip:

> Taking brighter views, she hoped that upon the whole this yoking of the young fellow with her, a portionless woman and his senior, would not greatly endanger his career. In such a mood night overtook her, and she went to bed conjecturing that Swithin had by this time arrived in the parish, was perhaps even at that moment passing homeward beneath her walls and that in less than twelve hours she would have met him, have ventilated the secret which oppressed her, and have satisfactorily arranged with him the details of their reunion. (242)

As Swithin leaves for the far distant Cape of Good Hope, he and Viviette lose touch with each other's movements. Viviette, now knowing that she is pregnant, tries to follow him but cannot guess which way he has gone, or even to what continent (279). The farther south Swithin travels, the more "new ideas" attract him and "absorb [his] attention that way" and the more grows

> a corresponding forgetfulness of what lay to the north behind his back, whether human or celestial ... Whoever may deplore it few will wonder that Viviette, who till then had stood high in his heaven, if she had not dominated it, sank, like the North Star, lower and lower with his retreat southward. (292–3)

When his work in the southern hemisphere is finished, Swithin begins to be re-attracted to the north and Viviette. He begins to think about her and consider a reconciliation with her (302) and "by chance" hears word of her. Once he has arrived in his home parish, Swithin lingers around Viviette's estate, until he feels compelled to see her: "Now that he was actually within her coasts again Swithin felt a little more strongly the influence of the past and Viviette than he had been accustomed to do for the last two or three years" (308). Catching a random glimpse of the tower, Swithin intuitively knows "somebody is on the column" and,

> instead of going straight to the Great House [Viviette's] he deviated through the insulating field, now sown with turnips, which surrounded the plantation on Rings-Hill. By the time that he plunged under the trees he was still more certain that somebody was on the tower. He crept up to the base with proprietary curiosity, for the spot seemed again like his own. The path still remained much as formerly. (309)

It is on the tower that the novel's final melodramatic scene takes place. Viviette, seeing Swithin's dismay at how much she has aged, releases him from his promise to her and sends him back down the tower's stairs. He, obeying "something [like] the natural laws that [were his] study . . . mechanically descended" (312). However, as he descends, he recognizes that their relationship has changed from passion to "loving kindness," a force, which, he suddenly realizes, is just as strong an attraction. He then rushes back up to her embrace.

When Viviette and Swithin are closest in their relationship immediately after their elopement, Hardy establishes an especially close association between them and the variable stars Swithin has been studying. Hardy places them arm-in-arm, newly bound as husband and wife, on the same road and moving in the same direction as Swithin had previously traveled alone several months before. Now they travel in the same orbit.

> They did not rejoin each other till they had reached a shadowy bend in the old turnpike road, beyond the irradiation of the Warborne lamplight. The walk to Welland was long. It was the walk which Swithin had taken in the rain when he had learnt the fatal forestallment of his stellar discovery; but now he was moved by a less desperate mood, and blamed neither God nor man. They were not pressed for time, and passed along the silent, lonely way with that sense rather of predestination than of choice in their proceedings which the presence of night sometimes imparts. (147)

The notion that one star of a binary pair can "eclipse" the other is also used by Hardy to describe aspects of the relationship between Swithin and Viviette. Swithin is warned by his uncle not to allow Lady Constantine to fall into "his path." Swithin admits to himself that Viviette often did "eclipse" his observational opportunities.

> There it had happened more than once that, after waiting idle through days and nights of cloudy weather, Viviette would fix her time for meeting him at an hour when at last he had an opportunity of seeing the sky; so that in giving to her the golden moments of cloudlessness he was losing his chance with the orbs above. (297)

Hardy extends the eclipsing binary metaphor at the moment of Viviette's demise, when as a dead star her attractive force would be diminished, and Swithin is simultaneously attracted to the "animated" Tabitha Lark "on the horizon." Hardy had described Tabitha just six pages earlier as one of those talented "Wonderful Women who had resolved to eclipse masculine genius altogether" (307). True to the astronomy of his day, Hardy uses the information that "binary" systems could often be composed of more than two members which could vary greatly in their distance from one another. Tabitha has been hovering in the distance throughout the book. She was first present as a member of the choir singing below Swithin, then as reading to Viviette in the Great House, then coming into contact with both Viviette and Swithin at the church. She has been mistakenly linked on various occasions with Swithin's "inconstancy" by Viviette, her brother and the Bishop (i.e., the "unseen something" as Hardy recorded in his notebook, that was perturbing his path). Hardy narrows

Tabitha's orbit toward Swithin as the novel closes in order to suggest the attraction and union the future holds for Swithin.

~

Hardy uses variations of the variable/multiple star metaphor to effect the large purpose of unifying the two main characters and to suggest that they, as matter in motion in the universe, behave as such. In describing the strength of their mutual attraction when close, its diminution when far apart, the perturbations that other neighboring bodies may introduce into their gravitational system, Hardy got the physics right. Unlike other celestial objects, however, Swithin and Viviette are matter with emotion, and for them (and by association, Hardy implies, for all of us), that makes all the difference. He extends this message about the physical and emotional dynamics interacting within human lives in two other extended astronomical metaphors (comets and a lunar eclipse) that serve simultaneously to complicate the action of the story as well as to enrich its philosophical substance.

A Comet Injects Energy into the System[17]

At the end of Chapter 9, Swithin is distraught to the point of endangering his health over his abortive attempt to publish his variable star theory. He believes he has lost all reason to live, all purpose to his astronomical observations, and all chance of becoming the "new Copernicus." Then the comet appears. Swithin immediately recovers, and Hardy then informs the reader that comets have all along been Swithin's first and foremost astronomical interest, holding for him an even greater fascination than variable stars. So positive is the change in Swithin's condition that Hardy credits the comet with saving Swithin's life (80). Hardy's use of the comet in the plot serves to bring about the important recognition scene in which Swithin becomes aware of his love for Viviette and her love for him. Hardy builds carefully toward the recognition by first having Swithin see Viviette in a new light – as a comet – an object that he (unlike Boldwood) knows how to observe.

> One evening a little later on he was sitting at his bedroom window as usual, waiting for a sufficient decline of light to reveal the comet's form, when he beheld, crossing the field contiguous to the house, a figure which he knew to be hers. He thought she must be coming to see him on the great comet question, to discuss which with so delightful and kind a comrade was an expectation full of pleasure. Hence he keenly observed her approach, till something happened that surprised him.

---

[17]   Newton, Halley, Whiston and others had all seriously considered that God might send comets into our solar system as a way to fine-tune planetary orbits and maintain the equilibrium of their complex and interrelated motions; for a discussion of cometary theory within the broader context of Newtonian astronomy and physics, see this volume's Chapter 3: 82–6.

When, at the descent of the hill, she had reached the stile that admitted to [his garden], Lady Constantine stood quite still for a minute or more, her gaze bent on the ground. Instead of coming on to the house she went heavily and slowly back, almost as if in pain; and then at length, quickening her pace, she was soon out of sight. She appeared in the path no more that day. (82–3)

The pattern of Lady Constantine's approach, turning and retreat, and change of speed, would no doubt remind an astronomer such as Swithin of the long elliptical orbit of the comet he has been observing. Until this point in the book, Swithin has not really "seen" Viviette as she is, but only as his benefactress. The next time they meet, they observe the comet together for the first time and Swithin, "the scales [fallen] from his eyes" (97) and with a "sudden sense of new relation with his sweet patroness" (101), confesses that he now has "two devotions, two thoughts, two hopes and two blessings in this world"– astronomy and Lady Constantine (93).

Hardy also utilizes the comet to allow him to foreshadow, through the country folks' speculations on the comet's meaning, the ways in which the comet may affect the later action of the novel. Haymoss predicts that Swithin's and Viviette's "ruling plannards" may end in a wedding. His companions assert that the comet foretells Viviette's downfall. Both forecasts of the folksy sky-readers come true.

The comet gathers more symbolic power as a representation of the shift in action from the superlunary realm to the sublunary region. In astronomical history Tycho Brahe's cometary observations shattered the notion of the perfection and changelessness of the superlunary universe and extended decisively, change and imperfection into the starry heights. Swithin's character shifts in a similar way, redirecting his energy from the stars to more earthly concerns:

The alchemy which thus transmuted an abstracted astronomer into an eager lover – and, must it be said: spoilt a promising young physicist to produce a common-place inamorato – may be almost described as working its change in one short night. (102–3)

Indeed, Hardy suggests a specific parallel between Swithin and the comet by mentioning the comet as approaching the sun at its closest point just as Swithin is glancing from the sun to Lady Constantine with this emotion,

half echoing the Greek astronomer's wish that he might be set close to that luminary for the wonder of beholding it in all its glory, under the slight penalty of being consumed the next instant. (103)

Without explicit statement, Hardy makes it clear with the juxtaposition of Swithin's two objects of desire that the youth is nurturing a dangerously consuming passion.[18]

---

[18] The Transit of Venus to which Swithin is looking forward in the book is related to the comet imagery here in that *Two on a Tower* is about "love crossing" the universe, and by the fact that the measurements obtained from Venus transits were used to estimate the distance

Almost in direct opposition to this warning-off, however, Hardy balances his presentation of the love of Swithin and Viviette by another direct correspondence with the comet. Just as the comet is peaking at its greatest proportions, stretching across the sky at such length that it dominates the horizon, but is poised to wane, Hardy chooses to express the sentiment that Swithin and Viviette are living at that moment, an instant of "human life at its highest excitement" – two human beings professing love for one another, and deciding to wed (116). Hardy concludes with some sympathy and some humor,

> He drew her yielding form to his heart, and her head sank upon his shoulder, as he pressed his two lips continuously upon hers. To such had the study of celestial physics brought them in the space of eight months, one week and a few odd days. (117)

Hardy used a similar humorous aside within the lunar eclipse scene in *The Return of the Native* to comment on how rapidly Clym and Eustacia had become attached to one another. Here, however, Hardy's comment provides a transition between the initial stage of Swithin's career during which he was an active observer, and the second stage, during which his love affair will be his first priority. In *Two on a Tower* the apparition of the comet serves Hardy as the carrier of tremendously varied metaphoric meanings, the intricacy of which rivals that of Donne's poetic use of elaborate conceits. Hardy may well have been so familiar with comets and their significance in history because of his own first-hand observation and study of them.

Within the novel, the comet's apparition extends from Chapter 10 through Chapter 15 (seven months). The characteristics of the comet as Hardy gives them are identifiable with a historic comet that he himself observed. Hardy describes the comet as not "Gambart's . . . Charles the Fifth's, or Halley's or Faye's," but as the largest in fifty years, of unknown period, reaching perihelion (nearest proximity to the sun) in the autumn and so bright it was visible in daylight. Both Carl Weber and Robert Gittings believe that the comet in *Two on a Tower* is drawn from the June 1881 apparition of Tebbutt's Comet. Weber speculates that the 1881 comet reminded Hardy of another one that he had observed back in 1858 (the estimated year of the novel's introductory action) and that he consequently transferred characteristics of the 1881 comet to the '58 comet for "fictional purposes."[19] Such an extrapolation is only necessary if one thinks (as Weber does) that the comet Hardy writes of seeing in 1858 or 1859 – "a very large one" – (Weber 133) is a reference to Encke's Comet visible for a short time in October, 1858. I believe that Weber is mistaken in this conclusion on several counts. Although Encke's was visible in the autumn of 1858, it was a faint comet, of "dim nebulosity without . . . outline" and did not display a tail or even much

---

from Earth to the sun.
[19] Carl J. Weber, *Hardy of Wessex: His Life and Literary Career* (New York: Columbia University Press, 1965) 133; hereafter: Weber.

elongation of the nucleus.[20] In his poem, "The Comet at Yell'ham," written about viewing the comet of 1858, Hardy specifically states that the comet showed a "fiery train." Hardy mentions that the comet "as described" in his poem was true to his observation of it (as in Weber 133). Encke's Comet, with its extremely short period (3.3 years), was, by mid-century, the best-documented comet of short periodicity and in no way fits the description of the comet in the novel (except for its year of appearance).

Donati's Comet, a fine bright comet, with a long (70 degree) curving tail also appeared in 1858.[21] It was visible in Italy in June and was at its brightest in England in September and October and remained visible into the early months of 1859. These dates approximate the early summer to late autumn visibility of the comet in *Two on a Tower*. It was the brightest comet since that of 1811 (about "fifty years") and was of unknown period, although it was later calculated that it would reappear in about 2,000 years. In Hardy's narration of the comet's perihelion passage he observes that it "would soon disappear for perhaps thousands of years" (111). As Watson describes the comet, "it would present a magnificent appearance in the western heavens soon after sunset" (135). This detail is true to Hardy's description of Swithin's experience, eagerly and anxiously awaiting sundown so he can view the comet out of his western-facing bedroom window (81). Also at one point, Donati's Comet was so bright that it could be seen in "bright twilight" before the sun was down and in the morning before dawn.[22] Further, Donati's was similar in brightness and size to the novel's comet and falls directly into the chronology of "Gambart's" (of 1826, so called by the French, but in England then and now currently known as "Biela's"), Halley's of 1835, and Faye's of 1843, 1851, and 1858. The mention of "Charles the Fifth's" comet especially supports my view as the return of the comet of 1556 which was credited with causing his abdication (perforce, retroactively, as Chambers points out, since Charles V abdicated in 1555) was expected in 1858 and was carefully watched for by astronomers and the public alike; but did not appear.[23] In fairness to Weber and Gittings, Tebbutt's Comet in 1881 probably did serve as inspiration for Hardy's choice of an astronomical setting for *Two on a Tower*, although the comet itself did not display many of the characteristics of the novel's comet. Tebbutt's, "a fairly bright

---

[20]   James C. Watson, *A Popular Treatise on Comets* (Philadelphia: James Challen and Son, 1861) 224; hereafter: Watson.
[21]   I originally offered these arguments supporting my view that Donati's Comet was the model for the fictional one observed by Swithin in my 1989 dissertation, *Poetic Resolutions of Scientific Revolutions* 487–90. Thirteen years later, Martin Ray used similar reasoning to conclude that Donati's inspired Hardy's poem, "The Comet at Yell'ham," although he does not extend his analysis to the comet described in *Two on a Tower*; see: "Hardy's 'The Comet at Yell'ham' and Donati's Comet" *Notes and Queries* 49.4: (Dec. 2002) 491.
[22]   See this book's cover for William Dyce's painting depicting this scene, "Pegwell Bay, Kent: A Recollection of October 5th 1858" (ca. 1858–1860, Tate Gallery)
[23]   George F. Chambers, *The Story of the Comets* (Oxford: Clarendon Press, 1909) 100–101; hereafter: Chambers.

comet," appeared in June 1881 but vanished from England's view in July, although it was observed in other parts of the world for a total of about nine months (Clerke 400–404). It had in common with Donati's and the novel's comet an extremely long period, estimated at 2,428 years.

~

However much the fictional comet may have depended upon the physical characteristics and behavior of its real-life astronomical peers, Hardy's use of the phenomenon exploits its symbolic value in multilayered ways. Like Newton's divine engineer, Hardy, as author, uses the apparition of the comet to inject energy into his story. The comet revitalizes Swithin's interest in his professional life and awakens him to love. Its presence in the plotline enables Hardy to shift emphasis from the celestial to terrestrial realms and, simultaneously, foreshadow the consequences his characters will experience because of that shift. With the comet's bright tail outstretched and poised above the narrative plane, Hardy, in imitation, pauses the action to remark on the momentous – but all too momentary – feelings shared by two human beings who are falling in love.

Celestial and Human Dynamics:
 A Lunar Eclipse, Revisited and the Melodrama of the Milky Way

Hardy drew upon his first-hand observation of a lunar eclipse to create a detailed account of the event in a poem and in a complex psychological scene in *The Return of the Native*. A lunar eclipse also occurs within the storyline of *Two on a Tower*, during what must have been one of the busiest astronomical years (albeit fictional) on record. Within the novel, the eclipse serves metaphorically to foreshadow important shifts in plot development and to introduce another "three-body problem" that will have consequences for the main characters. The eclipse occurs in Chapter 23 "one bright night in April" just before the Bishop arrives to perform a confirmation service for the parish. The occurrence of the eclipse and the arrival of the Bishop seem coincidentally juxtaposed within the novel's action, but, in fact, as Hardy shows, the two events will have grave significance for Swithin. The Bishop, as a powerful symbol of religious leadership and as a new love interest for Viviette, will "eclipse" and displace Swithin in Lady Constantine's favor both as her spiritual guide and as her husband. The relative importance of astronomy and religion will be directly called into question as Viviette must choose between the two men (172). Viviette will ask Swithin to be confirmed and recognize "God" as something to "cling to" greater than "each other" (157). As Swithin vacillates in making a decision, he will find himself outcast from Viviette's social "sphere" as she, as Lady of the county, entertains the Bishop during his visit (178).

The connection between the Bishop and the eclipse in relation to Viviette is adeptly and subtly portrayed in Hardy's poetic description of how the Bishop, one night, watches her through her window and silently professes his love for her. Viviette's brother (another perturbation among the interacting bodies in the plot) witnesses the scene.

> Last night, when everybody had gone to bed, I stepped out for a five minutes' smoke on the lawn, and walked down to where you get near the vicarage windows. While I was there in the dark one of them opened, and Bishop Helmsdale leant out. The illuminated oblong of your window shone him full in the face between the trees, and presently your shadow crossed it. He waved his hand, and murmured some tender words, though what they were exactly I could not hear.[24] (207–8)

The basic configuration of a lunar eclipse (the shadow of a body lit from behind falling across a second body that receives light from the same source) should have been familiar enough to a certain portion of Hardy's audience (as it is in the present) that it was unnecessary for him to offer any further explanation of the astronomical allusion in the above image. However, the same audience probably did not have a good idea of the shape or speed of a comet's orbit or a working knowledge of variable star theory. The complexity, pervasiveness, and ingenuity of astronomical imagery in *Two on a Tower*'s structure, character relationships, plot and themes support my supposition that the novel is not so "slight" a story as some, including Hardy himself, have said.

Although variable stars, the comet, and the lunar eclipse are the images most intricately interwoven into the storyline and its themes, Hardy masterfully fashions other astronomical metaphors to reinforce connections between astronomical matters and human concerns in *Two on a Tower*. As the relationship between Swithin and Viviette is just beginning to develop, Hardy details at great length the construction of the observatory dome and viewing "slit" through which Swithin's equatorial guides his telescope, its movement synchronized with the diurnal motion of the celestial objects that he is observing (for the sake of convenience, the whole passage, previously quoted, is re-cited below).

> The top of the column was quite changed. The tub-shaped space within the parapet, formerly open to the air and sun, was now arched over by a light dome of lath-work covered with felt. But this dome was not fixed. At the line where its base descended to the parapet there were half a dozen iron balls, precisely like cannon-shot, standing loosely in a groove, and on these the dome rested its whole weight. In the side of the dome was a slit, through which the wind blew and the North Star beamed, and towards it the end of the great telescope was directed. This latter magnificent object, with its circles, axes, and handles complete, was securely fixed in the middle of the floor.

---

[24]   As far as I have been able to determine, there was no particular historical lunar eclipse in April, 1859 (the estimated date of the novel's eclipse). However, Hardy saw a lunar eclipse and wrote a poem, "At a Lunar Eclipse" about it, approximately fifteen years before writing *Two on a Tower* (ca. 1867).

"But you can only see one part of the sky through that slit," said she.

The astronomer stretched out his arm, and the whole dome turned horizontally round, running on the balls with a rumble like thunder. Instead of the star Polaris, which had first been peeping in through the slit, there now appeared the countenances of Castor and Pollux. Swithin then manipulated the equatorial and put it through its capabilities in like manner. (66)

In a typically strange melodramatic plot twist, Lady Constantine, returning from her elopement with Swithin, is accidentally marked by a lash of a carriage driver's whip which makes a "vertical slit" upon her cheek. Because Viviette recognizes the driver as her brother who had come to visit her and who must not know about her marriage, she cannot go home until the wound has healed. These circumstances make it necessary that she hide-out with Swithin at the observatory's cabin for several days. While there, Swithin tends her diligently and in four lines, Hardy discloses the way in which Swithin's two loves and observational subjects have merged: "The morning was passed in applying wet rags and other remedies to the purple line on Viviette's cheek; and in the afternoon they set up the equatorial under the replaced dome, to have it in order for night observations (151). Swithin works half of a day upon the "slit" which guides his view to Viviette's "stars," her eyes, and the other half he arranges the equipment and dome slit so that he can view the heavens.

Later the same evening, Swithin and Viviette relish together the visual glory of the aurora borealis. For once, they turn their backs on the equatorial and astronomical instruments to enjoy the display through their unaided human eyes. With this scene Hardy illustrates one way in which the apparently mundane human appreciation of the universe can become truly sublime in its beauty as it bonds human beings together. The scene offers a contrapuntal point of view to a similar scene of emotional bonding in *Far From the Madding Crowd* during which Bathsheba is bedazzled by the colorful, flashy, light display of the "aurora militaris" of Troy's sword play. Standing motionless in awe, as he cuts and parries around her, she is "within half an inch of being pared alive two hundred and ninety-five times" (146). Although Bathsheba is eventually married to Troy, the relationship will ultimately break apart into confusion and shame, as does the scene during which she witnesses the spectacle of this artificial aurora. In *Two on a Tower*, the beauty of the celestial lights is produced by natural energy, and Swithin's and Vivette's love for each other is naturally kindled as well. The awe they experience as they observe the atmospheric phenomenon together is love-inspiring and hope-giving, not bewildering and endangering.

In *Two on a Tower*, Hardy's invocations of celestial phenomena carry psychological insights about the nature of love and life. Sharing the experience of discovery and together observing new, previously unknown or uncomprehended objects or events in the universe engenders a sort of cognitive dissonance within his main characters, who, then, find their minds and hearts open to experiencing new feelings of connection and caring. Feeling small in comparison to it all, looking into the face of the vast cosmos, at least his characters have each other.

Hardy extends the reach of such references in his use of recurrent allusions to the Milky Way which mark changes in Swithin's and Viviette's love relationship as it develops over time. In the paradisal place destined to be lost, and with direct Miltonic echoes, Hardy arranges for the pair to meet in springtime in Viviette's garden "by the long snowdrop bed, which looked up at [Swithin] like a nether Milky Way" (64). By autumn, the fading foliage appears as "black stars" (155). At their final meeting, Viviette's greying hair reminds Swithin of the Milky Way: " . . . the masses of [her] hair that were once darkness visible had become touched here and there by a faint grey haze like the Via Lactea in a midnight sky" (311). The association of the Milky Way with time passing – as a marker of universal seasons, as the aging of a human life – bespeaks the final avengers of the novel: time, decay, and mortality. The poignancy of the emotional effect of this reference is deepened by the fact that it is the physical toll that her pregnancy and motherhood have had upon Viviette's appearance that inspire the "mother's milk" comparison to the "Via Lactea." Having found herself alone upon that path, she experienced much illumination and joy, but also suffered emotionally and physically – to give life, takes life.

Ironically, it was Viviette's faith in the framework of her religious cosmology that causes her to interpret a chance event (the misdating of her marriage) as a sign from God and consequently release Swithin so that he can make the most of his chance with astronomy. That act of self-sacrifice, noble and generous as it seems within her world view, complicates her life, making it harder than it needed to be. Had she been able to accept Swithin's godless interpretation of that random accident, she need not have been alone, need not have faced pregnancy out of wedlock, need not have endured the ironic stress of deceiving the Church *because* she honored it. This apparently small difference in world views and psychological interpretative frameworks marks a turning point for Viviette's and Swithin's futures. The universe may well be an extremely complex place, but the ability that Swithin has (like Gabriel Oak had) to accept pragmatically the fact that sometimes the random is just random, could make our responses to life's circumstances simpler and easier. Sometimes, Hardy seems to indicate, we need to get our cosmologies out of our way to see the universe for what it really is.

In his allusions to the Milky Way, Hardy creates a profound and touching poetic comparison between our galactic surroundings and Milton's death-bringer in *Paradise Lost*. Whether because of the evil of Satan or the physical nature of the nebular cloud, death and decay are an inescapable part of life in our cosmos. Whatever our cosmological explanation for those phenomena, our human challenge remains how we will respond to it. The same associations were present in contemporary astronomy and cosmology as evidenced by William Herschel's description of the Milky Way in his "Catalogue of a Second Thousand of new Nebulae and Clusters of Stars; with a few introductory Remarks on the Construction of the Heavens" published in *Philosophical*

Transactions in 1789.[25] In his explanation of how the Milky Way is an optical effect caused by our solar systems's location deep within our galaxy, Herschel describes the difficulty of determining the relative age of star clusters by the degree of their sphericity.

> Youth and age are comparative expressions; and an oak of a certain age may be called very young, where a contemporary shrub is already on the verge of its decay . . . so that, for instance, a cluster or nebula which is very gradually more compressed / and bright towards the middle, may be in the perfection of its growth, when another which approaches to the condition pointed out by a more equal compression, such as the nebulae I have called *Planetary* seem to present us with, may be looked upon as very aged, and drawing on towards a period of change, or dissolution. (Hoskin 114–15)

As the elder Herschel points out, recognizing that similar appearing objects may have different relative ages is an important step in assessing the constitutive parts of the universe and its evolution.

> This method of viewing the heavens seems to throw them into a new kind of light. They now are seen to resemble a luxuriant garden, which contains the greatest variety of productions, in different flourishing beds; and one advantage we may at least reap from it is, that we can, as it were, extend the range of our experience to an immense duration. For, to continue the simile I have borrowed from the vegetable kingdom, is it not almost the same thing, whether we live successively to witness the germination, blooming, foliage, fecundity, fading, withering, and corruption of a plant, or whether a vast number of specimens, selected from every stage through which the plant passes in the course of its existence, be brought at once to our view? (115)

In *Two on a Tower,* Hardy reapplies Herschel's "vegetable kingdom" simile back to the case of a flower bed, retaining its astronomical significance as an indicator of evolution in the heavens and stages in celestial life-cycles. When he invokes the Milky Way in relation to Viviette's graying hair, the comparison joins the human experience of growing old and evidence of personal aging to that of star systems and their visual appearances. Our garden *is* the universe. Since we are all flora and fauna of this cosmos, subject to the same forces of change and decay, and since no master gardener appears to be at work, perhaps, such images imply, we ought to tend each other with mutual loving kindness and care.

Hardy uses two other minor poetic images of astronomical phenomena in *Two on a Tower* to suggest other important underlying conditions that universally affect human behavior. Hardy describes Viviette as Swithin's *primum mobile*, the one who "had set a certain machinery in motion" (280) by ordering Swithin away and who was obeyed by him "mechanically." Viviette, will soon find herself obeying a different "motive

---

25   The original paper appeared on pages 212–26 of volume LXXIX; see: Hoskin, *William Herschel and the Construction of the Heavens* 106–16; hereafter: Hoskin.

force," that of necessity: her pregnancy and unmarried state. Drawing such direct correlates between ancient Greek explanations of motion in the cosmos and his characters' motives, Hardy establishes the nineteenth-century "fact" that the universe is an impersonal place, not governed by or even begun by a benevolent divine hand. Necessity and circumstance are the mechanical laws controlling nature. Human nature may exercise some ability to predict the behavior of universal forces, but such predictive powers will always be imperfect. Elements of random chance will always be operating in our lives. Complementing this theme is the conclusion Swithin came to when at the Cape, that the nebular vortex, the "whirligig of time" (312), is the modern equivalent of the ancient "Wheel of Fortune" which has brought back around to him the opportunity of being reunited with Viviette. In the modern consciousness, Hardy implies, chance is now recognized as the creative force in the cosmos instead of divinity; and natural science has replaced religion – and superstition – as the most effective human response to that chance creation.

In addition to all of the astronomical metaphors Hardy invented for the novel, he also directly alludes to literary treatments of astronomy by other authors. He peculiarly inverts one very famous poetic astronomical allusion with great effect. At the end of Chapter 5, Hardy has Lady Constantine do a very odd thing.

> She became much absorbed in . . . very womanly reflections; and at last Lady Constantine sighed, perhaps she herself did not exactly know why. Then a very soft expression lighted on her lips and eyes, and she looked at one jump ten years more youthful than before – quite the girl in aspect, younger than he. On the table lay his implements; among them a pair of scissors which, to judge from the shreds around, had been used in cutting curves in thick paper for some calculating process.
>
> What whim, agitation, or attraction prompted the impulse, nobody knows; but she took the scissors and, bending over the sleeping youth, cut off one of the curls, or rather crooks, – for they hardly reached a curl, – into which each lock of his hair chose to twist itself in the last inch of its length. The hair fell upon the rug. She picked it up quickly, returned the scissors to the table, and, as if her dignity had suddenly become ashamed of her fantasies, hastened through the door and descended the staircase. (46–7)

The action, the tone, and the fantasy elements of the incident all harken back to the last thirty lines of Alexander Pope's "The Rape of the Lock" in which Belinda's cut-curl becomes a comet: "A sudden star, it shot through liquid air, / And drew behind a radiant trail of hair" (Canto V, 127–8). Belinda is supposed to draw comfort from the immortality she will attain because of her contribution to the universe. In Hardy's usage, however, instead of the lock becoming a comet, the comet watcher becomes a lock, that is, is seen in the beauty of his human youth and is eventually consecrated by Lady Constantine's love. Hardy paints a wonderful picture of how Swithin has used the scissors to cut crescent shapes for calculation purposes, how Lady Constantine cuts a crescent curl for love, and how both acts give meaningful shape to human life. Like the gentle satire of Pope's mock epic, Hardy's account also contains an implicit critique, that this kindest of cuts, a seemingly innocent act, will have far-ranging and life-altering consequences – a girlish whim can change the world.

As the tone of such scenes signifies, the message Hardy hoped to convey in *Two on a Tower* depends as much upon the novel's emotional melodrama as it does its metaphors. The story is decidedly melodramatic in that it often relies on improbable coincidence, sensational action, and dramatic shifts in tone and feeling; but the designation need not be entirely pejorative. If, as it has traditionally been described, melodrama is to tragedy as farce is to comedy, then here, Hardy complicates and elevates its conventional aspects, making melodrama the message of *Two on a Tower*, where the world of Swithin and Viviette is subject to the probabilities and improbabilities, horror and beauty of the new astrophysics, where human joy and tragedy exist one within the other and only gather meaning from their coexistence. Hardy's avowal in *Two on a Tower* is a reply to any who may think, as Swithin's uncle thought, that two in a million is as good as none. As Swithin's uncle put it:

> I have written with quite other views than to work up a sentimental regret on such an amazingly remote hypothesis as that the fact of a particular pair of people not meeting, among the millions of other pairs of people who have never met, is a great calamity either to the world in general or to themselves. (135)

Hardy, however, wrote expressly for that purpose. Hardy implicitly felt that it matters to them, the two people who meet; and so it will always be as long as there are two human beings alive in the universe who love each other. Against the cosmological dilemmas revealed by science, Hardy asserts that the power of the human mind and heart and the benefits of human companionship can mitigate the influence that the stars and their infinite loneliness have upon our souls and imaginations. The biological and physical facts of the universe can be filtered through our human psychologies and cosmologies. We may *be* alone, but we need not *feel* alone. Although the incoming forces and eventual outcome may ultimately remain outside of our control, human beings can and should continue *ad astra aspirare, ad amorem aspirare*. This sentimental message was within the grasp of Hardy's nineteenth-century readers, however much the astronomical details were not.

~

While *Two on a Tower* may have been written hastily, it was not conceived superficially. Hardy's significant understanding of the science of astronomy and the astronomical phenomena of his day allows him to depict accurately the personality and professional work of an astronomer and the attitudes of non-scientists toward that work. In describing the relationship between that new character and his more traditional mate, Hardy contrasts nascent with long-standing cosmologies, creating wide-reaching symbolic connections between humankind and the stellar universe which rival the accuracy and particularization of the metaphysical poets and was far in advance of such usage for long works of fiction.

Just as Gabriel Oak's natural astronomy and cosmology fit the genre of the life-story in which he finds himself – a postlapsarian pastoral – so Swithin's scientific astronomy and rational cosmology fit the melodramatic modern medley of conventional forces and competing interpretations of personal, social and universal phenomena that he perceives to be in operation in the cosmos around him. Gabriel can put the astronomy and cosmology of a past time to work in making a meaningful life for himself because he exists in a natural environment with which he is still able to maintain a nurturing and harmonious connection. Although some of the rural characters in *Two on a Tower* appear to live in a world where such pastoral resolutions remain possible, the circumstances of Swithin's life and education, make such paradises as lost to him as his dead father's belief system. Instead, caught between a defunct past and an unformulated future, Swithin must experience for himself the world of his present time and make his own observations and interpretations of the newly revealed universe of deep telescopic space, inventing his own cosmological perspective.

Synthesizing the lessons of physics with those of pathos gleaned from Viviette's example, Swithin is able to learn that to whatever extent we may be physical bodies caught in a web of natural and social laws, actions and reactions, individual human will, love and value are also forces to be reckoned with in this universe. In the final scene, when Swithin ceases for the first time to "obey . . . mechanically," he chooses, instead, to act upon his sense of loving-kindness – a deep emotional connection that Viviette's love and self-sacrifice has modeled for him. The power of such an act, of such a feeling, Hardy suggests, has the potential to save the day and someday may. But it does not now, in this story. Instead, the joy produced by Swithin's compassionate act kills his beloved. As Swithin's young son seeks his true father's protective hand, and they together confirm that Viviette has died, Hardy reports that "the Bishop was avenged." By those same four words, Hardy implicates his audience in the outcome.

Whatever possible futures the new cosmology may eventually attain, Hardy shows that for now they are unfortunately constrained by the moralistic expectations and melodramatic conventions of the Victorian society who reads and writes them. However good her intentions, however adaptative her coping strategies, Viviette's reading of personal and social signs has compromised her social and moral cosmology. She has – like the comet that Swithin first sees her as – fallen from her world's idea of "heaven" and society will exact payment from her for it. Hardy tracks the learning curve of Viviette's education into the cosmos as meticulously parallel to that of the empire of which she is a representative part: from her domestic seclusion within an abusive marriage and initial ignorance of astronomy; through her casual and tentative expressions of natural curiosity and scientific interest; to her poetic, motherly, and romantic patronage of the young scientist; her enlightenment into the horror and beauty of deep space and her subsequent religious reaction; her increasing practical proficiency in observing and note-taking; her altruistic support of her lover's career; and at last, her submission to cosmic laws of chance in melodramatic self-sacrifice. Yet it is not her self-sacrifice that kills her.

Nineteenth-century theory about the life cycles of stars and multiple star systems provides Hardy with a complex analogue for the fall of a woman who cannot overcome the effects of cosmic forces acting upon her, even when she has direct knowledge of them. Although throughout the novel Hardy makes it clear that Swithin benefits from his love of Viviette, is emotionally humanized by her, his involvement with the feminine sphere of romance and emotion (and religiosity) will not permanently alter the course of his profession or life in the way exposure to the masculine social world of rationality and science harms her. Swithin learns to value human empathy and passion (he even comes to believe in the "spiritual" fact that human love can transcend matters of physical attraction), but he learns too late, and she will not be the beneficiary of his education. Viviette, it seems, was half a generation too old to live on as a partner in a stylish scientific couple; but Hardy does not endorse this outcome as a good for humanity. While he seems to give society the last word in the novel, the final irony of the narrative, is carried, ultimately, by the multiple star analogy. In the business of social vengeance what goes around, comes around, and Hardy hints that when Viviette's successor enters the masculine realm, Tabitha will not fall victim to the same fate; rather it is the men around her who will find themselves endangered.

*   *   *

Hardy's conception of astronomy and cosmology was ahead of his time in two senses: ahead of the understanding of the general population around him and ahead of his own literary skill in dealing successfully with the problems of using subtle extended metaphor and elaborate plot development in the same story. Nonetheless, his incomplete literary development should not diminish the fact that he embodied his own goal: uniting within himself the deepest human emotions and the profoundest universal realities. *Two on a Tower* may itself be the best evidence we have of the process by which Hardy worked out for himself and came to terms with the effect that the popularization of astronomy had on his own life and thought. Whether formulating a sense of contemporary cosmology from mythopoetic or religious tradition, or from the direction of natural philosophy, mathematical and observational astronomy, Hardy is able to demonstrate for his Victorian readers, that they, like Viviette and Swithin, can arrive at a fundamentally similar conclusion about the best way to make sense of life in this universe. Whether inspired by Christian charity and grace or astrophysical awe and contemplation, the moral of both sets of cosmological stories appears remarkably the same: whatever you think may be out there, whatever your explanations may be for what happens, love one another.

Yet *Two on a Tower* is not the last Hardy novel in which astronomy figures strongly. *The Woodlanders*, *Tess of the d'Urbervilles* and *Jude the Obscure* all take place under contemporary astronomical skies where the objects of deep space have begun to confirm the reality of a cosmos and its life-forms generated by random activity. Hardy's insight into and understanding of how recent astronomical discoveries and theories complicated contemporary cosmology seems to have altered significantly his perception of the possibilities of late nineteenth-century life. Gothic romance, pastoral harmony, and melodramatic emotion all recede as bases for likely cosmological stories and give way to an increasingly probable vision that the genre of life in a fatalistic universe is a neo-Greek tragedy, weighted heavily with satiric and ironic elements.

The lessons that Hardy learned from the literary failings of *Two on a Tower* may have directly contributed to the success about ten years later of *Tess* in which he again attempts to interweave an extended scientific trope into the story. Instead of obscure astronomical images, Hardy chose highly popularized aspects of Darwinism; instead of melodrama, Hardy chose tragedy, and the result was a novel in which "God's *not* in his heaven: all's *wrong* with the world!" In *Tess*, the music of infinitely distant spheres strikes only tragic tones, and the final act of loyalty and faith on a tower gives way to a futile sacrifice at Stonehenge. In such a world, Hardy saw that it becomes even more important for human individuals not to thwart each other in the shared struggle to fulfill potential and desire. That lesson, for Hardy, was written in the stars.

Chapter 7

Universal Laws and Cosmic Forces
The Tragic Astronomical Muse in
The Woodlanders, Tess of the D'Urbervilles,
and *Jude the Obscure*

Hardy realized that most readers missed the astronomical message of *Two on a Tower*, but he continues to explore what Richard Proctor referred to as "the truths of astronomy" (*Essays* 37) in *The Woodlanders, Tess of the d'Urbervilles* and *Jude the Obscure*. In the third chapter of *Essays in Astronomy*, entitled "The Study of Astronomy," Proctor outlined his suggestions for what a comprehensive understanding of the subject should entail.

> It is not merely necessary that astronomical facts should be so presented to the student that he may become possessed with a feeling of their reality, but the student cannot be rightly said to 'have astronomy' at all (to use Shakespeare's apt expression) until he is capable of picturing to himself, however inadequately, the truths of the science. A man may have at his fingers' ends the distances, volumes, densities, and so on of all the planets, the rates at which they move, the physical features they present, and a hundred other facts equally important; but, unless he has in his mind's eye a / picture of the solar system, with all its wonderful variety, and all its yet more amazing vitality, he has not yet passed even the threshold of the science. (37–8)

To Proctor, "having astronomy" meant being able to situate visually our place in the universe relative to the solar system and relative to the farthest reaches of interstellar space. Proctor summons the best of his descriptive powers to offer a dazzling explanation of how the student of astronomy "must be able to conceive the mighty mass of the sun, ruling from the centre of the scheme the whole of that family" and each member of the solar system in turn.

> . . . small Mercury lit up with inconceivable splendour by the sun . . . Venus and Earth, the twin planets . . . ruddy Mars . . . . Then beyond the path round which Mar urges his course, the student must picture to himself the interlacing paths of hundreds of asteroids . . . each pursuing its independent course around the sun. . . . The vast globe of Jupiter circled about by his symmetrical family of satellites, the complex system of Saturn, with his gorgeous ring-system and a family of satellites the outermost of which has an orbit range of more than four and a half millions of miles; Uranus and Neptune, brother orbs, almost lost in the immensity of their distance – all these planets, and all

the wonders which the telescope has taught us respecting them, should be clearly pictured. In particular, the enormous distances separating the paths of these bodies from each other, and from the sun, should be clearly appre- / hended, and that strangely incorrect picture which defaces so many of our books on astronomy, wherein the paths of the planets are seen separated by nearly equal distances from each other, should be as far as possible forgotten. (my elisions, 38–9)

In Proctor's view, student astronomers have begun to grasp the significance of astronomical knowledge when they have taken the "important step" "towards that clear recognition of actual relations which should be the true end of scientific study" (39) and have begun to comprehend the distances involved. To form an accurate mental picture of the size of the solar system students must realize that "the whole family of the minor planets could not span the distance between the orbits of Jupiter and Saturn, where the distance between the orbits of Saturn and Uranus, or of Uranus and Neptune, almost equals the full span of the orbit of Jupiter" (39). More importantly, however, "the thoughts of the student of astronomy should range until [he/she] begins to apprehend to some extent the vastness of those abysms by which our solar system is separated on all sides from the realm of the fixed stars" (39).

And I know of no consideration which tends more clearly to bring this idea before the mind of the student than the thought that our sun, with his attendant family of planets, is speeding through those abysms with a velocity altogether past our powers of conception . . . . The clear recognition of this fact, and of its real significance, enables the thoughtful student to become conscious of the vastness of the depths separating us from the nearest fixed star, even though [he/she] can never form an adequate conception of their tremendous proportions. (39)

While the concept of solar and stellar velocity "serves most strikingly to impress upon us the vastness of the interstellar spaces," Proctor also believed that the case of comets could powerfully exemplify astronomical distances and, also, astronomical time.

We commonly find those comets which sweep round the sun in parabolic or hyperbolic orbits, spoken of as visitants from the domain of other stars. And so in truth they are. But how seldom do we find in our treatises on astronomy any reference to the enormous intervals of time which must have elapsed since these startling visitants were travelling close round some other star, making their periastral swoop before setting forth on that enormous journey which had to be traversed before they could become visible to our astronomers! Taking into account the directions in which certain comets have reached us, and assigning to the stars seen in such directions the least distances compatible with known facts, it yet remains absolutely certain that twenty millions of years at least must have elapsed since those comets were last in periastral passage. Where if, as one supposes, each comet (even those which now circle in closed orbits round our own) has glitted from star to star during a long interstellar existence, the mind shrinks utterly before the contemplation of the vastness of the time-intervals which have elapsed since those journeyings first commenced . . . (40)

As we have seen, Hardy incorporated each of these aspects of the "truths" of astronomy into *Two on a Tower*. His descriptions of the vastness, grandeur, and power of the universal frame rival Proctor's in accuracy, but far surpass them in beauty of expression. Yet Hardy may have learned something else about the "real significance" of astronomy from Proctor.

Proctor believed that the difficult process of forming an astronomically accurate picture of the universal scheme of things would provide a "valuable mental training" for those who attempted it. By focusing "the mind on the complete series of acts by which alone their real significance can be apprehended, we see in astronomy the apt means for disciplining the mind, and fitting it for the noblest work of which it may be capable" (41). The vast distances, wondrous variety, and "infinite vitality" of celestial objects, Proctor wrote, may well excite students' awe and admiration, but a sense of the *motion* of the universe allows them to experience the cosmic sublime.

> . . . the sense of wonder he would experience would sink almost into nothingness by comparison with that / which would overwhelm him could he recognise with equal clearness the movements taking place amongst the orbs presented to his contemplation – could he see moons and moon-systems circling around primary planets, these urging their way with inconceivable velocity around their central suns, where amid the star-depths, the suns were seen swiftly travelling on their several courses, star-streams and star-clusters aggregating or segregating according to the various influences of the attractions to which they were subject, and the vast spaces occupied by the gaseous nebulae stirred to their inmost depths by the action of mighty forces whose real nature is as yet unknown to us. *The mind cannot but be strengthened and invigorated, it cannot but be purified and elevated*, by the contemplation of a scene so full of magnificence, imperfect though the means by which the wonders of the scene are made known to us. The information given by the telescope is indeed but piecemeal, and as yet no adequate attempts have been made to bring the whole array of known facts as far as possible into one grand picture; but, seen as it is only by parts, and (even so) only as through a veil and darkly, the scene presented to the astronomer is the grandest and the most awe-inspiring which man can study. (emphasis added, 47–8)

This, the final passage of Proctor's chapter on the study of astronomy, may have struck Hardy as both an inspiration and a challenge. Finding that his own experience with astronomy essentially confirmed Proctor's grandiosely stated claims for its value as "mental training," Hardy had the additional insight that contemporary astronomy had potential as an agent of perspectival change within social and political life and thought as well. *Two on a Tower* may well represent a specific attempt by Hardy to fulfill Proctor's call for someone "to bring the whole array of known facts as far as possible into one grand picture." While Proctor no doubt envisioned a cosmological narrative that would exclusively treat astronomical "facts" from the most local to most distant, Hardy's story of human individuals and relationships – told within the context of a scientifically defined cosmos – far exceeded such intentions. Descriptive astronomy may well present the "grandest" object of human study, but it does not present the *whole* story.

Beyond Proctor's notions of how astronomy could act *upon* the human mind, Hardy seems to have understood that it interacted *with* it as well: astronomy *plus* psychology produces *cosmology*. Interactions between the natural realm and the human mind and body have been continuous throughout history. At all times and all places through human evolution, from our species' origins to the present, the universe has literally been *composed* by the individual psyches who observed, recorded, and interpreted their perceptions of the phenomena within it. In *Two on a Tower*, Hardy creates a scientifically "true" environment (à la Proctor) in which his characters are cosmically conscious of the latest human perceptions of and investigations into the nature of interplanetary and interstellar space. Attempting to impart to his readers a sense of what it means to be a living being on a planet hurtling through space, Hardy invokes a cosmic scale for the novel's setting, against which his characters act and interact as matter in motion. It was not entirely Hardy's fault that his fictional vision of the "grand picture" exceeded his readers' grasp.

Proctor himself was all-too-aware that even the most finely crafted word-pictures frequently failed to communicate cosmic realities. In the twenty-first century, readers of popular science have our visual imagination of distant inter- and extragalactic objects and structures aided by computer-enhanced images and animations provided by deep-space telescopes. In the nineteenth century, artistic and photographic images of newly made telescopic observations became increasingly available, but these generally represented *individual* celestial objects that could not convey (as Proctor felt so strongly was necessary) a sense of cosmic distances, velocities, and universal time, let alone a sense of the interrelated "whole." Proctor believed that the poetic descriptions of Milton's *Paradise Lost* were unsurpassed in their ability to evoke such a sense, exquisitely expressing the immensity of the universe and the loneliness of our little pendant world, suspended in an isolated sphere of order, surrounded by a chaotic abyss. He believed that the best prose descriptions of John Herschel's popular astronomy were their only near rivals. In the composition of *Two on a Tower*, Hardy produces a popular poetic cosmology, writing in an intermediate medium between imaginative epic poetry and popular scientific prose, bringing together the best of both modes to create a cosmological story that addresses the needs, desires and expectations of the readership of his time: dramatic and emotional narrative, visual description and scientific accuracy, all packaged in the highly readable and popular format of a serial novel. What he failed to achieve with the components and execution of this single work, however, Hardy was able to accomplish across the span of his life's work as a whole.

To some extent, Hardy seems to have shared Proctor's Platonically idealistic view of astronomy as an intellectually "elevating" pursuit, including some confidence that the human minds and souls who comprehended the magnificence of the cosmos could be "strengthened," "invigorated," "purified," and "elevated" by its study. Unlike Proctor, he was also aware that knowledge of astronomical truths was equally capable of producing an opposite set of results and responses: hopelessness and despair, selfishness and fatalism. Within every one of Hardy's novels, major or minor, the *possibility* of pastoral happiness – a harmonic relationship with the natural world, earthly and heavenly – exists, but that possibility is contained within an increasingly limited, and fast-receding, sphere. The odds that any human individual, or single set of human beings, will be able to achieve, act upon, and sustain an "elevated" relation to the cosmos and to each other (by whatever means they initially arrive at it – agrarian empiricism, magico-superstitious sympathy, religious faith, philosophical theory, or scientific investigation) grow less likely throughout Hardy's oeuvre, as each subsequent work appears.

Early in his career, by the shifting conventions within *A Pair of Blues Eyes*, Hardy had already suggested that the narrative spaces within which human heroes and heroines can act had experienced concomitant historical shifts: the open hearts, wide-ranging countrysides and free skies of romance narrow to the psychological enclosure of the Gothic mansion and curse, the modern confines of others' prejudices and misjudgements, and finally, death's tomb. In *Far From the Madding Crowd,* Hardy invokes Milton's heavenly muse of astronomy, Urania, to preside over the last remnants of the early Victorian rural paradise, poised before its final loss. While minor characters in other novels will retain some connection to natural harmony, Gabriel and Bathsheba are the last of Hardy's central couples who successfully take the lessons of celestial and earthly natural signs to heart and act accordingly to create a positive future for themselves. Just as the good shepherd's star-reading and calendar no longer keep physical time in later novels, so too the pastoral mode no longer encloses a safe biological space beneath heaven on earth in which Hardy's central characters can thrive. In *The Return of the Native*, Clym's modern, philosophically inspired "back to nature" project is blindsided by our nearest star, the sun, and Eustacia's visionary prescience enables her to read only the message of time's passage and the decay of love and life in the eclipse. In *Two on a Tower*, the remnants of pastoral existence make way for the possibilities of epic human action – Swithin *could be* the hero of a grand scientific–romantic journey across the globe and sky who successfully weds (at least temporarily) his science to Viviette's religion – but, in the end, the circumstances of time, chance, and audience allow mock epic and melodrama to prevail.

In all of these early works, Hardy closely correlates the contexts of astronomy, cosmology, and physics – the nature of nature – with his narratives' dominant tone and genre. While in the three earlier works the cosmic dilemma represented by astrophysics is subtly suggested by the settings, character descriptions, metaphors and analogies, in *Two on a Tower*, it becomes explicit. The two main characters actively seek out information about the cosmos, undertake the quest to understand their relation to the universe by exploring its very depths, deliberately plunge themselves visually into the abysms between the stars. Hardy's characters look into nothingness and learn to accept it what for it is. The shock and awe of that experience is mind- and life-changing. As Swithin openly comments to Viviette on their first night observing together, "whatever the stars were made for, they were not made to please our eyes. / It is just the same in everything; nothing is made for man" (31–2). After her first vision into the depths of space, Viviette cries out: "it overpowers me! . . . It makes me feel that it is not worth while to live; it quite annihilates me" (32).

As the cosmic Adam and Eve, Swithin's and Viviette's first glimpse into the vast universe outside the Edenic gates of Earth's solar system – their first direct awareness of the full reality of their human situation – is experienced in quick succession as paralyzing, bonding, and bracing. Yet no matter how profound the experience of exercising human curiosity and creativity to face the facts of the universe, Hardy's narrative clearly shows that such activity is no guarantee that the observers will be able to apply those lessons in a timely or appropriate way in the human realm of feeling and moral action, or will be allowed by society to enjoy what personal and interpersonal benefits such lessons might otherwise afford.

Swithin and Viviette gain perspective on the universal nature of things from their telescopic investigations and they successfully reconcile that perspective to their lives' philosophies, secular and spiritual; but the synthesis they achieve as individuals and as a couple is still not enough to save them from the flaws within their own human natures and from the matrix of social forces and temporal stresses acting upon them. Viviette, left alone by Swithin and pregnant with his son, succumbs to social pressure and acts out of expediency and not the sense of loyalty and moral choice that would otherwise have been her preference. Swithin's scientific nature enables him to turn his back on England without the slightest imagination of the difficulties in which he may have left Viviette. Unlike Gabriel Oak who can in the span of a single moment scan the night sky, glean its message, and turn his attention to the little lamb who needs his care, Swithin carries on his work at the Cape for four years with scarcely a thought for his lover's well-being. In the final scene, Hardy makes it clear that Swithin's scientifically objective approach to life and love is incomplete and unsatisfactory:

> He was a scientist, and took words literally. There is something in the inexorably simple logic of such men which partakes of the cruelty of the natural laws that are their study. He entered the tower-steps, and mechanically descended; and it was not till he got half-way down that he thought she could not mean what she had said (312).

The time it takes Swithin to process and reinterpret, intellectually and emotionally, what he has just heard, costs his beloved her life. The moral to this story, then, seems to be that while on the equally grand scales of astronomy, geology and biology, slow evolutionary processes may eventually result in dramatic change; on the scale of local, personal development, gradualism is experienced as catastrophe.

In the final scene shared by these two on the tower, Swithin and Viviette are able to just barely eke out a fleeting moment in which they share a meeting of minds, hearts, and cosmologies. The personal and social costs at which such a synthesis was bought were too great to sustain it. Viviette reconciles the values of her traditional religious faith to the new view of the cosmos that Swithin's telescope reveals to her, but the views of society around her were not so accommodating. Her sacrifice of marital bonds to Swithin's scientific career goals places her in social and spiritual jeopardy. For his part, Swithin comes too little, too late to his realization that the "universe" in her eyes and heart carries lessons as profound as those he has seen in the "profundity" of stellar space. While there may be a future for him and Tabitha, Hardy makes it explicit that any conjunction between them will not be easy either, as the union of a "new man" and "new woman" in this new universe will present its own challenging set of adaptations and accommodations. Although as modern society's rising star, Swithin proved himself a quick-study, by his personal failings Hardy demonstrates that the human limitations of even the most intrepid of learners in this cosmos can fall short of meeting the simplest needs of those around them. In his last major novels, Hardy will expand this final theme and explore how the cruelty of the laws of human nature and human society far exceed those operating in the natural world, biological, geological, or astrophysical.

In the poem "Parnassus" (1889), Tennyson described how the findings of astronomy and geology seemed to him a towering and fast-growing presence in human lives. Astronomy and geology revealed so powerful a vision of reality that they made the powers of the human imagination obsolete, subsuming the poets' function. It was this fearful view of human imagination dwarfed by its own discoveries that inspired Tennyson to make his famous declaration: "Astronomy and Geology, terrible Muses!" With the cosmic scales held in tension between Proctor's notion that facing the incomprehensibility of the earth's place in the cosmos would "strengthen" and "invigorate" humanity and Tennyson's insight that such knowledge might terrify and demoralize it, Hardy brings the contemporary findings of both sciences fully to bear upon his vision of the universe in his last three major novels. Astronomy is the tragic muse within the Darwinian universes of *The Woodlanders*, *Tess* and *Jude* in which Hardy treats its "truths" as axiomatic for the human condition as the processes of evolution – organic and inorganic – actively and relentlessly work within the world and upon his characters. Yet, as each of these stories inexorably reveals, to whatever extent physical and biological forces act upon and within us, it is the forces within ourselves and that we exert upon each other socially, politically, legally, economically, that have the most power to render this world good or evil. Since the sentimental irony of Viviette's story apparently missed its mark, Hardy employs increasingly realistic depictions of the social wounds inflicted by the epic agony taking place amidst the human life forms on this planet. Perhaps stronger social critique and more graphic catharsis might affect some enlightened reader in his audience somewhere to experience an upwelling of love and charity and tip the balance in our favor.

The Woodlanders (1887)

The *Woodlanders* appeared five years after *Two on a Tower*. Coming back down to earth for his choice of setting, Hardy also returns to familiar techniques of emplotment and characterization. The realm of astronomy – the dual "heavens" – that he had just explored as so physically present in Swithin's mind and Viviette's heart, respectively, is not entirely absent from this novel. Here, however, Hardy shifts critical attention from scientific realities and their philosophical implications to craft a narrative in which the facts of astronomy are perceived in contradictory ways by various individuals and different segments of human societies: as an accepted, even comforting, "given" of rural spaces and their inhabitants, and, conversely, as the ignored-reality behind the scenes of modern social life. In both responses, "astronomical truths" are the stage off-stage, so to speak, as in so many of Hardy's favorite works of classical drama and epic. Upon the freshly cleared *tabula rasa* of the woods, then, lit and backlit by the stars, sun and moon, Hardy is free to offer a new consideration of the *possibilities* of living a full and fruitful life in contrast to the *probabilities* of living an empty and meaningless existence.

To explore the personal and social dynamics of our common quandary, Hardy draws directly upon character types with which he had worked before. The "salt of the earth" rural working-class figures of Marty South and Giles Winterborne owe much of their psychology and values to Hardy's depictions of the work-folk in *Two on a Tower* as well as to Gabriel Oak in *Far From the Madding Crowd*. The temperament of the "modern man," Edred Fitzpiers, is assembled from various aspects (often the least admirable ones) of Henry Knight, Clym Yeobright, Wildeve, and Swithin St. Cleeve. Grace Melbury seems a refinement of Elfride Swancourt, as Hardy depicts her struggle to balance a rural upbringing with the education she has received in the ways of the more sophisticated modern world. In bringing together again this same basic cast of characters, Hardy varies their personal strengths and weaknesses, setting in motion new combinations of human nature, personality, social attitudes, beliefs, and behavior, running another iteration of the thought-experiments that so fascinated and haunted him: given a certain environment and certain sets of natural, human, and social forces, which cosmological combination will prove most successfully adaptive for the human population, if any prove adaptive at all: Old, rural folkways versus new, urban mores? Traditional religious faith versus new education? Some combination? How do cause–effect and contingency play out? To what extent, and how, are the possibilities of the present shaped out of and by the actions and events of the past and the human imagination of and intentions for the future?

In exchanging the cosmic point-of-view of *Two on a Tower* for a more local, rural perspective, Hardy is able to refocus his critique upon the actions and interactions of human and natural forces that he found so compelling in contemporary Darwinism. While the first harbinger of modern social Darwinism has arrived in this fictional environment, Hardy foregrounds the interconnected complexity of the active, biological natural domain of *The Woodlanders*, which rivals in its atmospheric effects that of the world he created for Swithin and Viviette. As Michael Millgate points out, the symbolic presence of the woods is palpable to both Hardy's fictional characters and the novel's readers.

> Working with established human ecology – men and women trained by the inheritance of generations to live in these particular circumstances – Hardy transplants exotic growths (Mrs. Charmond and Fitzpiers) from elsewhere. He also takes one promising plant (Grace Melbury) from its natural soil, forces it in hothouse conditions, and then transplants it back to its place of origin. Such metaphors seem justifiable in discussing a novel in which the relationship between man and nature is of such pervasive importance. (*Career* 250)

The woodlands serve not merely as the background for the novel's action, but as the symbolic representation of the biological forces behind it as well. In Millgate's words, the "woods may be beautiful, but they can also be terrifying, nor are the woodlanders themselves exempt from the fight for survival. Little Hintock becomes not a haven of 'sylvan peace' but the microcosm of a world in which the struggle for existence is everywhere the chief condition of existence" (*Career* 250–51). As in *A Pair of Blue Eyes*, astronomical realities are subtly present in this virtual terrarium, being most often felt simply, obviously and directly by the characters – as by most humans from time immemorial – through its influence upon the immediately surrounding environment and its atmosphere: in the effects of the changing seasons upon the works and days of the rural folk; through the light and warmth of the sun; through local weather patterns and fluctuations; and the effects of moonlight on human behavior. Also, as in his description of Elfride's world, Hardy employs allusions drawn from more technical stellar astronomy to mark certain characters as possessing overly idealistic (and potentially dangerous) philosophical stances or to remark upon how distant and remote their personalities have become from the common bonds that tie the less scientifically sophisticated individuals around them into a community.

Woodland Lives in Celestial and Terrestrial Force Fields

Hardy's descriptive introductions of this story's human actors establish the interconnectedness of celestial and terrestrial forces at work within them and around them. Each character embodies, in unique combination, the variable action and interactions of the laws of nature, human nature and society. He describes Mr. Melbury's quick recovery from a worried-filled night in terms of Darwinism and chemical physics: "he was hardly the same man as the man of the small dark hours. Even among the moodiest the tendency to be cheered is stronger than the tendency to be cast down; and a soul's specific gravity constantly reasserts itself as less than that of the sea of troubles into which it is thrown."[1] Here Hardy uses Darwin's conception

---

[1] Thomas Hardy, *The Woodlanders* (1974; London: Macmillan, 1986) 45; hereafter cited by page number within the text.

of the "tendency to joy" to indicate the particular quality of Mr. Melbury's character as an individual and also to establish species-specific aspects of humanity, i.e., the human soul floats. When Hardy introduces the novel's central female character, he makes it immediately clear that he is – perforce – focusing his primary attention upon human individuals in their natural *local* surroundings (not the greater cosmos) in this narrative. "It would have been difficult to describe Grace Melbury with precision, either then or at any time. Nay, from the highest point of view, / to precisely describe a human being, the focus of a universe, how impossible!" (52–3). Throughout *The Woodlanders*, Hardy's narration invokes cosmic perspective – not to exercise omniscience as might be expected – but rather, to admit and express the *limits* of both artistic and scientific observation and description.

In the woodlands, Hardy sets up a direct contrast between the natural cycles and long-established, predictable, astronomical patterns of change with the sudden intrusion and unknown consequences of human-made change in the environment. So repetitious, regular and predictable are the basic astronomical phenomena in these rural surroundings that they have become accepted by the locals as everyday givens, expected, even reassuring. New human inhabitants are not. When Grace returns from her schooling to live again in her girlhood home, she settles into her old familiar room and readies herself for sleep. Then she notices a strange light on the horizon.

> . . . she was watching the light quite idly when it gradually changed colour, and at length shone blue as sapphire. Thus it remained several minutes, and then it passed through violet to red.
>
> Her curiosity was so widely awakened by the phenomenon that she sat up in bed, and stared steadily at the shine. An appearance of this sort, sufficient to excite attention anywhere, was no less than a marvel in Hintock, as Grace had known the hamlet. Almost every diurnal and nocturnal effect in that woodland place had hitherto been the direct result of the regular terrestrial roll which produced the season's changes; but here was something dissociated from these normal sequences, and foreign to local knowledge. (61)

A reader recently conditioned by the imagery of *Two on a Tower* might be tempted to interpret the changing appearance of this light in the night sky as a variable star or supernova; and indeed it does belong to a man with astronomical connections and interests, Mr. Fitzpiers, a physician and amateur scientist. The light is shining from his laboratory where he is up late working. The Melbury's serving woman, "Grammer," describes him as "a man of strange meditations, and his eyes seem to see as far as the north star" (62). His philosophic views that "Everything is nothing" and "There's only Me and Not Me in the whole world" have the old woman baffled. By directly associating Fitzpiers with stellar astronomy, Hardy indicates his character's dissociation from his immediate surroundings, but he is also careful to ground the point in biological and Darwinian terms as well. As Grace muses on finding Fitzpiers in the village, "It was strange to her to come back from the world to Little Hintock and find in one of its nooks, like a tropical plant in a hedgerow, a nucleus of advanced ideas and practices which had nothing in common with the life around. Chemical experiments, anatomical projects, and metaphysical conceptions had found a strange home here" (63).

In Fitzpiers, Hardy presents a new type of "scientific" modern man, not a developing professional as was Swithin, not a serious student of science as was Knight, but a professional "dabbler," of a kind prevalent enough among the sons of upper-class families in nineteenth-century Britain. Hardy likens Fitzpiers'ever-changing scientific interests to the serpentine journey of the sun across the ecliptic:

> In the course of a year his mind was accustomed to pass in a grand solar sweep throughout the zodiac of the intellectual heaven. Sometimes it was in the Ram, sometimes in the Bull; one month he would be immersed in the Twins of astrology and astronomy; then in the Crab of German literature and metaphysics. (122)

Of course, as events transpire, Fitzpiers will zig-zag, vacillate, worm and snake his way through his love interests as well.

Just as Hardy had described the relationship between Swithin and Viviette in terms of both gravitational and sexual attraction, he traces the same two sets of forces operating between Grace and Fitzpiers. In a scene that Hardy recycled from *Two on a Tower*, Grace first comes upon the physician as he sleeps. As Viviette had used the moment to observe Swithin in great detail, so Grace gazes at Fitzpiers, "a specimen of creation altogether unusual to that locality" (125). After they have spoken, she knows that she should leave, but the "compelling power of [his] atmosphere still held her there" (129). Fitzpiers makes use of the opportunity to show her a slide of brain tissue under his microscope (Two at a Microscope!) and he falls in love with her at this "first sight" – or, rather, like Knight in the past and Angel still to come, he falls in love with his *idea* of her.

For all of his scientific and philosophically idealistic qualities, Fitzpiers is as subject to the laws of human nature as any other man. Fitzpiers's biological susceptibility to the effects of moonlight conflicts with (indeed, overrides) his intellectual aspirations and potential. During the enactment of a rural Midsummer Eve ritual, Fitzpiers catches Grace by the "blush" of early moonlight and according to local superstition this should mean that he and Grace will be "partners for life" (140). He lets her go, however, and soon after catches a local working-class girl by the light of the late-evening's "high moon," having been carried away by the chase, his own sexual desire, and the way the moonlight idealizes even this "hoydenish maiden" for him temporarily (143–4). Hardy consistently relates Fitzpiers's repeatedly misplaced affections in terms of astronomical allusions. Not long after his marriage to Grace, he begins an affair with an older woman whom he describes as the "loadstar of [his] one desire" (190). After an accident in which he is called in as medical consultant, he finds that the "intersection of his temporal orbit with Mrs. Charmond's for a day or two" (179) gave him opportunity to examine her face, "[her eyes] showing themselves as deep and mysterious as interstellar space" (180). A close reader of the astronomical passages in *Two on a Tower* could also have supplied the applicable missing adjective "empty" to this description; but Fitzpiers, equally deep and empty, does not see himself reflected in his lover's eyes.

Hardy consistently connects Fitzpiers and Mrs. Charmond – the two most alien of the village's current residents – with explicitly stellar astronomy, as objects far-removed from the daily and historical concerns of the locale. Mrs. Charmond even shuns the light of the local sun (185). In contrast (and in a way that echoes his earlier depiction of Thomasin), Hardy describes Grace, who was born and raised in the village, as directly and intimately connected with the local effects of the earth's nearest star and its cycles. Drawing upon the seemingly ceaseless pattern of days following days, the gradual change of seasons, the ebb and flow of Grace's contemplation of her approaching wedding day, Hardy evokes the inevitable and inexorable passing of Time. In this passage Hardy combines the skillful pacing and finely wrought detail that he had previously achieved in the cliff-hanging scene in *A Pair of Blue Eyes* as he attempts, once again, to convey to his Victorian readership how abstractions like time and space are experienced personally within the moment by moment quotidian flow of human life.

> From this hour there was no serious recalcitration on her part . . . .
> The interim closed up its perspective surely and silently. Whenever Grace had any doubts of her position the sense of contracting time was like a shortening chamber: at other moments she was comparatively blithe.
> Day after day waxed and waned; the one or two woodmen who sawed, shaped, or spokeshaved on her father's premises at this inactive season of the year, regularly came and unlocked the doors in the morning, locked them in the evening, supped, leant over their garden-gates for a whiff of evening air, and to catch any last and furthest throb of news from the outer world, which entered and expired at Little Hintock like the exhausted swell of a wave in some innermost cavern of some innermost creek of an embayed sea; yet no news interfered with the nuptial purpose at their neighbour's house.
> The sappy green twig-tips of the season's growth would not, she thought, be appreciably woodier on the day she became a wife, so near was the time; the tints of the foliage would hardly have changed. Everything was so much as usual that no itinerant stranger would have supposed a woman's fate to be hanging in the balance at that summer's decline . . . ./
> The narrow interval that stood before the day diminished yet . . . .
> Everything had been clear then, in imagination; now something was / undefined. She had little carking anxieties; a curious fatefulness seemed to rule her, and she experienced a mournful want of some one to confide in.
> The day loomed so big and nigh that her prophetic ear could in fancy catch the noise of it, hear the murmur of the villagers as she came out of church, imagine the jangle of the three thin-toned Hintock bells. The dialogues seemed to grow louder, and the ding-ding-dong of those three crazed bells more persistent. She awoke: the morning had come.
> Five hours later she was the wife of Fitzpiers. (162–4)

Hardy's handling of time here is reminiscent, almost certainly deliberately so, of Homer's evocation of natural cycles in his repetition of "the rosy-fingered dawn" and the ebb and flow of the "wine-dark sea." Hardy admired the way that the Greek poet interwove the diurnal and the seasonal into the life-cycles of his heroes and, here, Hardy does the same for Grace. Yet he is careful to indicate that what some may interpret as the effect of an impersonal force operating upon human individuals, may in reality be the result of his characters' own action or inaction in shaping their destinies. Time does not do this to Grace. She is not "fated" to marry Fitzpiers. She lets time bring the "fateful" day around to her. She could act otherwise, but does not. It is this aspect of how human beings respond to the conditions of their environments – what natural or social laws they accept as unchangeable, which they choose to act in accordance with or rebel against – that will form the underlying premise of the lives of Tess and Jude.

~

As in the case of Swithin and Viviette, the tragedy of Grace's story is caused by her awakening to cosmological reality too late: her life is not absolutely free and self-determined, but she does have access to degrees of freedom that she does not utilize. Also as in *Two on a Tower*, Grace's experiences teach her to value properly the relative magnitudes of "what is great and little in life" (202). By the time she discovers that she can act in accord with her true individual nature and her own preferences in choosing a mate, however (and not out of artificially imposed parental wishes and dreamily obeyed social aspirations), any pairing with her "natural" mate, Giles, is impossible. Human life is lived along time's arrow; missed opportunities do not pass by again.

Similar truths apply for the character of Giles, a planter of apple trees, and his workmate, Marty South. Together they exemplify the harmonic existence of humankind within nature. Like Gabriel Oak, Giles achieves a level of "intelligent intercourse with nature," can "read the hieroglyphs" of nature and its laws, accepts their conditions, and carries on with the world's work (292). In the woodlands, Giles does not merely acknowledge the reality of Darwin's mechanism for survival in the world, he *actively works* to fit as many specimens for survival within it as possible. Hardy depicts Giles as the heroic figure of *The Woodlanders*, "a good man" who "did good things" (323). He also depicts his hero as an endangered species. Unlike the "wonderful naterel" match made by Gabriel and Bathsheba, Giles is not able to conjoin his hard-earned natural wisdom to Grace's hard-won life-lessons, and they produce no offspring who might have carried, by nature and nurture, the best of both of their beings into the world of the future. In *Tess* and *Jude,* the possibilities of human beings achieving a life of harmony within the confines of the natural laws of biology and evolution are reduced to next to nothing as the world of the "moderns" (like Fitzpiers) continues to encroach upon the rural environment, thwarting the attempts of its inhabitants to fit themselves to an increasingly *unnatural* world that operates according to increasingly *unnatural* social, political, and economic laws.

Tess of the d'Urbervilles (1891)

In *Tess*, Hardy combines natural and astronomical images to create a cosmically whole environment for his characters that closely replicates his own world view, as evidenced by entries in his *Literary Notebooks*. As he had previously demonstrated most effectively by his narration of Henry Knight's experience on the cliff, nature is absolutely neutral in Tess's world. After the rape and the subsequent birth of her child, Tess begins to recover from her misfortune by returning to work. "Meanwhile," Hardy points out, "the trees were just as green as before; the birds sang and the sun shone as clearly now as ever. The familiar surroundings had not darkened because of her grief, nor sickened because of her pain."[2] As Millgate notes, Hardy's allusions to "fate," "chance," or "accident" in this world are intended as glosses on his characters' natures and flaws, not indicative of any reference to the supernatural: "The accidents that befall them, are rarely if ever a product of the random inexplicable intrusion of fate but rather the inevitable – or at least, credible – outcome of the immediate narrative context and of their own personalities as conditioned and limited by the forces of heredity and environment" (*Career* 272). As insightful as Millgate's view is, his description of the function of heredity and environment may be equally identifiable as the "chance" operation of biological determinism. Yet, surely, as he points out, Hardy's Tess "is not entirely helpless in the grip of a mechanistic universe, and a less passive, more self-confident character might have found avenues of escape not discovered by Tess herself" (*Career* 280).

As important as natural conditions are in shaping the lives of the characters in this novel, Hardy shows how the artificial conditions dictated by society and its conventions – the ways and means of social Darwinism – are formidable forces of often greater power. As Millgate so aptly puts it: "If Alec sacrifices Tess to his lust, Angel sacrifices her to his theory of womanly purity. The one obeys a natural law, the other a social law, and Hardy has no hesitation in assigning to the latter the greater blame" (*Career* 276). Yet despite all of the various vectors of force that Hardy shows to be acting upon his characters, he also clearly illustrates by their behavior that their own human natures, their own personal responses to these forces, ultimately decide their destinies. Religious doubt is the norm for the three main characters who have, for their own reasons, each lost faith in the God of orthodox Christianity.[3] In *Tess*, the human actors must depend on their own inner resources (including flaws) because "God's *not* in his heaven: all's *wrong* with the world!" (213). With these conditions, Hardy sets the stage for what has often been called a "modern tragedy in an ancient mode."

---

[2]   Thomas Hardy, *Tess of the d'Urbervilles*, ed. Scott Elledge, 2nd ed. (New York: W. W. Norton and Company, 1979) 77; hereafter cited by page number within the text.
[3]   William E. Buckler, introduction, *Tess of the d'Urbervilles*, by Thomas Hardy (Boston: Houghton Mifflin, 1960) xii.

Beneath the Stars

Astronomy is an elemental part of the stage-setting for this tragedy driven by social Darwinism. Solar imagery, especially its associations with Druidical sun-worship, is of primary symbolic significance for the story; yet Hardy also gives his readers important metaphoric insights into crucial moments of his narrative through his use of stellar and lunar images. When Tess and her younger brother, Abraham, set out late at night with the honey cart, the little boy observes the stars, "whose cold pulses were beating amid the black hollows above in serene dissociation from these two wisps of human life. He asked how far away those twinklers were, and whether God was on the other side of them" (25). As he continues his "childish prattle" he asks his big sister if the stars are worlds, and her reply both puzzles and fascinates him.

> "Did you say the stars were worlds, Tess?"
> "Yes."
> "All like ours?"
> "I don't know; but I think so. They sometimes seem to be like the apples on our stubbard-tree. Most of them splendid and sound – a few blighted."
> "Which do we live on – a splendid one or a blighted one?"
> "A blighted one."
> "'Tis very unlucky that we didn't pitch on a sound one, when there were so many more of 'em!"
> "Yes." /
> "Is it like that really, Tess?" said Abraham, turning to her much impressed, on reconsideration of this rare information. "How would it have been if we had pitched on a sound one?"
> "Well, father wouldn't have coughed and creeped about as he does, and wouldn't have got too tipsy to go this journey; and mother wouldn't have been always washing, and never getting finished."
> "And you would have been a rich lady ready-made, and not have had to be made rich by marrying a gentleman." (25–6)

When their horse is run through by the mail-cart, Abraham – exhibiting a child's intuitively commonsensical cosmology – suggests that "'tis because we be on a blighted star, and not a sound one, isn't it, Tess?" (27), but his sister takes personal responsibility for the accident, and reproaches herself for negligence. Because of her self-imposed guilt, Tess will sacrifice herself for the good of the family and pursue a tenuous connection with the Stoke-d'Urbervilles, ultimately putting herself at the mercy of Alec. This incident establishes the psychological and cosmological pattern that Tess will follow in responding to other tragic events in her life. Even when nothing more concrete than "the stars" ought to be blamed for some occurrence, Tess (like Elfride and Viviette before her) will blame herself and offer herself as atonement.

As in *The Woodlanders*, Hardy associates the stars in *Tess* with idealistic philosophy. Angel, in the process of rejecting his father's Christianity and his brothers' traditional Cambridge education, enters, like Clym, upon a nineteenth-century "back to nature" project, and decides to make himself into a Colonial farmer.

> Unexpectedly, he began to like the outdoor life for its own sake, and for what it brought, apart from its bearing on his own proposed career. Considering his position he became wonderfully free from the chronic melancholy which is taking hold of the civilized / races with the decline of belief in a beneficent Power. . . .
> He grew away from old associations, and saw something new in life and humanity. Secondarily, he made close acquaintance with phenomena which he had before known but darkly – the seasons in their moods, morning and evening, night and moon, winds in their different tempers, trees, waters, and mists, shades and silences, and the voices of inanimate things. (100–101)

Deep within this mood of appreciation for the natural world (which may well have been brought about because he allowed himself to experience nature as a fully sensory and sentient embodied being for the first time), Angel overhears Tess intimating similar feelings about the world around her. She recounts the sensation of an out-of-body experience she has had when looking at the stars. She feels, at such times, that her soul is set free (102). "A very easy way to feel [your soul] go . . . is to lie on the grass at night and look straight up at some big bright star; and, by fixing your mind upon it, you will soon find that you are hundreds and hundreds o' miles away from your body, which you don't seem to want at all" (102). Angel recapitulates her experience when he gazes at Tess and identifies her as his "Ideal" of a pure and natural woman. Tess, in turn, will have a similar response to hearing Angel's harp, the celestial associations of which Hardy makes so obvious. For this moment in time – and nearly only for this moment – Tess and Angel seem to possess commensurate world views.

At the turning-point of the novel – on the honeymoon eve when Tess and Angel exchange confessions about their past sexual experiences – Hardy ingeniously inverts the association of the stars and idealism, by using stellar imagery to illustrate Angel's disillusionment. At their wedding, Hardy describes Tess and Angel as at "stellar distances" from the congregation in the church. As they settle into their honeymoon home, Angel is struck with a full realization of how much their fates are joined together; he vows to never deny her or hurt her. At the peak of this emotion, he gives Tess a necklace, earrings, and other jewels – family heirlooms – that signify his vow and this bond. When she has put them on he exclaims, "My heavens . . . how beautiful you are!" (186). And indeed she does appear as his idea of "heaven" in the sparkling gems. As Tess is about to bring up the subject of exchanging confessions, Hardy identifies her explicitly as Angel's "star" by describing her in terms of two forms of radiance – the elemental and earthly warmth of fire and starlight.

> A steady glare from the now flameless embers painted the sides and back of the fireplace with its colour, . . . The underside of the mantel-shelf was flushed with the high-coloured light, and the legs of the table nearest the fire. Tess's face and neck

reflected the same warmth, which each gem turned into an Aldebaran or a Sirius – a constellation of white, red, and green flashes, that interchanged their hues with her every pulsation . . . . (188)

In creating this comparison, Hardy may have drawn upon John Herschel's descriptions of an open star cluster that he had observed in the southern hemisphere, NGC 4755, the "Jewel Box" cluster. The cluster contains several vivid blue and red stars which inspired its nickname and is located (with convenient irony for Tess's situation) in the constellation Crux (the Southern Cross). As Tess is about to learn, the cross of Angel's Christian idealism cuts both ways.

After she has heard Angel's story, Tess completely and utterly forgives him, and then tells her own. Her newlywed hope that her experience of the world and her knowledge of sexuality will be measured by the same standard as a man's is quickly dashed. As she speaks, Angel cannot see her celestial nature shining through her words. For him, the hearth light transforms itself into the hell fires of damnation and exposes her as sinful. Hardy foreshadows Angel's reaction by extending and negating the radiant imagery with Miltonic undertones. Radiance can enlighten and warm, and radiance can wither and burn.

> Their hands were still joined. The ashes under the grate were lit by the fire vertically, like a torrid waste. Imagination might have beheld a Last Day luridness in its red-coaled glow, which fell on his face and hand, and on hers, peering into the loose hair about her brow, and firing the delicate skin underneath. A large shadow of her shape rose upon the wall and ceiling. She bent forward, at which each diamond on her neck gave a sinister wink like a toad's; and, pressing her forehead against his temple, she entered on her story of her acquaintance with Alec d'Urberville and its results, murmuring the words without flinching, and with her eyelids drooping down. (190)

Tested in the alchemical crucible of her confession, the imagery of fire, heat and light, initially encapsulated in the lively brilliance of the jewels and the stars, is displaced by a dying fire with a damning aspect, and all of the basic elements of her relationship with Angel have suffered change.

> But the complexion even of external things seemed to suffer transmutation as her announcement progressed. The fire in the grate looked impish – demoniacally funny, as if it did not care in the least about her strait. The fender grinned idly, as if it too did not care. The light from the water-bottle was merely engaged in a chromatic problem. All material objects around announced their / irresponsibility with terrible iteration. And yet nothing had changed since the moments when he had been kissing her; or rather, nothing in the substance of things. But the essence of things had changed. (190–91)

Angel's re-illumination of Tess, the new light in which he sees her, leaves him in a state of absolute disillusionment, but he cannot see that it is the illusions that he has *retained* (not the ones he has lost) that are the primary cause of this pain. As they walk away into the night to separate, Tess feels "as sarcasm the touch of the jewels of which she had been momentarily so proud"(193). Fallen from Angel's idea of "heaven," Hardy again invokes the stars to show how Tess's universe instantly diminishes to the sadly mundane.

> The cow and horse tracks in the road were full of water, the rain having been enough to charge them, but not enough to wash them away. Across these minute pools the reflected stars flitted in a quick transit as she passed; she would not have known they were shining overhead if she had not seen them there – the vastest things of the universe imaged in objects so mean. (194)

Seeing herself reflected in the tracks, Tess realizes that Angel too "saw her without irradiation – in all her bareness; that Time was chanting his satiric psalm at her then – 'Behold, when thy face is made bare, he that loved thee shall hate; / Thy face shall be no more fair at the fall of thy fate. / For thy life shall fall as a leaf and be shed as the rain; / And the veil of thine head shall be grief, and the crown shall be pain'" (194).

Here Hardy revisits the emotional dynamics of the early confession scene in *A Pair of Blue Eyes* between Elfride and Knight (and he will later invoke that scene's "stonehenge" effect as well). Again, he holds the firelight and the starlight blameless for illuminating the human situation. Angel's own human nature and nurture are responsible for producing the overly idealistic and unrealistically judgmental perceptions of Tess by which he fails to see her – and value her – as she is. Tess is responsible for hearing this judgment as resonant with the teachings of her natural religion and internalizing it as true.

Angel's rejection of Tess is but one in a vast multitude of modern forces that Hardy implicates in her fate. In an episode that mirrors Tess's ride with her brother in the honey-cart, Hardy evokes similar stellar imagery to describe her night-time journey with Angel to deliver milk to the railroad station.

> They crept along towards a point in the expanse of shade just at hand at which a feeble light was beginning to assert its presence, a spot where, by day, a fitful white streak of steam at intervals upon the dark green background denoted intermittent moments of contact between their secluded world and modern life. Modern life stretched out its steam feeler to this point three or four times a day, touched the native existences, and quickly withdrew its feeler again, as if what it touched had been uncongenial.
>
> They reached the feeble light, which came from the smoky lamp of a little railway station; a poor enough terrestrial star, yet in one sense of more importance to Talbothays Dairy and mankind than the celestial ones to which it stood in such humiliating contrast. (157)

Hardy takes this opportunity to juxtapose Tess to the modern world as well. Just as the modern light of the mail-cart shone upon her after her horse was run-through, Hardy now allows the beam of this artificial "star" to catch her in its light:

The light of the engine flashed for a second upon Tess Durbeyfield's figure, motionless under the great holly-tree. No object could have looked more foreign to the gleaming cranks and wheels than this unsophisticated girl, with the round bare arms, the rainy face and hair, the suspended attitude of a friendly leopard at pause, the print gown of no date or fashion, and the cotton bonnet drooping on her brow. (157)

Through this scene Hardy is able to indicate how the railroad (and the industry of which it is a symbol) now drives human culture as the heavens and the gods were once thought to power the universe. The urban and rural worlds are not just different cultural places, they are different cultural *times*. Like an image made by strobe photography, Hardy freezes the frame, at once capturing the fact that the modern world has deeply encroached upon the fast-fading habitat of creatures like Tess and illuminating the full reality of her dilemma: she is caught and transfixed by the competing and accumulating vectors of force that exert their action upon her life and being.

Under the Moon

In *Tess*, as in *The Woodlanders* and other novels, Hardy associates lunar imagery with "past" rural rituals, unbridled sensuality, and violent lust. What is left of folk culture in the late nineteenth century still partakes of pagan abandon and reflects its primal origins. Hardy describes the country dance as an orgy of sexual selection, as the spinning and whirling motions of the dancers produce pairs that go off at tangents from the circle to leave together. As the participants begin their drunken walk home, their light-headedness affects them in astronomical terms:

They followed the road with a sensa- / tion that they were soaring along in a supporting medium, possessed of original and profound thoughts, themselves and surrounding nature forming an organism of which all the parts harmoniously and joyously interpenetrated each other. They were as sublime as the moon and stars above them, and the moon and stars were as ardent as they. (55–6)

When the Queen of Spades picks a fight with Tess along the moonlit way, she is similarly motivated by drunkenness, and the resultant primal feelings of territoriality and mating rights – all of which Hardy associates with effects of the "moon." When the fight is over, the crowd disperses into the mist and moonlight.

Then these children of the open air, whom even excess of alcohol could scarce injure permanently, betook themselves to the field-path; and as they went there moved onward with them, around the shadow of each one's head, a circle of opalized light, formed by the moon's rays upon the glistening sheet of dew. Each pedestrian could see no halo but his or her own, which never deserted the head-shadow, whatever its vulgar unsteadiness might be; but adhered to it, and persistently beautified it; till the erratic motions seemed an inherent part of the irradiation, and the fumes of their breathing a component of the night's mist; and the spirit of the scene, and of the moonlight, and of Nature, seemed harmoniously to mingle with the spirit of wine. (58)

Moonlight, and the lack of it, will play a part in another primal activity in the next crucial scene. When Tess hesitates to answer Alec's queries about her reaction to his past flirtations, the fog "seemed to hold the moonlight in suspension" in the tension of the moment. As they ride on into the forest, Tess becomes increasingly drowsy, the fog rolls in, she sleeps, and the moon sets. Equally susceptible to natural forces and human ones, at this fateful point in time, Alec takes her, and the narrator leaves no doubt that Tess is alone in the natural world:

> Darkness and silence ruled everywhere around. Above them rose the primeval yews and oaks of The Chase, in which were poised gentle roosting birds in their last nap; and about them stole the hopping rabbits and hares. But, might some say, where was Tess's guardian angel? where was the providence of her simple faith? Perhaps, like that other god of whom the ironical Tishbite spoke, he was talking, or he was pursuing, or he was in a journey, or he was sleeping and not to be awaked.
>
> Why was it that upon this beautiful feminine tissue, sensitive as / gossamer, and practically blank as snow as yet, there should have been traced such a coarse pattern as it was doomed to receive; . . . One may, indeed, admit the possibility of a retribution lurking in the present catastrophe. Doubtless some of Tess d'Urberville's mailed ancestors rollicking home from a fray had dealt the same measure even more ruthlessly towards peasant girls of their time. But though to visit the sins of the fathers upon the children may be a morality good enough for divinities, it is scorned by average human nature; and it therefore does not mend the matter. (62–3)

Solar Power

The connections Hardy establishes between the pagan or primeval moon and Alec, and the abstract ideal stars and Angel, will remain consistent throughout *Tess*; she will passively live out her existence beneath the light of both. Yet the celestial object most directly linked with Tess herself is the sun. Hardy alludes to Druidical sun-worship and related rural customs to emphasize how Tess responds to the universe with an essentially pagan, naturalistic outlook. Born in a Druid "vale," Tess retains an instinctual response to nature, feels herself to be *of* nature, not just within it.

> At times her whimsical fancy would intensify natural processes around her till they seemed a part of her own story. Rather they became a part of it; for the world is only a psychological phenomenon, and what they seemed they were. The midnight airs and gusts, moaning amongst the tightly-wrapped buds and bark of the winter twigs, were formulae of bitter reproach. A wet day was the expression of irremediable grief at her weakness in the mind of some vague ethical being whom she could not class definitely as the God of her childhood, and could not comprehend as any other. (72)

The narrator expresses his opinion that Tess is wrong to think that nature feels her presence as "sinful." "She had been made to break an accepted social law, but no law known to the environment in which she fancied herself such an anomaly" (73).

Hardy makes it clear, however, that the laws of nature are at work within Tess's world and he traces the probable origins of the human tendency to anthropomorphize them. His account may show the influence of his reading of Max Müller.

> The sun, on account of the mist, had a curious sentient, personal look, demanding the masculine pronoun for its adequate expression. His present aspect, coupled with the lack of all human forms in the scene, explained the old-time heliolatries in a moment. One could feel that a saner religion had never prevailed under the sky. The luminary was a golden-haired, beaming, mild-eyed, God-like creature, gazing down in the vigour and intentness of youth upon an earth that was brimming with interest for him. (73)

Hardy had earlier alluded to how easily similar tendencies were aroused in Knight in *A Pair of Blue Eyes*. Knight's fear made him see sunshine as a drunken leer. Tess's emotional state will have the opposite effect on her perception. Hardy explicitly connects Tess with the sun itself as the life-giving force in nature. He draws upon solar physics (probably the photospheric and coronal studies that he found in Proctor) to create images that illuminate Tess's essential optimism and capacity to hope, as well as her participation in the Darwinian appetite for joy.

> Her hopes mingled with the sunshine in an ideal photosphere which surrounded her as she bounded along against the soft south wind. She heard a pleasant voice in every breeze, and in every bird's note seemed to lurk a joy. . . . /
> The irresistible, universal, automatic tendency to find sweet pleasure somewhere, which pervades all life, from the meanest to the highest, had at length mastered Tess. (87–8)

Tess's deification of nature further manifests itself in an urge to sing the praises of the Lord as He is seen in his natural works: "O ye Sun and Moon . . . O ye Stars . . . ye Green Things upon the Earth . . . ye Fowls of the Air . . . Beasts and Cattle . . . Children of Men. . . bless ye the Lord, praise Him and magnify Him for ever!" (88). To this effusion, the narrator comments: "And probably the half-unconscious rhapsody was a Fetichistic utterance in a Monotheistic setting; women whose chief companions are the forms and forces of outdoor Nature retain in their souls far more of the Pagan fantasy of their remote forefathers than of the systematized religion taught their race at later date" (88). Hardy will later reveal the depths of her simple, but profound, theology by having her ask the one cosmic question that resonates throughout her life: why does the sun shine on the just and the unjust alike? (107).

Besides her role as a sun worshiper of sorts, Hardy also depicts Tess as a sun herself, in the way she gives warmth and life to those around her. She is Angel's star, but as he realizes too late, she is not one of the remote celestial bodies he has been idealizing, but the familiar, nearest, and because nearest, the most vital, of stars – the sun. Her personality is like the sun for Angel whose senses fill with her presence. She makes the sky throb and makes the world come to life for him (130). Yet Hardy also associates the sun, throughout the story, with sinister, death-giving activities. The male god-like sun so benevolent seeming in the passage above, bestows light upon the field in which a modern reaping machine harvests the field's crop *and* all of the living creatures in its path (74). As the old-time harvest scythe was a symbol of time and mortality personified by the Grim Reaper, now Hardy shows how the modern agricultural machinery of the harvest fulfills the same ritual and cultural function. Later, Hardy details how the threshing machine has replaced the sun as the "*primum mobile*" of the work-folk (269). It issues an unnatural call to country labor, having displaced the sun as a diurnal and seasonal "sign" in rural culture. In the modern agricultural world, the thresher is the "red tyrant that the women had come to serve" (269) and through their work, worship. Its arrival signals the beginning of their harvest rites, the sun does not.

The strongest and most troubling association of the sun with death and the encroachment of modernism occurs, of course, in the novel's closing scene. The story's final act occurs at Stonehenge, and Hardy draws upon the historical associations of the site (as well as Biblical and Miltonic echoes) to comment upon modernity and its human costs. According to British legend, Stonehenge was an ancient pagan temple where Druids were believed to have made human sacrifices to the sun. After Tess murders Alec, she and Angel wander aimlessly through the countryside, one step ahead of the law. Exhausted, she rests upon the altar stone and falls asleep. As the posse surrounds the site, Angel begs them to let her finish her sleep:

> When they saw where she lay, which they had not done till then, they showed no objection, and stood watching her, as still as the pillars around. He went to the stone and bent over her. . . . All waited in the growing light, their faces and hands as if they were silvered, the remainder of their figures dark, the stones glistening green-grey, the Plain still a mass of shade. Soon the light was strong, and a ray shone upon her unconscious form, peering under her eyelids and waking her. (328)

The ritual power of this moment reenacts the ancient ceremony that so strongly depended upon belief in the connection between human action and the elements of nature. The humans wait upon the sun. The sun rises. The sun shines. Falling across the altar stone with astronomical precision, its rays send forth one cutting beam: simultaneously awakening Tess to the reality of her fate and clearly illuminating the actions of the posse responsible.

~

In the conclusion of *Tess*, Hardy offers a Juvenalian critique of social Darwinism that rivals Swift's in its emotional intensity. Painfully torn between his loving compassion for the individual and his "savage indignation" and detestation of the "animal called man," Hardy offers a bitter dissection of humanity's inhumanity and abuse of reason.[4] Though spiritually in accord with natural law, Tess is judged and banished by personal edict. Upon the slab at Stonehenge, she is sacrificed to social laws as unrelenting and merciless as the whims of any pagan sun god; laws that judge the appearances of an act, and not the extenuating circumstances; a blind justice that cannot see the essential rightness of an apparent wrong, or the purity of spirit in a murderess. In the cosmic satire of this final scene, the weapon of choice has changed, but not the primitive urge that wields it. No sun god now demands such blood worship and the Christian God would forbid it. Yet for Tess, modern justice is devoid of jurisprudence, exhibiting neither the common sense of the Old Testament's "an eye for an eye" nor the compassion of the New Testament's *charitos*. At the height of empire, Hardy takes a hard look at the paradise that has been lost and asks: How can such a culture celebrate its progress in human nature or nurture? Three hundred years after the Reformation, Victorian sensibility still rejects Martin Luther's simple wisdom that a dairymaid can milk cows to the glory of God. Nineteen centuries after Christ's reconciliation of law and grace, we still refuse to grant it to each other. Such a society is as tragically self-blinded as Oedipus Tyrannus and wreaks equally devastating havoc on the human family. In *Jude the Obscure*, the gods of social law, abetted by the Malthusian calculus, will claim more victims.

Jude the Obscure (1896)

That social laws are more to blame than natural laws in determining human tragedies is the central theme of Hardy's final novel. As in *The Return of the Native*, Hardy patterns this story's trajectory after tragic Greek models. Chance and circumstance again join individual flaws as the causal agents of disappointment and senseless misery. In this story, the "satire of fate" further embitters its tragic tone, as Millgate explains:

---

[4] Swift's epitaph for himself reads, in part (from the Latin): "Here lies the body of Jonathan Swift . . . [gone] where savage indignation can lacerate his heart no more. Go traveler, and imitate if you can, one who to the utmost strenuously championed the liberty of man." His other famous comment is from a letter to Alexander Pope, 29 September 1725: ". . . when you think of the world give it one lash the more at my request. I have ever hated all nations, professions, and communities, and all my love is toward individuals; for instance, I hate the tribe of lawyers, but I love Counsellor Such-a-one, Judge Such-a-one: so with physicians – I will not speak of my own trade – soldiers, English, Scotch, French, and the rest. But principally I hate and detest that animal called man, although I heartily love John, Peter, Thomas, and so forth. This is the system upon which I have governed myself many years (but do not tell) and so I shall go on till I have done with them." As in *Jonathan Swift*, eds. Angus Ross and David Woolley, The Oxford Authors (Oxford: Oxford University Press, 1984) 470.

There does seem to be something gratuitous about Jude's sufferings, the death of Father Time and the other children, the violence of Sue's abnegation and self-flagellation. In view, however, of the Greek precedents Hardy seems to have had in mind, such turns of the screw can perhaps be explained, if not entirely justified, in terms of a deliberate determination to leave the reader precisely "stunned with a sense of the hollowness of existence." (*Career* 325)

In the Postscript to the 1912 edition of the novel, Hardy wrote that nineteenth-century marriage laws are the "tragic machinery" of the story. As modern industrial civilization "progressed," such laws had become, in his view (which agrees with that of Diderot), increasingly out of touch with the laws of nature. The gap was causing a "deadly war . . . between the flesh and spirit." The universal dilemma Hardy introduced in *A Pair of Blue Eyes* – how do human beings cope in the world of nature without a god? – also forms part of the background of the social crisis. The "struggle of ideas," as various philosophical, religious, social, and economic approaches compete for a chance to resolve that dilemma, creates problems for humankind as well. In *Jude the Obscure,* Hardy employs astronomical phenomena only rarely. The nebular hypothesis and cosmic scale of the universe are not of as much moment as the local operations of the mechanisms of social Darwinism for Jude and Sue. When astronomical imagery is invoked, Hardy will associate it significantly with various kinds of intellectual frameworks, internalized cosmologies, or philosophical stances, to query both the possible potential and the possible problems inherent in human perceptions and abstraction.

One of the earliest astronomical images in the novel occurs when Jude, at the age of sixteen, is teaching himself Classics. Driving the bread-cart home one night, he has been "stumbling though the 'Carmen Saeculare'" when he notices that:

> The light had changed . . . The sun was going down, and the full moon was rising simultaneously behind the woods in the opposite quarter. His mind had become so impregnated with the poem that, in a moment of . . . impulsive emotion . . . he stopped the horse, alighted, and glancing round to see that nobody was in sight, knelt down on the roadside bank with open book. He turned first to the shiny goddess, who seemed to look so softly and critically at his doings, then to the disappearing luminary on the other hand, as he began:
>
> 'Phoebe silvarum que potens Diana!'
> The horse stood still till he had finished the hymn, which Jude repeated under the sway of a polytheistic fancy that he would never have thought of humouring in broad daylight.[5]

---

[5]   Thomas Hardy, *Jude the Obscure*, ed., Norman Page (1978; New York: W. W. Norton, 1999) 29; hereafter cited by page number within the text.

The scene introduces many of the most significant themes of the novel: the juxtaposition of Classical, medieval, and modern cultures, personal aspiration and potential, and pagan versus Christian religion. When Jude arrives home "he mused over his curious superstition, innate or acquired, in doing this, and the strange forgetfulness which had led to such a lapse from common-sense and custom in one who wished, next to being a scholar, to be a Christian divine" (29). Hardy attributes the anomaly to Jude's eclectic self-education in which he had been "reading heathen works exclusively." Jude himself is aware of the "inconsistency": "He began to wonder whether he could be reading quite the right books for his object in life. Certainly there seemed little harmony between this pagan literature and the mediaeval colleges at Christminster, that ecclesiastical romance in stone" (29).

As events will show, the dangers of the pagan poets will not be responsible for forestalling Jude's goal of attending Christminster (the fictionalized Oxford). The next "pagan" danger Jude meets is Arabella, and she represents a far greater threat to his college preparations. Hardy emphasizes in his description of Jude's first meeting with Arabella, how the animal "magneticism" of her sexuality is powerfully attractive to him, overpowering his reason and will (35). Then, recalling a pattern he had created in *Two On a Tower*, Hardy shows Jude distracted from his studies (in this case, New Testament Greek) by thoughts of Arabella. Deserting his work for the chance to walk with her, the couple passes the place in the road where Jude had recited Horace's poem, but the significance of the sun and moon have now changed for him. With her beside him, "[he] passed the spot where he had knelt to Diana and Phoebus without remembering there were any such people in the mythology, or that the Sun was anything else than a useful lamp for illuminating Arabella's face" (38). Arabella will temporarily derail him from his long-term goal of a Christminster degree. Further echoing a passage from *Two on a Tower*, Hardy continues, "They were in absolute solitude – the most apparent of all solitudes, that of empty surrounding space. Nobody could be nearer than a mile . . . . They were, in fact, on one of the summits of the county, and the distant landscape around Christminster could be discerned from where they lay. But Jude did not think of that then" (44).

When Jude and Arabella part after their disastrous marriage, Hardy sets Jude back on the road he had left when Arabella crossed his path. He renews his dream to enter Christminster with these thoughts: "He might battle with his evil star, and follow out his original intention" (61). Then he sees a "faint halo," a "small dim nebulousness" on the horizon, his lodestar – Christminster. The aura of hopefulness around this scene lasts only until the beginning of "Part Second," where Hardy indicates by the opening epigram that Christminster will not be Jude's lucky star. The epigram is taken from Swinburne: "Save his own soul he hath no star." The next line of the poem, which Hardy does not quote, reads prophetically: "and sinks, except his own soul guide."

Jude's questing for some kind of intellectual "star" or guiding light can also be seen in his immediate reaction to his first vision of Sue. He sees her in a medieval light, "illuminating" texts, and decides then and there that she will be his "kindly star, elevating power, companion in Anglican worship, a tender friend" (74). He will be proven wrong on all counts, although Hardy does connect Sue's intellectual ideas and social philosophy with astronomical images. Her intellect "scintillate[s] like a star"(268). Because of her advanced views of marriage, she prefers an elevated, astronomically abstract kind of love between men and women which she designates "Venus Urania" (134). In her opinion this higher form of "marriage" should be instituted, instead of the current official recognition of animal desire (134). Sue sees social conventions in terms of an astronomical comparison: "the social moulds civilization fits us into have no more relation to our actual shapes than the con- / ventional shapes of the constellations have to real star-patterns" (162–3). By nature, Sue is "ethereal, fine-nerved, sensitive" and unfitted by temperament and instinct to be married or consummate a marriage (173). When her husband, Phillotson, questions her about her aversion to sex she blames "The universe, I suppose – things in general, because they are so horrid and cruel" (175).

Hardy uses most of the other direct references to astronomy in *Jude* to show how the circumstances of modern life have defeated and negated their original associations. Jude is rejected by Christminster and must suffer through the graduation parade, watching from a telescopically remote distance as "the new Doctors emerged . . . passing across the field of Jude's vision like inaccessible planets across an object glass" (257). When Sue gives up her intellectual ideals to become mother to little "Father Time," she does so because she believes that she has found something more profound than intellectual "stars" to care about: "There's more for us to think about in that one little hungry heart than in all the stars of the sky" (219). After the murder–suicide, Sue's and Jude's "stars" are utterly lost. Now her view of the universe has permanently altered.

> Vague and quaint imaginings had haunted Sue in the days when her intellect scintillated like a star, that the world resembled a stanza or melody composed in a dream; it was wonderfully excellent to the half-aroused / intelligence, but hopelessly absurd at the full waking; that the First Cause worked automatically like a somnambulist, and not reflectively like a sage; that at the framing of the terrestrial conditions there seemed never to have been contemplated such a development of emotional perceptiveness among the creatures subject to those conditions as that reached by thinking and educated humanity. But affliction makes opposing forces loom anthropomorphous; and those ideas were now exchanged for a sense of Jude and herself fleeing from a persecutor. (268–9)

The irony of Jude's circumstances intensifies on his death bed. He hears about a scholarship program being established for the poor students of the next generation, of the very kind that might have saved his own dream. Dying, he one last time compares Sue's intellect to a star and realizes that his own was merely a "benzoline lamp."

Although the direct astronomical allusions in *Jude* are few, they are significant. As in *The Return of the Native*, Hardy combines such references to create a neo-Greek atomistic universe for his late nineteenth-century characters. At one point Jude himself detects a direct parallel between Sue's modern dilemma as a wife and the ancient atomists' worldview: "Wifedom has not yet squashed up and digested you in its vast maw as an atom which has no further individuality" (151). Yet Hardy makes still grander, more sweeping, connections between cosmological conditions and his storyline. There are three sets of powerful laws at work within Jude's and Sue's universe. On a rural outing with Jude, Sue comments: "I rather like this . . . outside all laws except gravitation and germination." But Jude quickly reminds her of one other equally real force in her life: "you are quite a product of civilization" (111). As Sue knows, the source of her unhappiness in life is neither nature nor her own being: "It is none of the natural tragedies of love that's love's usual tragedy in civilized life, but a tragedy artificially manufactured for people who in a natural state would find relief in parting" (170).

Disparities between social law and natural inclination do not supply all of the ingredients in human tragedy. The physics of human nature plays a part as well, as Hardy indicates by the passage from Marcus Aurelius Antoninus that opens "Part Fifth": "Thy aerial part, and all the fiery parts which are mingled in thee, though by nature they have an upward tendency, still in obedience to the disposition of the universe they are overpowered here in the compound mass the body" (201). Jude recognizes that Sue is made of more refined human matter than he is. He is of a "grosser substance" possessing more animal passion. In relation to his disappointment in Christminster and life as a future parson, he also sees that he was just not of the "right stuff," was not evolved enough to be accepted as such: "He was as unfit, obviously, by nature, as he had been by social position to fill the part of a propounder of accredited dogma" (171). Jude realizes that neither human evolution or social Darwinism have progressed enough as far as he and his own dreams for an ameliorated future are concerned: ". . . it was my poverty and not my will that consented to be beaten. It takes two or three generations to do what I tried to do in one" (256).

In all of their personal disappointments and final tragic losses, Hardy makes it clear that the weak wills of his human actors are not entirely at fault. When Jude is trying to resist the temptation to see Sue anymore, he feels that "the human was more powerful in him than the Divine." Yet when he seems on the verge of succeeding, the narrator interjects that "other forces and laws than theirs were in operation" and by coincidence the two are thrown together (164). For all of their struggles to do well and be well, Sue and Jude can not win against all of the forces acting so inexorably upon them.

> And I was just making my baby darling a new frock; and now I shall never see him in it, and never talk to him anymore! . . . My eyes are so swollen that I can scarcely see; and yet little more than a year ago I called myself happy! We went about loving each other too much – indulging ourselves to utter selfishness with each other! We said – do you remember? – that we would make a virtue of joy. I said it was Nature's intention, Nature's law and raison d'être that we should be joyful in what instincts she afforded us – instincts which civilization had taken upon itself to thwart. What dreadful

things I said! And now Fate has given us this stab in the back for being such fools as to take Nature at her word! (266)

Sue has earlier asked "Why should Nature's law be mutual butchery?" (243). She could not help but feel that it was a "terribly tragic thing to bring beings into the world" (246). Even Phillotson, for all of his willingness to harmonize society's laws with nature's, realizes at last that "cruelty is the law pervading all nature and society; and we can't get out of it if we would" (251). After Father Time has hanged himself and his siblings, Sue, like Tess, gives voice to her own cosmological truth, murmuring that "It is no use fighting against God!" Although Jude tries to remind her that "it is only . . . man and senseless circumstance" to blame, she can no longer respond in her usual rational manner (269). The final knell of the novel rings in the tragic truth of the Doctor's opinion that:

> It was in his nature to do it . . . there are such boys springing up amongst us – boys of a sort unknown in the last generation – the outcome of new views of life. They seem to see all its terrors before they are old enough to have staying power to resist them. He says it is the beginning of the coming universal wish not to live. (264)

The collective tragedy of *Jude* is encapsulated in the fact that no matter what qualities of mind, body or spirit these characters bring to the struggle, none possesses, or develops, or happens upon a combination that works to "fit" them for survival within their natural and social environments. There seems to be no arguing with the despair inherent within the disparity Thomas Malthus had recently identified as operating between arithmetical–economic and exponential–biological rates of growth. While some of the central characters do live on, they must face the rest of their lives with full knowledge of their complete failures in the present as well as the utter futility of any future efforts. Unless something drastically changes for the better – within them or around them – this combination of nature, human nature and social realities will continue to prove deadly.

In this ironic tragedy of biological and social Darwinism, Hardy has fashioned a fictional narrative mode that closely resonates with what Alan Velie has identified as "perhaps the most common form in modern fiction"– ironedy.[6] In ironedy, "the hero faces obstacles, fails / to overcome them; and usually does not die but is trapped, and must live with his defeat. . . . no helper of the hero is fused with the receiver: the values he embodies or seeks are 'received' by neither the heroine, hero, nor helper, but by the opponent, the anti-hero" (Schleifer and Velie, 1144–5). And, indeed, Hardy gives the novel's last words to the antagonistic, pagan-Hobbesian, Arabella. By such a move, as in the biting irony of the final words of *Two on a Tower*, Hardy implicates

---

[6]   Ronald Schleifer and Alan Velie, "Genre and Structure: Toward an Actantial Typology of Narrative Genres and Modes," *Modern Language Notes* 102 (Winter 1987):1122–50.

his own readers as complicit in this tragedy. They may be surviving in their post-Darwinian world – even thriving – but by what means? Toward what ends?

In the final analysis, the members of Hardy's late Victorian audience prove immune to his irony. One doubts that it could have come as much of a surprise. After all, these consumers of cultural media were well-versed in denying the images held up to them by mirrors of satire. With practiced finesse, they could, one moment, blithely delight in Oscar Wilde's epigrammatic truisms that skewered their own attitudes and beliefs – "Life is never fair . . . And perhaps it is a good thing for most of us that it is not" and, the very next, force their author to feel the full irony of his own words as practiced by the "fairness" of their courts.[7] So, the readers of Hardy's *Jude* reject the burden of his story's truth and reflect it back, unheeded, to the author who, for his own sanity and survival, turns to poetry, deeding the message of this narrative to modern and postmodern generations. Yet next to Hardy's unflinching vision of a human future in which our intellectual and spiritual selves are crushed under social and economic pressures and our own damaged biological natures develop the power to will us out of existence, current cautionary tales about rampant artificial intelligence and selfishly self-protective genes pale in comparison.[8]

~

In the twenty-five years or so that have passed during his career as a novelist, Hardy has brought us from Henry Knight's astronomically and geologically realistic struggle to survive clinging to the cliff, to Father Time's surreal economic agony in which the struggle itself is so great that it daunts all hope. In the fatalistic evolutionary realism of *The Woodlanders* and the satiric and ironic tragedies of *Tess* and *Jude*, Hardy plays out three variant views of human history, demonstrating how different levels of cosmic law – personal, biological, social, economic, universal – act upon individuals over time, canceling and amplifying each other's effects like sound waves. As elemental astronomical phenomena of the inorganic universe constitute the essential and fundamental conditions for organic life on this planet, so, too, do the cosmic

---

[7]   From Act II, scene one of Wilde's play, *An Ideal Husband*, produced January 3, 1895. *The Importance of Being Earnest* opened February 14th. His criminal libel case against the Marquess of Queensberry commenced in March and Wilde was sentenced to two years' hard labor on May 27th; as in *The Complete Oscar Wilde* (New York: Crescent Books; Random House, 1995) 483.

[8]   Sadly, Dr. Lee Salk's studies of adolescent suicide appear to validate Hardy's insight here into the psychology of Father Time, as his work suggests that there may be in some sort of genetic trigger for self-destruction within developmentally disabled or damaged fetuses that the interventions of high-risk obstetrics and neonatology interrupt. The rate of suicide among the children "saved" by such interventions is higher than that among those who experienced complication-free gestations and births. See page 196 of the panel discussion, "Ethics in Embryo," in *Science and the Human Spirit*, ed. Fred White (Belmont, CA: Wadsworth Publishing Co., 1989) 193–207.

settings constrain the generic parameters of Hardy's narratives. Through carefully crafted allusions to the most basic astronomy – the stars, sun, and moon – he is able to recapitulate in these stories the essential range of ways that human creatures experience life upon our humble home in the universe.

Just as in our increasingly technologically educated and interconnected global world the vast majority of our planet's citizens pay little (if any) heed to the nature and movements of celestial objects and give even less thought to the implications their existence may have in relation to our own, Hardy was well aware that the scientifically sophisticated synthesis of Swithin's and Viviette's world views was hardly the norm for Victorian culture. Then, as now, how many of our fellow city dwellers really care which way the wind is blowing or expend the least energy to note the current phase of the moon? Realistically, then, in his final major novels, Hardy presents narratives set in ever more urban environments where most of the inhabitants have left behind or have lost touch with the practical and empirical understanding of natural phenomena and natural forces once possessed by their rural progenitors, and now engage the mundane realities of their lives in increasingly complex socio-politico-economic – not cosmic – contexts.

As the writer of "scientific realism," there can be little doubt that Hardy felt that what the "Greeks had suspected," his generation had confirmed. Where an indifferent nature, the characteristics of the individual and the species, chance, and society all interact to produce the effect of an "empty universe," he was convinced that tragedy was the most probable genre for the life stories of most of the human beings living within it. He was committed to telling himself and his readers that "truth." Yet Hardy's final solution to the existential dilemma revealed by astronomy and geology is not nihilistic. In every situation, life could have been otherwise for Grace and Giles, for Tess and Angel, even for Jude and Sue; if other choices had been made at crucial points, if certain circumstances had not intervened, if social laws had not thwarted them, if death and illness had not forestalled them, they might have been happy, even if "alone" in the universe.

*   *   *

Fervently holding a philosophical belief that some variation on the theme of the tragic is "most probable" is not equivalent to concluding that such an outcome is absolutely certain. As most readers of Hardy know, there has been a long tradition within Victorian studies for critics to read the "progress" of Hardy's novelistic productions and personal philosophy along the same developmental curve: from rural to urban, from optimistically hopeful to pessimistically bleak. Reducing the intricate and implicate order of Hardy's novel universe to a linear argument, however elegantly it may be drawn, may do his philosophical, scientific, and satiric sophistication a critical disservice.[9] I believe that a more telescopic perspective effectively reduces that

---

[9]   I have in mind here, in particular, the exquisitely researched and beautifully reasoned

hermeneutic risk. Focusing upon the astronomical and cosmological elements as they appear within his literary notebooks and creative prose works, we see them develop and accrue symbolic significance as important components of Hardy's set of personal constructs. In the three early works read here, *Two on a Tower*, and the three late novels, Hardy consistently insists on a cosmic connection between the inorganic and organic realms, and the essential continuity of evolutionary forces. The sum of those forces is always contingent on many variables, some controllable, some not. The final outcome is not invariably or inviolably determined, however; it all depends on who, and what, and where, and when, and why, as well as many factors beyond human comprehension. Read in the context of such an aesthetic, the harmonious resolution of *Far From the Madding Crowd* is just as "realistic" for those characters, in that time and place, as is the horrific ruin of Jude's world.

Whether "stunned" by the power of its "hollow" world view, or for the simple reason that it was the last of his novels, critics have often considered *Jude the Obscure* as Hardy's most complete and final word on the subject. Many of those same readers have assumed that Hardy's distinct break from his professional career as a writer of prose fiction was accompanied by an equally dramatic shift away from the artistic and philosophical issues he had explored within those novels' many pages. Such an assessment, I believe, misses the essential continuity of Hardy's aesthetic in prose and verse. I agree, substantially, with Peter Allan Dale's critical appraisal of Hardy's turn to poetic form.

> [Hardy] liked to talk about the change in generic venue as if poetry somehow gave him more license for expressing his unpopular views. But the object in going over to verse seems to me to have had less to do, after all, with a desire to reduce the pain inflicted by / critics than with Hardy's persistent Arnoldean pursuit of an aesthetic form appropriate to "scientific realism." The philosopher in him may have arrived at the "coming universal wish not to be," but the inveterate and, as he now seems to have recognized, obsessive artist persisted in wanting to find out how that wish might best be "structured."
>
> The process of collecting individual poems into single volumes always gave Hardy an opportunity he seemed eager to embrace [. . .] In one preface after another, we find him insisting that his poems are "dramatic" in the special sense that they are "impersonations" of the views of others, not himself, and that, in those cases in which they are clearly lyrical, they represent not any firmly held, systematic belief but contrasting moods and fancies. Moreover, the collections as wholes are, he insists, not wholes at all. They have no "cohesion" or "concord" but are simply "unadjusted

---

argument of Peter Allan Dale in the final two chapters of *In Pursuit of a Scientific Culture* 219–79. I disagree with him, however, that Freud deserves to retain the status traditionally assigned to him by early to mid-twentieth-century historians of science as the heir of the torch of scientific revolution after Copernicus and that Hardy's primary achievement was his "anticipation" of Freud. In my view, Hardy's literary cosmology is far more implicate than Freud's and has important implications (beyond Freud's) for scientific understanding, human psychology as well as aesthetics.

impressions" and "diverse readings" of phenomena. These are not expressions of modesty, still less of failure. In their conspicuous evasion of authorial and authorizing intentionality, they mean to announce something like an aesthetic principle, one aimed at conveying nothing so much as the "sense of disconnection." (277–8)

Dale uses this discussion to situate Hardy's work in relation to the French decadents, as well as to trace his "descent from Flaubert to Nietzsche to Derrida" (279) and beyond, and there is nothing degrading to Hardy in that literary and philosophical lineage. Yet, to my mind, the most salient insight here is the inadvertent reminder that Hardy, as he wrote his novels, was always already a *poet*. The novels, too, are "contrasting" and "dramatic," offering "'diverse readings' of phenomena." Across the span of his whole career as a prose fiction writer, Hardy's novels can be read as a comprehensive but "disconnected" set of prose poems, representing an aesthetic philosophy almost eastern in its detached, yet empathetic sensibility and its psychologically sophisticated apprehension of cosmic complexity in which localized moments only can be suspended in our perception, observed, described, appreciated and understood. As a poetic cosmologist, Hardy drew upon a strategy similar to the one that Richard Proctor had employed in his verbal tour of the solar system: describing the nature, size, and location of each planetary world separately and then each planet's place relative first to its own satellites, then its nearest neighbors within the local solar system, and finally, in relation to the vastness of the galaxy and the still greater cosmos as a whole. Read as partial, particulate, and provisional fictional spaces, the individually "pendant" worlds of Hardy's novel universe together compose a manifold montage of possible human futures, passions and dramas.

Having made, so it seems, some sort of a personal peace with nature's indifference, Hardy nonetheless mourned the fact that humanity seemed so often unable to value, preserve and enjoy the best of our human lives and selves. Seeing the world along Hardy's line of sight, we often survey with him the full range of the worst; yet, always, the Pisgah view is present on the distant horizon. As he so beautifully recounted in *Far From the Madding Crowd*, when human actors learn from their mistakes, learn to do "otherwise" than that which would bring them grief, learn to cooperate with each other and with nature, there is hope, and joy, and love "as strong as death." Such moments may be few and far between – and they may never last long – but the potential for experiencing them, however remote, *is* real. The loving kindness of Elfride, the loyalty of Viviette, the vitality of Tess need not be sacrificed in this world or to this world; and if they are not sacrificed to it, they may save it.

Chapter 8: Conclusion

Moral Astrophysics
Myth, Cosmos, and Gender in
Nineteenth-Century Britain and Beyond

By the form and content of this text I have tried to express my best understanding of how Hardy made sense of life in the universe and how he subsequently expressed that understanding within the form and content of his novels. It will always be impossible to identify and retrace exactly all of the pathways that Hardy's mind took to reach the syntheses of ideas he achieved in his fiction. The primary texts of the literary history of astronomy provide us with a list of the usual suspects that we can check against extant evidence in Hardy's fiction and nonfiction, letters and notebooks, literary references and allusions, stylistic modeling and echoes. As we saw in the opening chapters, such a process helps us map Hardy's participation in the long tradition of human writing about the cosmos, from archaeological artifacts to mythopoetic, classical and Biblical accounts, to narratives of anthropology and folklore, and the great works of western literature (past and contemporary). Likewise, revisiting significant primary texts of natural philosophy, the history of astronomy and cosmology, and natural history, we are able to suggest how their influences may have flowed into Hardy's consciousness through an eclectic variety of intellectual watersheds and tributaries.

In Hardy's mind, the two bodies of knowledge converge and merge with other essential personal constructs to formulate the insight that both literature and science have been engaged throughout human history in the process of making sense – making meaning – out of life and the world around us. Hardy realized that these narratives of origin, change, and development express and encapsulate the ideas and beliefs of the past cultures who created them and simultaneously inform and constrain the form and content of the cosmological narratives of the cultures that inherit them. Stories matter. The formal conventions of epic, pastoral, romance, melodrama and tragedy themselves contain "truths" about the possible range of human psychological response to environmental conditions. The stories we tell ourselves about ourselves and the cosmos have the power to describe and conscribe. We may live the lives that our stories tell us it is possible to live.

Hardy's novel universe offers literary stories that function as descriptive natural history *and* predictive cosmology. Both kinds of explanatory narratives about life and nature are products of human perception, personal, psychological, and social constructs; both are unavoidably influenced by nature itself as well as the imposition upon nature of orders of order of our own imagining. Although much of Thomas Hardy's "universe" may have been in his mind (à la Ernest Brennecke), it was not *all* in his head and he did not think it was all in everyone's else either. As a literary natural historian/literary cosmologist Hardy was interested in exploring and describing what he believed to be the nexus of human existence: *interaction between* the inner life of conscious awareness, perception, psychology, and personality and the outer life of nature and culture.[1]

Working within the constraints of then-current knowledge of the human mind, biology, astronomy and social, political and economic philosophies, each of Hardy's narratives can be read as a thought-experiment in which he establishes the initial environmental conditions in the novel's natural setting and particular local social crisis. He then places into those environments different sets of human characters with distinctive cosmologies, attitudes and beliefs. The stories that unfold test and recount the results of the interactions between the environment and these characters, reporting the significance of individual variations in affecting the overall outcome. Although he allowed that the forces of chance and circumstance could be overwhelming, singly or collectively, Hardy had no doubt that the nature of human psychology played an important, if not frequently decisive, role in determining our perceptions of the possible realms of action in our lives. Taking to heart the realistic assessment that we all have to take our chances in the universe and have only ourselves and each other to rely on, Hardy saw that his society would do well to use the power of the human mind to fend off succumbing to the equally treacherous extremes of fantastic idealism and fatalistic resignation.

As an active myth-maker, Hardy's descriptive experimental narratives provide a critique of the possibilities, limitations, and dangers of living out the storylines that our imaginative cosmologies project for us. Taken at face value, his cautionary tales should have been capable of operating at the same level as the critical philosophies of life offered by Matthew Arnold or John Ruskin or the literary social criticism of Charles Dickens or George Eliot. While various substantial readerships were able to appreciate sufficiently abstract intellectual and aesthetic arguments on the one hand, and sufficiently sentimental urgings toward charitable and "unhistoric" acts on the other, no sizeable audience was ready to receive the message of Hardy's moral astrophysics, the product of a quite literally *natural* theology. Having searched for God, as he said, for over fifty years, Hardy found Him right where William Whewell's

---

[1]   In my view, it may well have been the attractive complexity of just this set of problems that was responsible for keeping Hardy such an active reader and writer for the rest of his long life after he "retired" as a professional novelist. While the posse and jury in *Tess* had rendered a clear judgement against virtue being so, Hardy himself seems to have independently discovered – and apparently personally accepted – that for human life, our evolved intellect, ultimately, *was* its own reward.

Bridgewater Treatise said He would be: in the natural world of the cosmos and the human heart that lives to perceive it. Finding the divine in all the right places, but not for any of the theologically right reasons, Hardy saw that the stories of Christian cosmology and natural history (as told through the nebular hypothesis and biological evolution) carry the same philosophy of moral behavior – to love one's neighbor as one's self. Hardy's cosmic narratives repeatedly teach that this moral imperative (one of the central commandments of the New Testament covenant) emerges naturally from our understanding of our universal dilemma, as well as by revelation. By whatever pathway we obtain such insight, Hardy suggests we might well improve our experience of life by living by it.

Conjoining Darwinism with astrophysics, contextualizing organic evolution within the cosmic scale of the inorganic, provided Hardy with a more universal view of evolutionary theory than that becoming increasingly prevalent throughout Victorian culture. Popular interpretations of social Darwinism confused its major tenets with Hobbesian "dog eat dog" political philosophy and validated cut-throat economic competition and the struggle for resources with one's neighbors. When Hardy read Darwin he saw a complex story of the interaction of animate and inanimate forces, some controllable, some uncontrollable, some conscious, some unconscious. He saw the beauty and truth implicate in Darwin's tree of life (and death). Although he well knew that the history of science taught that humanity's comprehension of its own nature and the natural world would always be imperfect and provisional, Hardy's reading of Darwin yielded some slight possibility that conscious life could fit itself to the environment and could alter its environment to better fit itself. That the vast majority of those attempts would fail, he accepted as a fact of life. That fact, he acknowledged, could be discouraging, but it could also *en*courage each of us to try to better fit ourselves and each other, both materially and psychologically, to the realities around us.

Read collectively, Hardy's novels offer his Victorian readership a new testament to the state of humanity's place in the cosmos and propose a new means of salvation, a way to achieve (in the absence of an eternal paradise) a local heaven on earth, or failing that (as would more than likely be the case) a way at least to make this temporal life less hellish. The characters who embody the best values of both an Edenic paradise and classical Golden Age, those who bridge the past into the present and live in pastoral accord with nature, find few ways to extend that bridge into the future. All who do, after Gabriel and Bathsheba, are poised to fade into extinction. The men who attempt to rebuild that bridge by working from the perspective of modern education and social and political philosophies "back" toward nature, fall short and fail. Hardy's modern men blunder on, caught between the unrecoverable past and unrealizable future, torn by instinctual impulses and idealistic desires they inadequately understand, only partially aware of the victims they have left in their wakes, and tragically unseeing of the means to prevent or amend the damage they have created. While Swithin may be a new man of science with his heart in the right place, he too faces an uncertain future – he does not demonstrate the loyalty or the staying power under fire of Gabriel let alone establish a long track-record of being a good man who does good things, as does Giles. In no other novel does Hardy express even the slightest hope that other men of other sciences will successfully usher in an industrial, technological, scientific, or philosophical utopia that will ameliorate the human condition. Hardy's female characters appear to share similar fates, or ones even worse. Whether meeting a Gothic romantic demise, making a melodramatic last gasp, awaking to tragic violence, all serve as sacrificial victims to arbitrary social and moral conventions that seem to write them out of their own stories. Yet, significantly, in each narrative, Hardy makes it clear that it is the loving, life-giving, qualities of his cosmic heroines, the Elfrides, Viviettes, and Tesses of the world, that have the greatest potential to affect positive change in our matrix of interacting natural and human forces.

Taken as a magnum opus composed of numerous variations on the same cosmic theme – an aesthetically integral montage – Hardy's novels participate in a pervasive cultural trend among nineteenth-century scientific, historical and literary writers who were intent upon constructing a natural history of humanity, among them: James G. Frazer, Charles Darwin, Edward Tylor, Herbert Spencer, and Edward Gibbon. Taking their own time as endpoint, such histories offered a vision of the progressive development of contemporary social structures and the hierarchical ordering of species, races, nations and sexes. The collection and presentation of this information about the nature of human beings and their relations to each other seemed to tell the story of the evolution of culture itself, culminating in the *status quo* of nineteenth-century Britain. Educated readers must (as Darwin, for one, so frequently reminded them), squarely face "the facts" and admit their logical conclusion. To the collection of facts provided by expositors of comparative mythology and religion, biology and geology, anthropology and archaeology, social and political history, Hardy added those of astronomy and cosmology. Considering the sweep of human time from a God's-eye point of view, so to speak, enabled Hardy to see how literary history, human history, natural history, and the history of astronomy converge and manifest themselves in multifarious cosmological frameworks. This global and relativistic perspective provides a leveling effect to Hardy's evaluation of human-imposed hierarchies and arbitrary assignations of order within the natural and human realms, rendering categories of class, age and gender insignificant distinctions in comparison with our common dilemma beneath the stars.

Hardy surveys essentially the same natural and social terrain as other contemporary commentators but arrives at distinctively divergent conclusions. He does not share their positivist optimism. He does not see signs of inevitable and infinite progress. He does not see natural justification of social oppression by class or gender. Amidst the overwhelming aggregation of facts collected into and reported by the grand historical narratives of the nineteenth century was apparently irrefutable evidence of man's "natural" and historical superiority and woman's equally "natural" and historical inferiority. This evidence seemed to locate precedents for her restricted role within society that predated Pauline prescriptions as well as Old Testament accounts and those available in ancient mythologies. Stories gathered from cultures worldwide, from the distant past to near present, identified primitive woman as the inferior being she had been *a primo* and still was. Perhaps because of experiences in his own life's story or personal psychology,[2] Hardy developed an awareness of the present power past myths exert through the cultural narratives that enact and reenact them. Reinterpreting the confluence of early human myth and culture in light of biblical tradition and the contemporary findings of natural history, Hardy's cosmologically informed narratives offer a different prospect for men's valuation of women and for the lives of women themselves. The personal agony, the *psychomachia* of individuals, as well as the larger biological and social struggles of his local Victorian epics all have room for heroes *and* heroines; indeed, they have need for them both.

Cosmic Connections between Myth and Gender

As I have argued more extensively elsewhere, since ancient times, literary and artistic representations of humanity's relationship to the cosmos have reflected archetypal elements present in the Danaë myth.[3] Apollodorus, Homer, Vergil, Ovid and Horace all tell the story, with varying emphases and purposes.[4] Typically, classical versions are rarely concerned with the personal nature of the story's events as experienced by Danaë, directing attention instead to the responses of the male figures affected by those events and their social, political, and historical consequences. The Greek and Latin originals highlight her father's fear and anger, her son's heroism and accidental revenge, her restoration through her son to her rightful place in Argos, or her founding of Ardea, the future home of Turnus, with later import for the founding of Rome. Variant interpretations of the story by medieval and early Renaissance mythographers and artists all turn on the meaning assigned to the two key features – the nature of the "shower of gold" (supernatural force acting by secondary causes or local currency) and Danaë's reception of it – actively resistant, reluctantly seduced, passionately

---

[2]   Many biographers have suggested that his personal relationships with women, including his mother, wife, Emma, and others may have directly contradicted the stereotypical attitudes about women that he encountered in Victorian culture at large. Others suggest that his own experience with upward mobility through education may have inspired his sympathy for others who were making similar attempts. Another possible explanation may lie in the deeper psychological compulsion he felt to repeat the myth that he felt most unresolvable in his own life and thought (as Freud and a long line of Freudian analysts have suggested we all do). Dale offers this explanation for the persistence of some recurrent themes in Hardy's texts (270).

[3]   Pamela Gossin, "'All Danae to the Stars': Nineteenth-Century Representations of Women in the Cosmos," *Victorian Studies* 40.1 (Autumn 1996) 65–96.

[4]   For guidance to the primary sources, see: F. A. Wright, *Lemprière's Classical Dictionary of Proper Names mentioned in Ancient Authors* (London: Routledge and Kegan Paul, 1963) 191.

responsive, motivated by lust or avarice, or betrayed by the greed of her keepers. How these two basic elements are presented in large part determines whether the story takes on erotic or moralistic implications. What interpretations of the "golden shower" or "shower of gold" have in common is that no matter in what form Zeus arrived, he was something of value, coming from above. The visitation was a heavenly favor bestowed, whether it was delivered through the naturalness – perhaps even beauty and gentleness – of golden rain, through the colder exchange of a cash gift, payment or bribe, or by the violent force of a thunderstorm. What the classical stories tend to leave out is what happened after he arrived – rape, seduction, another transaction? In most post-classical versions there is an obvious confusion of rape/seduction/sexual desire/love – in Erwin Panofsky's infamous phrase, "rapture and relaxation."[5] Thus Titian and other Renaissance artists deliberately and graphically depict Danaë's story as a ravishment with its almost transcendent fusion of rape and passion.

Other medieval and early Renaissance versions focus on the nature of the act (rape/seduction) primarily to generate allegorical representations of and draw moralistic implications about women's personal and social behavior from a male perspective. In one Renaissance interpretation, Danaë's beauty, chastity and timely con-sensuality made her a perfect wife-mistress.[6] In Neoplatonic versions, Danaë's imprisonment in the tower was compared to the "soul's entrapment in the body" and the rain was interpreted "as wisdom that can free the soul from its confinement" (Nash 27). Christological exegesis of Ovid's *Metamorphoses* described Danaë as a chosen vessel for divine procreative power, "a prototype for the Virgin Mary, since . . . she was impregnated by a god in a bodiless form" (Nash, 27). Indeed, the most prominent examples of this type of story in western religious tradition are the visitation of the Holy Spirit upon the Virgin Mary and the reception of spiritual ecstasy by female saints. In paintings by Grünevald, Jan Van Eyck, and Titian, as well as in Bernini's sculpture of St. Teresa, the viewer instantly recognizes the confusion of supernatural imposition (however spiritual or incorporeal) and the rapt expressions on the faces and in the bodily positions of the recipients. The heavenly visitor may take the form of golden angels, a golden or white dove, beams of golden light (as in annunciation paintings) or the piercing of angelic golden arrows envisioned by St. Teresa. The subsequent iconographic status of these women, worshiped and admired though seduced by the spirit, suggests that women's expression of bodily pleasure – experienced as the reception of the divine cosmos – is appropriate primarily in circumstances that are explicitly transcendent, that deny the self to fulfill the desires of the divine other or through the sacrificial and altruistic acts of the production or nurturing of others. Each image connects male control of female value and sexuality with women's ultimate surrender to the power of spiritual, divine, or cosmic forces.

---

[5]   Erwin Panofsky, *Problems in Titian: Mostly Iconographic* (New York: New York University Press, 1969) 147.

[6]   Jane Nash, *Veiled Images: Titian's Mythological Paintings for Phillip II* (Philadelphia: Art Association Press, 1985) 26; hereafter: Nash.

Myths and legends of other cultures contain archetypal elements shared by the Danaë story that highlight the tension between these interconnections. James George Frazer's *The Golden Bough* made a detailed collection of these available to the late-Victorian readership he shared with Hardy. Frazer described how among the Ot Danoms of Borneo, certain Indian tribes of California, the Bella Coula of British Columbia and in Cambodia, girls at puberty were secluded in dark cells, or huts, forbidden to touch the ground, experience the natural world, look upon the sun, or see or be seen by men.[7] A Siberian tale tells of when a girl, thus long secluded, first "saw the bright world, [she] tottered and fainted; and the eye of God fell upon her, and she conceived. Her angry father . . . sent her floating away . . . over the wide sea" (Frazer 698). Noting the resemblances among these stories with that of Danaë, Frazer remarked: "the shower of gold in the Greek story, and the eye of God in the Kirghiz [Siberian] legend, probably stand for sunlight and the sun. The idea that women may be impregnated by the sun is not uncommon . . ." (698).

According to Frazer, in order to protect the tribe from the ill-effects of girls' burgeoning fertility, the mature members must exert social control upon them, simultaneously ensuring their worth for marriage and reproduction. These precautions dictated what a girl was allowed to eat, say, think and do; whether men and women could interact with her; what knowledge and awareness of her own bodily development and other natural phenomena and cosmic forces she could acquire. The notion that upon the verge of womanhood – for both their own and the social good – girls were to be literally kept in the dark, shielded from the light of the sun, secluded from knowledge of the outside world, protected from the gaze of men, and prevented from gazing on men, has several points of intriguing confluence with images implicated in nineteenth-century representations of women's inherent nature, education and social roles.

In nineteenth-century Britain, contemporary medical perspectives on female pubescence validated the attitude that girls entering sexual maturation presented a danger to themselves and others. Medical authorities urged diligent parental regulation of their daughters' sexual awareness and development.[8] Protective and restrictive

---

[7]   James George Frazer, *The Golden Bough: A Study in Magic and Religion* (New York: Macmillan, 1972) 692–5, 698; hereafter: Frazer.

[8]   For useful perspectives on the relations of gender, medicine and science and discussions of changing definitions of female sexuality, the body and feminine nature, see: Nancy Tuana, *The Less Noble Sex: Scientific, Religious, and Philosophical Conceptions of Woman's Nature* (Bloomington: Indiana University Press, 1993); Roy Porter and Lesley Hall, *The Facts of Life: the Creation of Sexual Knowledge in Britain, 1650–1950* (New Haven: Yale University Press, 1995); Michel Foucault, *The History of Sexuality: An Introduction*, vol. 1, trans. Robert Hurley (New York: Penguin, 1979); Londa Schiebinger, *The Mind Has No Sex?: Women in the Origins of Modern Science* (Cambridge, MA: Harvard University Press, 1989); Evelyn Fox Keller, *Reflections on Gender and Science* (New Haven: Yale University Press, 1985); Carolyn Merchant, *The Death of Nature: Women, Ecology and the Scientific Revolution* (San Francisco:

strategies employed by nineteenth-century British society to delimit women's knowledge of sexuality also constricted women's access to other aspects of education, including self-knowledge and personal development, knowledge of the public sphere, the world of business and the even greater outside world of nature itself. A woman's value and goodness were commonly measured in inverse proportion to her knowledge *per se*. Among things that men knew, but women should not, were the facts about the animal nature of sexuality exercised outside the home.[9]

In nineteenth-century fiction, young female characters who know too much are often placed literally in, and associated symbolically with, nature. This is true, for instance, of Maggie's relation to the river; Tess's connection to open fields and animals, wild and domestic, dead and alive; Arabella's earthy and animal sensuality; and L. T. Meade's Polly, whose inner untamed wildness and unbounded excursions outdoors leave tell-tale signs in the form of grass-stained clothing and twigs tangled in her unkempt hair.[10] To possess knowledge of nature, whether of her own desires, her physical body, the bodies of males, or of the creatures of the natural realm, indicated that a woman had ventured out into forbidden territory where the sexual and animal lurked. In acquiring such knowledge, a woman must have abandoned passivity and virtue and actively sought to lose her innocent state of un-knowing. Judged as having willed her own fall into the knowledge of the teeming, promiscuous and passionately alive nature of nature, such a woman could neither maintain nor feign the passionlessness that was commonly supposed (and medically believed) to comprise her true feminine nature (Reynolds and Humble, 12–13, 15–18, 49).[11] In Victorian representations of women and nature, audiences frequently encountered an unresolved tension between the nature of a woman out in nature – wild, active, abroad and free – and the controlled, passive, domestic and dependent nature that society generally expected her to express.[12]

Harper and Row, 1980) and Lynda Nead, *Myths of Sexuality: Representations of Women in Victorian Britain* (Oxford: Basil Blackwell, 1988).

[9]   Steven Marcus, *The Other Victorians: A Study of Sexuality and Pornography in Mid-Nineteenth-Century England* (New York: Basic Books, 1966) 29–32; hereafter: Marcus.

[10]   Kimberley Reynolds and Nicola Humble, *Victorian Heroines: Representations of Femininity in Nineteenth-Century Literature and Art* (New York: New York University Press, 1993) 33–4; hereafter: Reynolds and Humble.

[11]   See also: Erna Olafson Hellerstein, et al. eds., *Victorian Women: A Documentary Account of Women's Lives in Nineteenth-Century England, France, and the United States* (Stanford: Stanford University Press, 1981) 174–81.

[12]   For additional perspectives on representations of women and nature in nineteenth-century culture, literature and art, see: Joan Perkin, *Victorian Women* (New York: New York University Press, 1993); Elaine Showalter, *Sexual Anarchy: Gender and Culture and the Fin de Siècle* (New York: Viking, 1990); Helena Michie, *The Flesh Made Word: Female Figures and Women's Bodies* (Oxford: Oxford University Press, 1987); Philippa Levine, *Victorian Feminism: 1850–1900* (London: Hutchinson, 1987); Lynne Pearce, *Woman, Image, Text:*

At this locus the Danaë story intersects the duality that comprises what is perhaps its single closest analogue in nineteenth-century literature, art and social programs – that of the "domestic angel/fallen woman." The latter term Nina Auerbach described twenty-five years ago as "so pervasive [in Victorian treatments] . . . it takes on the status of a shared cultural mythology."[13] According to the usual pattern, fallen women, seduced, often pregnant out of wedlock, were later to rise again either by a transcendent exercise of will or rehabilitation through education, often through male graces. Both sets of stories perpetuate the belief that women must be protected from properly male knowledge and equate that knowledge specifically with knowledge of the male. For fallen women, as for Danaë, inappropriate knowledge of one's own body, sexual knowledge, becomes associated with socially unacceptable knowledge of the outside world and cosmos at large. As Auerbach records, fallen women, "cast beyond the human community," were often depicted in Victorian paintings and fiction as "associated with sweeping vistas of space" and "bare and open landscapes" (33, 43). She also notes both literary and artistic recurrent visual motifs in which a woman's "fall seems to open out space" and in which the woman herself is depicted as in kinship with the moon, observing it or cast in its light.

Auerbach (unlike Hardy) does not develop the symbolic implications of this astronomical imagery. In classical mythology, the moon (Diana/Cynthia) represented women in contradictory ways: symbolizing their beauty, chastity and fertility; or, their flux, fickleness, vanity, lunacy and lust. The duality of the mythological moon was thus easily adapted to the multiple tensions within its Victorian correlate. Moreover, within the social hierarchy of the heavens, the female moon was deemed the lesser of the two heavenly bodies shedding light on Earth (and only reflected light at that). She was of lower status than the male sun, and her influence, in the astrological sense, was considered to be more negative than his. There is also a long tradition of poetic associations between the moon and prostitutes since the moon inspired lustful behavior and provided a natural lamp for night-strollers.[14] The pervasive power of such associations helps explain why women who embodied knowledge outside their

---

Readings in Pre-Raphaelite Art and Literature (Hemel Hempstead, Eng.: Harvester Wheatsheaf, 1991); Griselda Pollock, *Vision and Difference: Femininity, Feminism and the History of Art* (London: Routledge, 1988); Sandra M. Gilbert and Susan Gubar, *The Madwoman in the Attic: The Woman Writer and the Nineteenth-Century Literary Imagination* (New Haven: Yale University Press, 1979); Cynthia Eagle Russett, *Sexual Science: the Victorian Construction of Womanhood* (Cambridge, MA: Harvard University Press, 1989; Avril Horner and Sue Zlosnik, *Landscapes of Desire: Metaphors in Women's Fiction* (Hemel Hempstead, Eng.: Harvester Wheatsheaf, 1990).

[13]   Nina Auerbach, "The Rise of the Fallen Woman," *Nineteenth-Century Fiction* 35 (1980): 29; hereafter: Auerbach.

[14]   The moon's phases also made a convenient metaphor for the waning caused by venereal disease. See my discussion of Jonathan Swift's "The Progress of Beauty" in *Poetic Resolutions of Scientific Revolutions* 333–50.

proper sphere were linked with the sublunar, fallen realm and labeled "women of the world," "worldly women" or "experienced" women, and why those labels were so pejorative. As Auerbach observes, a Victorian woman's fall left her personally "prone and punished" and threatened wide-ranging social and national consequences. In the case of the nineteenth-century Danaë – supine and surrendered– her individual intellectual quest will be of universal import, portending prospects for the survival and progress of the human species within the known cosmos.

Kept from knowledge by her family or father figure, introduced to the knowledge of men by a man, it is the woman in possession of such knowledge who is punished, by familial rejection, social banishment, exposure or death. In nineteenth-century literary accounts, women are depicted as paying the price of this fall into knowledge. The penalties are particularly painful when they fall into knowledge from the very great height of the outermost reaches of the universe. At about the same time that T. H. Huxley was articulating his views about "Man's Place in Nature," other writers and artists were inscribing images of Danaë into texts which described and prescribed woman's place in nature on a cosmic scale. Ludmilla Jordanova has described how gender operated as a "cosmic metaphor" in the discourse of Jules Michelet who "displayed a cosmological drive to assign meaning to everything" and treated, on a grand scale, themes of national "destiny . . . universal forces . . . feeling," history and natural history.[15] In places, gender is cosmic in the astronomical sense for Michelet, as in his descriptions of women as beings physiologically in harmony with the natural rhythms of the tides and the moon (Jordanova 79). More typically, by "cosmos," Michelet meant an abstract, ordered system in which "cosmic perspective" is important as a "source for individual liberation" and for achieving a "sympathetic relationship with nature" which could "[enable] people to combine knowledge of the natural world with an enhanced awareness of the human condition" (Jordanova 74). As we have already seen, Michelet's expression of a "philosophy of astronomy" was a common one, shared by nineteenth-century astronomers like William and John Herschel as well as popularizers of science, like William Whewell and Richard Proctor.

Among the many nineteenth-century writers besides Hardy who treated natural philosophy and science in relation to classical mythic and Biblical traditions (e.g., Arnold, Browning, Swinburne to name a few), Alfred Tennyson particularly and directly engaged elements of the Danaë myth and its attendant expectations, merging the myth with narratives of natural phenomena under construction by contemporary science, especially astronomy. Like Hardy, Tennyson does not flinch from realistically assessing the "facts" of the nineteenth-century universe in his verse, and again, like Hardy, he keeps alive the possibility that knowledge of humanity's place within the

---

[15]   Ludmilla Jordanova, *Sexual Visions: Images of Gender in Science and Medicine between the Eighteenth and Twentieth Centuries* (Madison: University of Wisconsin Press, 1989) 73 and 69, respectively; hereafter: Jordanova.

cosmos could have an elevating effect on individuals and society. In their versions of the Danaë story, both Tennyson and Hardy take the cosmos literally, creating heroines who obtain knowledge of astronomical phenomena and cosmology, and their direct relation, as organic beings, to the universe. For their Danaës, possessing such knowledge – personally, socially and universally – results in complex dangers, even fatality. Their cosmic heroines fall and fail, but the narratives that track their failures comprise vicarious and cathartic thought-experiments, exposing the flaws, accidents and mistakes that led to the falls and cosmographically charting potential ways to avoid them.

Before Hardy: Tennyson's Vision of Cosmic Heroes and Heroines

In the poetic generation just preceding Hardy, Tennyson experimented with the forms and conventions of western literary tradition to envision "paradises found" for his early Victorian audience. In the first decade of Victoria's reign (and just over twenty-five years before Hardy's *A Pair of Blues Eyes* would appear), Tennyson adapted the image of Danaë within his long poem, *The Princess* (1847). In this explicitly feminist poem, Tennyson tells the story of the failure of an experimental university, founded by women to educate women. Princess Ida, the idealistic heroine of the poem, has enacted her vision of equal education for women by inverting the male model, excluding men under penalty of death, rejecting women's proper sphere of domesticity by establishing a socialistic matriarchy, and by taking up scientific studies traditionally male, including the physical sciences of astronomy and cosmology. Some critics, including Reynolds and Humble, read Tennyson's use of sex-role inversion as effecting a positive "fusion between sexual and desexualizing images of women" by which he "implant[s] . . . [the] antithesis" of the "approved orthodoxy," expressing "the need for mingling the two sexes in equal and harmonious proportions" (21). In their interpretation, Princess Ida is intellectually knowledgeable but remains "technically sexually pure" so her partial fall requires only a partial redemption (22). This reading does not account for the narrative importance of how what Ida knows – and how she acts upon that knowledge – can hurt her and the world around her.

Ida has obtained insight into the male of the species – how education, aggression, oppression and exclusion give men power – and she adopts these strategies in her own female society. She has not achieved equally deep personal insights into how her own womanly qualities might shape her external world. Tennyson looks to nature for normative values, and his poem envisions male–female relationships between sexual and intellectual equals as the basis for an ideal society, rather than single-sex communities or those within which members of one sex dominate the other. Judged against this vision, Ida's utopia is found lacking. Tennyson's invocation of natural law, especially within pre-Darwinian evolutionary theory and astronomy, allows him to promote equality between male–female pairs as a fresh foundation for human society even as he conservatively legitimizes the necessity for male–female pairs. He avoids a complete overthrow of contemporary orthodoxy by suggesting moderate reforms that redirect and restructure the existing social organization. Ida's exclusion of men (not to mention death threat against intruders) represents, for Tennyson, a hostile stance. The hostile exclusion upon which her society is predicated is just as wrong as that of the male-dominated society against which she has rebelled. Hostility of either sex against the other constitutes an act of resistance to, and denial of, natural law. Such a revolt must fail if the human race is to continue. The universal laws of sexual attraction necessitate that the male and female cooperate for the species to survive, and some laws are too universal to be broken. This cosmic truth is communicated by abundant multilayered astronomical imagery throughout *The Princess*.[16]

When Ida is introduced in the medley, she is directly identified with the image of Uranian Venus embossed on her royal seal. Venus Urania presided over love in its celestial, abstract, intellectual and spiritual forms; as Christopher Ricks notes, she was "the higher love of Plato's *Symposium*."[17] By her surname, she is related to Urania, the muse of astronomy, who inspired the sublimity and transcendent spirituality of Milton's descriptions of the physical heavens in *Paradise Lost*. As we have mentioned before, according to Plato, the study of astronomy could purify the intellect and soul through contemplation and imitation of the highest and most refined material entities in the cosmos. Tennyson closely links these associations here as he did in the *Palace of Art* (1832), where his female "soul" meditates on the structure of the stellar universe as described by William Herschel (Korg, 150). Ida, as an earthly Venus Urania, is so extraordinary in her grace, power and vision that she seems extraterrestrial, "liker to the inhabitant / Of some clear planet close upon the Sun / than our man's earth" (i.e., Venus itself) (2.21–3). Although her refined nature and planetary status place her beyond the mean sublunary realm, Ida is not of quintessential stellar stuff – her actions are described as those of an "erring" or "wandering" star, a literal translation of the Greek "planet." Astronomical referents convey both the admirable high-mindedness and the unfortunate wrong-headedness with which she has established her female academy. Of a higher nature herself and devoted to enabling other women to "lift [their] natures up" (2.74), Ida, for her own space and time, "flies too high / she flies too high!" (5.271).

Astronomy and cosmology are significant components of the curriculum in Ida's university. Normally not a part of female education, the subjects provide her students with access to "all that men are taught" (Prologue 136) through both passive and active learning experiences. The lectures cover politics, human history, philosophy,

---

[16]   I can only touch on the most salient examples here. For more on Tennyson's use of science see: G. G. Wickens, "The Two Sides of Early Victorian Science and the Unity of 'The Princess,'" *Victorian Studies* 23 (1980): 367–88 and Dennis R. Dean, *Tennyson and Geology* (Lincoln, Eng.: Tennyson Society, 1985). For a concise overview of astronomy in Tennyson, see: Korg. For specific discussion of *The Princess*, see: John Killham, *Tennyson and The Princess: Reflections of an Age* (London: University of London, Athlone Press, 1958); hereafter: by surnames.

[17]   Christopher Ricks, ed., *Tennyson: A Selected Edition* (Berkeley: University of California Press, 1989) 239n.

ethics, physiology, geology, astronomy, natural history, zoology, botany, electricity and chemistry (2.353–62). Contemporary theories in astronomy and cosmology engender the narrative of the academy's feminist history which recounts the origins of the inorganic and organic through the nebular hypothesis, evolution and anthropology.

> This world was once a fluid haze of light,
> Till toward the centre set the starry tides,
> And eddied into suns, that wheeling cast
> The planets: then the monster, then the man;
> Tattooed or woaded, winter-clad in skins,
> Raw from the prime, and crushing down his mate;
> As yet we find in barbarous isles, and here
> Among the lowest. (2.101–8)

The story notably elides any mention of a male creator. Ida incorporates the facts of a mechanical universe into her cosmography and implies an evolutionary development toward sexual equality: only "the lowest" among modern men still "crush[es] his mate." The female students also engage the worst that the "terrible muses" of astronomy and geology have to tell through first-hand experiences in their observatory and direct investigation of the fossil record during field excursions. Joint contemplation of the awfulness of cosmic infinities will be invoked late in the poem as an experience which inexorably bonds the observers heart to heart (6.236–40). Like Hamlet, Ida remarks philosophically and empathetically upon the *memento mori* provided by the fossilized remains encapsulated within the layers of the earth (3.276–80). The only domain of male science that the female students eschew (ambivalently) is that of medical anatomy, which is deemed too violent in its "shameless" violation of the sanctity of living things; however, Ida herself learns "the craft of healing" for practical reasons, in case any of her students fall ill (3.288–304).

At the poem's crisis point, Tennyson uses astronomical images to represent both the negative and positive choices Ida can make to avoid surrendering herself to patriarchal law – a law which, by contrast, crudely expresses the natural relations of male and female in terms of the low science of animal husbandry.

>   . . . but this is fixt
> As are the roots of earth and base of all;
> Man for the field and woman for the hearth:
> Man for the sword and for the needle she:
> Man with the head and woman with the heart:
> Man to command and woman to obey;
> All else confusion. Look you! the gray mare
> Is ill to live with, when her whinny shrills
> From tile to scullery . . . but you – she's yet a colt –
> Take, break her: strongly groomed and straitly curbed.
> . . .   A lusty brace
> Of twins may weed her of her folly. (5.435–54)

To escape what male orthodoxy has deemed her natural fate as female breeding stock, Ida sees two options: to wage war against the male forces which seek to bind her to a marriage contract or un-repress her tenderer nature and feminine instincts, thereby surrendering to the Prince and trusting his pledge to create a marriage of equals between them.

At first, Ida would rather fight than switch. As the war between the sexes is about to begin, an astronomical simile compares Ida's three armored male captains to the three bright stars in the belt of the constellation Orion. This allusion to the giant hunter signifies the scale of the violence against nature that the coming clash will effect and also alludes to the omnipresence of warfare throughout human history by echoing Homer's similar comparison of armor to starlight in the *Iliad* (Ricks, 291n). As it becomes clear that this confrontation will do more harm than good, Ida's alternative is presented to her in the form of a child who has already awakened maternal tenderness within her. The baby girl, who was introduced early in the poem clothed "In shining draperies, headed like a star" (2.93–4), now appears "Half-lapt in glowing gauze and golden brede" and "Lay like a new-fallen meteor on the grass" (6.118–19). The child represents a cosmic test for Ida, who must decide in which realm the girl belongs. Is the meteoric child of the heavens or the earth? Should she stay with Ida, who wishes to be her adoptive, celestial, and intellectual mother, or be returned to the all-too-human woman who bore her? After being reminded of her astronomical bonding to the child's mother, she chooses the latter. Like many a fallen woman before her, the crestfallen Ida is compared to the moon.

> But Ida stood nor spoke, drained of her force
> By many a varying influence and so long.
> Down through her limbs a drooping languor wept:
> Her head a little bent; and on her mouth
> A doubtful smile dwelt like a clouded moon
> In a still water. . . (6.249–254)

The stage is set for Ida's final surrender.

In one of the most captivating and often anthologized lyric songs of the poem, the Danaë allusion appears at the crucial moment when the Princess realizes her utopian project of female education is doomed. After engaging the Prince's forces in battle, she finds herself tending his wounds. In fulfilling the traditional womanly role of nurse and nurturer – exercising the feminine art of healing more than the craft of medicine she has studied – Ida senses new feelings stirring within her. Reading softly aloud to herself at the Prince's bedside (from a book of women's poetry), the affective power of the song works its healing magic upon her inner nature. She subsequently admits her failure and surrenders. Indeed, who could resist the lyric sensuality of this song?

> Now sleeps the crimson petal, now the white;
> Nor waves the cypress in the palace walk;

> Nor winks the gold fin in the porphyry font.
> The fire-fly wakens; waken thou with me.
>   Now droops the milk-white peacock like a ghost,
> And like a ghost she glimmers on to me. /
>
>   Now lies the Earth all Danaë to the stars,
> And all thy heart lies open unto me.
>
>   Now slides the silent meteor on, and leaves
> A shining furrow, as thy thoughts in me.
>
>   Now folds the lily all her sweetness up,
> And slips into the bosom of the lake.
> So fold thyself, my dearest, thou, and slip
> Into my bosom and be lost in me. (7.161–74)

The song's imagery is simultaneously natural, sexual and astronomical. Its dreamy seductiveness participates in the emergent artistic obsession with the vulnerability and languor of the "Sleeping Beauty" figure more than the relaxed consciousness of the mythical women in Titian's paintings. With all of nature held in thrall – stilled, silent, asleep – the only visible flicker of life in the scene is the firefly's luminous sexual beacon, at which signal, the lover's voice bids his love to awake. Once the lovers share consciousness, the natural imagery suggests progressive stages of union, from the immaterial to physical, as each stanza describes a different site of surrender – the soul, the heart, the mind, the body. The ghostly spirit "droops" and "glimmers," the heart "lies open" to distant starlight and its influence, her intellection traces a transient, ethereal track across the substance of his mind. Only when unity of spirit, heart and intellect have been achieved is physical oneness intimated, and then the lover depicts "losing" one's self in another as a natural act of trust and personal volition ("fold thyself").

Although Tennyson's gloss on the Danaë line suggests that the astronomical association was not original to him, it represents an innovative interpretation of her story.[18] The body of the Earth is to the stars as Danaë was to the divine shower raining upon her from above. Lying open to the universe, the Earth's receptive state parallels that of the Princess, who in her study of astronomy, looked openly into the face of the

---

[18]   Tennyson's note reads: "Zeus came down to Danaë when shut up in the tower in a shower of *golden stars*" (my emphasis; as in Ricks, 319n). I am still searching for what source may have suggested to Tennyson that Zeus visited Danaë as "stars." Tennyson's awareness of Titian's painting of this subject may have come from his best friend, Arthur Hallam. Ricks, citing J. H. Buckley, also notes that Hallam's last letter to Tennyson included this remark: "and oh Alfred such Titians! by Heaven, that man could paint! I wish you could see his Danaë. Do you just write as perfect a Danaë!" (319n).

cosmos. As Tennyson uses it, the Danaë allusion elevates the woman, emphasizing her immaterial, celestial affinity (she is one with the cosmos) but also implies the immensity and absoluteness of the natural laws which control her relation to it. Although the Earth, as a heavenly body, plays some role in determining its own course on a local scale (diurnal rotation, annual revolution), the planet's place within the vastness of interstellar space is inconceivably insignificant, governed by a myriad of incalculable forces. With lingering reluctance and doubt, the Princess resigns herself to the universe and makes herself vulnerable to the reception of other kinds of knowledge from the man who loves her. It is not for nothing that the next lyric poem begins with these words:

> Come down, O Maid, from yonder mountain height;
> What pleasure lives in height (the shepherd sang)
> In height and cold, the splendour of the hills?
> But cease to move so near the Heavens, and cease
> To glide a sunbeam by the blasted Pine,
> To sit a star upon the sparkling spire;
> And come, for Love is of the valley, come,
> For Love is of the valley, come thou down
> And find him . . . (7.177–85)

The final destination of the Princess's "come down" is the Prince himself. Significantly, throughout the Danaë scene, he has lain "supine and surrendered" before the Princess, dreaming of her surrender in which she will remove the clothing that has veiled her true nature. As with most representations of femininity, Tennyson builds into this one its masculine counterpart. In the ideal society of male–female equality, it is the Prince who is the first to surrender in desire, love and trust to the Princess. Speaking valiantly on his own behalf, he invokes an image of a new-fashioned "domestic angel" that can serve them both as a model of ideal spousal behavior: his "celestial" mother. As the guiding force in his life, she taught him to love and respect women, curbed his "orbit," and redeemed him when he fell.

> Yet twas there one through whom I loved her [woman], one
> Not learned, save in gracious household ways,
> Not perfect, nay, but full of tender wants,
> No Angel, but a dearer being, all dipt /
> In Angel instincts, breathing Paradise,
> Interpreter between the Gods and men,
> Who looked all native to her place, and yet
> On tiptoe seemed to touch upon a sphere
> Too gross to tread, and all male minds perforce
> Swayed to her from their orbits as they moved,
> And girdled her with music. Happy he
> With such a mother! faith in womankind
> Beats with his blood, and trust in all things high

Comes easy to him, and though he trip and fall
He shall not blind his soul with clay. (7.298–312)

Ida's response to all this is faint hope. Here, what I would term the "natural idealism" of Tennyson's philosophy of history emerges from within the progress-through-procreation narrative of contemporary evolutionary theory to indicate the biological obligations of the Prince and Princess as a mating pair. If enlightened men and women do not reproduce, hopes for an enlightened future society perish. The Prince offers Ida a chance to reactivate her social experiment, this time within an optimum biological setting. Whether controlling for the crucial environmental variable will be enough to bring her ideals to fruition is left unresolved. Indeed, suspending the poem in the air of optimistic uncertainty, Tennyson closes it with a return to the framing device in which the young men and women who have been this myth's makers sit in silent contemplation of the uncharted darkness of cosmic space and the dim glimmer of what they (or their real-life counterparts) may make of the human future.

Post-Laureate: Hardy's "Next Generation" Cosmology

The interconnectedness of knowledge of men, knowledge of the natural forces of the cosmos, and a journey downward (even when undertaken by new women as in Tennyson's poem) is a pervasive theme in nineteenth-century fictional accounts depicting female characters in the role of receptors of contemporary popular astronomy. Hardy was a crucial member of the "next generation" that Tennyson imagined as the inheritors of the mythic task to build on the lessons of human history and write the next chapter of human cultural evolution. In his works, Hardy accepts this challenge, in turn, imagining other young men and women who struggle to process and produce viable social and personal cosmologies, making sense of their world and creating meaning in their lives. Unlike Tennyson's characters, Hardy's young couples need to look considerably farther than to their own mothers for successful examples of how to fit themselves domestically to the cosmos.

In the novels that I have discussed, Hardy creates narratives in which knowledge of distant realms is brought down to women by male characters, often with the aid of powerful instruments. His female characters may actively desire and seek initiation into the arcane world of astronomy, they may achieve competence in observational skills and calculations, but they usually do not aspire to theory. The reception of knowledge of the cosmos is interwoven in Hardy's narratives with a love relationship that leads to sexual intercourse, pregnancy, social ostracism and untimely death. The superficially apparent moral of such stories (which he may have calculated to simultaneously appeal to and critique the sentiments of his Victorian middle-class audience) seems to be that the only good new woman is a fallen woman and that the embodiment of cosmic truths for women is socially dangerous, personally deadly. The plots of these stories trace a female character's complex fall: on one level, from properly female behavior and pursuits into sexuality; and on another, from intellectual understanding of the universal and infinite into recognition of, and resignation to, the mortally finite. Male characters, who possess knowledge both bodily and cosmic, are typically able to transmit this knowledge to their female counterparts without suffering, as they do, by the exchange.

Tennyson and Hardy shared a strong interest in predicting the futures of new women in their narratives, but Hardy characterizes his fictional women as more primitive (in Frazer's sense) than men in their approach to natural phenomena.[19] Hardy's female characters most often form their ideas out of religious, superstitious, or uncritically traditional or authoritative sources. Their first response to new perceptions of nature tends to be emotional, often fear and awe. The shared experience of learning bonds the women to the men, though the reverse is not always the case. Hardy's men approach the universe as more modern, rational, scientific (Knight, Clym, Wildeve, Fitzpiers) than women, or as the more aptly adapted and more appropriately evolved gender of the species (Gabriel, Giles). When men serve as cosmic light-bringers, the light brings women death (Elfride, Eustacia, Viviette, Tess). It is only in the remotest of rural environments, safely distant in time and place from the madding crowds, that Gabriel and Bathsheba avoid the inevitable pattern that the reception of carnal knowledge and cosmic knowledge will lead to the woman's death. The closer his characters reside to modern civilization, the more urban ways and values encroach upon them, the less likely their chances of survival, let alone happiness.

Despite their more "primitive" associations, or perhaps, like Gabriel Oak, *because* of them, Hardy depicts his heroines as possessing some personal quality – some saving grace – that given appropriate opportunities and circumstances, would enable them to adapt successfully to the changes in the natural and social worlds around them and would help others to adapt successfully as well. In the cases of Bathsheba and Grace, their dual challenge is to properly identify and appreciate their natural place and recognize and select their natural mates. Bathsheba finally overcomes the flaws in her inner nature to become a successful recipient of Gabriel's natural instruction. Grace has been schooled to doubt her natural abilities so, like Swithin, learns too late.

---

[19] Strangely, although otherwise insightful, most scholarly studies of Hardy's women rarely mention their relation to contemporary science or nature. For generally useful discussions of Hardy and his female characters, see: Rosemarie Morgan, *Women and Sexuality in the Novels of Thomas Hardy* (London: Routledge, 1988); Penny Boumelha, *Thomas Hardy and Women: Sexual Ideology and Narrative Form* (Brighton, Sussex, Eng.: Harvester, 1982); John Goode, *Thomas Hardy: The Offensive Truth* (Oxford: Basil Blackwell, 1988); Patricia Ingham, *Thomas Hardy*, Feminist Readings (Atlantic Highlands, NJ: Humanities Press International, 1990); Margaret R. Higonnet, ed., *The Sense of Sex: Feminist Perspectives on Hardy* (Urbana: University of Illinois Press, 1993); Marjorie Garson, *Hardy's Fables of Integrity: Woman, Body, Text* (Oxford: Clarendon Press, 1991); and Jane Thomas, *Thomas Hardy Femininity and Dissent: Reassessing the 'Minor' Novels* (London: Macmillan, 1999).

Elfride, Viviette, and Tess each provide powerful *exempla* to the men in their lives, demonstrating how to live joyfully and lovingly through the setbacks and hardships of life. None lives to benefit from their male partners' modeling of their values and choices. The ethereal natures and visionary qualities of Eustacia and Sue, though misplaced in time and place, are nonetheless necessary to the spirit of a species that strives to progress. By the universal messages carried by the fallen and failed heroines of *Far From the Madding Crowd*, *A Pair of Blue Eyes*, *The Return of the Native*, *Two on a Tower*, *The Woodlanders*, *Tess*, and *Jude*, Hardy urged human individuals, male and female, not to thwart each other in the shared struggle to fulfill potential and desire. This mythic moral of Hardy's Danaë stories should have been equally applicable to both Victorian men and women beneath the stars.

*   *   *

If Frazer's epigrammatic "Men make the gods; women worship them" challenged Simone de Beauvoir to test its truth-value in *The Second Sex*, [20] it may continue to be worthwhile to examine the related truism that "men write the myths; women live them." Nineteenth-century texts by both male and female writers legitimated and questioned sexual orthodoxy in myriad ways. The narratives by which Tennyson and Hardy represent women's knowledge of the cosmos warrant close critical attention in relation to this issue because their production was historically ironic. Tennyson and Hardy were acting as perhaps two of the most effective receptors of nineteenth-century popular science. Each actively invested in the "trickle down" economics of popularization, serving as middle men – nonscientific intellectuals – who passed that knowledge from working scientists above them to general readers below. Building on his own reading in classical literature, comparative mythology and religion, early anthropology, social and political history, and popular science, Hardy developed complex configurations of astronomical metaphors through which he was able to envision, and display for his readers, a wide range of possible solutions to the existential dilemmas scientific knowledge of the universe presented to him. Although Hardy felt himself socially marginalized by his humble beginnings and lack of formal education, and Tennyson occasionally lamented his disciplinary difference, both men were accepted as worthy students and intellectual colleagues by some of the most influential scientists of the period; both were befriended and admired by the solar physicist, Norman Lockyer, for one. Still, neither man offered unqualified fictional projections that women could share in the kinds of positive learning exchange they had experienced, let alone their resultant rise in social and professional status.

Remarkable too, however, is the fact that the narratives of neither man reflected the reductively economic or cynically pornographic depictions of Danaë that were also

---

[20]   Simone de Beauvoir, *The Second Sex* (New York: Bantam, 1952) 71

produced during their lifetimes. In his study of *My Secret Life*, Steven Marcus himself deploys the image in his analysis of nineteenth-century sexual fantasies of "spending."

> ... the body is regarded as a productive system with only a limited amount of material at its disposal. And the model on which the notion of semen is formed is clearly that of money ... [and its scarcity] ... the fantasy of pornography ... is this idea's complement, for the world of pornography is a world of plenty. In it all men are infinitely rich in substance, all men are limitlessly endowed with that universal fluid currency which can be spent without loss. Just as in the myth Zeus descends upon Danaë in a shower of gold, so in pornography the world is bathed, floated, flooded, inundated in this magical produce of the body. (Marcus 22)

On both sides of the fin de siècle period, painters Carolus-Duran, Chantron, Antoine Auguste Thivet, Carl Strathmann, Max Slevogt, Edmund Dulac, Trouillebert, and Gustav Klimt, among others, all made graphic paintings of Danaës being impregnated by gold coins in which they promulgated negative stereotypes of woman, emphasizing her lust for money, her subjugation to the god's potent wealth, her sinful pleasure as a prostitute or the pornographic pleasure her posture gave male viewers.[21]

Unquestionably Tennyson's and Hardy's narratives resist the lowest common denominators that the image can generate. They mediate instead between enslaving female characters to the prurient interests of male others and transfixing them in the eternal passivity of their own purity. Their heroines fall, some passively, others actively, most sexually, all intellectually and socially, many fatally. Their narratives of failed female education represent Danaë figures who find the universe infinite but bounded. Although a number of Victorian educational experts warned that scientific investigations and study could be physiologically dangerous to women, weakening their maternal capacities as well as harming their naturally less intrepid minds, both Tennyson and Hardy were aware of real-life female astronomers who were successful professionally as well as physically robust, indeed very long-lived.[22] Maria Mitchell and Caroline Herschel (though both remained childless and unwed) were readily available as positive *exempla* of women with the ability to learn and embody knowledge of the cosmos. Yet neither Tennyson or Hardy patterned their plots upon the "scattered stars" of women of achievement; instead, they mapped into their narratives the probable locations of cosmic pitfalls that led to their heroines' surrenders and victimizations, providing potential routes of escape for their female readers. If their heroines ultimately failed to reach the stars, it was because they, and those around them, were perforce imperfectly or incompletely evolved humans. As

---

[21] Bram Dijkstra, *Idols of Perversity: Fantasies of Feminine Evil in Fin-de-Siècle Culture* (Oxford: Oxford University Press, 1986) 369–71.

[22] Sally Gregory Kohlstedt, "Maria Mitchell and the Advancement of Women in Science," *Uneasy Careers and Intimate Lives: Women in Science, 1789–1979*, eds. Pnina Abir-Am and Dorinda Outram (New Brunswick: Rutgers University Press, 1987) 129–46.

Hardy makes so clear in *Jude the Obscure,* individual goals of self-improvement often cannot be achieved in the space of one lifetime, but may require generations, even eons, of human evolution to fulfill. Jude comes up at least a generation short of his desire. Just as poignantly, Sue, as Venus Urania and a woman ahead of her time, seems to have fallen from the stars and the future.

Adding contexts and motifs drawn from the "abstract," "remote," "lifeless" and "cold" realms of the physical sciences of cosmology and astronomy brings a new dimension to our understanding of how the male/female and manly/womanly have been defined. Implicated in the cultural matrices of society, ideology, economics, ecology and medicine which historians, anthropologists, literary scholars and social scientists have previously described, human perceptions of natural, universal, and lawful cosmic forces simultaneously strengthened and broadened the compelling constructions of the masculine and feminine such matrices collectively produced. Querying the paradoxical effects mythic representations of men's and women's nature, education and social roles may have generated through art, literature, culture and science in the past, may help us discern similar constructions when they emerge in our own cultural productions.

In Lawrence Norfolk's novel, *Lemprière's Dictionary* (1991), the Danaë story is reenacted out of particularly virulent economic motives. In order to terrorize the son (and heir) of one of their male enemies, operatives of the East India Company force him to witness molten gold being poured down the throat of a kidnapped prostitute. The scene is made extraordinarily grisly not only because of the excruciating method of her murder ("liquidated" by their ill-gotten gains) but because the reader knows that the incident is just "D" in an alphabetical series of "object lessons" that this man will encounter as mythical incidents from his dictionary-in-progress are pervertedly performed live.[23] As Norfolk tells it, the myth is criminal: a crime against both the woman who dies by it and the male scholar who must read it and write it. The heinous deployment of the myth implicates and exposes the evil of the capitalistic conspirators, the madness of the experimental scientist who devised and tested the *modus operandi,* as well as the invasive activities of the medical and legal investigators whose attempts at forensic pathology reviolate the woman's body by redisplaying the hideous agony of her death.

Although in each of his narratives of failed possibilities, Hardy provides his cosmic heroes and heroines with glimpses of perfectible futures, the myth is not dead. Keener awareness of how permutations of such stories permeate our attitudes, institutions, and culture may engender deeper understanding and empathy for those of us it thwarts. Remnants of the Danaë story are still apparent within our society's views of who can and who should have access to knowledge of the natural sciences and how that knowledge ought to be personally and professionally expressed. As ongoing studies of women and minorities in science education and scientific and technological professions continue to show, critical attention to the climate within which instruction

---

23   Lawrence Norfolk, *Lemprière's Dictionary: A Novel* (New York: Ballantine, 1991) 153–4.

takes place, creative encouragement and timely support make a world of difference.[24] As the flawed optics of our most technologically advanced space telescope gather light from the limit of the material universe, and humanity once again discovers itself "All Danaë to the stars," this may be a good time to rewrite such myths into ones we all can live by.

[24]   See, for instance, Marguerite Holloway, "Trends in the Sociology of Science: A Lab of Her Own," *Scientific American* (November, 1993): 94–103; David Targan, ed., *Achieving Gender Equity in the Science Classroom: A Guide for Faculty* (Brown University, 1996); Sue V. Rosser, *The Science Glass Ceiling: Academic Women Scientists and the Struggle to Succeed* (London: Routledge, 2004).

Bibliography

Works Cited

Primary Works and Sources: Hardy

Novels

Hardy, Thomas. *Far from the Madding Crowd*. Ed. Robert C. Schweik. New York: W. W. Norton and Company, 1986.
—. *Jude the Obscure*. Ed. Norman Page. 1978. New York: W. W. Norton, 1999.
—. *A Pair of Blue Eyes*. New Wessex Edition. 1975. London: Macmillan; New York: St. Martin's Press, 1985.
—. *The Return of the Native*. Ed. James Gindin. New York: W. W. Norton and Company, 1969.
—. *Tess of the d'Urbervilles*. Ed. Scott Elledge. 2nd ed. New York: W. W. Norton and Company, 1979.
—. *Two on a Tower*. New York: Harper and Brothers, 1895.
—. *The Woodlanders*. 1974. London: Macmillan, 1986.

Other Works

Hardy, Thomas. *The Collected Letters of Thomas Hardy*. Eds. Richard L. Purdy and Michael Millgate. Vol. 1: 1840–1892. Oxford: Clarendon Press, 1978.
—. *The Literary Notebooks of Thomas Hardy*. Ed. Lennart A. Björk. 2 vols. London: MacMillan, 1985. ("*LN*")
—. *Wessex Poems and Other Verses* (New York and London: Harper and Brothers, 1899).
Millgate, Michael. *The Life and Work of Thomas Hardy*. Athens, GA: University of Georgia Press, 1985.

Other Primary Works: Literature, Art

Agee, James, and Walker Evans. *Let Us Now Praise Famous Men*. 1939, 1940, 1941. New York: Ballantine, 1976.

Cather, Willa. *Death Comes for the Archbishop*. New York: A. A. Knopf, 1927.

—. *A Lost Lady*. New York: A. A. Knopf, 1923.

—. *My Antonia*. New York: Houghton Mifflin, 1918.

—. *O Pioneers!* 1913. Boston: Houghton Mifflin, 1941.

—. *One of Ours*. New York: A. A. Knopf, 1922.

—. *The Song of the Lark*. Boston: Houghton Mifflin, 1915.

Dyce, William. *Pegwell Bay, Kent: A Recollection of October 5th 1858*. Tate Gallery. London.

Eiseley, Loren C. *All the Strange Hours: The Excavation of a Life*. New York: Scribner, 1975.

—. *The Immense Journey*. New York: Random House, 1957.

—. *The Innocent Assassins*. New York: Scribner, 1973.

—. *The Invisible Pyramid*. New York: Scribner, 1970.

—. *The Night Country*. New York: Scribner, 1971.

—. *The Star Thrower*. New York: Times Books, 1978.

—. *The Unexpected Universe*. London: Victor Gollancz, 1970.

Fontenelle, Bernard le Bovier de. *Conversations on the Plurality of Worlds*. Trans. H. A. Hargreaves. Berkeley: University of California Press, 1990.

Hazzard, Shirley. *The Transits of Venus*. New York: Penguin, 1980.

Janovy, John, Jr. *Keith County Journal*. New York: St. Martin's Press, 1978.

—. *Yellowlegs: A Migration of the Mind*. Boston: Houghton Mifflin, 1980.

Lopez, Barry Holstun. *About this Life: Journeys on the Threshold of Memory*. New York: Knopf -Random House, 1998.

—. *Arctic Dreams: Imagination and Desire in a Northern Landscape*. New York: Scribner, 1986.

—. *Of Wolves and Men*. New York: Scribner, 1978.

—. *Winter Count*. New York: Scribner, 1981.

Milton, John. *Paradise Lost*. Ed. Merritt Y. Hughes. New Edition. New York: Odyssey Press, 1962.

Morris, Wright. *Ceremony in Lone Tree*. New York: Atheneum, 1960.

—. *The Field of Vision*. New York: Harcourt, Brace, 1956.

—. *God's Country and My People*. New York: Harper and Row, 1968.

—. *The Home Place*. 1948. Lincoln: University of Nebraska Press, 1999

—. *Photographs & Words / Wright Morris*. Ed. James Alinder. Carmel, CA: Friends of Photography, 1982.

—. *Plains Song, for Female Voices*. New York: Harper and Row, 1980.

—. *Will's Boy: A Memoir*. New York: Harper and Row, 1981.

Norfolk, Lawrence. *Lemprière's Dictionary: A Novel*. New York: Ballantine, 1991.

Rutherford, Mark [William Hale White]. *Miriam's Schooling and Other Papers*. Ed. Reuben Shapcott. London: T. F. Unwin, [1913?].

Swift, Jonathan. Letter to Alexander Pope, 29 September, 1725. *Jonathan Swift*. Eds. Angus Ross and David Woolley. The Oxford Authors. Oxford: Oxford University Press, 1984. 470–472.

Tennyson, Alfred. *Tennyson: A Selected Edition*. Ed. Christopher Ricks. Berkeley: University of California Press, 1989.

Thomson, James. *The Poetical Works of James Thomson*. Boston: Houghton Mifflin; St. Clair Shores, MI: Scholarly Press, 1971.

Wilde, Oscar. "An Ideal Husband." *The Complete Oscar Wilde*. New York: Crescent Books; Random House, 1995. 461–530.

Secondary Sources: Hardy Criticism

Barloon, Jim. "Star-Crossed Love: The Gravity of Science in Hardy's *Two on a Tower*." *The Victorian Newsletter* (Fall 1998): 27–32.

Bate, Jonathan. "Culture and Environment: From Austen to Hardy." *New Literary History: A Journal of Theory and Interpretation* 30.3 (Summer 1999): 541–60.

Beech, Martin. "Thomas Hardy: Far from the Royal Observatory, Greenwich." *The Observatory* 110 (December 1990): 185–7.

Beer, Gillian. "Finding a Scale for the Human: Plot and Writing in Hardy's Novels." *Darwin's Plots: Evolutionary Narrative in Dickens, George Eliot and Nineteenth-Century Fiction*. Boston: Routledge and Kegan Paul, 1983. 229–41.

Bevis, Richard W. *The Road to Egdon Heath: The Aesthetics of the Great in Nature*. Montreal; Ithaca: McGill-Queen's University Press, 1999.

Blythe, Ronald. Introduction. *A Pair of Blue Eyes*. By Thomas Hardy. New Wessex Edition. New York: St. Martin's Press, 1985. 13–36.

Boumelha, Penny. *Thomas Hardy and Women: Sexual Ideology and Narrative Form*. Brighton, Sussex, Eng.: Harvester, 1982.

Brennecke, Ernest, Jr. *Thomas Hardy's Universe: A Study of a Poet's Mind*. 1924. New York: Russell and Russell, 1966.

Buckler, William E. Introduction. *Tess of the d'Urbervilles*. By Thomas Hardy. Boston: Houghton Mifflin, 1960. v–xxiii.

Cosslett, Tess. *The Scientific Movement and Victorian Literature*. Brighton, Eng.: Harvester Press, 1982.

Crowe, Michael. Letter to the author. 25 April, 1988.

Dale, Peter Allan. *In Pursuit of a Scientific Culture: Science, Art, and Society in the Victorian Age*. Madison: University of Wisconsin Press, 1989.

Draper, Jo. *Thomas Hardy's England*. Ed. John Fowles. Boston: Little, Brown, 1984.

Ebbatson, Roger. *The Evolutionary Self: Hardy, Forster, Lawrence*. Brighton, Eng.: Harvester Press, 1982.

Enstice, Andrew. *Thomas Hardy: Landscapes of the Mind.* New York: St. Martin's Press, 1979.

Firor, Ruth A. *Folkways in Thomas Hardy.* New York: Russell and Russell, 1931.

Garson, Marjorie. *Hardy's Fables of Integrity: Woman, Body, Text.* Oxford: Clarendon Press, 1991.

Goode, John. *Thomas Hardy: The Offensive Truth.* Oxford: Basil Blackwell, 1988.

Gossin, Pamela. *Poetic Resolutions of Scientific Revolutions: Astronomy and the Literary Imaginations of Donne, Swift and Hardy.* Diss. University of Wisconsin, 1989. Ann Arbor: UMI, 1990. 9010301.

Gregor, Ian. *The Great Web: The Form of Hardy's Major Fiction.* London: Faber, [1974].

Grimsditch, Herbert Borthwick. *Character and Environment in the Novels of Thomas Hardy.* New York: Russell & Russell, 1962.

Grundy, Joan. "Hardy and Milton." *Thomas Hardy Annual* 3 (1985): 3–14. Rpt in *John Milton: Twentieth-Century Perspectives, Volume 1: The Man and the Author.* Ed. J. Martin Evans. New York: Routledge; 2003. 329–40.

Heath, Desmond. "Roden Noel and Thomas Hardy: Correspondence, 1892." *Thomas Hardy Journal* 15.1 (Feb. 1999): 71–6.

Higonnet, Margaret R., ed. *The Sense of Sex: Feminist Perspectives on Hardy.* Urbana: University of Illinois Press, 1993.

Ingham, Patricia. *Thomas Hardy.* Feminist Readings. Atlantic Highlands, NJ: Humanities Press International, 1990.

Irwin, Michael. *Reading Hardy's Landscapes.* Houndsmill, Basingstoke, Eng.: Palgrave, 2000.

James, Harumi. "*Two on a Tower*: Science and Religion, Space and Time." *Hardy Review* 2 (Summer 1999): 141–56.

Kay-Robinson, Denys. *The Landscape of Thomas Hardy.* [Salem, NH]: Salem House, 1984.

Langbaum, Robert. "Hardy: Versions of Pastoral." *Victorian Literature and Culture* 20 (1992): 245–72.

Lencho, Mark. "Autobiography in *Two on a Tower*." Unpublished essay. Central (Oklahoma) State University, 1980.

Levine, George. *Darwin and the Novelists: Patterns of Science in Victorian Fiction.* Chicago and London: University of Chicago Press, 1988.

Millgate, Michael. *Thomas Hardy: A Biography.* Oxford: Oxford University Press, 1982.

—. *Thomas Hardy: His Career as a Novelist.* New York: Random House, 1971.

Moore, Kevin Z. *The Descent of the Imagination: Postromantic Culture in the Later Novels of Thomas Hardy.* New York: New York University Press, 1990.

Morgan, Rosemarie. *Women and Sexuality in the Novels of Thomas Hardy.* London: Routledge, 1988.

Neill, Edward. *The Secret Life of Thomas Hardy: 'Retaliatory Fiction.'* Aldershot, Eng.: Ashgate; 2004.

—. *Trial by Ordeal: Thomas Hardy and the Critics*. Columbia, SC: Camden House; 1999.

Newey, Vincent, ed. *Centring the Self: Subjectivity, Society, and Reading from Thomas Gray to Thomas Hardy*. Aldershot, Eng.: Scolar Press; Brookfield, VT: Ashgate, 1995.

Pinion, F. B. *A Thomas Hardy Dictionary*. Washington Square, NY: New York University Press, 1989.

—. *Thomas Hardy: His Life and Friends*. London: Macmillan, 1992.

Pite, Ralph. *Hardy's Geography: Wessex and the Regional Novel*. New York: Palgrave; Macmillan, 2002.

Radford, Andrew. *Thomas Hardy and the Survivals of Time*. The Nineteenth Century Series. Aldershot, Eng.: Ashgate, 2003.

—. "The Victorian Dilettante and the Discoveries of Time in *A Pair of Blue Eyes*." *Thomas Hardy Yearbook* 33 (2002): 5–19.

Ray, Martin. "Hardy's 'The Comet at Yell'ham' and Donati's Comet." *Notes and Queries* 49.4 (Dec. 2002): 491.

Sampson, Edward C. "Telling Time by the Stars in *Far from the Madding Crowd*." *Notes and Queries*, ns 14 (1967): 63–4.

Schur, Owen. *Victorian Pastoral: Tennyson, Hardy, and the Subversion of Forms*. Columbus: Ohio State University Press,1989.

Siebenschuh, William R. "Hardy and the Imagery of Place." *SEL: Studies in English Literature, 1500–1900* 39.4 (Autumn 1999): 773–89.

Smith, Margaret. "Lord Roden and Horace Noel." *Thomas Hardy Journal* 15.3 (Oct. 1999): 99–102

Squires, Michael. *The Pastoral Novel: Studies in George Eliot, Thomas Hardy, and D. H. Lawrence*. Charlottesville: University Press of Virginia, 1974.

Sumner, Rosemary. *Thomas Hardy, Psychological Novelist*. New York: St. Martin's Press, 1981.

Thomas, Jane. *Thomas Hardy, Femininity and Dissent: Reassessing the 'Minor' Novels*. London: Macmillan; New York: St. Martin's Press, 1999.

Thurley, Geoffrey. *The Psychology of Hardy's Novels: The Nervous and the Statuesque*. St. Lucia, Queensland, Aust.: University of Queensland Press, 1975.

Veater, Zoe. "Hardy's Use of Nature in His Novels." *Thomas Hardy Journal* 15.3 (Oct. 1999): 117–22.

Ward, Paul. "*A Pair of Blue Eyes* and the Descent of Man." *Thomas Hardy Yearbook* 5 (1975): 47–55.

—. "*Two on a Tower*: A Critical Revaluation." *Thomas Hardy Yearbook* 8 (1978): 29–34.

Weber, Carl J. *Hardy of Wessex: His Life and Literary Career*. New York: Columbia University Press, 1965.

Whitehead, Cintra. "Construct, Image and Prediction: A View of Hardy's *Jude the Obscure* through George Kelly's Psychology of Personal Constructs."

Constructive Criticism: A Journal of Construct Psychology and the Arts 1.2 (June 1991): 129–49.

Williams, Merryn. *Thomas Hardy and Rural England.* New York: Columbia University Press, 1972.

Secondary Sources: Literature, Art, Culture; Literature and Science (LS) Studies

Auerbach, Nina. "The Rise of the Fallen Woman." *Nineteenth-Century Fiction* 35 (1980): 29–52.

Brantlinger, Patrick, and William B. Thesing, eds. *A Companion to the Victorian Novel.* Blackwell Companions to Literature and Culture. Oxford: Blackwell Publishing, 2002.

Cornish, Alison. *Reading Dante's Stars.* New Haven, CT: Yale University Press, 2000.

Curry, Walter Clyde. *Chaucer and the Mediaeval Sciences.* 1926. London: Allen, 1960.

—. *Milton's Ontology, Cosmology and Physics.* Lexington: University of Kentucky Press, 1957.

Dainotto, Roberto Maria. *Place in Literature: Regions, Cultures, Communities.* Ithaca, NY: Cornell University Press, 2000.

Dean, Dennis R. *Tennyson and Geology.* Lincoln, Eng.: Tennyson Society, 1985.

Dijkstra, Bram. *Idols of Perversity: Fantasies of Feminine Evil in Fin-de-Siècle Culture.* Oxford: Oxford University Press, 1986.

Duncan, Ian. "The Provincial or Regional Novel." *A Companion to the Victorian Novel.* Ed. Patrick Brantlinger and William B. Thesing. Blackwell Companions to Literature and Culture. Oxford: Blackwell Publishing, 2002. 318–35.

Eade, J. C. *The Forgotten Sky: A Guide to Astrology in English Literature.* Oxford: Clarendon Press, 1984.

Geikie, Archibald. *English Science and its Caricaturists in the Seventeenth and Eighteenth Centuries,* Haslemere, Eng.: Haslemere Natural Historical Society, 1914.

Gilbert, Sandra M., and Susan Gubar. *The Madwoman in the Attic: The Woman Writer and the Nineteenth-Century Literary Imagination.* New Haven, CT: Yale University Press, 1979.

Gossin, Pamela. "'All Danaë to the Stars': Nineteenth-Century Representations of Women in the Cosmos." *Victorian Studies* 40.1 (Autumn 1996) 65–96.

—. "John Donne and the Astronomical Revolution." *Poetic Resolutions of Scientific Revolutions: Astronomy and the Literary Imaginations of Donne, Swift and Hardy.* Diss. University of Wisconsin, 1989. Ann Arbor: UMI, 1990. 9010301. 30–216.

—. "Jonathan Swift and the Newtonian Revolution." *Poetic Resolutions of Scientific Revolutions: Astronomy and the Literary Imaginations of Donne, Swift and Hardy.* Diss. University of Wisconsin, 1989. Ann Arbor: UMI, 1990. 9010301. 217–355.

Haynes, Roslynn D. *From Faust to Strangelove: Representations of the Scientist in Western Literature*. Baltimore, MD: Johns Hopkins University Press, 1994.

Henchman, Anna Alexandra. *Astronomy and the Problem of Perception in British Literature, 1830–1910* (Thomas De Quincey, Alfred, Lord Tennyson, George Eliot, and Thomas Hardy). Diss. Harvard University, 2004.

—. "Cinders of Stars, Solar Catastrophes: The Terror of Victorian Astronomy." Abstract. *Rethinking Space + Time Across Science, Literature + the Arts*. 17th Annual Conference of the Society for Literature and Science, October 23–26, 2003. 24.

Henry, Holly. *Virginia Woolf and the Discourse of Science: The Aesthetics of Astronomy*. Cambridge: Cambridge University Press, 2003.

Hooker, Jeremy. *Writers in a Landscape*. Cardiff: University of Wales Press, 1996.

Horner, Avril, and Sue Zlosnik. *Landscapes of Desire: Metaphors in Women's Fiction*. Hemel Hempstead, Eng.: Harvester Wheatsheaf, 1990.

Hunter, Shelagh. *Victorian Idyllic Fiction: Pastoral Strategies*. Atlantic Highlands, NJ: Humanities Press, 1984.

Johnson, Francis R. *Astronomical Thought in Renaissance England: A Study of the English Scientific Writings from 1500 to 1645*. Baltimore, MD: Johns Hopkins University Press, 1937.

Kay, Richard. *Dante's Christian Astrology*. Philadelphia: University of Pennsylvania Press, 1994.

Killham, John. *Tennyson and The Princess: Reflections of an Age*. London: University of London, Athlone Press, 1958.

Korg, Jacob. "Astronomical Imagery in Victorian Poetry." *Victorian Science and Victorian Values: Literary Perspectives*. Ed. James Paradis and Thomas Postlewait. New Brunswick, NJ: Rutgers University Press, 1985. 137–58.

Kucich, John. "Scientific Ascendency." *A Companion to the Victorian Novel*. Eds. Patrick Brantlinger and William B. Thesing. Blackwell Companions to Literature and Culture. Oxford: Blackwell Publishing, 2002. 119–36.

Levine, Philippa. *Victorian Feminism: 1850–1900*. London: Hutchinson, 1987.

Lucas, John. *The Literature of Change: Studies in the Nineteenth-century Provincial Novel*. 2nd ed. Brighton, Eng.: Harvester Press; Totowa, NJ: Barnes & Noble Books, 1980.

Meadows, A. J. *The High Firmament: A Survey of Astronomy in English Literature*. Leicester: Leicester University Press, 1969.

Mebane, John. *Renaissance Magic and the Return of the Golden Age: The Occult Tradition and Marlowe, Jonson and Shakespeare*. Lincoln: University of Nebraska Press, 1989.

Michie, Helena. *The Flesh Made Word: Female Figures and Women's Bodies*. Oxford: Oxford University Press, 1987.

Nash, Jane. *Veiled Images: Titian's Mythological Paintings for Phillip II*. Philadelphia: Art Association Press, 1985.

Nicolson, Marjorie. *The Breaking of the Circle: Studies in the Effect of the "New Science" on Seventeenth-Century Poetry.* Rev. ed. 1950. New York: Columbia University Press, 1960.

—. *Newton Demands the Muse: Newton's Opticks and the Eighteenth-Century Poets.* History of Ideas Series 2. Princeton: Princeton University Press, 1946.

—. *Science and Imagination.* Ithaca, NY: Great Seal Books, 1962.

Nicolson, Marjorie, and Nora M. Mohler. "The Scientific Background of Swift's *Voyage to Laputa.*" *Annuals of Science* 2 (1937): 299–334. Rpt in *Science and Imagination.* Ithaca: Great Seal, 1956.

—. "Swift's 'Flying Island' in the *Voyage to Laputa.*" *Annals of Science* 2 (1937): 405–30.

Orr, Mary Acworth. *Dante and the Early Astronomers.* 1913. Port Washington, NY: London, Kennikat Press, 1969.

Panofsky, Erwin. *Problems in Titian: Mostly Iconographic.* New York: New York University Press, 1969.

Pater, Walter. *The Renaissance: Studies in Art and Poetry.* 1893 text. Ed. Donald L. Hill. Berkeley: University of California Press, 1980.

Pearce, Lynne. *Woman, Image, Text: Readings in Pre-Raphaelite Art and Literature.* Hemel Hempstead, Eng.: Harvester Wheatsheaf, 1991.

Perkins, David. *Is Literary History Possible?* Baltimore, MD: The Johns Hopkins University Press, 1992.

—, ed. *Theoretical Issues in Literary History.* Cambridge, MA: Harvard University Press, 1991.

Pollock, Griselda. *Vision and Difference: Femininity, Feminism and the History of Art.* London: Routledge, 1988.

Reynolds, Kimberley, and Nicola Humble. *Victorian Heroines: Representations of Femininity in Nineteenth-Century Literature and Art.* New York: New York University Press, 1993.

Schleifer, Ronald, and Alan Velie. "Genre and Structure: Toward an Actantial Typology of Narrative Genres and Modes." *Modern Language Notes* 102 (Winter 1987): 1122–50.

Small, Helen, and Trudi Tate, eds. *Literature, Science, Psychoanalysis, 1830–1970: Essays in Honour of Gillian Beer.* Oxford: Oxford University Press, 2003.

Traister, Barbara. *Heavenly Necromancers: The Magician in English Renaissance Drama.* Columbia: University of Missouri Press, 1984.

Usher, Peter D. "Shakespeare's Cosmic World View." *Mercury* 26.1 (Jan./Feb. 1997): 20–23.

Vrettos, Athena. "Victorian Psychology." *A Companion to the Victorian Novel.* Ed. Patrick Brantlinger and William B. Thesing. Blackwell Companions to Literature and Culture. Oxford: Blackwell Publishing, 2002. 67–83.

Wickens, G. G. "The Two Sides of Early Victorian Science and the Unity of 'The Princess.'" *Victorian Studies* 23 (1980): 367–88.

Wood, Chauncey D. *Chaucer and the Country of the Stars: Poetic Use of Astrological Imagery*. Diss. Princeton University, 1963.

Wright, F. A. *Lemprière's Classical Dictionary of Proper Names Mentioned in Ancient Authors*. London: Routledge and Kegan Paul, 1963.

Secondary Sources: History of Science, Popular Astronomy; Science Studies; Other

Applebaum, Wilbur. *Kepler in England: The Reception of Keplerian Astronomy in England 1599–1687*. Diss. University of New York-Buffalo, 1969.

Aveni, Anthony F. *Skywatchers*. Rev. ed. Austin: University of Texas Press, 2001.

—, ed. *Native American Astronomy*. Austin: University of Texas Press, 1977.

—, ed. *World Archaeoastronomy: Selected Papers from the 2nd Oxford International Conference on Archaeoastronomy,* 1986. Cambridge: Cambridge University Press, 1989.

Beattie, William. M.D., ed. *Life and Letters of Thomas Campbell*. Vol. 2. London: 1849.

Beauvoir, Simone de. *The Second Sex*. New York: Bantam, 1952.

Berry, Arthur. *A Short History of Astronomy: From Earliest Times Through the Nineteenth Century*. 1898. New York: Dover, 1961.

Bono, James J. *The Word of God and the Languages of Man: Interpreting Nature in Early Modern Science and Medicine, vol. 1: Ficino to Descartes*. Madison: University of Wisconsin Press, 1995.

Brennan, Richard P., ed. *Dictionary of Scientific Literacy*. New York: John Wiley and Sons, 1992.

Brück, Mary. *Agnes Mary Clerke and the Rise of Astrophysics*. Cambridge: Cambridge University Press, 2002.

Chambers, George F. *The Story of the Comets*. Oxford: Clarendon Press, 1909.

Chambers, Robert. *Vestiges of the Natural History of Creation*. London: John Churchill, 1844.

Chapman, Allan. *The Victorian Amateur Astronomer: Independent Astronomical Research in Britain 1820–1920*. Chichester, Eng.: Wiley-Praxis, 1998.

Churchland, Patricia Smith. *Brain-wise: Studies in Neurophilosophy*. Cambridge, MA: MIT Press, 2002.

—. *Neurophilosophy: Toward a Unified Science of the Mind-Brain*. Cambridge, MA: MIT Press, 1986.

Clerke, Agnes M. *A Popular History of Astronomy During the Nineteenth Century*. Edinburgh: Adam and Charles Black, 1887; 4th ed. facsimile rpt. Decorah, IA: Sattre Press, 2003.

Cornell, James. *The First Stargazers: An Introduction to the Origins of Astronomy*. New York: Scribner's, 1981.

Crick, Francis. *The Astonishing Hypothesis: The Scientific Search for the Soul.* New York: Scribner/Maxwell Macmillan International, 1994.

Crowe, Michael. *The Extraterrestrial Life Debate 1750–1900: The Idea of a Plurality of Worlds from Kant to Lowell.* Cambridge: Cambridge University Press, 1986.

Curry, Patrick, ed. *Astrology, Science and Society: Historical Essays.* Woodbridge, Suffolk, Eng.: The Boydell Press, 1987.

Danielson, Dennis Richard. *The Book of the Cosmos: Imagining the Universe from Heraclitus to Hawking.* Cambridge, MA: Helix/Perseus, 2000.

Dick, Steven J. *Plurality of Worlds: The Extraterrestrial Life Debate from Democritus to Kant.* Cambridge: Cambridge University Press, 1984.

Edelman, Gerald. *Bright Air, Brilliant Fire: On the Matter of the Mind.* New York: Basic Books, 1992.

— . *Neural Darwinism: The Theory of Neuronal Group Selection.* New York : Basic Books, 1987.

Editors of Lingua Franca. *The Sokal Hoax: The Sham that Shook the Academy.* Lincoln: University of Nebraska Press, 2000.

Foucault, Michel. *The History of Sexuality: An Introduction.* Trans. Robert Hurley. Vol.1. New York: Penguin, 1979.

Frazer, James George. *The Golden Bough: A Study in Magic and Religion.* New York: Macmillan, 1972.

Genuth, Sarah Schechner. *Comets, Popular Culture, and the Birth of Modern Cosmology.* Princeton, NJ: Princeton University Press, 1997.

Grant, Edward. *Planets, Stars and Orbs: The Medieval Cosmos, 1200–1687.* Cambridge: Cambridge University Press, 1994.

— . "Science and Theology in the Middle Ages."*God and Nature: Historical Essays on the Encounter between Christianity and Science.* Ed. David C. Lindberg and Ronald L. Numbers. Berkeley: University of California Press, 1986: 49–75.

Gross, Paul R., and Norman Levitt. *Higher Superstition: The Academic Left and its Quarrels with Science.* Baltimore, MD: Johns Hopkins University Press, 1997.

Haraway, Donna Jeanne. *Primate Visions: Gender, Race, and Nature in the World of Modern Science.* New York: Routledge, 1989.

— . *Simians, Cyborgs, and Women: the Reinvention of Nature.* New York: Routledge, 1991.

Hellerstein, Erna Olafson, et al. eds. *Victorian Women: A Documentary Account of Women's Lives in Nineteenth-Century England, France, and the United States.* Stanford, CT: Stanford University Press, 1981.

Hetheringon, Norriss S., ed. *Cosmology: Historical, Literary, Philosophical, Religious, and Scientific Perspectives.* New York: Garland Publishing, 1993.

History of Astronomy Discussion Group. Archives. <http://listserv.wvu.edu/archives/hastro-l.html>.

Holloway, Marguerite. "Trends in the Sociology of Science: A Lab of Her Own." *Scientific American* (November, 1993): 94–103.

Holton, Gerald James. "Johannes Kepler: A Case Study on the Interaction of Science, Metaphysics, and Theology." *The Philosophical Forum* 14 (1956): 21–33.

—. *The Scientific Imagination: Case Studies.* Cambridge: Cambridge University Press, 1978.

—. *Thematic Origins of Scientific Thought: Kepler to Einstein.* Rev. ed. Cambridge, MA: Harvard University Press, 1988.

Hoskin, Michael. *The Herschel Partnership: As Viewed by Caroline.* Cambridge: Science History Publications, 2003.

—. *William Herschel and the Construction of the Heavens.* London: Oldbourne, 1963.

—, ed. *Caroline Herschel's Autobiographies.* Cambridge: Science History Publications, 2003.

"How to pick a telescope / Why buy a reflector?" Astronomics. <www.astronomics.com>.

Hoyt, Michael F., ed. *The Handbook of Constructive Therapies: Innovative Approaches from Leading Practitioners.* San Francisco, CA: Jossey-Bass, 1998.

Jordanova, Ludmilla. *Sexual Visions: Images of Gender in Science and Medicine between the Eighteenth and Twentieth Centuries.* Madison: University of Wisconsin Press, 1989.

Keller, Evelyn Fox. *Reflections on Gender and Science.* New Haven, CT: Yale University Press, 1985.

Kelly, George Alexander. *The Psychology of Personal Constructs.* 2 vols. New York: Norton, 1955.

King, Henry C. *The History of the Telescope.* 1955. New York: Dover, 1979.

Koch, Christof. *The Quest for Consciousness: A Neurobiological Approach.* Englewood, CO: Roberts, 2004.

Koertge, Noretta, ed. *A House Built on Sand: Exposing Postmodern Myths about Science.* Oxford: Oxford University Press, 2000.

Kohlstedt, Sally Gregory. "Maria Mitchell and the Advancement of Women in Science." *Uneasy Careers and Intimate Lives: Women in Science, 1789–1979.* Ed. Pnina Abir-Am and Dorinda Outram. New Brunswick, NJ: Rutgers University Press, 1987. 129–46.

Kuhn, Thomas S. *The Copernican Revolution; Planetary Astronomy in the Development of Western Thought.* Cambridge, MA: Harvard University Press, 1957.

—. *The Essential Tension: Selected Studies in Scientific Tradition and Change.* Chicago: University of Chicago Press, 1977.

—. *The Structure of Scientific Revolutions.* 2nd ed. Chicago: University of Chicago Press, 1996.

Latour, Bruno. *Science in Action: How to Follow Scientists and Engineers Through Society.* Cambridge, MA: Harvard University Press, 1987.

—. *We Have Never Been Modern.* Trans. Catherine Porter. Cambridge, MA: Harvard University Press, 1993.

Latour, Bruno, and Steve Woolgar. *Laboratory Life: the Construction of Scientific Facts*. Princeton, NJ: Princeton University Press, 1986.

Lindberg, David C. *The Beginnings of Western Science: The European Scientific Tradition in Philosophical, Religious, and Institutional Context, 600 B.C. to A.D. 1450*. Chicago: University of Chicago Press, 1992.

—. "Science and the Early Church." *God and Nature: Historical Essays on the Encounter between Christianity and Science*. Ed. David C. Lindberg and Ronald L. Numbers. Berkeley: University of California Press, 1986. 19–48.

—, ed. *Science in the Middle Ages*. Chicago: University of Chicago Press, 1978.

Lindberg, David C., and Ronald L. Numbers, eds. *When Science and Christianity Meet*. Chicago: University of Chicago Press, 2003.

Marcus, Steven. *The Other Victorians: A Study of Sexuality and Pornography in Mid-Nineteenth-Century England*. New York: Basic Books, 1966.

McCluskey, Stephen C. *Astronomies and Cultures in Early Medieval Europe*. Cambridge: Cambridge University Press, 1998.

Merchant, Carolyn. *The Death of Nature: Women, Ecology and the Scientific Revolution*. San Francisco, CA: Harper and Row, 1980.

Mitton, Jacqueline. *Concise Dictionary of Astronomy*. Oxford: Oxford University Press, 1991.

Nead, Lynda. *Myths of Sexuality: Representations of Women in Victorian Britain*. Oxford: Basil Blackwell, 1988.

Neimeyer, Robert A. *The Development of Personal Construct Psychology*. Lincoln: University of Nebraska Press, 1985.

Neimeyer, Robert A., and Jonathan D. Raskin, eds. *Constructions of Disorder: Meaning-making Frameworks for Psychotherapy*. Washington, DC: American Psychological Association, 2000.

North, John. *The Norton History of Astronomy and Cosmology*. New York: W. W. Norton, 1995.

Panek, Richard. *Seeing is Believing: How the Telescope Opened Our Eyes and Minds to the Heavens*. New York: Penguin Books, 1998.

Pannekoek, Anton. *A History of Astronomy*. New York: Dover, 1961.

Penrose, Roger. *The Emperor's New Mind: Concerning Computers, Minds, and the Laws of Physics*. New York: Penguin Books, 1991.

—. *Shadows of the Mind: A Search for the Missing Science of Consciousness*. Oxford: Oxford University Press, 1994.

Perkin, Joan. *Victorian Women*. New York: New York University Press, 1993.

Porter, Roy Porter, and Lesley Hall. *The Facts of Life: the Creation of Sexual Knowledge in Britain, 1650–1950*. New Haven, CT: Yale University Press, 1995.

Proctor, Richard. *Essays on Astronomy*. London: Longmans, Green and Company, 1872.

—. *Transits of Venus: A Popular Account of Past and Coming Transits. . . .* London: Longmans, Green and Co, 1874.

Richards, Pete. "Canary Islands, March, 1994." Excursion Report. University of Cambridge, Institute of Astronomy. <http://www.ast.cam.ac.uk/~ipswich/Events/Excursions/Excursion_Reports.htm>.

Roberts, Glenn, and Jeremy Holmes, eds. *Healing Stories: Narrative in Psychiatry and Psychotherapy*. Oxford: Oxford University Press, 1999.

Ross, Andrew. *Science Wars*. Raleigh-Durham: Duke University Press, 1996.

Ross, Andrew, and Bruce Robbins, *Lingua Franca* (July/August 1996).

Rosser, Sue V. *The Science Glass Ceiling: Academic Women Scientists and the Struggle to Succeed*. London: Routledge, 2004.

Russett, Cynthia Eagle. *Sexual Science: the Victorian Construction of Womanhood*. Cambridge, MA: Harvard University Press, 1989.

Salk, Lee. "Ethics in Embryo." Panel Discussion. *Science and the Human Spirit*. Ed. Fred White. Belmont, CA: Wadsworth, 1989. 193–207.

Schiebinger, Londa. *The Mind Has No Sex?: Women in the Origins of Modern Science*. Cambridge, MA: Harvard University Press, 1989.

Secord, James. *Victorian Sensation: The Extraordinary Publication, Reception and Secret Authorship of Vestiges of the Natural History of Creation*. Chicago: University of Chicago Press, 2001.

Showalter, Elaine. *Sexual Anarchy: Gender and Culture and the Fin de Siècle*. New York: Viking, 1990.

Sokal, Alan. "A Physicist Experiments with Cultural Studies." *Lingua Franca* (May/June, 1996): 62–64.

—. "Transgressing the Boundaries: Towards a Transformative Hermeneutics of Quantum Gravity." *Social Text* 46/47 (Spring/Summer 1996): 217–52

Sokal, Alan, and Jean Bricmont. *Fashionable Nonsense: Postmodern Intellectuals' Abuse of Science*. New York: Picador, 1999.

Targan, David, ed. *Achieving Gender Equity in the Science Classroom: A Guide for Faculty*. Brown University, 1996.

Tuana, Nancy. *The Less Noble Sex: Scientific, Religious, and Philosophical Conceptions of Woman's Nature*. Bloomington: Indiana University Press, 1993.

Unguru, Sabetai. *Physics, Cosmology and Astronomy, 1300–1700*. Boston Studies in the Philosophy of Science, 126. Dordrecht: Kluwer Academic Publishers, 1991.

Van Helden, Albert. *Measuring the Universe: Cosmic Dimensions from Aristarchus to Halley*. Chicago: University of Chicago Press, 1985.

—. "The Telescope and Authority from Galileo to Cassini." *Instruments*. Eds. T. L. Hankins and Albert Van Helden. *Osiris* 9 (1994): 9–29.

Van Helden, Albert, and M. G. Winkler. "Representing the Heavens: Galileo and Visual Astronomy." *Isis* 83 (1992):195–217.

Voelkel, James R. *The Composition of Kepler's <u>Astronomia Nova</u>*. Princeton, NJ: Princeton University Press, 2001.

Watson, James C. *A Popular Treatise on Comets*. Philadelphia: James Challen and Son, 1861.

Westman, Robert S. "Proof, Poetics, and Patronage: Copernicus's Preface to *De Revolutionibus.*" *Reappraisals of the Scientific Revolution.* Ed. David C. Lindberg and Robert S. Westman. Cambridge: Cambridge University Press, 1990. 167–205.

Works Consulted; for Further Reading

Andres, Sophia. *The Pre-Raphaelite Art of the Victorian Novel: Narrative Challenges to Visual Gendered Boundaries.* Columbus: Ohio State University Press, 2005.
Armstrong, Tim. *Haunted Hardy: Poetry, History, Memory.* Basingstoke, Eng.: Palgrave, 2000.
Baigrie, Brian S. *Scientific Revolutions: Primary Texts in the History of Science.* Upper Saddle River, NJ: Pearson Prentice Hall, 2004.
Baker, Susan. "'The Lover of All in a Sun Sweep.'" *Hardy Review* 2 (Summer 1999): 130–41.
Berger, Sheila. *Thomas Hardy and Visual Structures: Framing, Disruption, Process.* New York: New York University Press, 1990.
Bonica, Charlotte. "Nature and Paganism in Hardy's *Tess of the D'Urbervilles.*" *ELH* 49.4 (Winter 1982): 849–62.
Brick, Allan. "Paradise and Consciousness in Hardy's *Tess.*" *Nineteenth-Century Fiction* 17.2 (Sept. 1962): 115–34.
Brogan, Howard O. "Science and Narrative Structure in Austen, Hardy, and Woolf." *Nineteenth-Century Fiction* 11. 4 (Mar. 1957): 276–87.
Brooke, John Hedley. *Science and Religion: Some Historical Perspectives.* Cambridge History of Science Series. Cambridge: Cambridge University Press, 1999.
Bullen, J. B., ed. *The Sun Is God: Painting, Literature, and Mythology in the Nineteenth Century.* Oxford: Clarendon Press; New York: Oxford University Press, 1989.
Butler, Lance St. John. *Alternative Hardy.* New York: St. Martin's Press, 1989.
Casagrande, Peter J. *Hardy's Influence on the Modern Novel.* Houndmills, Basingstoke, Eng.: Macmillan, 1987.
Christ, Carol T., and John O. Jordan, eds. *Victorian Literature and the Victorian Visual Imagination.* Berkeley: University of California Press, 1995.
Christen, Eric. "Proud Poets Transformed: Hardy and Lucretius." *Thomas Hardy Journal* 17.3 (Oct. 2001): 64–7.
Clough, Peter W. L. "Hardy's Trilobite." *Thomas Hardy Journal* 4.2 (May 1988): 29–31.
Collins, Deborah L. *Thomas Hardy and His God: a Liturgy of Unbelief.* Basingstoke, Eng.: Macmillan, 1990.
Daleski, H. M. *Thomas Hardy and Paradoxes of Love.* Columbia, MO: University of Missouri Press, 1997.

—. "Thomas Hardy: A Victorian Modernist?" *The Challenge of Periodization: Old Paradigms and New Perspectives*. Ed. Lawrence Besserman. New York: Garland, 1996. 179–195.

Dalziel, Pamela. "Hardy's Sexual Evasions: The Evidence of the 'Studies, Specimens &c.' Notebook." *Victorian Poetry* 31.2 (Summer 1993): 143–155.

Daniel, Clay. "Science, Misogyny, and Tess of the D'Urbervilles." *Hardy Review* 1.1 (July 1998): 99–108.

Dave, Jagdish Chandra. *The Human Predicament in Hardy's Novels*. Atlantic Highlands, NJ: Humanities Press, 1985.

David, Deirdre, ed. *The Cambridge Companion to the Victorian Novel*. Cambridge: Cambridge University Press, 2001.

Davie, Donald. "Hardy's Virgilian Purples."*Arion: A Journal of Humanities and the Classics* N.S. 1 (1974): 505–26.

Davis, William A. *Thomas Hardy and the Law: Legal Presences in Hardy's Life and Fiction*. Newark, NJ: University of Delaware Press; London; Cranbury, NJ: Associated University Presses, 2003.

Dear, Peter. *Revolutionizing the Sciences: European Knowledge and Its Ambitions, 1500–1700*. Princeton: Princeton University Press, 2001.

Dessner, Lawrence Jay. "Space, Time, and Coincidence in Hardy." *Studies in the Novel* 24.2 (1992): 154–72.

Devereux, Joanna. *Patriarchy and its Discontents: Sexual Politics in Selected Novels and Stories of Thomas Hardy*. New York: Routledge, 2003.

Donne, John. *Poetical Works*. Ed. Herbert Grierson. London: Oxford University Press, 1967.

Draper, R. P. "Hardy and the Pastoral." *Thomas Hardy Journal* 14.3 (Oct. 1998): 44–56.

Dutta, Shanta. *Ambivalence in Hardy: A Study of His Attitude to Women*. Basingstoke, Eng; New York: Macmillan; St. Martin's, 2000.

Eakins, Rosemary L. "Tess: The Pagan and Christian Traditions." *The Novels of Thomas Hardy*. Ed. Anne Smith. New York: Barnes & Noble, 1979. 107–25.

Ebbatson, J. R. "The Darwinian View of Tess: A Reply." *Southern Review: Literary and Interdisciplinary Essays* 8 (1975): 247–53.

Ermarth, Elizabeth. "Fictional Consensus and Female Casualties." *The Representation of Women in Fiction*. Ed. Carolyn G. Heilbrun and Margaret R. Higonnet. Baltimore: Johns Hopkins University Press, 1983. 1–18.

Ferguson, Kitty. *Measuring the Universe: Our Historic Quest to Chart the Horizons of Space and Time*. New York: Walker, 1999.

Ferris, Timothy. *Coming of Age in the Milky Way*. New York: Anchor Books, 1989.

Friedman, Alan J., and Carol C. Donley, eds. *Einstein as Myth and Muse*. Cambridge: Cambridge University Press, 1989.

Gallivan, Patricia. "Science and Art in *Jude the Obscure*." *The Novels of Thomas Hardy*. Ed. Anne Smith. New York: Barnes & Noble; 1979. 126–44.

Garlock, David. "Entangled Genders: Plasticity, Indeterminacy, and Constructs of Sexuality in Darwin and Hardy." *Dickens Studies Annual: Essays on Victorian Fiction* 27 (1998): 287–305.

Gates, Barbara T. *Kindred Nature: Victorian and Edwardian Women Embrace the Living World.* Chicago: University of Chicago Press, 1998.

Gatrell, Simon. *Thomas Hardy and the Proper Study of Mankind.* Victorian Literature and Culture Series. Charlottesville: University Press of Virginia, 1993.

Gibson, James, ed. *Thomas Hardy: Interviews and Recollections.* Basingstoke, Eng.: Macmillan; New York: St. Martin's Press, 1999.

Gilmartin, Sophie. "Geology, Genealogy and Church Restoration in Hardy's Writing." *The Achievement of Thomas Hardy.* Ed. Phillip Mallet. Basingstoke, Eng.; New York: Macmillan; St. Martin's, 2000. 22–40.

Gose, Elliott B., Jr. "Psychic Evolution: Darwinism and Initiation in *Tess of the d'Urbervilles.*" *Nineteenth-Century Fiction* 18.3 (Dec. 1963): 261–72.

Goss, Michael. "Aspects of Time in *Far from the Madding Crowd.*" *Thomas Hardy Journal* 6.3 (1990): 43–53.

Gratzer, Walter, ed. *A Literary Companion to Science.* New York: W. W. Norton, 1989.

Greenslade, William, ed. *Thomas Hardy's 'Facts' Notebook: A Critical Edition.* The Nineteenth Century Series. Aldershot, Eng.: Ashgate; 2004.

Gussow, Adam. "Dreaming Holmberry-Lipped Tess: Aboriginal Reverie and Spectatorial Desire in *Tess of the D'Ubervilles.*" *Studies in the Novel* 32.4 (Winter 2000): 442–63.

Hallyn, Fernand. *The Poetic Structure of the World: Copernicus and Kepler.* Trans. Donald M. Leslie. New York: Zone Books, 1990.

Hands, Timothy. "Hardy's Architecture: A General Perspective and a Personal View." *The Achievement of Thomas Hardy.* Ed. Phillip Mallet. Basingstoke, Eng.; New York: Macmillan; St. Martin's, 2000. 95–104.

—. *Thomas Hardy: Distracted Preacher?: Hardy's Religious Biography and its Influence on His Novels.* New York: St. Martin's Press, 1989.

Hardy, Emma Lavinia Gifford. *Emma Hardy Diaries.* Ed. Richard H. Taylor. Ashington, Northumberland: Mid Northumberland Arts Group; Manchester: Carcanet New Press, 1985.

Hardy, Thomas. *Desperate Remedies.* Ed. Mary Rimmer. London: Penguin Books, 1998.

—. *The Hand of Ethelberta.* Ed. Tim Dolin. London: Penguin Books, 1997.

—. *Jude the Obscure.* Ed. C. H. Sisson. London: Penguin Books, 1978.

—. *A Laodicean.* Ed. John Schad. London: Penguin Books, 1997.

—. *Life's Little Ironies.* Ed. Alan Manford. Oxford: Oxford University Press, 1996.

—. *The Mayor of Casterbridge.* Ed. Robert B. Heilman. Boston: Houghton Mifflin, 1962.

—. *A Pair of Blue Eyes.* Ed. Pamela Dalziel. London: Penguin Books, 1998.

—. *A Pair of Blue Eyes.* New York: John W. Lovell, [1894?].

—. *The Pursuit of the Well-Beloved and the Well-Beloved.* Ed. Patricia Ingham. London: Penguin Books, 1997.

—. *Studies, Specimens &C. Notebook.* Eds. Pamela Dalziel and Michael Millgate. Oxford: Clarendon Press; New York: Oxford University Press, 1994.

—. *Tess of the D'Urbervilles.* Ed. William E. Buckler. Boston: Houghton Mifflin, 1960.

—. *Thomas Hardy: Three Pastoral Novels: Under the Greenwood Tree, Far from the Madding Crowd, The Woodlanders: A Casebook.* Ed. R.P. Draper. Houndmills, Eng.: Macmillan Education, 1987.

—. *Thomas Hardy's Public Voice: the Essays, Speeches, and Miscellaneous Prose.* Ed. Michael Millgate. Oxford: Clarendon Press; New York: Oxford University Press, 2001.

—. *Two on a Tower.* 1882. London: Macmillan, 1934.

—. *Two on a Tower.* New Wessex Edition. 1975. London: Macmillan, 1986.

—. *Under the Greenwood Tree.* Ed. Tim Dolin. London: Penguin, 1998.

Harris, Nicola. "An Impure Woman: The Tragic Paradox and Tess as Totem." *Thomas Hardy Yearbook* 26 (1998): 18–21.

Harvey, Geoffrey. *The Complete Critical Guide to Thomas Hardy.* London: Routledge, 2003.

Hazen, James. "Angel's Hellenism in *Tess of the D'Urbervilles.*" *College Literature* 4 (1977): 129–35.

Hennessee, Hella. "Science and Technology in the Works of Thomas Hardy: Cosmic Mystery and Modern Alienation." *The Image of Technology in Literature, the Media, and Society.* Ed. Will Wright and Steve Kaplan. Pueblo, CO: Society for the Interdisciplinary Study of Social Imagery, University of Southern Colorado, 1994. 51–6.

Henson, Louise, Geoffrey Cantor, Gowan Dawson, et al., eds. *Culture and Science in the Nineteenth-Century Media.* The Nineteenth Century Series. Aldershot, Eng.: Ashgate, 2004

Herrmann, Dieter B. *The History of Astronomy from Herschel to Hertzsprung.* Trans. Kevin Krisciunas. Rev. ed. Cambridge; New York: Cambridge University Press, 1984.

Higgins, Lesley, "Pastoral Meets Melodrama in Thomas Hardy's *The Woodlanders.*" *Thomas Hardy Journal* 6.2 (June 1990): 111–25.

Hirshfeld, Alan W. *Parallax: The Race to Measure the Cosmos.* New York: A. W. H. Freeman/Owl Book, 2001.

Hooker, Jeremy. *Writers in a Landscape.* Cardiff: University of Wales Press, 1996.

Horne, Lewis B. "The Darkening Sun of Tess Durbeyfield." *Texas Studies in Literature and Language: A Journal of the Humanities* 13 (1971): 299–311.

Hoskin, Michael, ed. *The Cambridge Concise History of Astronomy.* Cambridge: Cambridge University Press, 1999.

Howard, Tom. *Hardy Country.* London: Regency House, 1995.

Ingham, Patricia. "Hardy and The Wonders of Geology." *Review of English Studies: A Quarterly Journal of English Literature and the English Language* 31.121 (Feb. 1980): 59–64.

Irwin, Michael. *Reading Hardy's Landscapes*. London; New York: Macmillan; St. Martin's, 2000.

Jann, Rosemary. "Hardy's Rustics and the Construction of Class." *Victorian Literature and Culture* 28.2 (2000): 411–25.

Johnson, Trevor. "Hardy, Homer and Scott's Marmion." *Thomas Hardy Journal* 2.2 (May 1986): 52–55.

Jurta, Roxanne. "'Not-So-New' Sue: The Myth of *Jude the Obscure* as a New Woman Novel." *Journal of the Eighteen Nineties Society* 26 (1999): 13–21.

Kant, Immanuel. *Kant's Cosmogony, as in His Essay on the Retardation of the Rotation of the Earth and His Natural History and Theory of the Heavens*. Trans. W. Hastie. Ed. Willy Ley. Rev. ed. New York: Greenwood, [1968].

—. *Universal Natural History and Theory of the Heavens*. Trans. W. Hastie. Ann Arbor, MI: University of Michigan Press, [1969].

Kearney, Anthony. "Edmund Gosse, Hardy's *Jude the Obscure*, and the Repercussions of 1886." *Notes and Queries* 47 (245) (3)(Sept. 2000): 332–4.

Kepler, Johannes. *Epitome of Copernican Astronomy and Harmonies of the World*. Trans. Charles Glenn Wallis. Great Minds Series. Amherst, NY: Prometheus Books, 1995.

Kerridge, Richard. "Ecological Hardy." *Beyond Nature Writings: Expanding the Boundaries of Ecocriticism*. Ed. Karla Armbruster and Kathleen R. Wallace. Charlottesville, VA: University Press of Virginia, 2001. 126–42.

King, Jeannette. *Tragedy in the Victorian Novel: Theory and Practice in the Novels of George Eliot, Thomas Hardy, and Henry James*. Cambridge; New York: Cambridge University Press, 1978.

Kramer, Dale, ed. *The Cambridge Companion to Thomas Hardy*. Cambridge: Cambridge University Press, 1999.

Kroeber, Karl. *Ecological Literary Criticism: Romantic Imagining and the Biology of Mind*. New York: Columbia University Press, 1994.

Laird, J. T. "New Light on the Evolution of *Tess of the d'Urbervilles*." *Review of English Studies: A Quarterly Journal of English Literature and the English Language* 31.124 (Nov. 1980): 414–35.

Lang, Cecil Y., ed. *The Pre-Raphaelites and Their Circle*. 2nd ed. Chicago: University of Chicago Press, 1975.

Larson, Jil. "Sexual Ethics in Fiction by Thomas Hardy and the New Woman." *Rereading Victorian Fiction*. Ed. Alice Jenkins and Juliet John. New York; Basingstoke, Eng.: Macmillan; St. Martin's Press, 2000. 159–72.

Le, Jie. "Similar Phenomena, Different Experiments? A Study of Thomas Hardy's Literary Influence on Theodore Dreiser" *Midwest Quarterly: A Journal of Contemporary Thought* 45.4 (Summer 2004): 415–26.

Lovesey, Oliver. "Reconstructing Tess." *SEL: Studies in English Literature, 1500–1900* 43.4 (Autumn 2003): 913–38.

Lowe, Charles. "'A Complete Diorama': The Art of Restoration in Hardy's *The Return of the Native.*" *Hardy Review* 4 (Winter 2001): 148–55.

Lucas, John. *The Literature of Change: Studies in the Nineteenth-Century Provincial Novel.* 2nd ed. Brighton, Eng.: Harvester Press; Totowa, NJ: Barnes & Noble Books, 1980.

Mallet, Phillip, ed. *The Achievement of Thomas Hardy.* Basingstoke, Eng.; New York: Macmillan; St. Martin's, 2000.

Malton, Sara. "'The Woman Shall Bear Her Iniquity': Death as Social Discipline in Thomas Hardy's *The Return of the Native.*" *Studies in the Novel* 32.2 (Summer 2000): 147–64.

Massey, Jeff. "Why Wildeve Had to Die: Mimetic Triangles and Violent Ends in *The Return of the Native.*" *Hardy Review* 3 (Summer 2000): 117–26.

May, C. E. *Thomas Hardy: An Agnostic and a Romantic.* Lawrenceville, VA: Brunswick, 1992.

McDermott, Emily A. "An Ovidian Epigraph in *Jude the Obscure.*" *Classical and Modern Literature: A Quarterly* 19.3 (Spring 1999): 233–41.

McGhee, Richard D. "'Swinburne Planteth, Hardy Watereth': Victorian Views of Pain and Pleasure in Human Sexuality." *Tennessee Studies in Literature* 27 (1984): 83–107.

Millgate, Jane. "Two Versions of Regional Romance: Scott's *The Bride of Lammermoor* and Hardy's *Tess of the D'Urbervilles.*" *SEL: Studies in English Literature, 1500–1900* 17.4 (Fall 1977): 729–38.

Millgate, Michael. *Thomas Hardy: A Biography Revisited.* Oxford: Oxford University Press, 2004.

Mitchell, Judith. *The Stone and the Scorpion: the Female Subject of Desire in the Novels of Charlotte Bronte, George Eliot, and Thomas Hardy.* Westport, CT: Greenwood Press, 1994.

Morgan, Laura. *Educating Women: Cultural Conflict and Victorian Literature.* Athens: Ohio University Press, 2001.

Morrell, Roy. "Hardy, Darwin & Nature." *Thomas Hardy Journal* 2.1 (Jan. 1986): 28–32.

Morrison, Ronald D. "Love and Evolution in Thomas Hardy's *The Woodlanders.*" *Kentucky Philological Review* 6 (1991): 32–7.

—. "Two Responses to Victorian Science: Tennyson and Hardy."*Kentucky Philological Review* 7 (1992): 27–31.

Moss, Jean Dietz. *Novelties in the Heavens: Rhetoric and Science in the Copernican Controversy.* Chicago: University of Chicago Press, 1993.

Moxham, Jeffrey. *Interfering Values in the Nineteenth-Century British Novel: Austen, Dickens, Eliot, Hardy, and the Ethics of Criticism.* Westport, CT: Greenwood Press, 2002.

Murfin, Ross C. *Swinburne, Hardy, Lawrence, and the Burden of Belief.* Chicago: University of Chicago Press, 1978.

Murphy, Patricia. *Time is of the Essence: Temporality, Gender, and the New Woman.* Albany, NY: State University of New York Press, 2001.

Nicolson, Sarah. "The Woman Pays: Death and the Ambivalence of Providence in Hardy's Novels." *Literature & Theology: An International Journal of Religion, Theory, and Culture* 16.1 (Mar. 2002): 27–39.

O'Hara, Patricia. "Narrating the Native: Victorian Anthropology and Hardy's *The Return of the Native.*" *Nineteenth Century Contexts* 20.2 (1997): 147–63.

O'Malley, Patrick R. "Oxford's Ghosts: Jude the Obscure and the End of the Gothic." *MFS: Modern Fiction Studies* 46.3 (Fall 2000): 646–71.

Orel, Harold. *The Unknown Thomas Hardy: Lesser-known Aspects of Hardy's Life and Career.* New York: St. Martin's Press, 1987.

Otis, Laura. "Organic Memory: History, Bodies and Texts in *Tess of the d'Urbervilles.*" *Nineteenth-Century Studies* 8 (1994): 1–22.

—, ed. *Literature and Science in the Nineteenth Century: An Anthology.* Oxford: Oxford University Press, 2002.

Ousby, Ian. "The Convergence of the Twain: Hardy's Alteration of Plato's Parable." *Modern Language Review* 77.4 (Oct. 1982): 780–96.

Padian, Kevin. "'A Daughter of the Soil': Themes of Deep Time and Evolution in Thomas Hardy's *Tess of the D'Urbervilles.*" *Thomas Hardy Journal* 13.3 (Oct. 1997): 65–81.

Paganelli, Eloisa. "The Promethean Rebellion in Thomas Hardy's *The Return of the Native.*"*Res Publica Litterarum: Studies in the Classical Tradition* 18 (1995): 195–200.

Page, Norman, ed. *Oxford Reader's Companion to Hardy.* Oxford: Oxford University Press, 2000.

Pang, Alex Soojung-Kim. *Empire and the Sun: Victorian Solar Eclipse Expeditions.* Writing Science. Stanford: Stanford University Press, 2002.

Parker, Lynn. "'Pure Woman' and Tragic Heroine? Conflicting Myths in Hardy's *Tess of the D'Urbervilles.*" *Studies in the Novel* 24.3 (Fall 1992): 273–81.

Pettit, Charles P. C. "Merely A Good Hand at a Serial? From *A Pair of Blue Eyes* to *Far from the Madding Crowd.*" *The Achievement of Thomas Hardy.* Ed. Phillip Mallet. Basingstoke, Eng.; New York: Macmillan; St. Martin's, 2000. 1–21.

Pinion, F. B. *A Hardy Companion: A Guide to the Works of Thomas Hardy and Their Background.* London; Melbourne: Macmillan; New York: St. Martin's, 1968.

Platten, Stephen. "Hardy's Elusive God." *Thomas Hardy Journal* 15.3 (Oct. 1999): 110–12.

Pountney, Rob. "Moon-Gaze and Round Barrows." *Thomas Hardy Journal* 19.3 (Oct. 2003): 47–54.

Radford, Andrew. "The Excavating Consciousness in Hardy's *Two on a Tower.*" *Hardy Review* 4 (Winter 2000): 141–7.

Ray, Martin. *Thomas Hardy: A Textual Study of the Short Stories*. Aldershot, Eng.: Ashgate, 1997.

Regan, Stephen. "*Far from the Madding Crowd*: The Novel in History." *The Nineteenth-Century Novel: Realisms*. Ed. Delia da Sousa Correa. London: Routledge/Open University, 2000. 330–56.

Reilly, Jim. *Shadowtime: History and Representation in Hardy, Conrad, and George Eliot*. London; New York: Routledge, 1993.

Roberts, Jon. "Mortal Projections: Thomas Hardy's Dissolving Views of God." *Victorian Literature and Culture* 31.1 (2003): 43–66.

Robinson, Roger. "Hardy and Darwin." *Thomas Hardy: The Writer and His Background*. Ed. Norman Page. New York: St. Martin's Press, 1980. 128–50.

Rogers, Shannon L. "Medievalism in the Last Novels of Thomas Hardy: New Wine in Old Bottles." *English Literature in Transition 1880–1920* 42.3 (1999): 298–316.

Roy, Paula Alida. "Agent or Victim: Thomas Hardy's *Tess of the D'Urbervilles* (1891)." *Women in Literature: Reading through the Lens of Gender*. Ed. Jerilyn Fisher and Ellen S. Silber. Westport, CT: Greenwood, 2003. 277–9.

Ruskin, Steve. *John Herschel's Cape Voyage: Private Science, Public Imagination and the Ambitions of Empire*. Science, Technology and Culture, 1700–1945 Series. Aldershot, Eng.: Ashgate, 2004.

Salter, C. H. "Hardy's 'Pedantry.'" *Nineteenth-Century Fiction* 28.2 (Sept. 1973): 145–64.

Seymour-Smith, Martin. *Hardy*. New York: St. Martin's, 1994.

Shapin, Steven. *The Scientific Revolution*. Chicago: University of Chicago Press, 1996.

Simpson, Matt. "Pomp and Circumstance – Hardy's 'The Convergence of the Twin'." *Thomas Hardy Journal* 15.1 (Feb. 1999): 33–8.

Smith, Margaret. "Thomas Hardy and the Watery Landscape." *Thomas Hardy Journal* 16.2 (May 2000): 59–62.

Southerington, F. R. "The Return of the Native: Thomas Hardy and the Evolution of Consciousness." *Thomas Hardy and the Modern World*. Ed. F. B. Pinion. Dorchester, Eng.: Thomas Hardy Society, 1974. 37–47.

Sprechman, Ellen Lew. *Seeing Women as Men: Role Reversal in the Novels of Thomas Hardy*. Lanham, MD: University Press of America, 1995.

Stave, Shirley A. *The Decline of the Goddess: Nature, Culture, and Women in Thomas Hardy's Fiction*. Westport, CT: Greenwood Press, 1995.

Steele, Jeremy V. "Thoughts from Sophocles: Hardy in the '90s." *The Poetry of Thomas Hardy*. Ed. Patricia Clements and Juliet Grindle. Totowa, NJ: Barnes & Noble, 1980. 69–82.

Sternlieb, Lisa. "'Three Leahs to Get One Rachel': Redundant Women in *Tess of the d'Urbervilles*." *Dickens Studies Annual: Essays on Victorian Fiction* 29 (2000): 351–65.

Summer, Rosemary. *A Route to Modernism: Hardy, Lawrence, Woolf*. Basingstoke, Eng.; New York, NY: Macmillan; St. Martin's Press, 2000.

—. "The Experimental and the Absurd in *Two on a Tower.*" *Thomas Hardy Annual* 1 (1982): 71–81.

Taylor, Richard Hyde. *The Neglected Hardy: Thomas Hardy's Lesser Novels.* New York: St. Martin's Press, 1982.

Tiefer, Hillary. "Clym Yeobright: Hardy's Comtean Hero." *Thomas Hardy Journal* 16.2 (May 2000): 43–53.

Trezise, Simon. "Ways of Learning in *The Return of the Native.*" *Thomas Hardy Journal* 7.2 (May 1991): 56–65.

Vance, Norman. "Secular Apocalyptic and Thomas Hardy."*History of European Ideas* 26.3–4 (2000): 201–10.

Voelkel, James R. *Kepler and the New Astronomy.* Oxford: Oxford University Press, 1999.

Waldoff, Leon. "Psychological Determinism in *Tess of the d'Urbervilles.*" *Critical Approaches to the Fiction of Thomas Hardy.* Ed. Dale Kramer. London: Macmillan, 1979. 135–54.

Whitlock, Ann. "Science and Symbolism in the Language of Hardy's Novels." *Thomas Hardy Journal* 16.1 (Feb. 2000): 84–92.

Wickens, G. Glen. "Hardy and the Aesthetic Mythographers: The Myth of Demeter and Persephone in *Tess of the d'Urbervilles.*" *University of Toronto Quarterly: A Canadian Journal of the Humanities* 53.1 (Fall 1983): 85–106.

—. "Literature and Science: Hardy's Response to Mill, Huxley and Darwin." *Mosaic: A Journal for the Interdisciplinary Study of Literature* 14.3 (Summer 1981): 63–79.

—. "'Sermons in Stones': The Return to Nature in *Tess of the D'Urbervilles.*" *English Studies in Canada* 14.2 (June 1988): 184–203.

Widdowson, Peter. *Hardy in History: A Study in Literary Sociology.* London; New York: Routledge, 1989.

Woodfield, Malcolm J. "Tragedy and Modernity in Sophocles, Shakespeare and Hardy." *Literature & Theology: An International Journal of Theory, Criticism and Culture* 4.2 (July 1990): 194–218.

Wright, Terence. "Space, Time, and Paradox: The Sense of History in Hardy's Last Novels." *Essays and Studies* 44 (1991): 41–52.

Index

Italics are used for figure references.